MW01165020

"This latest valuable addition to Walter Laqueur's insightful and extensive chronicle of European Jewry's fate in the twentieth century is an exceedingly well-crafted and fascinating collective biography of the younger generation of Jews: how they lived under the heels of the Nazis, the various routes of escape they found, and how they were received and ultimately made their mark in the lands of their refuge. It is a remarkable story, lucidly told, refusing to relinquish its hold on the reader."
—*Rabbi Alexander M. Schindler,*
President emeritus, Union of American Hebrew Congregations

"Picture that generation, barely old enough to flee for their lives, and too young to offer any evident value to a world loath to give them shelter. Yet their achievements in country after country far surpassed the rational expectations of conventional wisdom. What lessons does this story hold for future generations? Thanks to Walter Laqueur's thought-provoking biography, we have a chance to find out."
—*Arno Penzias, Nobel Laureate*

"*Generation Exodus* documents the extraordinary experiences and attitudes of those young Austrian and German Jews who were forced by the Nazis to emigrate or to flee for their lives into a largely unknown outside world. In most cases they left behind family members who would be devoured by the infernal machines of the Holocaust. Yet by and large, some overcoming great obstacles, some with the help of caring relatives or friends, or of strangers, they became valuable members of their adopted homelands. Their contributions belie their small numbers. I myself described my sense of identity as 'an American, a citizen of the world, a Jew, and a former Austrian.' Others see themselves differently. This is a book which brings joy and pain: joy for the rescue of these valuable lives; infinite sorrow for those that were extinguished. The book's significance for our harsh times far exceeds its specific subject."
—*Walter Kohn, Nobel Laureate*

"Walter Laqueur has always been an historian with an eye to significant, and sometimes neglected, historical episodes. *Generation Exodus* is a prime example of that talent. It is an absorbing story of the 'saving remnant' of the German Jewish generation that survived and so often became famous—with surprises such as the Nobel Laureates Arno Penzias and Konraad Bloch, and Dr. Ruth Westheimer. It is not an 'exotic' story, but a sober one, reminding us of the shame of the United States which limited the entry of Jewish refugees before the war and doomed many of them to their death."
—*Daniel Bell,*
Henry Ford II Professor of Social Sciences Emeritus,
Harvard University

"I am deeply impressed by Walter Laqueur's new book. He provides us with moving portraits of human fates in the last century. What he describes is my generation. Both of us went to school in Berlin at the same time. The sufferings of those who had to emigrate, their incredible challenges to find new roots, their astounding success in many cases, and, last but not at all least, the never-healing losses to their former homes tell the story to the young generation in our part of the world that it should never forget." —*Richard v. Weizsäcker,*
former president of the German Federal Republic

"Walter Laqueur's fascinating account of the fate of teenage nobodies who became superstars after they had been driven from their homelands by the Nazis is an inspirational counterpoint to the well-known post-emigration stories of the members of the elder generation (the Bertolt Brechts, Albert Einsteins, Thomas Manns), who were already famous when they turned into refugees."
—*Gunther S. Stent, University of California at Berkeley*

"Although I am a member and a friend of many members of Generation Exodus, I was totally unprepared for the multitude of different fates and adventures with which members of my generation of Jews from Germany survived the Second World War and which are described in this fascinating book. Laqueur shows that these people did not merely survive; they mastered their lives creatively and aggressively under the most adverse circumstances. This book is based on thousands of published and unpublished interviews, memoirs, diaries, and letters which Laqueur pulled together from individuals and archives in literally all corners of the world. It is a fascinating and gripping story which has not been told so far and needed to be told." —*Ernest Fontheim, University of Michigan*

"Walter Laqueur's skillfully woven tapestry vividly portrays the achievements of the widely dispersed members of this group who have been a blessing to the countries where they found refuge. Looking back over the past fifty years one might conclude that no other wave of refugees left their imprint in so many diverse fields and in so many countries than did those who were given the opportunity to leave Germany while there was still time. With his skillful style, Laqueur has collected their story." —*Stanley Rabinowitz, Rabbi Emeritus,*
Adas Israel Congregation, Washington D.C.

GENERATION EXODUS

Walter Laqueur

GENERATION
EXODUS

*The Fate of Young Jewish Refugees
from Nazi Germany*

—⁓⁓—

TEMPLE ISAIAH
RABBI HASKELL M. BERNAT LIBRARY
55 LINCOLN STREET
LEXINGTON, MASSACHUSETTS 02421

Brandeis University Press
Published by University Press of New England
Hanover and London

A
940.52
L   29.95

Brandeis University Press

Published by University Press of New England, Hanover, NH 03755

© 2001 by Brandeis University Press

Originally published in German as *Geboren in Deutschland:*

Der Exodus der jüdischen Jugend nach 1933

by Propyläen

in 2000.

All rights reserved

Printed in United States of America

5 4 3 2 1

Every effort has been made to trace and acknowledge
ownership of copyright for the photographs.

Library of Congress Cataloging-in-Publication Data

Laqueur, Walter, 1921–
    Generation exodus: the fate of young Jewish refugees from Nazi Germany /
Walter Laqueur.
        p.   cm. — (The Tauber Institute for the Study of European Jewry series)
Includes bibliographical references (p.   )
ISBN 1-58465-106-7 (cloth)
    1. Jews—Germany—History—1933-1945. 2. Refugees, Jews—Biography.
3. Jewish youth—Germany—Biography. 4. Jews—Germany—Migrations.
5. Germany—Ethnic relations. I . Title. II. Series.
DS135.G3315 L37 2001
943'.004924—dc21   00-010538

THE TAUBER INSTITUTE FOR THE
STUDY OF EUROPEAN JEWRY SERIES

Jehuda Reinharz, General Editor
Michael Brenner, Associate Editor

The Tauber Institute for the Study of European Jewry, established by a gift to
Brandeis University from Dr. Laszlo N. Tauber, is dedicated to the memory of the
victims of Nazi persecutions between 1933 and 1945. The Institute seeks to study
the history and culture of European Jewry in the modern period. The Institute has
a special interest in studying the causes, nature, and consequences of the European Jewish catastrophe within the contexts of modern European diplomatic, intellectual, political, and social history.

Gerhard L. Weinberg, 1981
World in the Balance:
Behind the Scenes of World War II

Richard Cobb, 1983
French and Germans, Germans and French:
A Personal Interpretation of France under
Two Occupations, 1914–1918/1940–1944

Eberhard Jäckel, 1984
Hitler in History

Frances Malino and
Bernard Wasserstein, editors, 1985
The Jews in Modern France

Jehuda Reinharz and
Walter Schatzberg, editors, 1985
The Jewish Response to German Culture:
From the Enlightenment to the
Second World War

Jacob Katz, 1986
The Darker Side of Genius:
Richard Wagner's Anti-Semitism

Jehuda Reinharz, editor, 1987
Living with Antisemitism:
Modern Jewish Responses

Michael R. Marrus, 1987
The Holocaust in History

Paul Mendes-Flohr, editor, 1987
The Philosophy of Franz Rosenzweig

Joan G. Roland, 1989
Jews in British India:
Identity in a Colonial Era

Yisrael Gutman, Ezra Mendelsohn, Jehuda
Reinharz, and Chone Shmeruk, editors,
1989
The Jews of Poland
Between Two World Wars

Avraham Barkai, 1989
From Boycott to Annihilation:
The Economic Struggle of German Jews,
1933–1943

Alexander Altmann, 1991
The Meaning of Jewish Existence:
Theological Essays 1930–1939

Magdalena Opalski and
Israel Bartal, 1992
Poles and Jews:
A Failed Brotherhood

Richard Breitman, 1992
The Architect of Genocide:
Himmler and the Final Solution

George L. Mosse, 1993
Confronting the Nation:
Jewish and Western Nationalism

Daniel Carpi, 1994
Between Mussolini and Hitler:
The Jews and the Italian Authorities in
France and Tunisia

Walter Laqueur and
Richard Breitman, 1994
Breaking the Silence: The German
Who Exposed the Final Solution

Ismar Schorsch, 1994
From Text to Context:
The Turn to History in Modern Judaism

Jacob Katz, 1995
With My Own Eyes:
The Autobiography of an Historian

Gideon Shimoni, 1995
The Zionist Ideology

Moshe Prywes and
Haim Chertok, 1996
Prisoner of Hope

János Nyiri, 1997
Battlefields and Playgrounds

Alan Mintz, editor, 1997
The Boom in Contemporary Israeli Fiction

Samuel Bak, paintings
Lawrence L. Langer,
essay and commentary, 1997
Landscapes of Jewish Experience

Jeffrey Shandler and
Beth S. Wenger, editors, 1997
Encounters with the "Holy Land":
Place, Past and Future in
American Jewish Culture

Simon Rawidowicz, 1998
State of Israel, Diaspora, and Jewish
Continuity: Essays on the
"Ever-Dying People"

Jacob Katz, 1998
A House Divided:
Orthodoxy and Schism in Nineteenth-
Century Central European Jewry

Elisheva Carlebach, John M. Efron, and
David N. Myers, editors, 1998
Jewish History and Jewish Memory:
Essays in Honor of Yosef Hayim Yerushalmi

Shmuel Almog, Jehuda Reinharz, and
Anita Shapira, editors, 1998
Zionism and Religion

Ben Halpern and
Jehuda Reinharz, 2000
Zionism and the Creation of a New Society

Walter Laqueur, 2001
Generation Exodus:
The Fate of Young Jewish Refugees from
Nazi Germany

For Susi

CONTENTS

⚬

PREFACE

—∽∾∿—

This is a first attempt to sketch the portrait of a generation, the young people from Germany and Austria who were forced to emigrate after the Nazis came to power. I refer to the cohort of those born, roughly speaking, between 1914 and 1928, not the Einsteins and Freuds but those still at school or university or in apprenticeship, who had no finished education and were, in the language of the statisticians, not yet gainfully employed. I do not include the even younger ones, because their recollections were limited and their roots not very deep. About eighty thousand belonged to this age group, three quarters of whom escaped in time.

It was in many ways a truly remarkable generation. Fate dispersed them all over the globe, but many of them made a mark, largely, no doubt, out of dire necessity. They had to try harder, because for most of them there was no safety net. Some of this generation have distanced themselves from their origins, in the hope that drawing a veil over them might expedite the social integration in their new homelands. But the great majority behaved differently; this is reflected in the staggering number of recollections, published and unpublished, produced by members of this generation. It is shown perhaps even more strikingly by the great number of reunions of the class of 1933 (and 1936 and 1939) that have taken place in recent years in many parts of the world.

Difficult as it is to write the biography of an individual, it is infinitely more difficult to compose a collective portrait. There is no ideal approach that does justice to all aspects involved. By necessity many names and places have to be mentioned briefly, without the opportunity to relate the full story, to enlarge on what happened to certain individuals before and after.

Voltaire once wrote that those who write history are bound to be up-braided both for what they said and for what they omitted, and this book will not be an exception. He could have added that the historian is bound to step on a variety of toes: some may take umbrage for not having been mentioned, others for having been included but not as they see themselves.

One should never forget that the young men and women (or the boys and girls) of the 1930s were in no way a homogenous group. Some left early, others came with the proverbial last train or ship, and a few thousand escaped only after war had broken out, or survived under-ground in Nazi-occupied Europe. Some went abroad alone, others with their families. They went to every known country in the world, including some unlikely ones, a few went east (or became Commu-nist), but most went west or south. Never before in the history of the Jewish people, or indeed any other people, had there been so wide a dispersal. Some migrated first to one country and later to another, for certain destinations (Shanghai is an obvious example), by necessity, provided only temporary shelter. A few returned to Germany or Aus-tria when the war was over, some because of ideological conviction went to East Germany, others to West Germany, because they thought that professional prospects were better, or because they had not felt at home in the country to which they had originally emigrated. Some found integration easy in their new homelands, others faced enormous difficulties.

The great geographical dispersal quite apart, there were consider-able social and cultural differences between these young refugees of the prewar years. Some came from well-to-do families who had lived in Germany or Austria for many generations, and others from poverty. The majority was secular, but a significant minority practiced their re-ligion. There were Zionists among them, for whom leaving Germany was not a trauma but redemption, the realization of an old dream, the return to a Jewish homeland and the building of a new and better soci-ety. But many others came from highly assimilated homes, and some were Jews only by interpretation of the Nuremberg laws, children of mixed marriages or of parents who had been converted. Some were deeply rooted in German culture and language and continued to write and speak German; a few even became German writers, poets, and playwrights only in exile. Many others distanced themselves out of conviction or circumstances from their German heritage, and a few even came to deny their origins (German and Jewish), considering them either disgraceful or insignificant.

Their subsequent fates were as disparate as their backgrounds. Many of them saw military service in the Allied armies in World War II, or in the Israeli defense forces, subsequently the Israeli army. A few hundred fought in the Spanish Civil War, and about an equal number in the French Foreign Legion. Some became generals or spymasters. Hundreds, perhaps a few thousand, had hair-raising adventures escaping from Germany in the middle of the war or living inside Germany as "submarines," sometimes in Nazi uniform. They had as much excitement and danger in a day, in an hour, as normal people in normal circumstances would face in a lifetime.

For others the transition would be relatively smooth, either because they went abroad with their family, or because they had a good war and never faced real danger. They chose every conceivable profession including that of a Benedictine abbot, Hindu guru, and West African chieftain. On the whole, they did rather well, perhaps because they had to start from scratch, because there was no helping hand, no money, no connections, no safety net. For them it was a question of swimming or sinking. For some of this generation it can certainly be said that but for Hitler and the Nazis they would never have gone as far in life as they did. Some spent their later years in the limelight, others remained in the shadow. And there was, of course, always the memory of the many thousands—relatives, close friends, acquaintances, classmates—who had not survived.

I belong to this generation, and sometimes while writing this book I had the impression that I knew every single one of them, that I could picture every one of them. This, of course, was an optical illusion. But I graduated from a German school the last year (1938) Jews were permitted to do so, lived subsequently for fifteen years in what was then Palestine and later became Israel, and I have divided my time since between the United States and Europe. Thus I have had the opportunity to meet at one time or another many of those I am writing about. And others mentioned in the narrative were the friends of friends or the acquaintances of acquaintances. Over the years I have read many of the memoirs written by members of this generation, published and unpublished. In addition I have interviewed over a long time, more or less systematically, friends as well as chance acquaintances about their fate in war and peace. I found all of their accounts interesting, and sometimes the more artless ones seemed even more authentic than the more sophisticated. The problem facing me was the abundance of material rather than the lack of it. I hope I shall be forgiven for not mentioning or quoting from every single narrative. This account, like all history, had to be selective in approach. There simply were too many stories—for each I mentioned, there were five or even ten others I had to leave out.

The surviving boys and girls of the 1930s are now in their seventies and eighties, and their number is rapidly dwindling. Wherever they are, they celebrate the anniversaries of their rescue. One generation passeth away and a new one cometh, and the world goes on for the time being. Does this generation have a heritage to bequeath? Was there a common denominator or at least common features in the first place? It might be too early even to try answering these questions, and I shall attempt to do so only tentatively and in passing. But the story so far seems to me so interesting that, even if it should appear at some future date that this generation did not have a lasting impact, its story should still be told, and I hope that this book takes a step in this direction.

Being a member of this generation, my interest in its fate went beyond mere academic interest. I do know only too well, for I experienced it in my own life, what crucial role accident played in the fate of individuals. The stories of survival against nearly overwhelming odds and of great achievement among members of this generation are many, but so are the many incredibly sad and tragic stories. A feeling of "there but for the grace of God . . ." was never far away.

One August evening a few years ago I was admitted to Hadassah Hospital, Jerusalem. The hospital was full and I was lucky to find a bed in a dark corner, sharing a room with five other patients. None was very ill or sleepy and, at a late hour, after the nurses had taken the temperature, blood pressure, and glucose level for a last time, they began to tell stories from their lives. One had been in the underground in Iraq in the 1940s. Another came from the neighborhood of Lublin, Poland; he had been a boy at the time of the German invasion and spent the next five years in a so-called family camp in a very distant part of the Soviet Union. There was someone of vaguely French background who had spent the war years in the French Foreign Legion, but it had been an existence not quite as romantic as in the Hollywood films of the period. I also made my contribution, and the hours passed rather quickly with these stories, something like a latter-day Arabian nights. There was also a younger Israeli Arab man, perhaps a schoolteacher, with exquisite manners, always willing to help his neighbors, who eventually said with some envy: "What interesting lives you all have had." We tried to explain without evident success that he may not have missed that much, and that, in any case, a price had to be paid for an eventful life.

That night the idea first occurred to me that the time had come to attempt to tell the story of my generation.

Acknowledgments

I am obliged to a great many men and women belonging to this generation who put their unpublished memoirs at my disposal or shared with me their recollections in letters, telephone conversations or personal interviews. If I could not make use of all this evidence, it is still true that every memoir, every conversation helped broaden my understanding of the period in question and of local conditions in various parts of the world.

But I have to single out several whose help went beyond supplying evidence and who went to great lengths by guiding my steps in my research, providing background papers, or reading and commenting on parts of the manuscript, eliminating factual mistakes or querying doubtful generalizations. Among them were Andreas Mink (the present editor of *Aufbau* in New York), Eva Neisser, Richard Schifter, Ernest Fontheim, Frank Mecklenburg and the Leo Baeck Institute in New York, Isaac Green, John Weitz, Herbert Strauss, Walter Roberts, Rabbi Joshua Habermann, Rosemarie Steinfeld, Zvi Yavetz, Abraham Ascher, all in the United States. Vera Tomkins helped with regard to the Soviet Union, Sonja Muehlberger and Ernest Heppner concerning Shanghai, Irene Runge on East Germany, as well as Rosemarie Nief and Ben Barkow in London, Lilo Stone and Eli Tzur in Israel. My old friend, Bo Parsson, neither Jewish nor belonging to this generation, provided much guidance with regard to wartime conditions in Sweden and helped put me in touch both with survivors of that period and scholars dealing with the refugees in wartime Sweden. Shoshanna Hermann lived underground in wartime Holland and France and provided both literature and valuable contacts. Edith Kurzweil, whose wartime odyssey as a young girl through Western Europe is briefly described in this book, shared with me her as yet unpublished memoirs. The same is true of another old friend, Ernst Beier, who became a German prisoner of war at the time of the Battle of the Bulge. Herbert Cohen in Australia, Ernst Cramer, Ruth Piek, Tom Freudenheim, and Marc Svetov in Berlin, and Shlomit Laqueur in Jerusalem helped me get valuable and rare source material, as did Alfredo J. Sadler of Sao Paulo, who generously provided much literature that was difficult to obtain, and answered innumerable questions. The same is true with regard to Werner Guttentag of La Paz, Bolivia. In Israel, Esther Herlitz, among many others, was a mine of information. Steve Kary and his father, Hans, once a classmate of mine, helped as far as Australia is concerned. Anita and Renate Lasker as well as Klaus Harpprecht read sections of the manuscript and checked facts concerning their own fate and that of others.

Jehuda Reinharz, president of Brandeis University, an old friend and a member of the "second generation" took a personal interest in the fate of this project; my gratitude goes to him, to Sylvia Fuks Fried, and to the editors of the University Press of New England that the book appears in the present series.

My sources are listed in the biographical essay. Many personal accounts have been published by the younger generations of refugees. Some of them have been widely read, such as Marcel Reich-Ranicki's *Mein Leben* and Markus Wolf's *Troika. The Diary of Anne Frank* is the best known of this literature but has not been included in the present book simply because the author, while technically a refugee, left Germany as a small child. Many other manuscripts have not been published, either because the authors could not find a publisher, or because they were written for family and friends, not a wider public, in the first place. It could well be that no other wave of refugees has produced so many memoirs. There are, in addition, many books and articles, not to mention television documentaries, about the exodus of 1933 and the years after; the great majority deal with the older generation, especially the great and famous among them. But this is only of marginal interest in the context of my story, for the problems and the prospects of the younger generation were quite different.

The Leo Baeck Institute in New York has the greatest collection, well over a thousand, of unpublished memoirs of the German and Austrian Jewish emigration, but most of these accounts were written by members of the older generation. The same is true with regard to the eyewitness accounts of the Wiener Library in London, which has the most comprehensive collection of published material readily accessible, and this has greatly helped me in my work.

Among those who left Germany and Austria there was a great deal of cohesion in their new homes, and the publications, some of which continue to appear to the present day, have been of considerable help. They include above all *Aufbau* in New York, the *Mitteilungsblatt* of the Association of Olim from Germany and Austria in Tel Aviv, and the monthly bulletin of the AJR (Association of Jewish Refugees) in London. But there have been in addition many local publications, for instance, by German Jewish congregations in Latin America, including Buenos Aires, Sao Paulo, but also Montevideo, and, at one time, La Paz. Those who came to England with the children's transport (Kindertransport) published a circular letter in the 1990s, as did the Gross Breesen group for over six decades. These last two publications cover the age group that is the subject of the present book. The Gross Breesen newsletter is particularly interesting, because its first issues were published in the 1930s when the farm in Silesia had just come into being. Subsequent issues include detailed accounts about their emigration from Germany, their arrival in their new home, their fate during the war and postwar period, up to the reunions of the surviving members in the 1990s in the United States, Israel, Australia, and elsewhere. Kibbutzim in Israel founded by German Jews have also published historical accounts from their early days in the country to the present day, based on documents and the recollections of their members.

Among my assistants at CSIS in Washington, it is a pleasure to single out Daniel Silverman, Albena Russeva, Alexander Cynamon, and Elliot Hentov, Jeff Thomas, Jeff Abosolo, Pebe Teebom, and James Lambert who helped me greatly to obtain and sift much of the source material. Marek Michalewski and Benjamin Graham helped, not for the first time, to sort out the inevitable problems confronting a member of the pre-computer generation.

Washington, D.C., June 2000   W. L.

GENERATION EXODUS

INTRODUCTION

Growing Up between Weimar and Hitler

⸺⫶⸺

When Hitler came to power in 1933, about half a million Jews lived in Germany. Their number had been declining because of both a decrease in the birth rate and a movement away from the community, through conversion to Christianity or simply through religious indifference and the erosion of ties. For more than a century, German Jews had moved from villages and little towns to the big cities; over one third lived in the capital, Berlin. The demographers, amateur and professional, predicted the disappearance of German Jewry in the not too distant future. Of this half million, less than one-fifth belonged to the generation that will be the focus of our story, those in their teens and early twenties. All generalizations about age cohorts are bound to be imprecise, and this will be true for our group. Some of them came from rich families, others from poor; some had a strongly Jewish background be it religious or Zionist, whereas, for others, the fact that they were born Jewish was of no vital importance and certainly not of paramount interest. The families of some had lived in Germany for many generations, whereas others were of Eastern European origin, their parents, and in some cases they themselves, having arrived in Germany only within the previous decade or two.

But there were also common patterns, and it is to them that we shall turn first. According to its social structure, German Jewry was predominantly middle class: there were quite a few artisans but not many manual workers and virtually no farmers. But the German middle class had suffered as much as the rest of the population from the inflation of 1922/23 and the great depression after 1929. The living standards of many families had gone down, and Jewish social services had to deal with an increasing number of needy people. The political tensions of the late twenties and early thirties had affected young Jews as much as, if not more than, the rest of the population; they had created an interest and involvement in politics among young people who in other times would have preferred other pastimes. It manifested itself in a Jewish re-awakening, an interest in things Jewish that had not existed to the same extent for the last hundred years. Zionism, which did not initially have a strong following in Germany, attracted many new supporters after 1933, more among young people than among the older generation.

The main formative influences on young people were home, school, and the youth movements. Families had traditionally played a central role in Jewish life, and though ties had loosened throughout the nineteenth and especially the twentieth century, and there had been a generational revolt, family links were still important. They became more important as the situation worsened for Jews; because they were under siege, people were looking for protection in groups. Whether a family could emigrate after 1933 often depended on whether one or more of its members, close or more distant, had settled in other countries and were willing to assist those who had remained behind. Families, whenever possible, would emigrate together.

School and University

Most Jewish schoolchildren in Germany attended German schools. The number of Jewish elementary schools had been steadily declining since the end of the nineteenth century, and by 1932, it was little more than a third of what it had once been. This was the result (as Michael Brenner has pointed out), on the one hand, of the urbanization of German Jewry, since the smaller communities that remained could no longer sustain schools of their own, and, on the other, the growing belief among liberal Jews that abolishing separate schools would help further integrate Jews into German society. It should be added that, whenever their numerical presence warranted it, Jewish children in German schools received Jewish religious tuition, usually from a local rabbi. The quality of these lessons was in my own experience fairly high, but the students were not particularly interested, except perhaps when they had truly charismatic teachers.

There were considerable differences from town to town and region to region. In some cities, such as Frankfurt, Hamburg, and Cologne, every second Jewish child attended a Jewish school, whereas in Berlin, the biggest community by far, at most one in five attended. These figures do not tell the whole story, however, and to some extent they are even misleading. Most of the established Jewish schools that had closed down in the decades before 1933 had been very small or private, whereas the new schools that opened after World War I were more substantial. And, on the other hand, what did it mean to attend a Jewish school? How Jewish in character were they? Less so than commonly believed. Specific Jewish subjects (including the teaching of Hebrew) constituted only a small segment of the curriculum, partly, no doubt, because these schools had to be accredited by the state authorities, and their diplomas had to be recognized by institutions of higher learning. Attending a Jewish school certainly had a major impact on the social life of the students—most of their friends would have been Jewish— but the knowledge imparted to them would not have greatly differed from what children were taught in German schools.

How comfortable did Jewish children feel in non-Jewish schools? Again, conditions varied from place to place. There were incidents of antisemitism, but probably not more than in, say, Britain or France, and probably considerably less than in state schools in Eastern Europe. Most Jewish children growing up in Germany, except perhaps those from strictly Orthodox families, had non-Jewish friends, shared their interests and experiences, fought and competed with them in sports. Cases of blatant discrimination or persecution were few. While a majority of German teachers sympathized with the nationalist parties of the right, not many were Nazis prior to 1933, and, in any case, as state employees they were forbidden to take part openly in political activities. There were no doubt in every school, probably in every class, a few rabid antisemites, but for the great majority of non-Jewish pupils the presence of Jewish classmates in their midst was not a matter of vital concern.

All this began to change, in some cases quite suddenly and drastically, in 1933, and it is precisely because relations earlier on had been more or less harmonious that discrimination, broken friendships, and gradual isolation often had a major impact on Jewish schoolchildren. It was frequently worse in the smaller towns than in the big cities. When Zvi Aharoni, born Hermann Aronsheim in Frankfurt (Oder) in

1921, was invited many years later to be a guest at the three hundredth anniversary of the school he had attended as a youngster, he wrote in his reply that there were too many unhappy memories, and that he preferred not to come. (After joining a kibbutz, Aharoni became an officer in the Israeli army and eventually one of the top officials of Mossad, the Israeli secret service; he was the man who identified Adolf Eichmann in Argentina.) But Georg Iggers in Hamburg was advised by well-meaning classmates to join the Hitler Youth; why did he have to mention the fact that he was Jewish? Peter Levinson, who attended a famous school in Berlin, the Grey Monastery (Graue Kloster), when Hitler came to power, reports that he was treated well. Levinson studied for the rabbinate in Berlin under Leo Baeck as late as 1940/41, and he returned as a rabbi to Germany after World War II.

Marcel Reich-Ranicki, who later became Germany's leading literary critic, participated in 1963 in the twenty-fifth reunion of his Berlin class. "Why," he asked, "did you not treat your fellow Jewish students much worse, conforming with Nazi propaganda?" They answered that they could not possibly believe in Nazi propaganda concerning Jewish inferiority if the one who knew most about German literature was a Jew and also the best sprinter. But Reich-Ranicki was not altogether happy with this answer—what if a Jew had not excelled in athletics and another in German literature? He thought that the true answer was that his fellow students behaved as they did because the teachers, who included a fair number of Nazis, treated the Jews relatively decently, and that in the milieu from which the non-Jewish students came, the educated upper middle class, the crasser forms of antisemitic attack were frowned upon. But he also noted that the general attitude vis-à-vis the fate of the Jews was one of indifference. They did not want to know about the fate of the Jews at the time, or twenty-five years later.

The Exodus from German Schools

After 1933, there was an exodus of Jewish schoolchildren from German schools and of Jewish students from German universities, and new Jewish schools were founded in Berlin, Breslau, and other cities. But the laws aiming at the expulsion of Jewish schoolchildren were by no means consistently applied. Children of Jewish war veterans were permitted to stay on, as well as those of non-German nationality and a few other categories; only in 1938 did the last Jews graduate from senior high school *(Gymnasium)*—I was one.

In the universities, the exclusion was more rigorously applied, with only a very few exceptions, mainly of foreign nationals; the great majority was thrown out the year Hitler came to power. Nazism was widespread in German universities, more than in the country at large; there had been violent demonstrations against Jewish and left-wing professors even before 1933. Since there were few universities and the total number of students was relatively small, it was easier from an administrative point of view to expel the Jews. However, there was inconsistency even in the universities, and while most Jews could no longer graduate, a few were permitted to attend lectures up to 1938. Among the "anomalies" was Heinz Kellermann, later a prosecutor in the Nuremberg trials and an American diplomat, who graduated in 1937 from the law faculty of Berlin University.

Youth Movement

Every Jewish boy and girl went to school, but not everyone belonged to a *Bund*, a youth group; only about half of this age group did after 1933. And yet these countrywide organizations had a considerable formative influence on two generations of young Jews in Germany. The youth movement was a specific Central European phenomenon. Similar in some ways to the Boy Scouts and Girl Guides, it was in some respects quite different: it had come into being as a protest movement against established social conventions, and so, was far more ambitious in its aims, and it was led not by adults but by young people. The German youth movement (the Wandervogel) had come into existence shortly before the turn of the century; young Jews wanted to join it but were often rebuffed, and, therefore, they created their own organizations.

By 1933 only a small minority of Jews belonged to German *Buende*; the great majority were members of Jewish youth groups, which existed in every kind of ideological orientation, style, and social composition. The Zionists had their own organization, originally called Blau Weiss, which educated its members toward life in Palestine with emphasis on work in a kibbutz. It taught them Hebrew, Jewish history, and traditions, but at the same time the organization was steeped in

German culture. There were weekly discussion meetings, and members went on hiking trips on weekends and during school holidays. In the early thirties when Blau Weiss ceased to exist, there were various successor groups—Kadima, Maccabi Hatzair, and Habonim—and also party political youth organizations of the left (Hashomer Hatzair) and of the right (the "revisionist" Betar). The most influential non-Zionist group in the 1920s was Kameraden (the Comrades), which eventually split into three groups. The Werkleute (a name chosen under the influence of Buber and Rilke) became more Jewish in outlook and, eventually, strongly Zionist. The assimilationists, while not ignoring Jewish heritage, put more stress on being German, politically as well as culturally. The smallest faction opted for the extreme left, be it the Communist party or one of the many Communist opposition groups that existed at the time.

Furthermore, religious Jews had their own youth groups, and there were active sports associations, again divided along ideological lines. The Zionist groups were called Bar Kochba or Maccabi, according to the national heroes in early Jewish history. The more German-oriented youth belonged to the sports clubs sponsored by the association of Jewish war veterans (RJF). Competitive sports and interest in sports played an important role in the life of Jewish youth in Germany, and perhaps even more in Austria, where the swimmers and waterpolo players of Hakoah Vienna won many national championships, as well as playing important roles in soccer, fencing, and other sports.

Such a brief summary cannot possibly convey an impression of what it meant to belong to a group of this kind. It certainly involved much more than being a member of a group of young philatelists or a synagogue choir. The *Buende* wanted the whole human being, a far-reaching commitment. They propagated ideas and ideals, and they wanted their members not just to pay lip service to them, but to live according to them. "Verwirklichen" was a key word of this time. It meant, to give an obvious example, forgoing one of the traditional Jewish professions, such as trade or academe, to become a farmer and join a kibbutz in Palestine. In brief, some *Buende* wanted not to entertain their members, not just to have them enjoy themselves in the company of like-minded contemporaries. They wanted a commitment for life.

Not all *Buende* made such total demands, and, as mentioned earlier on, not everyone was a member of a *Bund*; in the smaller communities they hardly existed. But they were still very important as part of growing up, they made it easier to confront the tensions of the time as members of a group, provided leadership in an era of great confusion, and gave cohesion and camaraderie in situations in which a single young person was finding it exceedingly difficult to make his or her way in the face of growing pressures of every kind.

Joining a certain *Bund* was usually accidental—one went because a friend or a relation belonged—so the ideological element should perhaps not be overemphasized. Young people would move from one group to another, from left to right and vice versa. At a reunion in Israel fifty years after their exodus, an American professor noted if he had not at age twelve been persuaded by an acquaintance to join a non-Zionist organization, he would probably now be a worker in a kibbutz; some of his contemporaries in Israel could just as easily be teaching history or sociology in the United States. As much depended on the personality of the group leader as on other considerations. In some communities only one or two *Buende* existed and the young generation had little choice. Despite all these accidental factors, the *Buende* played a very important educational role. And it should also be mentioned that after 1933 there was a marked increase in their membership. When members of such a group would meet many years later there would often be an instant feeling of having things in common, based on shared experiences, on books read and songs sung, on holiday camps and campfires and adventures long ago, on common friends and acquaintances. The bond was something between an old school tie and membership in a Masonic lodge.

Under the impact of the rapidly deteriorating situation, the assimilationists among the young Jews quickly lost their patriotic enthusiasm. As more and more countries closed their doors, radical young Zionists found their way to America, whereas not a few previously ardent German-Jewish patriots came to what was then Palestine and over the years turned into staunch Israeli patriots. With radicalization in the general political situation, young Zionists went over to Communist groups, preaching that only world revolution could solve the Jewish question and that in the meantime admiration and support for all things Soviet was the commandment of the hour. But this infatuation with Communism too, was rarely deep and lasting. Having read the works of Marx, Engels, Lenin, and Stalin in illegal study circles did not prevent many from following in their later lives careers and activities far removed from the dreams of radical politics.

Youth in Germany Remembered: Soccer and Avant-garde Culture

How in later years did the generation of 1933 remember the early days in Germany? It depends to a considerable extent on age and background. Some were at the time of the Nazi takeover in primary school, others in secondary school, and yet others were at university or underwent an apprenticeship in one profession or another. The older ones would remember the rich cultural life of the last years of the Weimar Republic, especially if they happened to live in Berlin or another major town. It was a time of unprecedented blossoming in the German theater, music, and the plastic arts; virtually every evening (if one could afford it) there was some performance or exhibition or concert of interest. With the exception of the plastic arts, which still had their mecca in Paris, Germany was the cultural center of the world, and for a young person to witness and partake of it was a matter of great excitement, even if he or she was a radical critic of society or a Zionist dreaming about a new homeland far away from the shores of the Spree, the Elbe, and the Rhine.

The cultural interests of the younger ones were by necessity more limited, more in line with the usual preoccupations of their age groups. For them the magic names were not Max Reinhardt, Piscator, and Furtwaengler; they followed with bated breath the results of the soccer games each Sunday between Hertha BSC (of Berlin) and Schalke 04, the leading club in the Ruhr. Their heroes were not Elizabeth Bergner or Emil Jannings or Albert Bassermann but Hanne Sobeck and Richard Hofmann, the leading goal scorer of the day. Just as the older ones would grow sentimental in later years when recalling a historic performance of *Jedermann* or a revival of a classical play, younger ones such as Henry Kissinger or Peter Gay or Zvi Yavetz (a distinguished professor of classics at Tel Aviv, New York, and Munich) would be able to recite fifty years later the composition of a leading German or Austrian soccer team confronting England or Hungary or Italy.

Alfred Grosser, who came to France as a boy, relates in his autobiography that he remembers by heart the names of all the players of the soccer team of the Racing Club, Paris, the French champions at the time; and Abraham Ascher, now teaching Russian history in New York, has the same expert knowledge for the first division of the British soccer league for several decades. This is the generation that followed with passionate interest whether Helene Mayer, Gretl Bergmann, and Rudi Ball, sportsmen and sportswomen of Jewish descent (even though uninvolved in Jewish affairs), would be permitted to represent Germany in the Olympic games of 1936. However grave the political situation, sports were still of absorbing interest.

It was an exciting period, and in this respect, at least as onlookers, the involvement of young German Jews was total. Such involvement in and identification with the general culture, high and low, of their country, existed perhaps for young Jews in the United States, Italy, and the Netherlands, but less frequently in France and Britain and seldom in Eastern Europe. To realize this is to understand the rootedness of most young German Jews in their country of origin, even if it was usually a one-sided love affair, despite discrimination and the persecutions after 1933.

The psychological attitudes, the mental makeup of the young Jews in Germany cannot be understood if one regards them merely as the reaction to Nazi Germany. They were the children of Weimar Germany, a democratic country with free institutions; they were the products of its educational system and its specific culture. For them emigration meant a poorer life not just materially but also culturally. This is true primarily for their parents' generation, but it also applies to a considerable degree to the younger ones and it explains their difficulty adjusting once they left the country in which they grew up.

A Happy Youth?

In later years, when the children of 1933 had become parents and grandparents, they wrote a great many memoirs about their early years in Germany and Austria. There is, of course, a well-known tendency to embellish in old age events that happened long ago, to show them in a rosy light and to suppress less pleasant occurrences. There is an inclination to forget that growing up is often, even in ideal conditions, a painful process, full of problems with oneself and one's surroundings, of failures and disappointments. But it is still remarkable that the picture that emerges from the overwhelming majority of recollections of pre-Nazi Germany is a happy and sometimes even idyllic one. Not everyone lived in comfort; Ignaz Bubis, later the head of the Association of Jews in Germany, the son of Polish immigrants, tells a grim tale of life in a Breslau suburb, of six or seven people living in two rooms, of grinding poverty and general misery. (The family moved back to Poland in the mid-thirties and Bubis was the only one of a big family to survive.) But unhappy memories of poverty, while not unique, had much more to do with the economic than the political situation.

On the other extreme there is the story of Angelika Schrobsdorff, whose erstwhile Jewish mother had married into a well-to-do, almost aristocratic Prussian family. Part of Angelika's childhood was spent in a family mansion in the countryside, she had a pony of her own, and whatever toys and dolls she and her sister wanted would be given by doting parents and grandparents. Henry Wallich was the scion of a famous and very rich Berlin banking family, his father was Jewish but his mother "Aryan"; the chauffeur would drive him each morning to school in an impressive car. Being a little self-conscious about the family wealth, Henry would alight from the car in a side street and make the rest of the way on foot. In 1932 he was sent for a year to Oriel College, Oxford, to polish his tennis stroke (in the words of his biographer) and to get acquainted with sherry. (Henry Wallich became a Yale professor and a member of the Federal Reserve Board.)

Angelika and Henry were technically merely half Jews; they were not candidates for Auschwitz. In their families the Jewish origins were not mentioned, even though the grownups were all aware of it; Henry's father committed suicide by jumping in the Rhine after Kristallnacht. Angelika had not the faintest notion that she was of Jewish origin, and when everyone else was hoisting red flags with the swastika in 1933, she was very unhappy that her parents, for once, did not instantly fulfill her wish—to have her own swastika hanging from the window of her room. Only much later, when hiding with her mother in Bulgaria, did she learn the truth.

George Mosse (later a distinguished professor of history at the University of Wisconsin and the Hebrew University of Jerusalem) came from a wealthy family; his grandfather had established a press empire in the capital. George remembered the palace and the art gallery that his grandfather had built at Leipziger Platz, but closest to his heart were the manor, parks, lake, and castle at Schenkendorf, south of Berlin, with Medici tapestries and Empire chairs, with eight guest rooms, a winter garden, and large terraces. Young George had a castle tower for himself; there were many servants, and always a governess, usually British or French, for the children. On his birthday, George would be serenaded beneath the castle's large terrace by the village band.

Such a lifestyle was not typical for most of German Jewry, but it was not unique. Even those who did not grow up in castles or travel to school in a chauffeur-driven limousine could look back on a carefree and fairly comfortable childhood, often in a villa or a spacious apartment in one of the more exclusive garden suburbs. They remembered family gatherings, sometimes boring, sometimes enjoyable, weekend excursions with family or friends down the Rhine or to the Black Forest or the lakes and forests near Berlin. The more affluent families would travel to St. Moritz or Pontresina in summer or winter (and sometimes both); those overweight would try to shed a few pounds in Meran. True, there were resorts on the North Sea and the Baltic that made it known that they did not want Jewish patronage, but there were more than enough beautiful places in Germany and abroad where German Jews were welcome. Those less well off would rent a room in an inexpensive hotel in the Taunus or the Riesengebirge.

The children belonging to the youth movements would camp or hike in the summer, and discover foreign countries. Life on these occasions would be frugal, the food sometimes barely edible, but they would return happy and sunburned and look forward to the next camp or group excursion. They would rediscover a closer relationship with nature, which had been lost for most Jews when they moved to the cities. They would visit museums and other tourist attractions, and once back home, they would have many stories to tell. George Weidenfeld of Vienna, subsequently Lord Weidenfeld of Chelsea, the publisher, wrote in his memoirs that he had a sunny childhood; I believe the feeling was shared by most of his contemporaries. It is, in any case, what emerges from the written and oral recollections. It explains, at least to some extent, why many found the departure from their homes so difficult, despite the persecutions and the dangers looming. It was not the separation from the country as such, certainly not from the German people, but from their home in the wider sense, or *Heimat*, to use the German term, the familiar sites connected with the joys and dreams of youth, with friendships and sometimes first love.

A Rude Awakening

Of course, not everything was rosy: world economic depression hit Germany particularly severely. But the Jews shared these problems with their German neighbors. Did they feel insecure, was there a great fear of things to come in the years and months prior to 1933? No one thought of emigrating, very few thought of transferring at least some of their money abroad. There were threatening demonstrations in the streets, and the anti-Jewish propaganda of the Nazis could not be overlooked. The governments were weak and rapidly changing, many people were worried but few anticipated that one day Hitler would come to power. And even if he did, was there any good reason to believe that he and his henchmen would last longer than the previous governments? There were no massive physical attacks against Jews; a few cemeteries were desecrated and a few Jewish students beaten up, but this happened in other countries too.

The situation was far from idyllic, and it required no deep political understanding to realize that Germany was approaching a dangerous crisis. But there had been crisis situations as far as most people could think back, certainly almost without interruption from the outbreak of World War I in 1914. Young Jews do not appear to have lost much sleep over these dangers.

And then came January 1933—the torchlight parades, the boycott of Jewish shops—when antisemitism became official policy. Those who were not expelled from German schools had to put up with all kinds of humiliations. Their classmates appeared in school in Hitler Youth uniforms, the teachers opened each lesson with the "German greeting" ("Heil Hitler"), there was a new discipline called *Rassenkunde* (racial studies), and in subjects such as German literature and history, Nazi doctrine prevailed. Above all, friendships between Jews and non-Jews came to an end, and Jews were asked not to participate in class excursions or, of course, in assemblies, which were more and more political in character. Teachers behaved on the whole correctly, which is to say that there were no insults during the lessons, but it became difficult for a Jewish pupil to score high on tests. This was easier to bear for those who had only a year or two to go before graduation, but the younger ones found it more and more difficult to accept their new status as pariahs.

The Shock and the Reaction

How did the adolescents of 1933 face the new situation? Some were hardly affected in their personal life. Yehuda Amichai, born Ludwig

Pfeuffer in Wuerzburg in 1924, later one of Israel's leading poets, remembers that he grew up in totally Jewish surroundings. He went to a
Jewish school where Hebrew was taught from the very beginning, and
though his father had business relations with some non-Jews who told
him to remain in Germany because Hitler did not really mean what he
proclaimed, and would not last long in any case, the parents did not
listen. The whole family, grandparents, parents, children, uncles,
aunts, and cousins emigrated to Palestine in 1935. "I had a very beautiful childhood," Amichai said in an interview many years later. For
him leaving Wuerzburg was anything but traumatic.

To some extent this was true also for those who had attended a Jewish school even before 1933, for young people with a religious background, and for some of the Ostjuden, whose roots in German society
had not been very deep in the first place. Pnina Nave (née Fass), later
an editor of Buber's writings and a coeditor of the *Encyclopedia Judaica*,
came from Berlin and went with her family to Palestine in 1935. Her
home was Zionist; over the desk in her room was a map of Palestine.
She attended a German school, but at the age of twelve she had herself
transferred to a Jewish school. She too remembered many years later
that she had never regarded leaving Germany as a kind of emigration
but as *aliya*, that is to say returning home, ascending to a better life.

Others felt less sanguine at the time. Hilde Hoffmann, born in 1922
in Frankfurt's Westend, had to leave her German school in 1933, and
ride a long way on her bike to the Jewish school. More than once she
had unpleasant encounters on the way to school and her brother, who
looked "more Jewish," was often abused. Naomi Laqueur, born Barbara Koch, attended the Schiller school in Frankfurt; she did not have
to leave in 1933, and relates in her memoirs that she suffered no physical harm but only vague, or not so vague, psychological harassment:
"Nevertheless, I was deeply insulted because I was no longer considered as good a German as my classmates. Probably the first insult I
suffered consciously was when our beloved headmaster, Dr. Bojunga,
who had frequently gone out of his way to be friendly to me, behaved
as if I no longer existed. Nothing changed among my classmates."

Eva Herrmann, born in Berlin in 1923, relates that she was called
by the teacher to stand in front of the class so that he could demon-
strate the specific physical characteristics of the semitic race. Physically she was never molested; on one occasion someone shouted "ass-
hole," but "I was never beaten and there was no panic or fear but

rather a kind of general oppression." Marianne Frey (née Steinbock), also born in Berlin, eventually went to Palestine and became a farmer. She recalls that she had many non-Jewish friends at her school in Karlshorst even after 1933, and "we did everything together. But then, one after another, they came to me and said that they had joined the BDM (the girls' section of the Hitler Youth) and that we could no longer meet." From that time on she was very much alone.

Erwin Leiser, born in Berlin in 1923, the son of a lawyer, later became one of the most prominent European documentary filmmakers. He claims that even at the age of ten, having been beaten up at school and in the streets, he and his Jewish friends realized that there was no future for them in Germany. His parents and their friends, meanwhile, could not imagine that Hitler's threats were serious.

The Expulsion of Students: Where to Turn?

Most university students had to live from one day to the next. Even those who had virtually concluded their studies and had only to hand in their dissertations or sit for their oral examinations could not graduate, unless a well-meaning professor was willing to turn a blind eye to the instructions given by the ministry of education. One of these lucky students was Abraham Cutomuth (later Abraham ben Menahem), who received his doctorate in law from a sympathetic professor at the University of Giessen. Ben Menahem may have asked himself in later years, when he worked in a kibbutz, whether the effort had been worthwhile. But the ways of providence are inscrutable, and twenty-five years later Ben Menahem became the mayor of Netanya, one of the more important cities in Israel, north of Tel Aviv. He had never practiced German law, but he was probably at the time the only Israeli mayor with such a doctorate.

To have one's studies interrupted was a disaster if one aimed at a professional career. Heinz Bauer of Vienna had begun his studies in medicine but could not continue them, and it took years as a house painter, a farmer, and a sausage manufacturer in Kenya before he became what he originally had wanted to be, a professor of pathology at an American university.

There were other cases in which leaving the university in the middle of the studies did not, finally, matter. Gideon Ruffer (later Rafael) began his studies in Berlin, but could not continue. Instead he was among the founders of a kibbutz, became its secretary, and ended his career as the director general of the Israeli foreign ministry, even though he had no academic title. George Weidenfeld, born in 1919, could not graduate in Vienna, but acquired a substantial education in any case, and later revolutionized British publishing and became a member of the House of Lords.

Where could a Jewish student turn to conclude his studies? If he was studying law, he might as well consider retooling as a carpenter or locksmith, because the demand for people trained in German law was virtually nonexistent outside Germany. If he studied another subject and if his parents had the means to support him, he could apply for a place at a German university in Austria, Switzerland, or Prague. There were only few openings, though, and the transfer of money was rarely permitted. Lastly, he could continue his studies in an English- or French-speaking country, but there was, all other difficulties aside, the problem of language. There were also very few stipends for students from abroad. Stefan Heym, the well-known writer who later settled in East Germany, had the good luck to find such an opportunity in Chicago, as did Reinhard Bendix, the sociologist. George Mosse discovered that Harvard had a fellowship specifying that the recipient had to have been born in Berlin-Charlottenburg; few people at Harvard were eligible.

A sizeable number of students, about two hundred, went to Italian universities, mainly because it was easier to transfer money from Germany to Italy than to most other countries. This arrangement came to an end in 1938 when Mussolini proclaimed his anti-Jewish legislation. Lastly, there was the Hebrew University in Jerusalem, but this was a small institution at the time with barely five hundred students; it had neither a medical nor a law faculty, and did not offer many scientific subjects. Nevertheless, a few hundred Jewish students from Germany and Austria passed through the Hebrew University over the years; most of them had not studied abroad and chose subjects such as history, philosophy, and Jewish studies.

The road toward a professorship was seldom straightforward. Uriel Heyd, a Turkologist, came to an academic career via the Arab department of the Jewish Agency; Gabriel Baer, an expert on the Egyptian economy, had taught Arabic to schoolchildren in a boarding school; Joshua Arieli, a modern historian, had joined the British army, was taken prisoner in Greece in 1940, and spent the next five years in a prisoner of war camp before returning to the Hebrew University.

There were some attempts to establish schools for Jewish children outside Germany. The famous boarding school at Herrlingen in southwest Germany was transferred almost in toto to Bunce Court in England. In Moscow the Karl Liebknecht School (which we will discuss more later on) absorbed the children of Communist emigrants, including some who would to rise to fame in later years (Markus Wolf, the East German spymaster, was one of them). In Italy, several boarding schools were founded, including one near Florence and another near the Mediterranean coast. Dr. Werner Peiser, the head of one of the schools, had close relations with Gentile, the philosopher and Fascist minister of education. But the German consul did what he could to close the school. Whenever Hitler or another leading Nazi visited Italy, the local police took some of the teachers of the schools into protective custody. Another director was Robert Kempner, formerly a junior official in the German ministry of interior, who later became a central figure in the Nuremberg trials. Most of these schools ceased to exist even before Italy passed its racial legislation in 1938.

These institutions could absorb only a small number of the young people who had been thrown out of German schools, and the number of parents who could afford to send their children to English or French schools was even smaller. But financial difficulties and lack of opportunities apart, there was a more general question: school should prepare young people for life, but what was their life to be? The professions for which German Jews had traditionally opted were not in demand abroad, and thus in the Jewish community *Umschichtung* (social restructuring or retooling) became one of the great slogans of the period. *Umschichtung*, which was to affect both young and middle-aged people, meant that those involved should become skilled laborers and farmers, and training centers were set up for this purpose.

It was a praiseworthy undertaking, but not always very well thought through. True, there was no need for German physicians and lawyers abroad, nor for businessmen with experience in Germany. But working-class unemployment was even higher in most industrial countries following the great depression, and agriculture faced a worldwide crisis.

There may have been a greater future for manual laborers and farmers in Palestine than for German lawyers, but a significant Palestinian industry did not yet exist, and within the lifetime of those trained to become farmers, a major scientific and technological revolution in agriculture would lead to a significant reduction of manpower needs.

Training in Agriculture

All this could not, of course, be foreseen in the 1930s, and there was a feeling that something ought to be done to prepare young people for life abroad. By 1936 there were fifty centers where young people acquired a training in farming for their life in Palestine. Among the most famous were Winkel, Schniebinchen, and Neuendorf im Sande, all within one hour's drive from Berlin, but there were many others within and outside Germany (in the Netherlands, Denmark, and even Poland and Italy). There were also Halutz homes (Bate Halutz) in major German cities; they were communes, the members of which attended courses for metal work, carpentry, electrical engineering, plumbing, and other crafts expected to be useful in their future lives. Most of these centers aimed to prepare young people for life in Palestine, but there were others, like Gross Breesen in Silesia, headed by Curt Bondy, an erstwhile professor of education, which focused on emigration to other countries.

Thousands went through these centers for a year or two, and sometimes even longer. There are many accounts of the hard work and life in difficult conditions, of getting up at four in the morning to milk the cows and work in the kitchen, of sleeping with six or more in one room. They had been accustomed to having a private sphere of life, of which little if anything remained in the new surroundings, where the emphasis was on the group and on community. It was difficult to maintain cleanliness in these conditions, and city children did not change their negative attitude toward manual labor overnight. Their (professional) supervisors were often near despair with the youngsters who preferred talk to hard work and who sometimes had to be shocked into action. In the evening there were supposed to be language courses, as well as some general instruction on Jewish topics. But the students were far too tired and most of them fell asleep. It took at least a year to make workers out of those who stayed the course.

Some of these centers were more attractive than others, for instance those preparing applicants for work at sea, be it shipping or deep sea

fishing. But there, too, entrants were warned that life on ship was hard
work and dangerous and not just romantic, and that not every graduate would become an officer or captain. The training center was eventually transferred to the Danish island of Bornholm in the Baltic, a decision that saved the life of the trainees because it made the escape to
Sweden (on which more later on) a practical possibility. Those in the
agricultural training centers who had not been able to emigrate by
1940 were less lucky: Winkel was liquidated by the Gestapo in 1941,
Neuendorf in April 1943. A few escaped and went underground but
most perished in Auschwitz.

The value of these training centers was not always obvious. Though
a tractor was always a tractor, a cow was always a cow, and knowing
how to milk could do no harm, there were great differences between
farming in a moderate European climate and in Palestine. Those
working on these farms did learn to live in primitive conditions and to
work hard, something that could not be taken for granted among
young people of their background. However, there was yet another
reason for establishing and maintaining these centers: After 1936, immigration into Palestine became restricted, only a limited number of
immigration certificates were issued for workers, and there was a ever
lengthening waiting list. People had to wait for years until their turn
came, and though attempts were made to shorten the process, through
illegal immigration or fictitious marriages (in such cases a couple
would count as one individual), the lines remained long. Some young
people individually found jobs or even apprenticeships in Jewish enterprises in Germany, but these opportunities became fewer and fewer
as Jewish businesses were "aryanized." In those that were still in Jewish hands up to 1938, the Nazi labor organization had the decisive say,
and young Jews were thrown out sooner or later, even if they worked
as interns, without any compensation.

Ghettoization and Emigration

The Nazi takeover had been traumatic, and was followed by a slow
but relentless ghettoization of German Jewry. But the signals were
sometimes contradictory. The Nuremberg laws, a milestone toward the
eradication and eventually the destruction of German Jewry, appeared
in 1935. But the year after, the Olympic games took place in Berlin, and

the Nazis, wanting to score a global propaganda victory, were on their best behavior. Once the sportsmen and women and the journalists had departed, the anti-Jewish measures became more intense, and they reached a climax with the great pogrom of November 1938, the Kristallnacht.

And yet it would be a mistake to believe that the young generation, prior to 1938, was constantly feeling deep unhappiness, panic, and fear, or that they were dancing (if dance they did) on the edge of a volcano. The sports meetings and cultural events continued, and though the economic situation steadily deteriorated, few went to bed hungry at night. Young people are resilient in the face of adversity and they have a capacity to hope for the best and ignore the dangers ahead. They were also held back by the older generation's reluctance to emigrate. Many of their parents' generation thought that the persecution would not go much further; in any case, what would they do abroad and what country would let them enter in the first place? It is probably fair to say that the overwhelming majority of young German Jews, rationally or instinctively, had concluded well before the pogrom of 1938 that there was no future for them in Germany. But most of them, including their leaders, thought that there was more time to prepare themselves for life abroad than there actually was. The sense of urgency was often missing. The Jewish schools, youth groups, and agricultural and nautical training centers were islands of relative peace, and they created an illusion of shelter and of safety.

Early Departures

A closer look at the emigration statistics from Germany tells the story in a nutshell. In 1933, under the immediate impression of the Nazi terror, some thirty-seven thousand people left Germany, but many of them were political rather than "racial" refugees, and several thousand returned to Germany later on. There were, of course, emigrants who were neither anti-Nazi militants nor ardent Zionists, and who still read correctly the signs of the times. One of them was Dr. Max Marcuse, a Berlin physician and one of the founders of the German school of sexology. His books were among those burned during the famous book burning ceremony on May 10, 1933, at which point, he and his family left for Palestine. Dr. Marcuse did not know a word of Hebrew and his professional life in Palestine was an uphill struggle. His son Hans, later Yohanan Meroz, was twelve years old at the time. Some forty-five years later he was to return to Germany as the ambassador of the state of Israel.

Alfred Grosser was ten years old when his parents took him from his native Frankfurt to Paris; his father, a professor of pediatrics, had lost his chair at the university along with all other Jewish professors. Within a short time Alfred would speak and write French better than German, and after the war he would emerge as a leading political scientist and French Germanist. Esther Herlitz was a little older when she went in 1933 from Berlin to Jerusalem; her father had been director of the Zionist archives and the move came neither as a surprise nor a trauma to the family. At the border, Esther and her mother were stripped naked by custom officials looking for smuggled gold and foreign money. The humiliating experience certainly did not make the farewell from Germany any more difficult.

Also among the early emigrants were a group of Zionist pioneers aged twenty or thereabouts who set out to establish a new kibbutz in Palestine. Some of them decided to visit the sites in Italy that had once been part of the grand tour on which every educated young gentleman and woman went if they could afford it. They rightly assumed that this would be the last opportunity for a long time, perhaps forever. Their knowledge and experience of agriculture was minimal and they faced more difficult years than they had ever imagined. But eventually their idealism and enthusiasm prevailed, and the place they established, Hazorea, southeast of Haifa, with about a thousand inhabitants, is now one of the largest and most prosperous of such settlements.

But these early emigrants were the exceptions. The number of those leaving Germany declined to twenty-three thousand in 1934 and twenty-one thousand the year after. This figure remained stable in 1936 and 1937 (twenty-three thousand and twenty-five thousand respectively). As a result of the intensification of the anti-Jewish measures, the number of those leaving rose to forty thousand in 1938 and some eighty thousand in 1939, even though after the outbreak of the war in September 1939 it became exceedingly difficult to leave the country. Nevertheless even in these impossible circumstances, fifteen thousand Jews left greater Germany (which by that time included Austria and Czechoslovakia), either to Shanghai usually by rail through the Soviet Union or by way of Italy, which did not enter the war until June 1940. Even in 1941, some eight thousand Jews departed from Germany before October, when Himmler gave the order to stop emigration altogether.

But even this order seems to have been ignored on occasion; another few thousand Jews appear to have left Germany, legally or illegally, between October 1941 and the end of the war. Altogether it is estimated that some 250,000–280,000 Jews, about half or slightly more of the total, left Germany. Not all of them escaped the gas chambers, for many emigrated to neighboring countries, such as France, Belgium, and Holland, which were occupied early on during the war by the German forces, and they did not succeed in escaping a second time.

In Germany the process of ghettoization took over five years. In Austria and Czechoslovakia the process took between five days and five weeks; by May 1939 some 75 percent of the Jews of Vienna depended on the help of the community. The shock was much more immediate, and, what with Eichmann in charge of promoting Jewish emigration, so was the urge to leave the country as quickly as possible. Thus one hundred twenty-eight thousand Austrian Jews left the country while they could, a higher percentage than in Germany. Some twenty-six thousand, or about a third of the total, managed to leave the Protectorate (German-occupied Bohemia and Moravia, the Sudeten having been incorporated in the Reich). They went to eighty-nine different countries, including colonies and other dependent territories.

Where Did They Go?

Who were the emigrants and what were their countries of destination? There are no reliable statistical breakdowns regarding age groups, but it stands to reason that far more young people left Germany than elderly ones. More is known about the destinations of the refugees than about their ages, but the figures can be misleading. France accepted more refugees in the early years of Nazi rule than any other country, but for about 80 percent of them, France was no more than a country of transit. While it was at first relatively easy to enter France, it was virtually impossible to obtain a labor permit. Almost all refugees were destitute, and since the assistance extended by the French Jewish community was modest at best (they were afraid of a growth of antisemitism), and there was strong resentment among wide sections of the French population against Germany and against Jews, the emigrants were under considerable pressure to look for another asylum.

Many years after the exodus from Germany, a young generation of writers wondered why many more had not left Germany earlier. Such questions are based on ignorance and the benefit of hindsight and leave a bitter taste. The traditional countries of asylum and havens for the oppressed were Switzerland, Britain, and of course, the United States. But political considerations quite apart (the appeasement policy vis-à-vis Germany), Britain was willing to give access only to people in transit to other countries and to certain categories of people if they could prove that they had sufficient means. But this was next to impossible given the German currency legislation, which made it possible to take out ten marks only.

If the French immigration policy became more and more restrictive after 1933, the British became slightly more liberal after 1938, inasmuch as domestic servants and farm laborers were also admitted, if they could find sponsors in Britain, and ten thousand children were accepted during the last months before the outbreak of the war. Switzerland was a small country, where there was both fear of provoking the Germans and antisemitism. "Racial persecution" was not a valid reason to be admitted to Switzerland or the Scandinavian countries. Up to 1938, the number of Jewish refugees living in Switzerland was never higher than five thousand and labor permits were virtually never granted.

Knocking on Closed Gates

The sad story of United States immigration policy has been told many times and only the most essential facts need be recalled. According to the National Origins Law of 1924, some 160,000 immigrants were to be permitted to enter the United States yearly, of which some 26,000 were to be from Germany. But political resistance and bureaucratic sabotage made it impossible to reach these quotas; for the period of 1933 to 1945 only 36 percent of the quota was actually used. American consulates reported back to Washington that the anti-Jewish persecutions of the Nazis had been greatly exaggerated, and Martin Dies, the head of the House Unamerican Activities Committee, declared that "we must ignore the tears of the sobbing sentimentalists . . . and permanently close, lock and bar the gates of our country to new immigration waves and then throw the keys away." Breckinridge Long, who became head of the Special War Problems Division in the state department and as such responsible for visas, disliked foreigners and Jews and gave instructions to prevent as far as possible the granting of a visa.

There were individual consuls who tried to help, just as the British passport control officer in Berlin (and a representative of the British Intelligence Service MI–6), Victor Foley did, but these were few and far between. Even if a prospective immigrant could provide all the necessary papers, such as the famous affidavit of support, he was routinely told to return in three or four years. The result was that up to 1938 only a tiny number of those desperate to leave Germany could move to the United States. When in 1939 Senator Robert Wagner tried to pass a law according to which twenty thousand Jewish children from Germany were to be admitted to the United States, the initiative was easily defeated by a coalition of anti-Jewish forces including the Catholic welfare conference and conservative women's organizations, which argued that there was no particular emergency justifying such a measure.

There was one Jewish community, Palestine, willing and eager to accept Jews from Germany and Central Europe. But Palestine was under British mandatory government, and though between 1933 and 1935, immigration was more or less open, provided the prospective immigrants could pay for the trip, new regulations were passed in 1936, partly as the result of the Arab riots, which reduced Jewish immigration to a mere trickle, and the White Paper of 1939 virtually led to the stoppage of immigration altogether.

Decades after these events some writers claimed that more Jews had not left Germany because they were so deeply rooted in Germany that they found it psychologically impossible to emigrate. At the same time other authors claimed that antisemitism had always been deeply ingrained in the German people and that it had aimed at the physical elimination of the Jews. If this had been true, more Jews would certainly have fled during the early years of Nazi rule, when it was relatively easy to do so. German Jewry in its majority was spiritually rooted in its country of birth, but this was less true of the younger generation, which had not fought for the fatherland in World War I, and which was politically less patriotic, loyal, obedient than their elders.

The leading organizations of German Jewry could have done more
to expedite emigration. The reasons for their hesitation were not igno-
ble: they felt a responsibility for what remained of the community and
did not want to endanger it by illegal action—such as buying illegal
ships for transports to Palestine or illegal visas for emigration to Latin
America—or by failing to cooperate with the Nazi authorities in
charge of Jewish emigration. They were, after all, German by origin
and had been educated to be good citizens. They lacked the instinctive
distrust that, with good reason, Eastern European Jews nurtured toward their authorities. This lack of distrust, the unwillingness even to
consider worst-case possibilities, was a grave, sometimes fatal, handicap as they faced the Nazis. They should have tried to escape before
and after the outbreak of war, even if their chances of being saved
were not good at all. Instead, despite warnings from abroad, all too
often, even among the young generation, the attitude prevailed that
"whatever fate has in store for us, let us face it together." It was a
noble sentiment of solidarity, but it prevailed at the wrong time and in
the wrong place.

Pauperization

In the meantime, on the eve of the war, the pressure to leave Germany
dramatically increased. The cruel pauperization of the German Jews
was accompanied by the sudden realization (after the November pogrom of 1938) that time was running out. The young people left behind in schools and youth groups saw their best friends depart one by
one, and little did it matter that many of them left for places no one
had ever heard of before—Ecuador, Bolivia, Shanghai, the Dominican Republic. There were endless lines in front of the foreign embas-
sies and consulates in Berlin. John F. Baer, who in 1938 was a twenty-
year-old student from Breslau, has described what was a fairly
common experience:

> I went to Berlin and called on a large number of embassies such as the
> United States and the Latin American countries. This proved to be an
> exercise in futility as almost every country had closed its borders to Jew-
> ish refugees. Through a travel agency in Berlin I learned that there was
> a possibility of obtaining a tourist visa to Peru through rather devious

means. While the Peruvian consul in Germany refused to issue any visas, the Peruvian consul in Paris was issuing a number of such visas in exchange for a little compensation.

Baer (today an attorney in California) was better prepared for such a transaction than most, for he had a good working knowledge of English, French, and Spanish. But languages alone would not solve his problem: he needed $280 for the Peruvian consul, and according to German law it was strictly forbidden to possess foreign currency, let alone take it out of the country. So he wrote to every Baer in United States telephone directories with the request for a loan. In the end he found one in Gastonia, North Carolina, who had a mother in Breslau, who agreed, if Baer paid the equivalent in marks to the lady in Breslau, to send dollars to the consul in Paris. But even this was not the end of the story, for on the way to Latin America, a man in a bowler boarded the ship in Antwerp and announced that he was the new consul in Paris and that all the visas issued by his predecessor were invalid. Either he was a very honest man or, more likely, he wanted his own cut. This hurdle too was overcome, and eventually the ship reached Mollende, at that time a small port in southern Peru where officials were likely to be less attentive with regard to the authenticity of the immigrants' visas than in Callao, the main port. Baer was one of those who got away, as were the lucky youngsters who obtained a place on one of the ships bought or hired by Aliyah Bet, the organization illegally shipping immigrants to Palestine. There were several such organizations: the official Zionist one, which had offices first in Berlin, then also in Vienna and Prague; right-wing revisionist organizations engaged in rescue attempts; and a few private entrepreneurs (mainly in Vienna). Emissaries from Palestine had arrived in 1939, among them Pino Ginsburg and Max Zimmels, working for a mass exodus of young people on the shortest possible notice. There were negotiations with Hapag, the biggest German shipping company, about hiring a ship that would take 3,800 *chalutzim* (pioneers) to Palestine. But it was too late, the money was not available or was not given, the negotiations dragged on throughout July and August, and on September 1, the Nazis invaded Poland. The day after, a few hours before Britain and France declared war, Ginsburg and Zimmels crossed the German Dutch border. True, illegal emigration continued even after that date and a few thousand were evacuated, even though illegal immigration was a risky venture.

Some of these illegals were four years or even longer on the way, having been stuck in the Balkans or deported by the British to the island of Mauritius. Some ships were sunk, such as the *Struma*, which was torpedoed by a Soviet submarine in the Black Sea, and the *Patria*, which went down in Haifa harbor following an attempt by the Hagana to disable the ship. Some illegal immigrants were discovered in Kladovo on the Danube, south of Belgrade, by German troops and murdered.

During the last months and weeks before the outbreak of the war, desperate attempts continued in other directions: children were sent posthaste to Britain, some Zionist pioneers were transferred to farms in Denmark and Sweden, emigration to Palestine continued via Italy up to June 1940 and to Shanghai via the Trans-Siberian Express even later, and a few ships reached North and South America up to 1941. But by and large the trap had sprung.

The statistics report emigration even after the fall of 1941, but these figures mainly refer to escape from countries other than Germany and Austria, such as the flight of refugees from Holland, Belgium, and France to Spain and Portugal. True, a few managed to escape in the middle of the war over the Swiss border and were lucky enough not to be returned by the Swiss who had decided in July 1942 not to admit Jewish refugees anymore because "the boat was full." (This order remained in force for about a year; it did not apply, for instance, to members of Mussolini's family who were looking for shelter in Switzerland after the fall of the Duce in 1943.)

A few, following incredible adventures, managed to reach Sweden, Turkey, and North Africa. Some of their stories will be related in the course of our narrative, but these were few and far between. Lastly there were those desperate or courageous enough to hide in Nazi Germany or in Austria or to assume a false identity. This was particularly difficult for young men because anyone of this age group not in uniform was immediately suspect. Some of them were caught but a few hundred did succeed; "Hitler Youth Salomon" was not the only one.

Who had the misfortune to remain behind? To some extent it was a matter of money and, more important, connections abroad. But enterprise and accident also played crucial roles. Those belonging to an organization such as a youth group were in a better position than lone young people. Not a few stayed behind because they wanted to finish their vocational training or because they did not want to emigrate

without their families. Some parents refused to let their children emigrate because they thought them too young to travel on their own,
even though there were opportunities to leave; conversely, young men
and women stayed out of obligation to care for their elderly and sometimes sick parents. There were many tragic cases, and the unwillingness to accept separation did cost the lives of some who could have
been saved. Such separation occurred even among those lucky enough
to emigrate. John Baer managed to have his fiancée, Ursula, join him.
It was difficult, for Bolivian law prohibited the immigration of unattached females, but since Bolivian law did permit marriage by proxy,
Ursula, at that time in London, could rejoin her beloved. Wolfgang
Neisser, who emigrated to Peru, was not as lucky; it took him seven
years to be reunited with his fiancée in upstate New York. There were
others whom cruel fate separated forever. These were not exceptional
cases; for each one of those mentioned by name, many hundreds could
be found whose fate was the same or similar.

The Great Dispersal

Those who left Germany and Austria were dispersed all over the globe;
there was hardly a country in which not at least a few refugees could be
found. Members of my own family went to a dozen European countries, to Turkey, Iran, Palestine, Shanghai, Canada, Australia, the
United States, Argentina, Brazil, Chile, Peru, and Bolivia. About a
thousand German and Austrian Jews went to India, including a student
from Cologne (Ruth Prawer) who in later life became a well-known
writer on India and the author of some of the best known Indian films,
such as *Heat and Dust* and *Shakespeare Wallah*. Another girl from
Frankfurt named Ruth became America's most famed sexologist. Some
made their way to Japan and to various exotic African countries, even
to South Sea islands. Eva Siao, the Chinese photographer, was born
Eva Sandberg in Breslau, but became a patriot second to none of her
new homeland; not a word of criticism would emanate from her lips
even though she was for years a victim of the lunacies of the Maoist cultural revolution. A young Jew born in Fuerth, Bavaria, became secretary of state of the United States; a boy from Chemnitz (I. Foighel) became minister of taxation in Denmark; and a third boy, born in
Cologne, represented South Africa as its ambassador in Washington.

Yet another became editor of the *New York Times*. Paulus (Guenter) Gordan ended his days in a Beuron monastery, having attained the top position in the order of the Benedictines, serving as editor of their leading journal and their representative at the Vatican. A lady from Breslau, a few years older, reached even more elevated status: a martyr of the church, she was eventually beatified and canonized. But there were even more exotic cases. A young Jew who had somehow reached Nigeria became one of the chief experts on and promoters of Yoruba art and eventually also an honorary tribal chief. One initiated the official Bolivian encyclopedia and a postage stamp now commemorates the achievement of Señor Werner Guttentag Tichauer on behalf of Bolivian culture. A young man of similar background, after an adventurous life, which included not only service in the Israeli army but also travel in the Amazon jungle and the Gobi Desert, settled in Nepal and headed a small Buddhist institute dedicated to meditation.

There were common patterns, but in the final analysis each story was different.

ESCAPE

—⁓—

As their situation became more desperate, more Jews left Central Europe during the last months of peace than ever before. But with the outbreak of war, emigration from Nazi Germany became even more difficult. True, only with Italy's entry into the war (June 1940) did legal emigration to Palestine come to a halt, and organized illegal emigration with ships sailing down the Danube to the Black Sea continued even longer. Ships from Rotterdam still went occasionally to the United States (up to the fall of 1941) and Latin America, but fewer and fewer vessels of neutral nations dared to enter the war zones. Until the German invasion of the Soviet Union in June 1941, refugees still went to Shanghai by way of the Trans-Siberian Railroad.

A boy aged ten remembered the circumstances of leaving Germany as follows: Only one door out of Germany remained legally open for Jews—a remote border station between Oldenburg and the Dutch city of Groningen. After customs came a last German passport check by two Blackshirts, who asked, "Will you have more oranges to eat there? Do you realize that the ocean is full of our mines? Can you swim?" Max Frankel, future editor of the *New York Times*, managed to leave Germany early in the war owing to his mother, a remarkable woman of singular determination and persistence who had, against overwhelming odds, procured all the necessary permits, stamps, and visas. But she did not manage to get her husband out as well. He had gone to take leave from his family in eastern Poland, and could not rejoin his wife in time. He would finally be reunited with them six years later, on Columbus Day, 1946, in New York, following long detours through the Gulag.

Wolfgang Hadda, a native of Breslau, was twenty when he left with his family in May 1941, one of the last to leave legally. An uncle who had served in the German flying corps in World War I told them that Shanghai was not a civilized place, and he had a very sad leave-taking from his girlfriend, whom he was never to see again. Relations came to wish them well, some envied him, others pitied him. They had to stay a few days in Berlin and Allied bombers were attacking the city at the time; one bomb landed near their hotel. When they were in the train just outside the German borders, the news came that Hess, Hitler's second in command, had parachuted into Scotland with a peace offer. Perhaps it was a mistake to leave, perhaps the war would be over soon? Two weeks later the German armies attacked the Soviet Union and this escape route too was closed.

Altogether some twenty to twenty-five thousand Jews left Germany and Austria after the outbreak of the war, until, on October 23, 1941, Himmler, head of the SS and the German police, gave a final order to stop the emigration of Jews altogether. By that time the decision to destroy European Jewry had been made and in part already carried out through the Einsatzgruppen (special police units), killing hundreds of thousands in the Soviet Union. But the Nazis wanted to keep the mass murder secret, at least for the time being, and this was one of the main reasons for the total stoppage of emigration.

Nevertheless, several thousand German and Austrian Jews managed to escape even after the Himmler decree. The exact figure will never be known but it could have been between five and ten thousand. In addition, thousands managed to survive in Nazi-occupied Europe in hiding or assuming a non-Jewish identity.

Routes of Escape

How did they escape? Those Jews who got out illegally established an "underground railway" from Holland and Belgium by way of France into Spain and Portugal. They went with sailing boats from the Danish island of Bornholm to Sweden and from Romania and Bulgaria to Turkey and from there to Palestine. They walked by night over the German-Swiss border, or climbed over some of Europe's most difficult terrain from France into Switzerland. They made their way through Slovakia to Hungary and further south. These were not even the most exotic ways to escape. Some hid in crates and containers shipped from Germany to neutral countries; this was one of the riskiest ways to escape and only a few who opted for the crates succeeded. Such escapes demanded both daring and agility, and therefore those who did escape were almost without exception young people.

Organized groups, on the whole, stood a better chance, because all kinds of logistic preparations were required for an escape: maps, railway tickets, money, sometimes a uniform of sorts, forged papers, addresses of guides or safe houses near the border. However, the more thorough the preparations, the more one had to depend on outsiders over whom there was no control, and the greater therefore the danger of discovery by Nazi security forces. It is difficult to generalize, for there were also some cases when individuals or very small groups succeeded in fleeing with only minimal help.

Communist Underground

There were only two groups with organizational networks, however rudimentary, through which they could extend logistical help for an escape, the Communists and the Zionists. The Communists, or at least some of them, had conspirational experience from the prewar underground. But the Communist cells inside Germany and Austria had been effectively destroyed and all they could or would do was to help some of their Jewish or half-Jewish comrades find hiding places in the big cities. Such help was given to only a very few people; the Communists were more effective in saving their comrades in concentration camps.

They certainly saved the lives of Hermann Axen, Kurt Bachmann, Kurt Goldstein, and Emil Carlebach. Axen became a member of the East German politburo after the war, an important figure behind the scenes in East German foreign policy; Bachmann became a leader of the Communist party in West Germany; and Carlebach had a postwar career as an editor in Frankfurt, an enthusiastic Stalinist even in the Gorbachev age of reforms.

Communists had often key positions in the camp administration as *Kapos* (foremen with considerable authority) and secretaries in the camp administration. Communist inmates in many concentration camps had, roughly speaking, an even chance to survive; the prospects of Jews were infinitely worse. The Communist camp officials could not organize mass escapes, but the bigger the camps, the more the SS needed the Communists to help run them. In their positions, they could give warnings to their comrades, and make them (officially) die and reappear in the camp under a new identity. As a result, several dozen Jewish Communists were saved who otherwise would have perished. Thus, to give yet another example, Thomas Sandberg, born in East Berlin in 1952, relates that his father, a young Jewish Communist who spent altogether eleven years in Nazi prisons and camps almost certainly survived only because the party comrades in the Buchenwald administration got him out of work in a quarry, where hardly anyone lasted for more than a few months.

Outside Germany, in countries such as France and Belgium, a Communist underground existed that could provide temporary shelter and forged travel documents for German party comrades in good standing. However, saving Jews who were not party members was not a matter of priority for the Communists, unless specific instructions were given from the supreme party authorities, which, as far as can be established, was seldom if ever the case. In wartime, with resources so limited, every group was primarily interested in protecting their own, be it the Orthodox Jews, the Zionists, or the Social Democrats, and even Varian Fry, the American guardian angel in Marseilles, had instructions to save, above all, well-known writers, artists and public figures. The Communists, not surprisingly, were an extreme case of limiting their help to loyal party members.

But it is only right to add that, as always, there were exceptions. Franz Leitner, an Austrian Communist, was made *Kapo* of Block 8 in Buchenwald, where Jewish children from Russia, the Ukraine, and Hungary were kept. He did what he could to keep them alive by allocating them greater food rations, and by saving them from work that would have killed them and from deportation to Auschwitz. He even bribed the SS man in charge to save the children. His successor as *Kapo*, Wilhelm Hamann, behaved equally well. Among the children saved was Israel Lau, who, almost fifty years later, became chief rabbi of Israel. Yad Vashem named the Communist Leitner a Righteous among Nations in 1999.

Zionist Networks

The Zionists, more specifically the Zionist youth organizations such as Hechalutz, had little conspirational experience, they never had enough money, and they had to rely on the enthusiasm and the inventiveness of their own members as well as the goodness and courage of some non-Jews willing to endanger their lives to carry out rescue activities. The Zionist youth groups had succeeded during the months before the outbreak of the war to get many hundreds of their members to third countries since the British had virtually stopped immigration to Palestine. Thus, in addition to the 10,000 children who went to England (Kindertransport), hundreds went to work on farms in Britain, others went to Holland. Some 650 went to Denmark (including 265 belonging to youth *aliya*), several hundred children to Switzerland, and about 300 to Sweden.

But hundreds were left inside Germany even though attempts were made to organize illegal immigration. Those who had reached the shores of Britain were safe, those in mainland Europe were not. Places of work had been found with Swedish farmers owing to the help of Emil Glueck, a Swedish Jewish doctor who also was an officer in the Swedish army. The pioneers were concentrated predominantly in the south of the country, the Helsingborg/Malmö area. They even had their own kibbutz, called Swartingstorp, but were subject to stringent restrictions, such as not settling near the big cities like Stockholm and Göteborg. These restrictions were removed only after the tide of war had turned in 1942/43, when some of the youngsters from Germany were permitted to enrol in the universities. But in 1940 when the German forces occupied Denmark and Norway there was reason to fear that Sweden would be next and the pioneers deliberated what could be done in the event of such a calamity. They reached the conclusion that there was not much they could do, except have their bicycles ready and move to the north of the country as fast as they could, a distance of about a thousand miles assuming that the Allies would land there to fight the German invaders.

The young people in Denmark were more directly exposed to danger, even though after the occupation (April 1940), life seemed to continue more or less as before. There were some confused plans for a mass exodus and buying arms, but these were fantasies and had to be abandoned. Hechalutz had the good fortune of having enlisted the help of a remarkable Dane named Niels Siggaard, who acted as their coordinator; his official title was "head of the agricultural travel bureau." He was in his fifties at the time and had been active as a teacher and in the Danish Agricultural Society. He was helped by a number of dedicated Danish Jews, such as Abraham Margolinski and Melanie Oppenhejm, who was able in the middle of the war to dispatch a legal group of forty-seven youth *aliya* children to Palestine in a round-about way (through Sweden, Finland, the Soviet Union, and Turkey). To get one country to agree to a venture of this kind in March 1941 was exceedingly difficult; to get four to collaborate must have seemed utterly impossible.

But what of the 547 who were left behind?

There was trouble brewing. In the beginning relations had been idyllic, but the children who had arrived three years earlier had become teenagers and they had become rebellious. Some of the farmers who acted as foster parents complained that their behavior was shameless, that instead of working they were running away to be together with their comrades elsewhere.

The unruly youngsters also had their complaints. None of their clothes fit anymore and their shoes and boots had worn out. They had no raincoats or bicycles. These were not unjustified complaints, but they were too young and immature to understand that no one owed them anything at all. They might have grown physically, but their mental horizon was still that of children, they were incapable of realizing the magnitude of the danger facing them and the simple truth that their very survival depended on the good will of the people who sheltered them, and against whom they rebelled. Their leaders in Copenhagen issued stern admonitions. They were told not to leave their homes, not to use main roads, not to appear in groups or attract attention, not to use the telephone. Many youngsters probably never understood the need for such strict discipline, but it helped save their lives. It was easy to be deceived by the calm reigning in Denmark, for the situation had hardly changed since the German occupation. However, by late 1942, the older ones among them had heard about the fate of the Jews in Holland and Norway, and the change of government in Copenhagen (the takeover by a more collaborationist government) acted as yet another warning sign.

A group of some fifty activists among the *chalutzim* developed an escape program called "the third way," which aimed at escaping, if only possible, to Palestine. Five of them tried to smuggle themselves on board trains or trucks leaving for abroad, for Switzerland in one instance, and for Turkey in another. But they were caught, and only one of them survived—in Auschwitz. A few joined the Danish resistance, but this was obviously a solution for individuals only. Lastly, a daring escape by sea to Sweden was undertaken with the help of three German Jewish youngsters named Marx, Julius, and Bamberger, who had trained in Bornholm as fishermen. They stole a cutter on March 31, 1943, and together with six others went out to sea in a dark night with high winds when the chances of being caught were small. They safely reached a Swedish harbor; the theft had been a charade, for the owner had given his consent, provided he would be compensated for loss of earnings.

One of the participants, Heinz Mosse, sent a detailed report to the Hechalutz office in London, which was read with interest by British intelligence. However, this escape of the nine did not pass unnoticed, and the authorities warned the leaders of Hechalutz in Denmark that such escapades could have grave consequences not only for the remaining youngsters but for Danish Jews in general. Thus, there were no more flights of small groups, but the Bornholm escape still had some positive consequences: the Swedish Hechalutz, with money received from London, decided to buy the cutter *Julius* for evacuating their comrades from Denmark if need be. In November of that year, when Danish Jewry were warned of the impending deportation, this fishing boat saved almost four hundred people in a series of trips.

The story of the mass escape of Danish Jewry has frequently been told and need not be reiterated in any detail. It was difficult to warn the youngsters staying with farmers dispersed all over the country, but through messengers, telephone calls, mailmen and even policemen, this task was more or less accomplished. Only twenty-eight *chalutzim* and thirty-eight youth *aliya* youngsters were caught by the Germans and transported to Theresienstadt. They had dropped out of the organization and could not be reached in time, had disbelieved the warnings, or had fallen into German hands by sheer ill luck. But even they would survive, owing to constant Danish pressure on and inquiries with the Germans. Only one young woman of this group, Ruth Nebel, died in Theresienstadt, and she died of disease. The rest, unlike most other inmates, were not shipped to Auschwitz but released a few days before the end of the war owing to the intervention of Count Bernadotte, acting as a go-between in negotiations between Himmler and the Allies.

Most of the young men and women who had spent the war years in Denmark went to Palestine after the end of the war, joining kibbutzim such as Neot Mordehai, or went elsewhere to rejoin their families. Almost

all kept in touch with and revisited the families in Denmark who had
sheltered them. Of those who had spent the war years in Sweden, a
fairly high percentage remained there after the war, even though the
Swedish government and society had not exactly encouraged their social integration. Some had married Swedes, others had begun their
studies at Swedish universities, and a few of the agricultural trainees
ended their careers as university professors.

From Holland to Spain: The Underground Railway

Whereas in Denmark the evacuation of the *chalutzim* was an unqual-
ified success, and those deported to the German camps also survived,
the thousand pioneers who lived and worked in Holland at the time of
the German invasion were less fortunate—almost half of them perished. Their great majority was German Jewish, most of them worked
in agriculture, some received vocational training in other professions.
Most belonged to secular youth movements, others were members of
religious Zionist groups. Some were concentrated in major groups
such as the Werkdorp in North Holland, others worked with individual
Dutch farmers. The majority were Zionists, but some wanted at the
end of their training to emigrate to other countries.

In contrast to Denmark, the persecutions in Holland started in 1941,
even before the mass deportations got under way. In 1941 some nine
hundred young Jews were arrested and shipped to Mauthausen concentration camp, where they were killed within weeks. The news from
Mauthausen reached Holland quickly; the intention was to demoralize
the Jews, and show that all resistance was hopeless. To a certain extent, it worked: the Jewish Council in Amsterdam opposed all illegal
activity (including illegal immigration), and among the *chalutzim*
there was deep dejection.

By the time the systematic deportations began in July 1942, more
than 700 pioneers were still in agricultural training, slightly more than
half (387) decided to go underground, and 80 percent of them survived. Of those who obeyed the German authorities and accepted deportation, only a quarter survived. Even this was a much higher percentage than usual, and it probably happened because their
deportation came relatively late during the war; furthermore, some
were brought to labor camps and Belsen, where many people died

from starvation and disease, but which was not, strictly speaking, an extermination camp.

The decision to go underground was by no means unanimous. The Dutch Jewish leaders opposed it and many *chalutzim*, too, were demoralized, for there seemed to be no help from the outside; where would they hide, how could they survive? The decision not to obey the deportation order was made not in the Werkdorp, the greatest concentration of pioneers, but in smaller places such as Loosdrecht and Gouda. The leading spirits, Joachim Simon ("Shushu"), Kurt Hanemann, and Menachem Pinkhof, succeeded in establishing contact with Joop Westerweel, a "Christian anarchist" who, together with a few friends, found temporary shelters for the illegals. These included a number of youth *aliya* members aged between fifteen and seventeen. Shushu went on a reconnaissance tour of southern France to contact the Jewish resistance in Toulouse and Lyons and find ways and means to escape. But French Jewish resistance was not yet well organized, and Shushu mistakenly believed that Switzerland was the only country to which escape was possible, and that crossing to Spain was next to impossible. In truth, Switzerland had closed its borders at the time and Spain had not. A more realistic assessment prevailed only in early 1943 when a handful of *chalutzim* (including Adina, Shushu's wife) crossed into Switzerland and another small group into Spain.

From March and April 1943 onward the illegals, using forged identity papers, moved southward into France working for Organization Todt (semimilitary German building construction). By the end of that year preparations to smuggle small convoys of German Jewish pioneers from Holland by way of Pau to the Pamplona district or by way of Andorra and the Massif de Maladetta were far advanced, and in early 1944 the operation was in full swing. The smugglers who acted as guides over the mountains charged a high price, but by that time some funds had been received from Jewish organizations such as the Joint and World Jewish Congress and the Jewish Agency Rescue Committee.

In the meantime, the emissaries of the Jewish Agency had hired the ship *Nyassa*, which carried some 750 young refugees from Portugal to Palestine. This figure included, however, escapees from Holland, France, and Belgium who had reached the Iberian peninsula singly or in groups; there were only eighty members of the German Jewish underground from Holland among them. The others who survived did so with false papers in Holland and France.

Unfortunately, the decision to go underground and to try to escape from Holland was made only at the last possible moment, and for some it came too late. We now know that Spain could have been reached at the time with greater ease than generally thought. As early as February 1943 a group of four who had made their way from the agricultural training centers in Holland walked more or less accidentally from France into Spain, not far from a German outpost, without the help of smugglers and guides. Nor was Spain the only haven; three groups of pioneers found temporary shelter in the most unlikely place, namely Germany. Following the bombing of the industrial centers of the Ruhr, they joined the army of foreign workers mobilized by the Germans at the time to carry out repairs in the city that had been damaged.

Of the leaders and heroes of the rescue activities, Joop Westerweel was arrested in March 1944 while attempting to smuggle two young girls into Belgium. He was executed in August of that year. Joachim Simon (Shushu) had been arrested even earlier, in January 1943 in southern Holland. He committed suicide in prison fearing that he might reveal secrets under torture and endanger his comrades. After Simon's death, Kurt Reilinger became a leading figure in organizing the escape, but he and others of this group were arrested in April 1944 in a hotel in Paris. Considering their lack of experience, they had been astonishingly successful, having managed to place one of their members as a secretary in the building department of the local Gestapo. Most of those arrested in Paris were shipped to Buchenwald but survived. Kurt Reilinger tragically died in a traffic accident in Holland soon after the end of the war.

Help from Switzerland

How were links maintained between the members of Hechalutz in occupied Europe and its center abroad? The young Zionists on the farms in Denmark needed little material help up to the time of their evacuation in October 1943. The situation in Holland, Germany, and elsewhere was quite different once the deportations began. Liaison was kept through the Hechalutz office in London, but its head, Peretz Leshem (Fritz Lichtenstein) could pay only short visits to the continent (Portugal and Spain), and thus played only a minor role as far as rescue activities were concerned. These were concentrated in the hands of Nathan Szwalb (later Dror), a man in his thirties, born in Poland, a member of a kibbutz who had moved to his post in Switzerland just before the outbreak of the war. Szwalb maintained contact with individuals and groups in many countries. He had only a tiny budget, but sent almost daily letters and parcels by means of couriers who also carried Latin American passports as well as money and medicine. He helped to organize legal as well as illegal emigration. Since Switzerland was wholly surrounded by Axis powers after the occupation by the Germans of Vichy France, Szwalb was virtually cut off for a year and a half from communicating with Washington and Jerusalem. Only after the War Refugee Board had been established by Roosevelt in early 1944 and the embargo on the transfer of money to Europe had been lifted, could Szwalb provide money to those who needed it most, and even these funds were not always readily given by his superiors. Szwalb and some local colleagues prepared lists of still living members of the youth organizations, and from an early date tried to persuade them in very slightly coded messages, using Hebrew terms, that only Uncle Yezia (exodus) or Aunt Brecha (escape) could save them.

But some of those he tried to help and protect in Holland and Germany were slow to understand the gravity of the situation and even slower to accept his advice. They could not read Swiss newspapers and had no access to information other than German. The difficulties involved in escape were enormous and thus a tacit (and sometimes explicit) consensus was reached in Germany and the occupied countries not to engage in individual escape but to continue acting as a collective. The reasoning behind this show of solidarity was that the young Jews could perhaps escape their bitter fate if they took a low profile and continued to work quietly and inconspicuously doing jobs that were, after all, of some importance for the German war effort.

There was yet another reason, particularly among those in Germany. The leaders of the Reichsvereinigung, the roof organization of what remained of German Jewry (such as Paul Eppstein, later killed in Theresienstadt) believed that emigration from Germany had to be coordinated with Eichmann who, up to 1941, had been the head of the Nazi organization responsible for Jewish emigration and who still had, it was believed, an interest in promoting it. Eppstein and his colleagues thought that escape of which Eichmann was not informed would lead to sanctions with regard to those remaining behind, and thus, at best, save a few but fatally endanger many. Eppstein seems not to have known that from the summer of 1941 the Eichmann organization had ceased to promote emigration but had been transformed into an apparatus for coordinating the murder of the Jews.

Underground in Germany

When war broke out, hundreds of young pioneers were still concentrated in a dozen or more farms and afforestation stations throughout Germany. Others lived in Berlin and were mobilized early on during the war for work in factories important to the war effort. Until the introduction of the yellow Jewish star in 1941, which had to be prominently displayed on the sleeve of a coat, they could still move and communicate relatively freely; after that it became next to impossible. In 1942 deportations began on a massive scale. In the beginning the younger Jews working in agriculture and industry were often exempt, but during the first part of 1943 they too were affected.

The prevailing attitude in the beginning was still "whatever faces us, it will be easier to bear if we face it together." This attitude, the belief in the power of solidarity, was shared by Alfred Seliger, who then headed the remaining youth groups. It was a tragic mistake, but it ought to be borne in mind that while there were rumors about what faced those deported to the East, there was no absolute certainty that deportation meant death. It took several months for information to trickle back to Berlin about the fate of those who had disappeared. Late in July 1943, a letter was received in Berlin from Auschwitz, written by Karla Wagenbach, who had decided not to go underground and was now working in the kitchen of the extermination camp, and also part time in the famous Auschwitz orchestra. She said that most of their comrades were "already with Alfred" (Seliger, whose death in Auschwitz had become known earlier) and that hundreds were gassed and burned daily in the oven next to the kitchen. Another letter was received from Josef Rotenberg reporting that he was "now alone." But since Rotenberg had departed as member of a group, the meaning of the statement was clear.

These letters led to the decision in 1943 among those remaining behind to go underground, to stop wearing the Jewish star. Their leader was Joachim (Jizchak) Schwersenz, born in 1915, who had gone to school in Berlin and later worked as a teacher and youth leader. He and his companion, Eva Wolff (Ewo), were in close touch with Szwalb in Switzerland and established what became known as the Chug Chalutzi (the pioneer circle) in Berlin. The kernel consisted of no more than twenty to thirty members, but together with its periphery there were about a hundred. They also kept contact with Jewish friends outside the capital. But Schwersenz, too, initially hesitated to go underground; it was only owing to the persistent urging of Ewo that he decided to take this step.

Their story has been told by surviving members of the group: how youngsters aged fifteen, sixteen, and seventeen celebrated the Jewish holidays in the middle of the war, how they went on excursions in the neighborhood of the city, singing their old songs, talking about their future in Palestine, even going to the opera and concerts together. True, a significant proportion were children of mixed marriages who enjoyed special status, even though no one could know how long this would last. However, for the authorities they were still considered *Geltungsjuden* (they had been brought up as Jews). The question has often been asked how could they have survived against virtually impossible odds? The brief answer is that the Gestapo was a relatively small organization and by no means as omnipresent as frequently thought. Once the big Allied bombings began in 1943, as hundreds of thousands Germans lost their homes and needed new papers, as millions of foreign guest workers (or rather slave laborers) were employed in Germany, the Gestapo lost much of its control. Quite often those suspected were not arrested in the street or their homes but received a summons by registered mail to appear next day in the Gestapo offices.

Underground existence was still very dangerous and demanded enormous courage and inventiveness. The young pioneers (like all Jews underground) had more reason to fear denunciation by spiteful neighbors or the handful of Jewish agents of the Gestapo, such as Stella Kuebler, Ruth Danziger, Rolf Isaakson, and Siegfried Goldstein, who had sold their souls to the devil in order to save their own skins.

Survival without the help of non-Jews was virtually impossible in Germany as in other European countries. But such help did exist, ranging from deeply religious people to prostitutes and simple, apolitical, but profoundly decent men and women willing to endanger their own lives to save another's. These people were ready to hide Jews and provide useful contacts for both survival and escape. But some help could be obtained only for money, such as forged identity papers and ration cards. Official documents enabling the bearer to enter German border zones (and escape from there to Switzerland) had to be bought for between four thousand and six thousand marks, a considerable sum by any standard. German farmers who had holdings near the border had to be paid to act as guides. Beginning in 1944, couriers from Switzerland began to arrive in Berlin with money. On the first such occasion a courier handed to Gad Beck (who had taken over from Schwersenz as leader and coordinator) one hundred thousand marks, much more than he had ever seen in his life.

Escape in Wartime

Most of the members of the Chug Chalutzi survived, even though Schwersenz had to escape with the Gestapo in hot pursuit. (Ewo, his companion, had been arrested earlier on, but being "half Aryan" survived in prison.) He described the circumstances of his escape after the war both in writing and on television. He had genuine papers obtained from a noncommissioned Wehrmacht officer stationed near Berlin. His papers stated that he was an engineer employed by the air force, and he traveled in uniform with a Nazi newspaper prominently showing from the pocket of his overcoat. He made his way to Lake Constance, where there were the usual delays of wartime and police controls. The last control took place in the border town, when in the middle of the night there was a knock on his door—"Gestapo, open up." Schwersenz compensated for his non-Aryan looks with a loud and smart "Heil Hitler," explaining that he was looking for temporary quarters for his family, which had been bombed out. These nightly checks were routine and the explanation satisfied the Gestapo representative.

Schwersenz continued the next day by way of a local railway to the village, where he met the two farmers who gave him and his companion, a middle-aged Jewish lady, the necessary instructions. He was also given two big white linen sheets for camouflage, so that it would be more difficult to spot them against the snow. Schwersenz handed them his (fake) documents so that they could again be used by future escapers.

For the last and most difficult mile, Schwersenz and his companion were on their own. They saw a German border patrol and then, in the darkness, continued uphill in the general direction of Switzerland. (There was during the war a total blackout in force in Germany but not in Switzerland; however, to save electricity, lamps in the streets of Switzerland were switched off after 10 P.M.) Schwersenz' companion, who was neither young nor fit, had to be half carried by him, but after a while the road went downhill and after several more minutes they entered a village. They did not know whether they were still in Germany. They had crossed no iron curtain, no barbed wire entanglement, nothing to indicate that there was a state border. Great was his joy when Schwersenz discovered on the wall of one of the houses a poster that said Sports Club Helvetia. It was Thayngen, Switzerland. They threw the white linen away, embraced and kissed and wept, thinking of those whom they left behind. Schwersenz said the prayer for having been saved from mortal danger.

But the danger, they thought, was not quite over. They had been warned that if they were apprehended by the Swiss police near the border, it was possible, indeed likely, that they would be forcibly returned to Germany, whereas once they reached the interior and the bigger cities, the danger would be much less. The warning had been correct at one time, but was out of date by February 1944. It had been Swiss practice for almost a year after August 1942 to send all Jews back who had managed to cross the border. However, after the summer of 1943, following much opposition at home (and in consequence of the changing war situation) this practice was discontinued. Schwersenz and his companion were detained in Schaffhausen, but the day after his arrest he was invited to dinner by the mayor of the city, Bringolf, who apologized in the name of the Swiss people for the arrest and said that despite the proximity to Germany they had not been able for a long time to comprehend the full extent of the disaster. Schwersenz spent several months in a work camp, where Szwalb and others came to visit him, and worked for the rest of the war as a teacher among Jewish children who had escaped to Switzerland from various European countries.

In the meantime, attempts were made to enable other members of the Chug Chalutzi to escape, in view of the relative ease with which Schwersenz had crossed the border. But only a few came, because of unforeseen difficulties. The German soldier who had provided the fake documents had been arrested, and a meeting near Konstanz where

Beck's sister was to collect Latin American passports fell through because of a misunderstanding concerning the meeting place.

Race against Time

After the Allied landings in France and Italy, the end of the war seemed only a few months away. Some members of the Chug Chalutzi found a place to live in the countryside; following the massive bombings the appearance of strangers no longer provoked much surprise and suspicion. The circle continued to function under the leadership of Gad Beck, who moved with inexhaustible energy between various hiding places providing money, food, drugs, and above all encouragement at a time of crisis. He helped to organize the escape of three comrades, three brothers named Wallach who were in a camp for those to be deported. The son of a Viennese Jewish father and a Prussian Protestant mother Beck had connections with homosexual circles in Berlin as well as "Aryan" relations, and thus had access to and was helped by people with whom young Jews did not normally have contact. When Szwalb writing from Geneva upbraided him, implicitly, for not doing enough, he wrote back, "We are no cowards. If one is persecuted and pursued every single moment, if every knock on the door could be the end and yet one continues to function nevertheless, liberating from police detention some of our comrades, this should be enough evidence of our courage."

In late February 1945, Beck and a companion, Zvi Abrahamson, were arrested and interrogated by the feared Gestapo officer Dobberke. They thought that this was the end of the road, but in their despair chose the right approach; to spin out the interrogation. They intimated that they had much knowledge that would be of interest to Dobberke but that time was needed to remember everything and put it on paper. A full hit by a bomb on the prison in which Beck was kept caused additional delay, since Beck had to be excavated from underneath the rubble and had to spend some time in the hospital. By mid March, the Allies had broken through on all fronts and their arrival in Berlin seemed only a matter of days. In the circumstances, Dobberke ignored orders given from above to have all surviving Jews in Berlin (some eight hundred) shot. Thus Beck and Abrahamson were released even before the war ended. Most members of the Chug went to Palestine, five to the United States, and five, including Beck, returned to Berlin after spending several years abroad.

In some of the pictures of the members of the Chug Chalutzi there appears a striking looking woman, a little older than the rest, always carrying a strange cervical collar (she suffered from an incurable tubercular infection). Her name was Sonja Okun and she acted as a guardian angel of the Chug as long as she could. She appears in many of the memoirs of the Berlin survivors, and everyone seemed to love and admire her—even Eichmann inquired about her when he came to Theresienstadt. Few knew her story. Born of Russian parents in Hamburg, she moved in artistic circles and met Erich Engel, one of the great stage and movie directors of his time, and they became lovers. Engel was a man of the left, he had directed the original performance of Brecht's *Threepenny Opera* and was a master of comedy and musicals. He continued to make wholly apolitical films under the Nazis and had yet another successful career after 1945.

The two never married, for Engel had a wife whom he did not want to divorce. He could have done more to save Sonja Okun, but she apparently did not want to leave her young friends in the lurch. (Her whole family was in the United States and tried to persuade her to leave.) She stayed on, first in Berlin in the office of the central organization of German Jews and later in Theresienstadt. She probably could have survived Theresienstadt because she was not on the list of those to be sent to Auschwitz, but she wanted to be with her younger friends on their last journey. It was one of the few cases in which someone did have a choice, and Sonja Okun chose death.

"Submarines" in Big Cities

These then were the fates of some of the members of one of the organized groups of young Jews that existed in Germany throughout the war. But many were not organized and yet more than a few tried to escape the fate the Nazis had in store for them. They did not mind forced labor and the persecutions, but from 1941 there was the acute danger, even the certainty, of deportation. They could obey the instructions received by the authorities and turn up on the specified date at a place that served as a concentration point for deportations, usually not far from a railway station. Or they could ignore the instructions, go underground, and become "submarines" (U-boats) in German parlance.

The decision was not easy because, in addition to the uncertainties of an illegal existence, their own inexperience, and their lack of resources, there was also the feeling that they could not abandon their families and friends when they needed them most. The decision to join or not to join a transport always entailed anguish and agony. To go underground was easiest for young, unattached people or in cases when a whole family decided to do so.

This was next to impossible on short notice. One needed new identity papers to face the frequent wartime raids and police controls, one needed money, and one needed above all friends who could provide a hideout and other such help. How would they obtain food in a situation in which almost everything was rationed, how would they get medical help if needed? Would it at all be possible to stay in Germany or should they try to reach a neutral country?

Most of the Jews left in Germany were elderly and not very adaptable to conditions for which they had not been prepared. They had been educated to respect and to obey authority—this was, after all, Germany. They were poor and did not have the means to live underground for any length of time, and many did not have close "Aryan" friends willing to help despite great danger to themselves and their families. The punishment for hiding Jews was three to six years' imprisonment, more if it involved helping them to cross the border.

Without the help of non-Jewish friends or well-wishers it was virtually impossible to go underground. Without the help of a Nazi official, Edith Hahn Beer in Vienna would certainly not have survived. He gave her exact instructions as to what kind of documents she needed and how they could be obtained through a non-Jewish friend. He also told her to volunteer for the Red Cross in another city because this was the organization least controlled by the police. And so Edith went to Munich, worked in a hospital, met a young German, and married him. She told him the truth about her real identity but he did not care. At the end of the war, she lived in East Germany and after her liberation she was made a local judge before emigrating to and settling in England.

To Hide or Not to Hide?

The immediate decision to be made in 1942/43 was whether to obey the authorities and accept deportation or go into hiding. The decision would have been easier had they been certain of what fate was in store for them, for in that case they would have understood that they had nothing to lose by trying to escape. But in the summer of 1942 there were only rumors, however pervasive, but no certainties. No one had ever returned from the East and reported on the fate of previous trains. The optimists thought that while many would perish, some might survive, and perhaps they would be among the lucky ones. From a breakdown of reports made of survivors after the war it emerges that several months later, toward the end of 1942, almost all had heard about the mass murder.

There are no precise figures concerning the numbers of those who tried to escape this fate. It is estimated that altogether twelve to fifteen thousand Jews in Germany went into hiding, and that perhaps 25 to 30 percent of them survived. This is not a high percentage, but the alternative was Auschwitz and almost certain death. There were fourteen young men and women in the last graduation class of the Berlin Jewish school in 1940, and we know the fate of every one of them. Peter Levinson was among the lucky few who came to America as a legal immigrant in 1941. All five of those who went underground survived, three by escaping over the Swiss border in 1943, one by hiding outside Berlin until the end of the war, and one was apprehended by the Gestapo but survived in a camp. Of the remaining eight, only one survived in a camp; seven perished. One was executed as a member of the Communist Baum group; another committed suicide; one was killed in mysterious circumstances, probably by a group of gangsters/black marketeers. The last, a native of Slovakia, returned home and probably perished there. But, to reiterate, six of fourteen survived, five of them because they had opted for life in the underground. Some people hid in big cities, some in small villages. As one of these illegals, Ilse Rehwald, later wrote, "By removing the yellow star of David we decided against the only certainty that was left, that of being deported. In 1943, for a Berlin Jew, there was no other prospect than uncertainty or certain death." We do know from a sample investigation that the majority of those who were hiding were young or relatively young, a majority was single; they had found a place through non-Jewish friends or acquaintances. Sometimes the decision to hide had in fact been taken following the advice of non-Jewish friends. The number of survivors was perhaps even larger because we know about only those who wrote about their experience or made an oral deposition after the event. But most of the survivors did not write, either lacking the ability or the urge to tell their stories, or wanting to suppress them altogether, because they could not confront these memories or because they wanted to detach themselves from their Jewish origins once and for all.

Hiding in Austria, or to be precise, in Vienna, was more difficult. It is estimated that there were seven hundred Jews hiding there in 1942, but of them only about two hundred survived underground up to the end of the war. It is likely, however, that after the outbreak of the war many hundreds crossed the border illegally to Hungary, Italy, Romania, and, up to early 1941, also to Yugoslavia. Many of them continued their journey to freedom, others were caught following the German invasion of these countries. Of the six hundred Jews who survived "legally" in Vienna, some worked for an industrial enterprise (Wittke and Grimm), some had foreign passports issued by neutral countries and had not been deported, and some were in jail.

There were, in theory, many potential hiding places, including garden allotments in the suburbs, monasteries, huts in isolated areas, boathouses, attics or cellars, storerooms, hidden cubicles, and so on. But without the help of at least one person on the outside, no one could hide for any length of time. They needed food coupons and cash. Very few of those hiding stayed in one place all the time; quite often they had to move every few months.

There was an infinite number of ways to evade the net of the Nazi authorities, but unfortunately also an even greater number of ways to get caught. Still, some generalizations about chances and dangers are possible. It was, of course, far easier to hide or to change one's identity in a big city than in a small town or village where everyone knew everyone else. This began to change in late 1943, however, with the evacuation of part of the civilian population from the cities that were massively bombed. It was easier for young women to pass than for young men of military age, about whom the question would arise, "Why isn't he at the front defending the fatherland?" Young men of this age had to appear either younger than they were (by wearing short trousers and Hitler Youth uniforms), or appear older, or appear to be war invalids. They had to decide whether they would try to hide in a room or a cellar, or perhaps in a vegetable garden in a suburb and leave it only in the dark, or whether to try to get a part time, temporary job, of which there were a great many in wartime, cleaning or repairing windows, cleaning carpets, washing dishes in restaurants, carrying coal or food, doing odd jobs in houses or gardens. Was it safer to change one's domicile often or to stay in one place, so that the neighbors would get accustomed and would stop asking questions?

Ernest Fontheim graduated from a Jewish school in Berlin after the war had broken out. He then worked as a forced laborer for Siemens, a giant electric concern, and went underground following the deportation of his parents in December 1942. With the help of another illegal, Walter Joelsohn, he got false identity papers, and from Frieda Kunze, who had been supervisor of his father's law office for many years, he rented a little hut in an allotment garden in a village southeast of Berlin, where he lived underground with his future wife and her parents.

Living in such huts became quite common among Germans as the Allied bombing of Berlin increased and since, strictly speaking, all those living there were illegals because they had not surrendered their apartments inside Berlin to the authorities, controls were not too strict and everybody minded his or her own business. But Fontheim reports that it was still dangerous to travel into the city because of the many patrols, and that control broke down only a few months before the end of the war. Both Fontheim and Joelsohn, members of the graduating class of 1940, emigrated to the United States after the war; the former became a research physicist at Ann Arbor and also worked for NASA, and the latter became chief economist at General Electric.

Rules for Survival

The golden rules for survival: not to appear in any list of Jewish organizations; not to attract attention, but not to look scared or furtive; to appear to walk with a purpose, not too fast and not too slowly. In some cases it was desirable to improve on one's "Aryan" appearance by, for instance, dyeing one's hair. But this had to be done expertly, for nothing was more suspect than badly dyed hair. And since most Germans, from Hitler and Goebbels downward, did not look very

"Aryan" either, self-assurance was more important than German looks. Gerhard Badrian, from Beuthen, Upper Silesia, was an extreme case of self-assurance, playing the role of Scarlet Pimpernel in wartime Holland. He appeared in SS uniform in the Amsterdam police head-quarters demanding the handover of several political prisoners, and repeated this exploit in a hospital to spirit away a Jewish woman about to be deported. He became a legendary figure, and was betrayed and shot in an ambush in June 1944. Guenther Gerson obtained faked Ges-tapo papers and an SS uniform and checked during the Berlin black-out whether passersby were carrying the necessary identity papers. He seized the briefcases of those who were not, which gave him the money and the ration cards to survive. He was arrested toward the end of the war, but lived to tell his story.

The possibilities of hiding or disguising one's identity were end-less. One frequently used stratagem was the legal approach, namely to argue that one's legal father was not one's natural father. At a time when many registration offices had been destroyed, it was always possible to submit documents and declarations by distant relations to this effect, thereby making a half Jew out of a full Jew, and a "real German" out of a half Jew (in cases when the mother was "Aryan" in the first place). German courts were surprisingly liberal in dubious cases and at the very least some months of valuable time could be gained this way.

Inge Deutschkron and her mother (who became Fräulein and Frau Richter) were saved by friends of the family both in the center of Ber-lin and in the suburbs; the father had been an active Social Democrat, and his erstwhile comrades stood by him and his family. The fate of Hans Rosenthal was similar; he was to become in postwar Germany one of the most popular radio and television entertainers introducing innumerable shows. Aged seventeen when he went underground, he was in hiding part of the time outside Berlin. Later, in March 1943, he moved to a five-by-six-foot tool shed belonging to the owner of a small dress shop for whom he kept the sales records and by whom he was made to read the Bible. But then Frau Jauch, the owner of the shop, suddenly died and some friendly neighbors continued to provide the occasional bit of food and even took him to an air raid shelter. He was much more afraid of the neigbors than the bomb, but though half of them knew the truth, no one talked.

Shlomo Perel ("Hitlerjunge Salomon") came from a family of Polish

Jews, expelled from Germany like all other Polish Jews in October 1938. He found himself in the Soviet occupied region in Eastern Poland when war broke out, but after the German invasion of Russia, he became a German prisoner. He pretended to be an ethnic German, and a German officer who took an interest in him came to like him and sent him to boarding school in Germany, where he successfully played the role of a Hitler Youth up to the very end. Perel-Salomon was not an accomplished actor but a mere boy without much learning and life experience who instinctively did all the right things to survive against hopeless odds. Seemingly hopeless, for in 1941 Germany was victorious on all fronts and the end of the Nazi regime was nowhere in sight. Why should anyone even have attempted to make the effort, to go underground, to change his identity, if the German final victory seemed at hand? The brief answer is that those living underground wanted to gain time; they were motivated by the eternal Jewish optimism that something perhaps would turn up.

Neither Hitler Youth Salomon nor Helga Fruehauf belonged to any group or organization. Helga was twenty-three when she left Frankfurt in the middle of the war to escape deportation. Her aim was to reach Belgium, where she had friends and where she thought, rightly, the chances for survival were better. But how to cross the border without travel documents? She had been given the address of a restaurant close to the border and went there. A few soldiers were drinking there and Helga told them her story about a fiancé, a soldier, who was seriously ill and whom she had to see. Every hour counted and in the hurry she had not been able to get all the stamps needed. The soldiers volunteered to take her into Belgium as the fiancée of one of them. Once in Belgium, they even bought her a fourth-class railway ticket to Brussels, where she arrived on February 10, 1943. She was smuggled by her friends from one hiding place to the next and lived to see the liberation of Brussels in September 1944.

She was by no means the only one to escape from Germany in the middle of the war in the belief that the long-term chances of hiding were better even in the occupied countries. Hundreds if not thousands tried to reach Switzerland or, less frequently, Hungary (prior to the German invasion); a few, like Helga, went to Belgium and France. A very few considered escaping to Sweden. We have no precise figures with regard to success and failure of these escapes. But escape was sometimes possible even in the least promising conditions.

Among those who got away were Herbert Strauss and Ernst Ludwig
Ehrlich, then in their early twenties and studying for the rabbinate in
Berlin; they were among the last students of Rabbi Leo Baeck, the most
prominent figure among German Jews. When the courses were termi-
nated and when they felt that deportation was imminent, Herbert
Strauss and his companion (and later wife) Lotte went underground in
October 1942. Through contact with anti-Nazi non-Jews, they received
addresses and forged documents. Lotte traveled to a small town near
the Swiss border, went on a little walk to a nearby forest—and was in
Switzerland. It had been almost unbelievably easy. Herbert Strauss' escape a few weeks later in June 1943 together with Ehrlich was more
complicated. They needed genuine documents issued by the Ministry
of War Production for the many check points they were likely to encounter on their way. The documents were effective, they safely
reached Singen, and their guide walking ahead at a distance showed
them the general direction of the border. They waited for darkness and
then crawled over a field to the trees that marked Swiss territory. There
are no precise figures as to how many people crossed the border at this
very point at Gotmadingen, but there seem to have been at least forty
to fifty. Neither of these people had any experience evading the security
organs but, as Dr. Johnson said, "when a man knows he is to be hanged
in a fortnight, it concentrates his mind wonderfully." Through German
contacts they got advice on where and how to escape.

Private Enterprise or Stories of Individual Escapes

Another case of individual enterprise was that of Juergen Hermann, a
boy aged sixteen, the son of German Jewish parents who were hiding
in Amsterdam in conditions not dissimilar to those of Anna Frank's
family. Being very active and impatient by nature, he found it impossible to be cooped up in a tiny place; his parents feared for his sanity
and let him go when he insisted. He had a little money to begin with,
picked up some quasi-Dutch documents, which no one outside Holland understood anyway, and made his way through Belgium to
France. There he did odd jobs for Organization Todt, a kind of German labor army employing foreigners for construction work. (Organization Todt seems to have employed at the time many dozens of Jews
living illegally.) Later he was employed by a German cavalry unit as a

local hand cleaning horses. On one occasion a coworker said that he looked like a Jew, which meant that he had to show great indignation, to be restrained with difficulty from fighting the man. Over a number of months he made his way to southern France, crossed the border into Spain and later to Portugal, and less than a year after he had left home he reached Palestine, where he went to work at the Dead Sea.

Harry Zucker (Zvi Yavetz) in Czernowitz, Romania, was one year older than Juergen Hermann at the time of the German invasion of Russia in June 1941. Czernowitz, the capital of Bukowina, had been part of the Austrian empire and after World War I became part of Romania. In 1940, it became part of the Soviet Union. Like most of his friends, Harry belonged to a Jewish youth movement, which had advised its members not to let themselves be deported by the Soviet authorities who arrested and exiled to Siberia many thousands of the Jewish inhabitants of the city. After all the members of his family had been deported, Harry heard that there was a way to escape. But it involved substantial funds, for the destination was Palestine: a ship had to be bought, and the Romanian authorities also wanted their cut.

Harry remembered having been told that his parents had hidden a certain sum of money in their front garden on the very day he had been born. He dug out dollars, pounds sterling, and even Maria Theresienthaler (a currency dating back to the eighteenth century), but it was not enough. However those responsible also accepted two golden watches and three fur coats. First the Romanian authorities had to be bribed, but by that time the tide of war had turned and was no longer in favor of the Germans, and Antonescu, the Romanian dictator, was more accommodating. An old yacht of sorts was bought from an ethnic German neighbor named Nasta, and in the end six ships made their way, one by one, first to Sulina on the Black Sea (Constanza, the bigger port, had become a German naval base) and then along the Black Sea shore to Turkey. But these little ships were never meant to operate on the high seas, the Czernowitz sailors had no map except a page from an atlas used in school. The yacht on which Harry was sailing eventually ran ashore on a small, rocky, uninhabited island named Karaburnu, off the Turkish mainland. Unlike the others, Harry could not swim, but was eventually rescued. He was kept in a Turkish prison, later detained in Syria, and in the end had to spend many months in Cyprus, since there was no legal migration to Palestine. Before the end of the war he was smuggled to Palestine in a British uniform.

Altogether some 350 natives of Czernowitz were rescued with this flotilla, but not all were to stay in Palestine. What of the school and youth movement friends whom Harry had left behind and whom he did not expect to meet anymore? Many years after the war, he met Willy Trebitsch again in Montreal; he met another close friend, believed to be dead, in Australia; and under Gorbachev, after a delay of fifty years, his cousins arrived from Siberia, together with the other surviving members of the trainload that the Soviets had dispatched from Czernowitz on June 13, 1941.

The amazing story of Edith (Dita) Kurzweil and her brother Hansl, natives of Vienna, should be told, however briefly. They were in a Belgian Jewish children's home at the time of the German invasion. Her father had left France for America a few weeks earlier. The children were to follow, but the German offensive changed all this. Dita was fourteen at the time, her brother two years younger. Those in charge of the children's home showed a great deal of foresight; they arranged for a train south, just ahead of the German tanks, and the children ended up in Toulouse. Dita established contact with her parents, and after a few months received a United States visa and even a few dollars. But to leave France in this imbroglio, to get Spanish and Portuguese transit visas, was a daunting task even for older and wiser people, and not a few of them gave up in despair.

But Dita was resourceful and made of stern stuff. She put on her most adult looking dress, a lightweight navy print with huge white flowers, and went to the prefecture, the Jewish rescue committee, the consulates, in brief all the places where hundreds of frantic people were gathering. (The layer of sophistication probably did not help her; playing the lost child would have been easier, since it was closer to the truth, and it might have been more effective.) In the end, she encountered a number of good people who took pity on the lost children, and steered her through the melée of Toulouse, at the time and for years after the center of refugees, and Dita ended up with tickets for Barcelona and Lisbon. But even the "legal" trip to Lisbon was complicated and dangerous in wartime; the children had only a few dollars and did not know whether they would make the next ship leaving Lisbon, which, for all one knew, could be the last. Having crossed the Spanish border they had to share a hotel room with a dozen drunk males. They starved on a diet of dry bread and bananas, always paying attention to how the other travelers behaved in critical situations, and following their example. But they made it to Lisbon, by that time the only port of departure for America, and on August 31, 1940, left Europe on SS *Excalibur* belonging to the American Export Lines.

When Dita Kurzweil made her way through France to Toulouse, many other refugees were trying to do the same. Among them was sixteen-year-old Marianne Loring, who also went to Toulouse, and from there to Spain and Portugal. But her trip was relatively luxurious, for she traveled with her family, and her father (Friedrich Stampfer, the Social Democrat) had been a well-known politician in Weimar Germany. He knew French politicians and this still opened some doors, even in wartime, even outside Paris. However well connected, they still faced many surprises on the road, and there was no certainty that they would escape from France in time. Marianne got all the traveling and excitement she needed during those weeks; when she wrote her recollections almost fifty years later, she stated that she was happy to report that she had spent the last four decades in the same house in California.

Survival against All Odds

There is an old German popular song according to which those who have been traveling have a story to relate. ("Wenn einer eine Reise tut . . .") But those who did not travel also had stories to tell. Each account of a "U-boat" inside Germany was different from the other. "David" (Joel Koenig, Ezra BenGershom) was both U boat and escapee. He was the son of a rabbi and grew up in Upper Silesia. Born in 1922 he went into hiding in Berlin in 1942, having spent the previous two years in a Zionist agricultural training camp. He somehow obtained a Hitler Youth uniform of sorts, which he used day in, day out. According to his documents his name was Herbert Schneider and he made himself look younger than he was to escape attention. He stayed together with Leon, a brother, in one of the poorer quarters of town with an old shoemaker. But the shoemaker wanted to get rid of his lodgers and kept them only because of the money he was paid and the occasional supply of food.

In April 1943, having celebrated Passover with other (mostly illegal) Jews, he decided that the time had come to leave Germany and to find a way out for his few remaining friends and relations. He had worked

as a cleaner in Berlin for a Hungarian Jew named Farkas, who had as-
sured him that in Hungary he would be safe. But David realized that
he would not reach Vienna, let alone Budapest, without some docu-
mentation making it clear that his trip in the middle of the war was officially sanctioned. He approached Dr. Sell, the head of the laboratory
in which he had been working. This was a great risk, and friends had
warned David against ever revealing his Jewishness. But within a few
seconds, it appeared that Dr. Sell was an old Social Democrat, that he
felt a duty to help a human being in trouble. Not only did he invite
David to dinner at his home and let him stay there overnight, he also
provided the travel documents needed and advised David to travel on
Easter Sunday, when the trains were likely to be overcrowded and the
controls less strict.

In Vienna, David found "how superbly the invisible network of the
U-boat helpers worked. Rarely did I risk being seen twice by the same
janitor, though spending two nights under the same roof. Each helper
told me where to find the next, and they all received gladly the refugee
who placed their own lives in jeopardy." At the second attempt, with
the help of a Hungarian smuggler named Imre, David crossed into
Hungary, and later, with the assistance of the same man and his little
network, he succeeded in extricating his brother Leon and twenty others from Germany. After the Nazi invasion of Hungary, David fled to
neighboring Romania and, following a further odyssey, reached Palestine in 1945.

The case of Valentin Senger is remarkable because he and his family, stateless rather than German Jews, survived the war unharmed in
their own apartment inside Germany. The parents had come from
Russia and, in order to live undisturbed in Germany had, even before
World War I, prepared a "legend" for the authorities. However, this
legend was not perfect inasmuch as the police registration of the Sengers (the real name was Rabizanovich) still revealed that their religion
was Jewish. A far-sighted local police sergeant crossed out the "Jewish" on their file in 1933 and substituted "Nonconformist." ("Why, the
reader may ask, should Sergeant Kaspar have stuck his neck out for
us? I honestly don't know," writes Senger, "We were not close friends,
we were no friends at all. We were acquainted only through his official
functions and he had never met with us out of office hours. He may
have known something about my parents' political opinions
[Valentin's mother was a Communist], but he never wasted a word on

the subject and I doubt whether he had any particular sympathy . . .")
The friendly sergeant realized that a card that had been corrected by
hand was still suspect, and two years later he destroyed the old card
and replaced it with a new one.

But this alone would not have saved the Sengers, for in the little
street where they lived, Kaiserhofstrasse in the old center of Frankfurt,
every second person either knew or suspected that they were Jews. It
was a street of the lower middle class, with, no doubt, a fair number of
Nazis. But no one ever talked. Valentin, born in 1918, and his brother
and sister spent their childhood and youth there. Valentin went to work
in a factory as his father did, who, incidentally, never shook his strongly
Yiddish accent. Valentin had a variety of love affairs, he was vaguely
active in anti-Nazi circles, succeeded in shirking service in the Hitler
Youth, and half a dozen doctors who examined him over the years did
not see (or did not want to see) that Valentin was circumcised.

Such luck made him incautious, for in the middle of the war he took
Mimi, his girlfriend, for a short holiday in the border zone near Switzerland. In the middle of the night there came the infamous knock on
the door by the Gestapo. "As if it weren't enough to be a Jew," he recalls, "a Russian Jewish stateless Communist, to have a false name and
a father with a Yiddish accent and a forged passport and to belong to
an illegal political group, I had, just to give me and Mimi a little fun, to
register at a hotel in the border zone and throw myself into the arms of
the Gestapo."

This trial passed too, but six months from the end of the war, Valentin and his brother Alex were drafted by the army. Valentin was lucky
and never saw action; a physician who liked him sent him to recover in
a spa. Alex was killed in one of the last battles of World War II.

Valentin arrived back in Frankfurt on May 8, 1945, the day after
the German capitulation and "with a wet jacket and beating heart"
he ran through the field of ruins and the mountains of rubble. The gas
lamp in front of Kaiserhofstrasse 12 was still there and so was the
house and papa standing at the window: "He looked as if he had been
standing like that for weeks and months, day and night waiting for
Alex and me." Valentin Senger married one of his wartime girlfriends
and worked as a reporter for the German media after the war. The little street, once the street of the small people, has now become very
fashionable indeed with shops like Yves St. Laurent, Vidal Sassoon, a
discotheque and the Buffalo Steakhouse, Frankfurt's best.

Valentin Senger survived because the family lived quietly, inconspicuously. The same cannot be said about two others, Konrad Latte
and Larry (Lothar) Orbach, who were constantly on the move, not because they wanted to, but because there was no other way. Born in
1923, Latte showed promise as a musician; even as a child he received
tutoring with excellent teachers and later became friendly with some
of the leading composers and conductors of the time, including Gott-
fried von Einem. He had been hiding with his family first in a village
in Silesia, and later in Berlin, where they were arrested. Latte escaped
from the Grosse Hamburgerstrasse prison in September 1943 and was
hidden by the dancer Tatjana Gsovsky and others. Eventually he became conductor of a small ensemble entertaining the troops on the
eastern front, for there was little demand for his field of specialization,
Baroque music. But there were rumors about his real identity: He
convened the group of musicians, announced that he would complain
about such calumnies to the Gestapo, retired to an adjacent room,
and collapsed. For the rest of the war he was hidden by the singer of
the ensemble whom he married after the end of the war.

Larry Orbach's story was one of constant adventures and crises.
Born in 1923, he had been a member of one of the (non-Zionist) youth
groups; when war broke out, the family was living in Berlin's unfash-
ionable east. After his father had been arrested and killed in a German
concentration camp, both Larry and his mother, separately, went
underground. He became Gerhard Peters, and with his friend Tad, a
streetwise young man, did odd jobs, moving from shelter to shelter,
but much of the time living and operating on the fringes of the criminal underworld. In Dahlem he had stolen a police badge saying "Air
Warden," and this gave him some additional security while walking
the streets of Berlin.

Their headquarters was a billiard room frequented by criminal
types who, whatever their ethical beliefs and practices, were not Nazis
and few acted as informers. He stayed for much of the time in the incredibly dirty and run-down apartment of an old man ("Opa") who
acted as a fence for the local thieves. Whenever a search was feared he
moved to the bathroom of a nearby bordello. The story he tells is not a
pretty one and should not be judged according to the values of normal
times. He and his friends, also illegals, had no money, so they broke
into shops, stealing from cash registers, and they comforted ladies in
their thirties and forties whose husbands were at the front or had been

killed and who urgently needed male companionship, especially at night. They also pretended to be members of the Berlin vice squad and robbed homosexuals.

But eventually someone informed on Larry and he was arrested and interrogated by the feared police commissar Dobberke, whose name has already been mentioned in connection with the arrest of Gad Beck. But Larry was lucky: he was arrested in August 1944 and by the time he reached Auschwitz it was mid September. At that time the Russians were not far and the killing machinery was no longer working at high speed. Larry, physically in good shape, was sent to work with a group in an aircraft factory and liberated by the Americans in Buchenwald in April 1945. At that time, at six feet tall, he weighed eighty pounds. He returned to Berlin, where he was reunited with his mother and his brothers, who were now back in Germany in American uniforms working for United States army intelligence.

The case of Ernest Fontheim, who hid in a hut in an allotment garden just outside Berlin, also shows that in critical situations, the help of German neighbors was decisive. Fontheim was betrayed by a fanatical Nazi in the village a few months before the end of the war. But Fontheim was told almost immediately about the denunciation by another neighbor, and together with the Jewish family hiding with him he went to yet another neighbor to ask for advice and help in a desperate situation. These good people did not hesitate for a moment, provided food, buried incriminating papers, and gave them the use of their apartment in Berlin. The son of the family, a German army officer on sick leave, gave Ernest a revolver with the advice that if the Gestapo should turn up before they managed to escape to Berlin next morning, they should "shoot the pigs without hesitation." The story of Michael Degen, a few years younger, was quite similar. He told it for the first time fifty years after the event: together with his mother he hid in various allotment gardens just outside Berlin. This would have been impossible without the help of German well-wishers. Degen became a well-known actor in postwar Germany.

The subsequent fates of some of those mentioned as escapees and U-boats should be mentioned, however briefly. Herbert Strauss emigrated to New York, and became a professor and editor of a standard reference work on the German emigration. Lutz Ehrlich settled in Basel, Switzerland, where he represented an international organization dealing with Christian-Jewish relations. Schwersenz and his wife made their home in Haifa, Israel, where he worked as a teacher. But he went on long visits to Germany, where he was a frequent lecturer, especially in schools and among young people. Edith Kurzweil finished school in America and, after an interval of fifteen years, attended university. She became a distinguished university professor and the editor of *Partisan Review*. Harry Zucker became Zvi Yavetz, a professor of classics, founded two universities (Tel Aviv and Addis Ababa), wrote many learned papers and books, and taught at Queens College, New York, as well as Munich, Florence, Oxford, and Paris, lecturing in English, French, Italian, Hebrew, and even in Latin. Valentin Senger's work as a journalist has been mentioned, Konrad Latte became a conductor of a small orchestra in Berlin, and Larry Orbach had a new and successful career in the American jewelry industry. "David," Joel Koenig, studied chemistry and became chief chemist of a company near Tel Aviv. Shlomo Perel, alias Hitler Youth Salomon, also settled in Israel.

Of those deported to the camps, the overwhelming majority was killed, the very young and the elderly and the weak were gassed almost immediately after arrival. Those able to work survived a little longer, until starvation and epidemics took their toll and they were killed too. They worked in factories in Auschwitz and in the whole archipelago of little camps belonging to it. But some still survived the horrible conditions and the death marches following the evacuation of Auschwitz. Among them was Norbert Wollheim, who had been a leader in the youth movement before the war, and Heinz Galinski, who became head of the Berlin Jewish community for many years after the war, as well as president for ten years of the Jewish communities in West Germany. Another was Ignaz Bubis, a mere seventeen at the end of the war, who succeeded Galinski as president of the Jewish communities.

The Fate of the Survivors

Two other Auschwitz survivors were Renate and Anita Lasker. Born in Breslau in 1924 and 1925, respectively, they had been members of a Zionist youth movement, but unlike their third, older sister, missed the last train to England. They were sent to an orphanage after their parents had been deported and even earlier had started work in a factory. In this factory there was also a group of French prisoners of war and the two sisters helped them prepare to escape. Eventually they, too, decided to flee to Paris, but the Gestapo had been on their tracks for a while, and they were arrested at the main Breslau railway station. In an unobserved moment they swallowed cyanide capsules, but they lived to tell the story because the friend who had supplied the pills (none other than Konrad Latte, the musician mentioned earlier on) had replaced the poison with powdered sugar.

There was a trial and the two girls were given a prison sentence, which probably saved their lives, because it meant that they would not be deported to Auschwitz until December 1943. This was the perverse logic of bureaucracy, owing to which a few dozen Jewish political prisoners survived who otherwise would have perished. Charlotte Paech, a member of the Communist Baum group (about which more below), was one of these survivors. She had been sentenced to death in June 1943, but since she was in prison at the time and was in an isolation ward suffering from scarlet fever, there was a delay of many weeks. Then she was taken to Berlin, but there was another quarantine, followed by an Allied air attack, in the course of which her files were destroyed. No one remembered anymore why she had been arrested in the first place and she continued to work for six months as a nurse in prison, until she succeeded in escaping—into a camp of French "guest workers," or forced laborers.

Renate and Anita Lasker arrived at Auschwitz in late 1943. Anita was an accomplished cellist; there is a picture of her, aged three, pretending to play the cello with a broomstick and a comb. She was, in fact, the only cellist in the camp, and so she was drafted to play in the famous orchestra, led by Alma Rose, a Viennese woman from a well-known musical family. (Her father had been leader of the Vienna Philharmonic, her mother a sister of Gustav Mahler.) This meant that Anita did not have to work and received better living conditions and more food. As for Renate, Anita later wrote:

> She became a total wreck in no time at all. It was horrifying. Her appearance and general state were so bad that she was not allowed to reenter our block. So she came and stood outside and waited for me to bring her some soup or whatever else I could give her. She developed huge festering sores on her legs which would not heal . . . Eventually she contracted typhus and all seemed lost. There were times that I hoped that she would quietly die and her misery would come to an end.

But Renate survived the disease and her sister helped her to get a new assignment as a courier in the camp, which involved less work.

Like other surviving inmates of Auschwitz, Renate and Anita were transported to Belsen in West Germany as the Allies closed in. Anita had contracted typhoid, but she was alive, barely, when British units entered the camp in early April. A British Broadcasting Corporation van with equipment was touring the camp, desperately looking for someone to be interviewed. Anita was chosen and her broadcast reverberated around the world; it was the first indication that at least a few had survived. The two sisters went to England, where Anita continued to play the cello and became a founding member of the English Chamber Orchestra; she continues to play to this day. Renate became a writer and today works her garden in the south of France. Another young woman to survive Auschwitz was Karla Wagenbach, who had smuggled the famous letter out of the camp warning her comrades in Berlin of the fate in store for them.

There is the story of a few other young German Jews, Albrecht and Friedel Weinberg and Bernie Walheimer, who had trained as agricultural workers in Gross Breesen and missed the last opportunities to emigrate. They too had the good luck not to arrive at Auschwitz until 1943, and were dispatched not to the main camp but to Buna Monowitz, which belonged to I. G. Farben, and where the chances of survival were slightly better. But all those who became ill or too weak to work were also sent to the gas chambers, and Walheimer, who was sick much of the time, said in retrospect that he owed his survival to the solidarity of his fellow prisoners who made him get up from his sickbed even when he felt like dying so that he would not be listed as incapable of working and sent to the gas chambers. A few weeks after the liberation in mid May 1945, the British burned down Bergen Belsen.

Why did the two sisters survive? Why did anyone survive? Anita asked herself this question and so did others. Was it because of any special physical and mental strength? There was the case of H. H., a graduate of Auschwitz, one of those who wanted to stay anonymous. He was small of stature and likely to be overlooked at the time of a "selection." Or was it perhaps because he was an electrician of sorts and repaired the lamps in the living quarters of the SS guards? (He became head of a big air and space corporation in the United States after the war, and, after his retirement, an adviser to the U.S. government.) According to

Anita Lasker, the short answer to the question of survival is that the odds were about a hundred to one against it: "If you did witness the day of liberation—you were simply lucky." In other words, there were a great many factors that could increase or diminish the chances for survival, but since the chances were so poor, accident played the decisive role.

How many Jews from Germany and Austria did survive the extermination camps? For reasons indicated earlier, there can be only rough estimates, but their number was in the hundreds rather than in the thousands. No one returned from Izbica, and only a handful from Riga, a few more survived Auschwitz and the death marches and the transport to Belsen. The majority of camp survivors left Germany as soon as they could, some of them never to set foot again on German soil.

RESISTANCE

—◦◦◦—

German Jews had every reason to resist the persecutions, but how could they have done so? They were a small minority, less than one percent of the population in 1933, less than half a percent six years later when war broke out. The very young among them realized that their families and other Jews were mistreated but they could not understand the reasons. If they were beaten up at school or in the street, they were hopelessly outnumbered. Individuals could on occasion fight back but as a collective they could not.

What of those in their late teens who had a fuller political understanding? Their first reaction was bound to be one of confusion—why should they be singled out for mistreatment? Were they not as good Germans as the other? In what way had they merited such treatment? This was true mainly with regard to the offspring of the assimilated families, which were the majority in 1933. It was not true with regard to those from Orthodox homes or with a Zionist background who had been taught from early on that they were indeed different and/or that they belonged elsewhere.

Young people thirst for action, and as they grew up in Nazi Germany and were groping for explanations, some of them were eager not to suffer passively, not just to leave the country, but to get together and act in some way against their persecutors. But there were insurmountable difficulties. One was the sheer power of the Nazi dictatorship, with the Gestapo, the concentration camps, and its other tools of suppression. Nazi propaganda created the impression that the "national revolution" was invincible, that all those trying to resist had already been smashed. And it was of course true that all legal anti-Nazi organizations had disappeared within a few months of January 1933. Their leaders had fled abroad or were under arrest. Their illegal cells had been penetrated and destroyed. How could a handful of young people without experience and resources succeed where the big political parties with millions of voters had failed?

But there was another, even more formidable obstacle on the road to active resistance. Would-be active opponents of Nazism faced not just a dictatorial government but a people that in its great majority was either opposed to them, having been influenced by Nazi propaganda, or at best indifferent. The young Jewish opponents confronted a dictatorship of a new type, not yet quite totalitarian but on the road to becoming so. They had to fear not only the police but also their neighbors and this made effective resistance well nigh impossible. True, there were certain sectors of the population that resented Nazi rule or even hated it. These were the men and women of the left who had not surrendered their convictions in 1933, some believing Christians and other upright individuals. But the Jews were not particularly welcome as allies even in these circles; they constituted a political embarrassment and a physical threat from a practical point of view.

Jews in the Anti-Nazi Underground

If there were still some illusions in 1933/34 among Jews and non-Jews as to the depth and durability of the roots of the Nazi regime, by 1935/36 all but a handful had reached the conclusion that however detestable and dangerous the Nazi government, young Jews could not play a significant role in the active anti-Nazi struggle. The liberation of Germany would have to be the task of non-Jewish Germans, or as it eventually came to pass, of outside military powers. It could not be the work of a group of people who had become pariahs. This conclusion was reached not just by individuals but also by political parties. The Communist party had advised its Jewish members either to leave Germany or, if they could not do so, to form their own Jewish cells, outside the Communist underground.

Jewish anti-Nazi militants of the older generation had left Germany or were in prison or concentration camps. But there were small groups of younger people who had been members or fellow travelers of the Young Communist League or other such groups. The younger brothers or sisters or cousins of those who had to leave the struggle now volunteered for all kind of activities. They were in a better position for the illegal struggle simply because they had no police record, and being young they were less likely to attract attention. They met in small study groups and read the Communist Manifesto and *Das Kapital*, even if they did not understand a single word of it. They listened to Radio Moscow about the great successes of the Five Year Plan and from time to time an older comrade would turn up and give a survey of the world situation as seen by a revolutionary Marxist. They would then proceed to more active undertakings, such as acting as couriers with comrades abroad, in Paris, Prague, and Brussels. They would carry correspondence, instructions, propaganda brochures, and occasionally money. They would write slogans on the walls of houses, leave leaflets in buses, and cautiously try to gain new members.

Most of these illegal groups were caught by the Gestapo and their members arrested, not because the police was all powerful but because of the circumstances that have been mentioned. Sometimes the Gestapo had infiltrated by placing a mole or two in the leadership of the illegal group; at other times they had apprehended the illegals by sheer accident or because the names of the others had been given away by one who had been arrested. The few cells that still existed by the late thirties had largely become inactive because they felt isolated, incapable of bringing about any change through their activities.

There had been many left-wing groups in pre-Nazi Germany but only in two of their youth organizations had significant numbers of young Jews been active. This was the Communist party with its youth league, and the KPO, a Communist splinter faction, which had protested the suicidal line of the Communists in pre-Hitler Germany, according to which the Social Democrats rather than the Nazis were the main enemy. (There were other left-wing groups with a sizeable Jewish membership, such as the SAP, ISK [the Nelson Bund], and Neu Beginnen, all ideologically located somewhere between the Social Democrats and the Communists, but they had no separate youth groups and therefore do not directly bear on our discussion.)

Many young Jews had earlier belonged to one of the apolitical youth movements, but in the wake of the general politicization and radicalization of the early 1930s, some of them had moved into the orbit of the extreme left. They had come to believe that only the victory of the world revolution would solve the Jewish question and do away with antisemitism once and for all. Those who could left Germany after 1933, but some were unable to.

Some six hundred KPO members were arrested in 1933/34. They were lucky because in those early years only short prison terms were imposed on most of the younger ones among them. The subsequent fate of one of the biggest branches (Breslau) is not atypical. Marianne, a young militant not yet aged eighteen at the time, was given a sentence of less than two years, and not long after her release emigrated to Palestine. Ernesto Kroch did not get a long sentence either but was rearrested after his time was up and taken to a concentration camp. Eventually, he was permitted to leave for Yugoslavia, and found a new home of sorts in Uruguay. Heinz Putzrath, also released after having served his prison sentence, made his way to England and joined the Social Democrats and, after the war, worked for many years in the party's central office in Bonn. Two other members escaped to Sweden.

The local branch was headed by three brothers named Blass, one of whom escaped to Brazil, another to Palestine, and the third was caught and given a lengthy sentence. Miraculously, he survived prison and concentration camps, but his wife, who had emigrated to Britain, remarried thinking that he had died. He had a modest political career in East Germany after the war. Two other militants, Walter Rosenthal and Ernst Fabisch, went to the Soviet Union to work as technical specialists. Rosenthal was lucky and left in time for Latin America, but Fabisch was caught up in the maelstrom of the Stalinist purges, was extradited to Nazi Germany after the nonaggression pact of 1939, and was killed.

Those who continued to be active illegally and were arrested in 1938 fared worse. Helga Beyer, aged eighteen, who had acted as a courier, received a three-and-a-half-year sentence. Her letters to her sister in Shanghai have been preserved. On her birthday, May 4, 1941, she wrote that she was now working in the garden of the prison, that she liked her work and was sunburned. She was studying English, and her emigration affairs were managed by Dr. Spitz, a Breslau lawyer. A month later she wrote that this was her last letter but one from prison, and that she was overjoyed by the prospect of being reunited with her sister so soon. Helga Beyer did not anticipate that the Gestapo would be waiting for her at the gate of the prison on the day of her release, that she would be taken to Ravensbrueck concentration camp, where she would die a horrible death within a year of her release from prison. Ursel, her sister, who had only been marginally involved in the activities of the group had been acquitted in the trial, and moved to Shanghai; eventually she settled in New York.

Ten people, ten different fates.

Heroism and Futility

Were the sacrifices worthwhile? The futility of political resistance by a small group of people that had been effectively removed from the body politic of the German people is highlighted by the activities of the Herbert Baum group in Berlin. Herbert Baum had been a Communist youth leader before 1933. He was assisted by his wife and two other party comrades. They were in their twenties; most of their followers were six to eight years younger. They had all belonged to German Jewish youth groups, some Zionist, others non-Zionist, some Communist moles in search of a legal cover, others bona fide members won over by Baum to the Communist party line. When these legal youth groups were dissolved in 1938, the Baum group became a refuge for those who had not emigrated. Altogether the group consisted of thirty to forty members and camp followers; many of them had been sent by the authorities to do forced labor in the Siemens factory. They were studying the classics of Marxism-Leninism but while the Nazi-Soviet pact was in force, their anti-Nazi activities were bound to remain restricted to meetings and discussions in accordance with the then Communist party line.

It was only after the Nazi attack on the Soviet Union that the group began to distribute leaflets and paint slogans on the walls of houses. Since they had no access to duplicating machines, only a few copies were actually distributed. Their main exploit was the attempt to put fire to an anti-Communist exhibition in the Berlin Lustgarten entitled "The Soviet Paradise," showing the great danger and wickedness of the "Judaeo-Bolshevik world enemy." This attempt of sabotage was a total failure: it was barely mentioned in the local media and within ten days it led to the arrest of the members of the group. The Gestapo announced that it had penetrated an illegal Communist group, but it is more likely that the group had been betrayed by someone who was never identified. Joachim Franke, a non-Jewish Communist, had provided technical material to the group and had been arrested a few days before the operation; he might have given the information under torture. But these are mere suspicions; no evidence was found after the war, and Franke was executed along with the members of the Baum group. It is also possible that violating elementary rules of conspiracy had invited the disaster. They needed money and under the guise of Gestapo agents had "expropriated" fellow Jews. Those robbed had complained to the police, and the police had informed them that for once the Gestapo had not been involved.

Herbert Baum committed suicide, or more likely was driven to suicide two weeks after his arrest. Twenty-two members of the group and several more who had belonged to its periphery were sentenced to death, executed, or sent for "special treatment" to an extermination camp. Four survived, escaping abroad or hiding inside Germany. In addition, the Gestapo arrested five hundred Jews who had been in no way connected with these activities; half of them were immediately shot, the other half were killed within a few days in the nearby Sachsenhausen concentration camp. Leaders of the Berlin Jewish community were ordered to witness the executions.

After World War II, the Herbert Baum group became the symbol of Jewish resistance in East Germany and a Berlin street was named after its leader. Other streets in East Berlin were named after Rudi Arndt and Hans Litten, Communist militants who had come from the German Jewish youth movement and were killed in Nazi concentration camps. No street has been named so far in East Germany in honor of their erstwhile comrades who had emigrated to the Soviet Union and perished in Stalin's camps or were shot in Soviet prisons without benefit of a trial.

The story of the Baum group is also related with admiration in some works published in the West. And it is indeed impossible to deny their brave stand when arrested, making no secret of their convictions. But in their propaganda they never stressed Jewish concerns or anti-Jewish persecutions. This, too, conformed with the Communist party line, which argued until about 1936 that Nazi persecutions were directed against only poor Jews, not against rich ones. The party later changed its line, but was fully aware that this issue was not popular, and with one exception (after the November 1938 pogroms) made no mention of the persecution of the Jews. In its propaganda the Baum group was preoccupied with issues such as the class struggle in general and the difficulties Berlin housewives faced in obtaining sufficient food in wartime conditions. The Baum group accepted the basic tenets of Communist doctrine—Judaism as a religion and an ethnic group was bound to disappear, and the victory of Communism would bring about a new world order in which the Jews would no longer be persecuted but have equal rights.

One can sympathize with members of a small, isolated group in the center of Nazi Germany, who felt that something ought to be done to fight the evil monster. Neither Baum nor his followers were students of political philosophy or even reasonably well informed about the state of world affairs. But it is still true that they lived in a fantasy world, their ideas were at best unrealistic and their actions utterly futile. Their courage was matched only by their political blindness. Given the circumstances, there simply was no room for them in the antifascist struggle. Baum claimed on occasion that they were doomed in any case, but he had preached for years that the place of young Jewish antifascists was in Germany fighting Nazism side by side with German Communists. For some of this group, there was perhaps no escape, but others had the opportunity to emigrate yet were not encouraged by Baum to do so; the few who did were treated more or less as deserters. They were victims and made others victims in a struggle that was not their struggle.

More effective but less well known were the activities of a small group called Society for Peace and Reconstruction, active in Berlin and neighboring cities in Brandenburg. The leading spirits were Hans Winkler, politically unaffiliated, who worked at a local court in a subordinate capacity, and Werner Scharff, a young Jew, one of the few who had succeeded in escaping from Theresienstadt and returned to Berlin. Consisting mainly of lower-middle-class opponents of the Nazi regime, the group hid and helped dozens of Jews to survive and distributed thousands of anti-Nazi leaflets. Toward the end of 1944, most of the members of the group were arrested—their conspiratorial experience was virtually nil and they had failed to take elementary precautions. But most, including Winkler, survived as the trial against them dragged on, and most of the Jews they had protected also were saved.

Helmut Hirsch and Hilda Monte

Hundreds of young Jews were arrested after 1933 for active participation in the anti-Nazi struggle; dozens paid with their lives. Their resistance did not make the slightest difference. But did it mean that resistance was altogether impossible? Was political activity the only way to resist? Werner Scharff did not think so, nor did Helmut Hirsch. Born in Stuttgart in 1916 and a student of architecture, Hirsch had belonged to an elite (non-Jewish) German youth group, the DJ 1st of November. He went to Prague where he associated with Otto Strasser, who had once been a prominent follower of Hitler but had left the Nazi party because he believed in a national revolutionary orientation, whereas Hitler, as he saw it, was a reactionary. Strasser was by that time a genuine opponent of Nazi rule, but among his lieutenants there were Nazi agents, and the Gestapo learned almost immediately of Hirsch's plan to plant bombs on the grounds of the annual convention of the Nazi party in Nuremberg, possibly killing Hitler. Hirsch was followed from the moment he reentered German territory, and arrested soon after. He was executed in June 1937 despite U.S. diplomatic protests, for Hirsch also had U.S. citizenship.

There were other ways to resist Nazi rule. Toward the very end of the war, on April 17, 1945, German border police arrested a woman trying to cross the Swiss-Austrian border near the town of Feldkirch. When she tried to escape, she was shot. According to the papers found on her body, she was a secretary named Schneider; the authorities never established her true identity. Her real name was Hilda Monte, born Meisel, and she had belonged to the extreme left that had split away from one of the nonpolitical German Jewish youth groups. She later joined the ISK, a left-wing neo-Kantian group headed by the philosopher Leonard Nelson. Having emigrated with her parents to Britain, she became a militant and published books and articles about the future of Germany and Europe *(Where Freedom Perishes)*. But she also acted as a courier, entering Germany more than once during the war, serving both British intelligence (without whose help these missions could not have been undertaken) and the remnants of her own group, which were reorganizing toward the end of the war for political work during the years to come. It is impossible to calculate the importance of the contribution of Hilda Monte (and others like her) to the Allied war effort to defeat Nazi Germany. But there can be no doubt that she did contribute, just as did the Allied commandos who landed behind the German lines.

Helmut Hirsch was a politically naïve youngster; it is doubtful whether he ever heard of dialectical materialism. Young people like him were not trained for terrorist action, nor was it easy for them to

obtain suitable weapons. The chances of killing a Nazi leader, including Hitler, were remote but not impossible, as the assassination of
Heydrich in 1941 was to show. It was, in fact, the only danger of which
Hitler was truly afraid, as he said on more than one occasion, for he
knew that against one truly determined sniper all the precautions of
the security forces would be in vain. If Hirsch or someone like him had
succeeded, such an assassination might have changed history, in a way
the Baum group's leaflets appealing to the Berlin housewives could
never have done.

German Jews in the French Maquis

The cases of Hirsch and Hilda Monte attracted some attention and they
appear, albeit as mere footnotes, in the annals of the resistance to Nazism. But there were others, younger yet, who survived, and whose actions became widely known only many years after. Among these are
Herbert Herz, born 1923, Leo Weil, born 1921, and Lothar Martin, born
1924, to choose three out of perhaps three hundred who were fighting in
the French underground. They came from the Augsburg region and,
like many refugees from southern Germany, escaped to Western Europe. Herbert Herz went with his mother and brother to France; the
mother survived, the brother tried to enter Switzerland, was sent back
by the Swiss police, and perished at Auschwitz. Leo Weil went to Amsterdam in 1936, and Lothar Martin passed the French border at
Kehl/Strassburg in 1939 underneath a railway carriage. Weil learned
Dutch quickly and Herz picked up enough French in his years of apprenticeship to pass for a native. Weil joined a Communist underground group and after several narrow escapes—the first from the
Westerbork camp, the second from a train to Germany—went to
France where he joined the FFI (Forces Françaises d'Interieur). He was
involved in bank raids to obtain money for his maquis, as well as in the
assassination of Gestapo informers, was arrested in Paris in July 1944
and shipped to Buchenwald with one of the last transports. He survived
the camp and returned to Paris, where he joined the French army, was
promoted to the rank of lieutenant, and received the Croix de Guerre.
Herbert Herz, aged eighteen, also joined the armed underground
(Carmagnole-Liberté), was renamed Raoul, and, being an electrician,
was in charge of the armory of his group. From September 1943 he

participated in many attacks, first in the Grenoble region, later in Toulon. He returned to Grenoble in 1945, and after three years graduated as an electrical engineer.

Lothar Martin had reached France relatively late and his knowledge of the language and the people was not sufficient to hide for any length in the underground. But he was experienced and courageous enough even at the age of sixteen to travel to the south of France and to cross the Pyrenees near Perpignan—all this with a broken arm, which he had suffered during an escape from a camp. In Lerida, Spain, he joined a group of Frenchmen who traveled to North Africa, where he became a soldier, subsequently a lieutenant in the Second Armored Division, the best of the French units at the time. He took part in the battle of Bir Hakim, and later participated in the Normandy landing, the liberation of France, and the Battle of the Bulge. He was twice wounded.

What made these youngsters fight? They could have hidden their identities, lived quietly underground, or tried to escape to Spain. Was it the desire for adventure or the wish to avenge the murder of members of their family, or a vague feeling of duty, or perhaps a mixture of these and other motives? Both Weil and Herz belonged to Communist underground groups, but in interviews many years later they said that this was more or less by accident. Weil related that while his friends in Holland belonging to The Group (Huis Oosteinde) were studying and discussing *Das Kapital*, he was not a member of the party, and preferred playing table tennis and hiking. Herz, also interviewed decades later, said that he might as well have fought in a Zionist cell, but it so happened that being a young worker he established at work contact with a Communist group. While fighting he was politicized and became a Communist for a while, but this had not been his original motivation. On the contrary, he related that the party had not helped him escape from Westerbork camp.

Young Refugees and the British War Effort

For the great majority of young refugees, tens of thousands of them, resistance meant military service in the war against Nazi Germany, in Britain, the United States, and, of course, Palestine. Their motivation, the way they served and were treated, varied greatly from country to country (and sometimes from unit to unit), but for all of them the years of military service were of decisive importance as far as their later life was concerned.

In Britain during the early years, those wanting to volunteer had to go through an obstacle course; most, in fact, were shabbily treated, except only the few who had the good fortune to have been naturalized before the outbreak of the war. A few fared better because of special talents or connections—such as, for instance, Robert Kronfeld, the Austrian holder of glider records who was immediately accepted and given the rank of squadron leader in the Royal Air Force. But Kronfeld was an exceptional case, a man of international fame, having established a number of world records; he was the first before World War II to fly one hundred kilometers, the first to reach a height of two thousand five hundred meters, the first to fly over the Alps and to cross the British Channel.

Some six "alien" pioneer companies were set up in 1939/40; they were not issued arms but expected to engage in road construction work, setting up Nissen huts and other such work. These units consisted of older non-refugee conscripted men or those suffering from a physical defect and their slogan *(Labor Omnia Vincit)* was quoted more often humorously than in earnest. The officers appointed to head these units were those unwanted in other parts of the army. Their camps were miserable. Eventually, some of them found themselves in France prior to the surrender in 1940. Among the many other inequities to which these volunteers were exposed was the fact that they were not given British nationality upon enlisting (or at least upon being sent abroad) which meant that they would have no protection if they were taken prisoners of war, because the name change that was common practice was hardly likely to deceive the Germans.

When the bedraggled remnants of Seventy-Fourth Company Pioneer Corps arrived in Southend on Sea having been evacuated from Dunkirk, they were inspected by their commander, a brigade general, the marquess of Reading, the scion of one of the leading Anglo-Jewish families, who told them that never in his army career had he seen such a display of filth and dirt, an absolute disgrace. The marquess may well have been right, but as Sergeant Pelican later wrote, it was still a case of monumental chutzpah; he should have shown some tact, understanding and compassion vis-à-vis men who, in contrast to him, had not eaten, received anything to drink, shaved, or slept for days. In a report to the War Office written after the end of hostilities, Lord Reading complained about the Tower of Babel atmosphere prevailing in these units. But he also conceded that the general dishevelment was not entirely the Pioneers' fault; the physique of his men was different from those of the average Englishman, the garments issued did not fit, and larger caps were needed. In brief, the climate in these companies could have been better.

After the fall of France there was a long pause as far as enlistment was concerned; most of those who wanted to volunteer were detained or had been shipped to Canada and Australia. As British policy with regard to the detainees became more liberal, they were offered the choice of volunteering for the Pioneer units or remaining in the camps for an indefinite period. This was not an exhilarating prospect and the number of volunteers increased, but there were other motives as well, the feeling that they should do their duty against Nazism, the restlessness and expectation of adventure among the very young—as one of them put it: "We were absolutely too young to sit around doing nothing."

From 1941 on British policy gradually changed—first it was decided that aliens could be commissioned in the Pioneer Corps; by the end of 1941 the pioneers were at long last issued rifles; and from early 1943 aliens were permitted to serve in units other than the Pioneer Corps, with the exception of the Royal Signal Corps. At the same time, women could join the ATS (Auxiliary Territorial Service), the WAAF (Women's Auxiliary Air Force), and as doctors and nurses in the RAMC (Royal Army Medical Corps), where they could even serve as officers. Most of the women saw service as clerks, drivers, waitresses, and radio and telephone operators, but a few also made it as radar operators, bomb plotters, and flight mechanics. Altogether some three thousand refugee women served in the United Kingdom in the ATS and WAAF, and about the same number served in the Middle East, having volunteered in Palestine.

Individuals did have eventful war careers. Captain J. Kennedy, an Austrian serving with the French Foreign Legion, who had been evacuated to Britain after Dunkirk, joined the Eighty-Seventh Company Pioneer Corps, volunteered for special services, took a leading part in a commando raid on Tobruk in North Africa and gained both the M.M. and M.C. (the Military Medal is the highest distinction for enlisted men, the Military Cross one of the highest for officers.) But it ought to be recalled that the great majority of the British army (as distinct from the air force and the navy) was not involved in fighting prior to the invasion in June 1944, with the exception of North Africa and India. There is the temptation to quote the accounts of those who made spectacular careers or went through particularly exciting situations. But even those who fought in the front line in regular or commando units did so mainly during the last twelve months of the war. The stories they have to tell concerning the earlier months and years were mainly about training, which was interesting and challenging in the case of special units, but boring and often frustrating in other cases.

The Commandos

The story of Stephen Dale born in Berlin in 1917, another graduate of the Jewish youth movement, is fairly typical. He was detained in 1940, shipped to Australia, returned to Britain and served at first with the Pioneer Corps. He applied for a transfer, was ordered to come for an interview in the War Office, and, having been found suitable for the assignment (what the assignment would be was not revealed to him and the others for many months) he was sent to various training centers in England and Scotland, where he learned about weapons and had his first parachute jumps. Eventually, it was made clear to him that he and the other trainees would operate in units of four on behalf of the Special Operations Executive, which had been established in 1940 to engage in subversion and sabotage on the continent. He was sent on a mission into northeast Italy in October 1944, but had the misfortune to be taken prisoner very soon after.

One of the more interesting units was the X Troop (with the mysterious official designation, 3 Troop 10 Commando), established by Lord Mountbatten, at one time chief of combined operations. Some three hundred refugees from Germany and Austria served in these units, the very existence of which was kept secret for reasons unknown until long after the war, except that Mountbatten revealed on one occasion that these had been very brave people and that half of them had been killed in active service. Peter Masters, born Peter Aranyi in Vienna, describes his interview for joining this unit in the seedy Grand Central Hotel in Marylebone High Street in London in April 1943. His unit became 3 Troop 10 Commando. Carlebach became Andrew Carson; Nomburg became Harry Drew; Geiser became Henry Gordon; Manfred Gans became Freddy Gray; Abramowitz became Arlen; Landau became Langley; Levy became Maurice Latimer; Weinberger became Webster; and Oskar Henschel became Sergeant Major O'Neill. Someone in the London War Office must have thought, that from now on, there could be little doubt about the truly British character of this unit, given the fact that the British authorities were still unwilling to give these men British citizenship.

These young people had excelled in sports and they were further toughened on various training grounds. They saw a great deal of fighting after the invasion of Europe; out of eighty-seven in Masters' unit, twenty were killed, eighteen became commissioned officers, four of them receiving battlefield commissions. Masters wrote in retrospect that "had we been British born, many of us would have begun their military careers in cadre school and reached high rank. Handicapped not only by being foreigners but also being enemy aliens, we were held back further by being in a Commando troop we did not want to jeopardize (our unit) by leaving when it was about to go into action."

The parachutists were later attached to various brigades and saw action in North Africa as well as Sicily and Italy. They suffered heavy losses in operation "Market Garden" (Arnheim) and operation "Dragoon" in the south of France, near Toulon. On this, as on other occasions, such as in Greece, they landed behind enemy lines, acting as pathfinders for Allied gliders and other regular units.

Some became officers because of leadership qualities, others because they had been to the right school (those who had attended a private school were thought to be officer material, but few refugees had been to such schools). In some cases persistence paid off. Albert Lisbona belonged to an old Sephardi family but had been born and educated in Berlin. When war broke out he was engaged in business in Cairo. He wanted to volunteer for the British army but all they offered him was the Pioneer Corps in which he would not see combat. After various futile attempts he had an interview with an ill-disposed senior RAF officer. The fact that Lisbona's citizenship (lapsed) was German certainly did not help. The officer eventually asked him what made him so eager to see action, whereupon Lisbona replied that being a Jew he was at least as highly motivated as the man who interviewed him. This argument proved to be persuasive: he was sent for training in Rhodesia, and became an RAF pilot and eventually a flying instructor in various theaters of war. Had he been of British nationality he would

have become a squadron leader; since he was not, he ended the war as
warrant officer (a rank roughly equivalent to staff sergeant). But at
least they let him fly.

An elite unit was like an exclusive club: it was difficult to enter but
once a person had been admitted, he was treated like a member—the
esprit de corps extended to all. Ernest Goodman was nineteen when he
joined the Coldstream Guards, one of the elite British regiments; he
was one of only two refugees to be admitted. (The Guards had suffered
heavy losses in Italy and were looking for replacements.) He was severely injured in fighting on the continent, and back in the hospital in
Britain, it was not certain whether he would live. In an unpublished
memoir, he was full of praise about the way he was treated. The nurses
informed the many visitors to sick and injured soldiers from nearby
mills and factories in and around Birmingham that a very sick and
lonely soldier needed company:

> As a result people saved some of their very meagre rations for me, they
> brought eggs, and some of the teenaged girls from the nearby factory
> kept chicken especially for me. I never knew how many people had
> adopted me, but when these marvellous people came to visit me on Sun-
> days, after expensive and complicated bus trips, they loaded me with
> presents of food and other things. The girls baked cakes and at one time
> I had ten cakes on my bed with heartfelt messages.

Wartime created a new climate, a new camaraderie not only within
the fighting units but between the refugees and the rest of the population. And yet, the aliens were still aliens and Goodman as well as Peter
Masters and many others went to live in America after the war. Once
they were demobilized in 1945/46 having faithfully served king and
country, the alien soldiers and officers still had to proceed to the nearest police station in their hometown to register as aliens.

By the end of the war refugees could be found in virtually all units
of the British army, including those engaged in highly secret scientific
work. As in the U.S. army, German speakers were in particular demand during the last months of the war and thereafter in intelligence,
the search for war criminals, the preparations for the Nuremberg
trials, and also the administration of occupied Germany and Austria.
Throughout the war certain circles in the Austrian emigration had
tried hard to differentiate between German and Austrian refugees, in-
sisting on the establishment of special Austrian units, always on the

assumption that Austria was "Hitler's first victim" and that many if not most of the refugees would return to Austria after the war. There even was a Free Austria committee in Palestine demanding the repatriation of refugees to their homeland. But in the end, as the extent of the Nazi atrocities and Austrian collusion in these acts became known, very few Austrians chose to return.

Even earlier on refugees had taken a very active part in psychological warfare such as monitoring enemy broadcasts, broadcasting, and composing leaflets to be dropped over Germany. Martin Esslin, who in later years attained fame as an expert in the field of modern drama, and George Weidenfeld began their career in the BBC monitoring service. There were at the time several Allied radio stations, the BBC quite apart, broadcasting to Germany from England as well as the Mediterranean and later on from Italy (Bari). Hundreds of German writers and speakers were employed in these stations. However, few of the younger generation took part in these activities, for preference was given to those who had an earlier career in Germany and Austria as journalists.

In Occupied Germany

The number of translators and administrators needed in Germany was considerable, and many young people were pulled out from their units because of their proficiency in German. Some interrogated German political and military leaders; others searched for war criminals. Fred Pelican describes how a search could concern one specific incident, such as the murder by the local Nazi chief in the city of Neuss of a British pilot shot down in December 1943. The culprit was hiding, but following extensive detective work, Sergeant Pelican got his man. In another case Pelican and Captain Freud searched for a major criminal, Dr. Bruno Tesch, who had provided Zyklon B, the poison gas for Auschwitz. He was also caught and punished.

Many refugee soldiers stationed in Germany were hoping against hope that some members of their families who had remained in Germany had survived. In the great majority of cases these hopes were in vain, but there were a few incidents in which at least one or two of those missing were located. Pelican, a native of Upper Silesia, was reunited with his mother, who had survived Auschwitz, and he related how the joy was shared by many of his comrades in arms and even officers and that he left for Berlin loaded with presents. Franz Loeser had hoped to find his mother hiding in Amsterdam, and he describes how he made his way in a jeep to the address he had, Weteringschans 49. He found a pale, starved man clad only in pajamas who had been hidden in a hole under the roof, his brother Peter. His mother had been deported, never to return, like the rest of the family. Master Sergeant Werner Angress of the U.S. army also found his mother in Amsterdam. Lieutenant Freddy Gray (Manfred Gans) of a British commando unit went in a jeep through the Soviet zone of occupation to Theresienstadt. There he found his parents in this showcase ghetto. "Freddy looked at his father. He had been prepared for a shock, but in spite of that, he had to clench his teeth not to show it. He could hardly recognize him; had he met this starved wreck of a man, his clothes hanging too loose on his gaunt body, in the street he would not have known him. The parents could not stop crying."

While many former Pioneers were now hunting war criminals, others were helping to build a new Germany. The story of Michael Thomas (Hollaender) was not atypical. When the gates of the British detention camp closed behind him in 1940, the prospects for a military career were not rosy, though Thomas swore that he would end the war with the rank of major. His friends did not even laugh. Thomas was half Jewish, his father had been a well-known writer of texts for musicals and revues performed in Berlin in the 1920s. Thomas had belonged to the Berlin *jeunesse dorée* and had studied with some of the best-known professors. When he was released from detention, owing to connections in high places in London, he did not have to join the Pioneers but was transferred to a regiment of the line. It consisted of men from North Lancashire, and though Thomas spoke English well he needed a translator to understand what the soldiers were telling him. He became a second lieutenant and then an instructor.

At the time of the invasion of the continent, Thomas was made liaison officer with a Polish division and, after the capitulation of Germany, an influential figure on the staff of General Templer in Bad Oeynhausen, which was at the time the center of the British command. By now Thomas had the rank of major and was in a position of considerable influence. He granted licences to German newspapers and periodicals, including some that would later become most important, such as the weeklies *Der Spiegel* and *Die Zeit* in Hamburg, which was part of the British zone. Thomas had known professor Carlo Schmid as a teacher before the war; Schmid now emerged as a leading Social Democrat. He also came to know most of the German politicians of the first hour, including Adenauer (whom the British disliked) and Ernst Reuter, burgomaster of Berlin. Captain Marion Bieber, Thomas' deputy and another bilingual German Jewish refugee, was his liaison with the German left. She introduced him to a man who, she claimed, would one day play a leading role in German politics—Willy Brandt. Thomas was not in a decision-making position as far as high politics were concerned but his reports, oral and written, were influential as far as appointments in the early postwar period were concerned.

The story of Major Lindford, a Jewish refugee from Austria who had fought with the armored corps, was similar. An Oxford student at the outbreak of the war, he made it from the Pioneer Corps to intelligence officer of a division and eventually deputy secretary in the Allied Commission for Austria. Soon after his demobilization, Thomas joined a German business engaged in steel imports and exports. A few other refugees, both from England and the United States, had similar postwar careers in Germany. Some were in charge for a while of British and U.S. radio stations (such as RIAS in Berlin), but hardly any chose to become German citizens, except two who became judges and a handful who returned to an academic career and thus became state employees.

Several thousand refugees of German Jewish origin continued to serve in the armed services up to 1947, and some continued to belong to the territorial army (the volunteer standing army) even after their release. Meanwhile those who had been released earlier on had founded various veteran associations partly to keep contact with each other but also to defend common interests. In addition, company reunions took place and regimental Old Comrades associations were set up. Above all there was the two-year fight for British nationality. All other alien soldiers who had fought in the British army were naturalized after the war but the German Jews were still enemy aliens subject to many restrictions especially as far as employment was concerned. In theory they had to observe even the curfew regulations, meaning that they had to be at home once darkness fell. Those who had been wounded in the army received army pensions but the others were not automatically eligible for the various government schemes for released soldiers, modest as they were, and they had to fight for them.

The younger ones among the veterans seldom had the time and energy to engage in these activities. Normal life for them had been interrupted for six years or more; they wanted to get on with their lives.
Employment opportunities in postwar Britain were limited. Those who
succeeded in finding a niche for themselves stayed on; others emigrated to America and other parts of the world.

Among the G.I.s

It is relatively easy to trace the fate of the young refugees who had
joined the British army, since the majority were kept together, first in
the detention camps and then in the Pioneer Corps. Their paths did
not diverge until the last two years of the war. In the United States on
the other hand the process was quite different; there was no volunteering, but those who had been found fit to serve received their call-up
notice in due time and were then shipped to Fort Dix, Fort Smith, Fort
Bragg, Fort Jackson, or one of the other main training centers. As in
Britain, the army drafted enemy aliens, who as such, in theory at least,
were subject to countless restrictions including the right to carry arms.
But within several weeks or months this anomaly was usually put right
in the nearest courthouse, where a certificate of naturalization was issued. Having done their basic training, those who showed promise and
adjusted well to army routine were promoted, receiving two, three, or
four stripes, and after a while were shipped off to England, North Africa, the Far East, or one of the Pacific islands.

The story of these young refugee soldiers (there were few women
among them outside the medical corps) during the early years of the
war is more or less identical to that of all other recruits: they were
treated the same, received the same rations, went through the same exercises. Most went to the infantry, only relatively few made it to the
navy or the air Force. Many were found in camps in Britain during the
months before the invasion of Normandy; they also fought in Italy
under General Clark. It was only as the U.S. army made its way toward
the German border in September 1944 that the army command realized
that German speakers would be needed on a massive scale for intelligence, the administration of occupied Germany, and the interrogation
of prisoners of war. And it was at this stage that army intelligence

began to pull out refugee soldiers and to use them where and in the way they were needed most.

Many hundreds congregated in Camp Ritchie, the military intelligence training camp in the Blue Ridge Mountains not too far from Washington. Following some routine investigation of their background by the FBI they were taught essential techniques and upon graduating from their courses were sent back to serve in S-2 and G-2 intelligence units from the regimental to the army level. Others went to CIC, the Counter Intelligence agency, which had its own training center at Fort Holabird, Maryland, but also used the Camp Ritchie facilities. Yet others went to the OSS (Office of Strategic Services) or to one of the psychological warfare agencies.

In later years the research department of the OSS attracted more interest among historians than any other branch, not so much because of its contribution to the war effort, which was minimal, but because it was manned by a group of academics who attained great fame (and in some cases notoriety) in the 1950s and 1960s, including Herbert Marcuse, Franz Neumann, Stuart Hughes, and Otto Kirchheimer. Later some were accused of deliberately having suppressed information about the Holocaust. But this had not been their assignment in the first place and in any case the employees of the research department of the OSS, with perhaps the exception of the very youngest, belonged to another, older generation.

The younger generation went where the real action was, the battlefield. Later on, their daily work was often humdrum, interrogating German prisoners of war with regard to the positions of their units and other such details, reading and analyzing written material that had been seized by the advancing American armies. But on occasion, by using bluff and force of personality, these intelligence trainees took whole units of German soldiers prisoner. Sergeant (later Captain) Walter Midener received the Silver Star and a battlefield commission for having more or less singlehandly taken scores (of admittedly demoralized) German soldiers prisoner in the Battle of Falaise-Argentan. Sergeant Walter Eichelbaum achieved a similar feat during the battle of the Bulge when he spotted a German special unit that was in American uniform, and through commands shouted in German led them into U.S. captivity. He was decorated by General Patton. Lieutenant (later Captain) John Weitz, an agent of the active branch of the OSS was reportedly parachuted behind German lines. Midener in later life became a well-known sculptor, and Weitz had a distinguished career as a fashion designer. The most spectacular postwar career was of course that of Henry Kissinger, an infantryman and interpreter with the Eighty-Fourth Infantry Division at the time, later chief adviser of the municipal government of Krefeld and of the Bergstrasse district south of Frankfurt.

During the last, desperate German counterattacks, some refugee soldiers had the misfortune to fall into German hands, as did Sergeant Werner Angress in the fighting for Normandy and Sergeant Ernst Beier at Cherveaux during the Battle of the Bulge. (The former later became a history professor, the latter professor of psychology). Together with many others Beier was shipped to Stalag 9B, a prisoner of war camp where the Gestapo tried to carry out a "selection." Jewish prisoners for war were to be segregated and be sent to an unknown destination. The spokesmen of the prisoners of war told the Gestapo that this was not the way things were done in America, whereupon he was included among the 450 suspected Jews to be deported. In actual fact, many of those selected by the Gestapo experts were not Jewish at all, and most of them survived. In another camp, however, two Jewish prisoners of war were murdered by their captors.

Strange are the ways of providence. At the very time Sergeant Beier was discussing *Faust* with Dr. Schatler, the Gestapo representative in the camp who tried to trip him up and prove that he was a Jew and therefore subject to "selection," his cousin Ulli Beier, a native of Berlin and the son of a Jewish doctor and a Protestant mother, was in a British camp in Palestine. Blond and blue-eyed, Ulli was suspected of being a German agent. In these boring months of detention he took a correspondence course in phonetics and thus laid the foundation for a career that took him to Africa. He became a world famous scholar of Yoruba art and literature and was made an honorary chieftain; his wife became a priestess. Later on he specialized in native art in New Guinea, founding the important museum in Port Moresby. He was not the only one to be arrested at the time as a suspicious character, possibly a spy, by the British police in Palestine. When "David" (Joel Koenig) arrived in Haifa in 1944, having lived underground in Berlin and escaped against all odds by way of Hungary and Romania, his story was not at first believed and he was put under arrest.

As the war ended, the demand for soldiers of German and Austrian background became even greater, and old friends and comrades met for the first time since they had left Germany. Those who had been at the farming school in Gross Breesen were dispersed, quite literally, all over the world. Many had joined the U.S. army and in their bulletins postcards and letters began to appear, such as that from Staff Sergeant Henry Kornes: "I had the surprise of my life when I came up into the orderly room and stared into a face which seemed rather familiar to me—it was Isi [First Lieutenant Isi Kirschrith] who has been assigned to U.S. forces in Austria." Kirschrith was to stay with the army for the next thirty-two years.

A postcard from Bad Homburg, Germany, turns up in the archives:

> This is to report the meeting of the three of us, Schorsch, Walter and Pimpf. I was assigned a billet near the resort promenade and ran into Schorsch two days later. The following afternoon we went swimming and met Pimpf who works for the local military government.

The joy was great but did not last long, they parted ways again, quite frequently forever. And those who went back to administer Germany could not fail to remember their many friends and comrades who had been murdered. As Staff Sergeant Angress wrote from somewhere in Germany, "let us not forget that for most of us there is bad news." He had been among the lucky ones, finding some of his family alive in Holland. Yet another, a first lieutenant, wrote, "let us not forget that we do not belong to them [the Germans] anymore." The writer of this letter was to return to Germany a few years later, but he was one of the very few who did. Actors returned and some writers and established academics, but not those of the younger generation. During the years after the capitulation of Germany there continued to be many jobs there for German speakers. There was a considerable American presence in Germany and also in Austria called OMGUS, the office of the military government; people were needed to administer a country that did not yet have its own government, to establish and direct the media, to hunt down Nazis and prepare the Nuremberg and other trials. More experts than before were needed for the various intelligence agencies. Translators were in demand at every level and other opportunities opened up. But to repeat, at least for a number of years, most of those who chose Germany as a career belonged to an older generation, and were those who had finished their academic educations or even practiced their professions in Germany before Hitler.

Among them were former German government officials like Robert Kempner and John Herz who played a role in the preparation of the Nuremberg trials, or journalists like Hans Habe and Hans Wallenberg who were involved in editing the new newspapers and running the new radio stations. Some of the OSS old-timers such as Peter Sichel joined the CIA and were given key positions in postwar Germany. The younger men who had been trained at Fort Ritchie and worked in intelligence in 1945/46 were on the whole eager to return home and be demobilized. They were collecting "points" to return home as soon as possible, rejoin their families, continue their educations where they had been interrupted. As the result of the G.I. Bill of Rights they had access to educational opportunities they had been able only to dream about before the war.

But there were other reasons as well for not staying: The German postwar experience for them had been fascinating, and they returned as conquerors to the country that had expelled them. But after a little while they realized that this was no longer their country. They understood finally that America for them was not exile but their new home.

No one put it more succinctly than Henry (Heinz) Kellermann, who had been before 1937 a leader of one of the German Jewish youth groups, not at all inclined toward Zionism, but assimilationist, steeped in German culture and tradition. He had worked for the OSS but was later seconded for the preparation of the Nuremberg trials and later yet became a U.S. diplomat. Asked about his experiences in 1947, he wrote that he had just stayed for two days with Norbert Wollheim, who had been a close colleague in prewar Berlin and spent the war years in Auschwitz. Kellermann wrote, "It became utterly clear to me why we, i.e. people of our circle with sound reactions will never be able to regain a so-called normal relationship to the country of our past, why this will be eternally a foreign country to us, why there can never be an identity between our memories and the present reality." He also noted that what he had seen in Germany had neither weakened nor strengthened his resentment; he had been able to face and interrogate the blackguards at Nuremberg such as Frick and Ley without any trace of hatred. And it was not just that he had to be "objective" by virtue of his office, he simply could not identify these shabby, sorry, and utterly unimpressive characters as the men responsible for the most gigantic crimes in history.

You Can't Go Home Again

There are many accounts by young soldiers returning to the houses where they had grown up, if these houses were still standing, accounts of being confronted with scenes that seemed superficially familiar, of meeting old neighbors and distant acquaintances or even contemporaries who had survived the war. Some of these encounters were moving, others shocking, but virtually everyone felt that all this belonged to a past that had gone forever. (Many said, "You could not go home again, even if the home still existed.") And it was not only the fact that Germany was a country in ruins and that prospects for the future seemed bleak. For the great majority of the younger ones this was a chapter in their lives that had irrevocably been closed.

Gunther Stent had never quite overcome the fascination of the Berlin of his youth, which he had left as a boy of thirteen. When the opportunity arose eight years after his involuntary departure, he applied to be a member of a scientific intelligence mission. He was at the time a promising Ph.D. student at the University of Illinois, Champaign, and he became a junior member of the Technical Industrial Intelligence Branch (TIIB) screening documents inside Germany. His second encounter with Berlin took place in November 1946 and it could not possibly leave him cold—some of the old cinemas were still standing, the theater was playing again, and there was marvelous skiing in the mountains. And yet, seven months and several passionate love affairs with German women later, he left Germany without regrets to embark on a career that was to make him a leading figure in the field of neurobiology.

The "Jewish Brigade"

Of those who went to Palestine in the 1930s virtually every able-bodied young man and woman did military service one way or another, full time or part time. They were mobilized by the Hagana, the defense force of the Jewish community, with the outbreak of the riots in 1936. The military service was done in the settlements and cities, and included guard duty especially at night, with often illegal weapons, maintaining telephone or telegraph or radio contact with outlying settlements, and military exercises in small units.

With the outbreak of World War II, young men and women volunteered for the British army. Whereas the Zionist authorities were fighting for a Jewish army within the framework of the British army, the war
cabinet in London opposed the idea and it was only in 1943/44 that a
Jewish brigade was set up in Egypt. Prior to that date, Jewish volunteers
joined existing British establishments such as the Buffs regiment, some
went to the engineers or the infantry, some were sent to special artillery
courses, physicians were employed in the Middle East and India, and a
small number of volunteer pilots for the Royal Air Force were sent to
special training in Rhodesia. Jewish volunteers saw action in France,
prior to Dunkirk, as well as in Greece and Crete, and later in North Africa. The British and the Jewish authorities collaborated in setting up
commando units to be employed behind the German lines and later on
also in training parachutists to be used in Nazi-occupied Europe. A significant proportion of these volunteers were of German (and Austrian)
Jewish origin. Some went because the authorities had called on them,
others because they felt that they had a special patriotic duty to fight
Nazism having been its principal victims, still others joined the army
to escape from the difficulties they experienced in the process of integration in Palestine. There are no accurate figures with regard to the
percentage of German Jewish volunteers as compared with other ethnic groups but their numbers were certainly high.

Martin Hauser, whose diary we have mentioned, noted that in the
critical summer of 1940 about half of the two thousand who went with
him to Sarafend, the biggest army base in Palestine, were German and
Austrian Jews. He also wrote that for him, as for many others, the decision to join the army was not easy, for the British had virtually closed
the doors of immigration to Palestine, and it was only at this critical
time, after the fall of France, that he had realized that duty was calling
him to join up. The ritual was always the same: in Sarafend they took
the King's Shilling. That is, they took an oath on the Bible, were given
their uniforms and rifles, and underwent at least three weeks of exceedingly boring basic training. After that initial period they went by
rail to Egypt and joined the units to which they had been attached. In
Hauser's case this was the Middle Eastern headquarters of the Royal
Air Force. He was employed first as a clerk in a transport department,
but later, when it was discovered that he was a native German speaker,
he was transferred to intelligence. Hauser had been sworn in on July
22, 1940; by the first week of September he was stationed in Cairo

where he remained for almost four years. He was put off by the attitude of the local (rich) Jews who at first showed no interest in the Palestinians and had no wish to associate with them, but notes that later on relations improved.

As early as 1940, Jewish volunteers from Palestine attached to such units as the Fifty-First Commando in the Middle East theater of war did see action and gained recognition. Fritz Jordan and Fritz Hausmann received medals for gallantry, having escaped in dangerous circumstances from German prisoner of war camps. Several Palestinians of German Jewish origin were quoted in dispatches, having participated in commando raids; the most senior RAF medical officer during this early period of the war was Richard Harsher-Levi. An army doctor, Captain Ferdinand Zangen, received the Military Cross for having shown particular courage during heavy enemy shelling at the Anzio bridgehead.

But the Palestinian battalions and regiments stationed in Egypt were doing boring work for years—guard duty in ammunition dumps, airports, prisoner of war camps—until at long last the British government announced in September 1944 the establishment of the Jewish Brigade, which, Churchill added in explanation, would see action and take part in the occupation of enemy territory. The Jewish Brigade was concentrated first in Bourg el Arab in Egypt and later on in Fiuggi, not far from Rome. But it was not until March 1945 that it saw action in Italy in the Lake Comacchio area in the weeks leading to the German surrender.

Martin Hauser, employed in a tactical RAF intelligence unit in Upper Italy, visited his comrades of the Brigade, took part in the Seder celebrations and, a few days before the end of the war, saw the first Jewish survivors of the death camps. On May 8 he was in Trieste, exactly twelve years after having embarked from there to Palestine. In the days after he and the men of the Brigade entered Austria, the Villach-Klagenfurt area, and it was there that they first encountered displaced persons, the survivors from Eastern Europe, who had left their former homes and were desperately looking for food, clothing, and a way out of Europe.

From this point on, the Jewish Brigade and also many individuals from other units engaged mainly in social work, extending first aid and acting as Scarlet Pimpernels, helping to organize the exodus from Eastern Europe and illegal immigration to Palestine. A small group of Palestinian volunteers called *hanokmim* (the avengers), engaged in their private de-Nazification, hunting down local Gestapo officials and others who had been actively involved in the murder of the Jews. Some of the surviving partisans from Eastern Europe, who had in the meantime reached the Brigade, wanted to engage in more ambitious forms of vengeance such as poisoning water supplies. But these partisan schemes, intelligible against the background of time and place, were vetoed by the Jewish authorities.

Far more important were the rescue activities. Captain Casper, chief chaplain of the Brigade, estimated that the Brigade helped to smuggle some eight thousand refugees into Italy to wait there for transport to Palestine. Individual soldiers took leave with and without permission trying to find remnants of their families in Germany and Austria, and even in Poland and Romania; sometimes they were away for weeks and months. This did not escape the notice of the higher military authorities, and eventually the Jewish Brigade was transferred to Belgium to reduce these extracurricular activities to a minimum.

While Jewish soldiers from Palestine were stationed outside their country, thousands of others were mobilized for the defense of the homeland, beginning in 1941/42 when a German invasion from both Egypt and the north (Syria and Lebanon having been occupied by Vichy French forces) seemed a distinct possibility. This was the time when the Palmach was born, the military elite units that played such a crucial role in the Israeli war of independence, and also the militia field units (Chish and Chim), and when, in general, the foundations were laid for an Israeli army.

The Struggle for Israel

Jews of Central European origin played a leading role in establishing the Israeli defense forces in the early years. In their overwhelming majority, they belonged to the Hagana; only a very few were members of the Irgun and the Stern Gang. Vladimir Jabotinsky had been prophet and leader of the right-wing nationalists called Revisionists, but his teachings had never been very influential in Germany and were only a little more so in Austria. It was in the revisionist youth organization Betar that the terrorists of the right found their recruits in Palestine. One rare exception was a young man named Meir Shamgar (Sternberg), a native of Danzig, who joined the Irgun, was detained by the

British authorities, and was exiled to a camp in Eritrea where he planned escape tunnels. He became even more famous in later life as chief justice of the Supreme Court of Israel, and, in other circles, as the honorary president of the Israeli Friends of Jazz.

Probably the most important weakness in these early years and up to 1948 was the shortage of arms and ammunition and modern, sophisticated arms in general (Hagana had no artillery prior to 1948 except a few mortars). No one was more successful in purchasing and smuggling such weaponry than Ehud Ueberall (Avriel), a native of Vienna, a veritable dynamo of a man and a key figure, behind the scenes, in these activities before and after statehood. Jews from Central Europe played a crucial role in establishing Israeli military intelligence, over and above a purely tactical level. In fact, the other intelligence services, such as Mossad and Shin Bet (active inside Israel only) were headed and manned in the early years to a considerable extent by people with a Central European background, including Josef Hermlin, Avraham Achitov, Avraham Shalom, and in the pre-state days, by David Shaltiel and Asher Ben Nathan. Shaltiel, born in Hamburg, whose Foreign Legion background has been mentioned earlier, was commander of Jerusalem during the siege of 1948, Ben Natan became a diplomat ending his career as a successful and popular ambassador to Germany.

It is also true, to round out the picture, that some of the most noteworthy spies acting for and against Israel during the early years were of Central European origin. This includes Israel Baer, an Austrian whose real name and identity is not known to this day; he claimed to have had profound military knowledge and long experience in Spain and elsewhere, and, while he was never given an active command in Israel, he was privy to much inside knowledge that was of interest to his Soviet spymasters. Another major mole in the early days of Israeli statehood was a young man of Eastern European background named Avni, who had become a Soviet army intelligence agent in Switzerland. He joined both the Israeli foreign service and the Mossad but was apprehended relatively early. In the course of a long stretch in an Israeli prison he was given the opportunity to retrain as a psychologist, which became his second career. The "third man," who had been prominently involved in some disastrous Israeli sabotage activities in Egypt in the early 1950s, and who was found to be an enemy agent, had also been of German-Jewish background, but so was Wolfgang Ludz, the successful Israeli "champagne spy" in Egypt.

It would be invidious to single out individuals, for in the war of independence every citizen of Israel was involved, and civilians were victims as often as soldiers, particularly in the agricultural settlements
but also in Jerusalem. The heroism of the Jerusalem housewives lining
up for the daily water ration while the shelling was going on was as
noteworthy as the courage of the Palmach's trying to reopen the supply
route to Jerusalem. Hans Beyth, the managing director of youth *aliya*
was among the many civilians killed in the battle for Jerusalem. The war
of independence was the bloodiest war by far of all the Israeli wars, and
it is the only one for which statistics exist. Of those who were killed in
this war, the percentage of those born in Germany and Austria was
higher than the average. Among the victims were many, such as Fritz
Jordan, who had distinguished themselves in the battles of World War II.

German Jews in the Red Army

Jews of Central European origin served in most Allied armies during
World War II, including some that have not yet been mentioned. Konrad Wolf, the brother of spymaster Markus Wolf and a future president
of the East German Academy of Arts, and Moritz Mebel were officers
in the Red Army. Fritz Markuse, a native of Berlin, had escaped to
Riga after 1933 and joined the Red Army after the occupation of Lat-
via. He lost an arm in the fighting at the Belorussian front and lived to
witness victory day in Alma Ata as a student of medicine. Friedrich
Koch, born in Frankfurt in 1922, served in the Soviet army, having migrated to the Soviet Union in the 1930s with his father, a well-known
professor of medicine; the family had survived the Stalinist purges far
away from Moscow in a Caucasian resort.

One of the largest concentrations of German and Austrian Jews was
in the French Foreign Legion. They had joined the Foreign Legion in
order to legalize their perilous status as emigrants in France, or because they had fled from Spain after the end of the Spanish Civil War
or because after the defeat of France they feared deportation. The
Foreign Legion quite often used considerable pressure to induce people to join their depleted ranks, especially during the war. But those
who had enlisted or were press-ganged were by no means employed as
soldiers but had to work on the construction of the trans-Saharan railroad, connecting the Algerian and Tunisian ports and Dakar. They

were concentrated in camps that, while not officially named concentration camps, were hardly distinguishable from such installations. A few fortunates escaped, bought themselves out, or were taken to Britain after the fall of France and joined the Pioneer Corps. But for most, their lot began to improve only after the liberation of North Africa by the Allies in late 1942.

Of the roughly eighty to one hundred thousand refugees from Germany and Austria who were of military age, about half, if not more, took an active part in the war. Their fates varied enormously; for some it was a relatively short war, whereas others served five, six, even seven years. Some were severely injured, became prisoners of war, or were killed in action; others had what is commonly known as a good war. Some began and ended their military career as privates; others rose from the ranks to the elevated status of colonel, or, in the case of Israel, of general. For some, the war was a painful interruption of a civilian career, not to mention a separation from their friends and families; for others, on the contrary, the war constituted the great chance in their life, the springboard for an education and a subsequent professional career that would have been impossible in normal circumstances. For all the war was the decisive watershed in their personal lives.

ISRAEL

Immigration Jeckepotz

—ᴔᴔ—

For a young refugee there were basic differences between Palestine and all other destinations. Palestine had as yet to be built as a country of absorption for hundreds of thousands of immigrants. "Building" and "construction" were the key words in Zionist ideology and in the songs the young pioneers were singing; the largest Zionist youth movement was Habonim, the builders. America, Britain, and Shanghai were exile, but Palestine for a Zionist, was the opposite of exile, the ingathering of the exiles, the return to a Jewish homeland. A young refugee arriving in Britain would be instructed by the Chief Rabbi: be considerate, quiet, and polite, above all be grateful. Other institutions would tell him (or her) not to talk loudly, not to congregate in public places—in brief, not to attract attention. The refugee should never forget that he was a guest, perhaps even a welcome guest, but still an outsider and a stranger. It was the same in New York and La Paz and wherever the refugees went. They should be aware of their precarious status, they should retrain themselves so as not to provoke hostile feelings. There was no room for exuberance; they could not behave (and especially misbehave) like citizens of London, New York, or La Paz because they did not belong, at least not for the time being, and perhaps for a long time to come. They had been given the same advice by their parents and teachers in Germany.

Those who went to Palestine were also given good advice of various sorts, but they were not subject to the special injunctions to be inconspicuous, to be grateful, to be on their best behavior. In brief, the element of self-consciousness was missing. They would suffer various hardships, they would encounter antagonism even on the part of their fellow Jews, but there was no need to look constantly over their shoulders.

There was yet another difference. Those who went to England, America, and other countries were above all concerned with creating a new existence for themselves. Among those who went to Palestine, though, a significant number of young people were motivated by idealism, the desire to create a new society, a new form of life not just for themselves and their families but for a whole generation of the Jewish people. It is quite immaterial whether this endeavor was successful or whether the idealism eventually faded under the harsh realities of the new country, or that many had not shared this idealism from the very beginning. What matters is that this idealism did exist at the time and that this constituted an essential difference from emigration to other countries.

Early Immigrants

Prior to 1933, relatively few people in Germany knew much about Palestine, and there was no great interest in the subject. True, there had been a trickle of immigrants to Palestine even before World War I, among them people whose names became well known in the history of the country. In later years, there were physicians, architects, economists, lawyers, and other professionals, but also Chalutzim belonging to one of the pioneering organizations in Germany such as Blau Weiss and the KJV (the student Zionist organization). Scholars came to the Hebrew University after its foundation in 1925 and employees of the central Zionist organization also settled in Jerusalem. Young people from Germany and Austria were found in some of the kibbutzim and kvutzot from Givat Brenner in the south, to Givat Haim in the center of the country, and Markenhof (Bet Sera) in the Jordan Valley. But there were few of them and their stories somehow did not percolate back to Germany.

The bigger Jewish organizations in Germany were only mildly interested in Palestine. True, some of their leaders had visited the country, but they had reached the conclusion that Palestine was too small and too poor to absorb substantial numbers of Jews, the political situation was inauspicious (the conflict with the Arabs had turned violent in 1929), and culturally it was not attractive. Above all, there was no urgent reason why German Jews should become more deeply involved in Palestine, because the question of emigration was far more likely to arise in Poland than in Germany. The German Zionists who had made their home in Palestine were critical as far as Zionist policies were concerned. The businessmen, bankers, and managers among them frowned upon the official ideology that stressed the return to the soil, to change the lopsided Jewish professional structure in the diaspora. The German Zionists admired the pioneers battling malaria in the valley of Esdraelon in their attempts to build a collective agriculture. But they felt that this was not the best way to build an economy that should absorb tens and hundreds of thousands in Palestine.

Attitudes among German Jewry changed dramatically with the Nazi takeover in Germany; for the next few years up to 1936, Jewish Palestine became the single most important country of refuge for Jews from Germany, in particular the younger ones among them. Up to 1940 about sixty thousand reached Palestine, not counting those who came illegally (for instance on tourist visas) or German-speaking arrivals from other parts of Central Europe. Altogether this *aliya* (immigration wave) constituted about one third of the total immigration to Palestine in the period before World War II. It reached its height in 1935 but declined thereafter as a result of the immigration restrictions imposed by Britain, the mandatory government.

Of the German Jews who went to Israel, slightly more than one quarter worked in agriculture, a considerably higher percentage than in the former major immigration wave from Poland (1925). Of those who settled in the cities, about sixteen thousand went to Tel Aviv, eleven thousand to Haifa, and only six thousand to Jerusalem. Of the younger generation, the percentage of immigrants who worked in agriculture at least for some years after their arrival was probably closer to 50 percent.

Arrival and Culture Shock

Most of those who arrived came by ship via Trieste or another Italian port. They could not take money out of Germany except in the framework of a special transfer agreement (Ha'avara) according to which certain sums of money were transferred to be accounted against German exports to Palestine. However, these new immigrants were relatively well equipped in comparison with the arrivals from Eastern Europe. They came with small containers (called lifts) and they had plenty of clothes, leather coats, raincoats, and leather bags in the form of portfolios, which were one of their distinguishing marks. The older immigrants were formally dressed in suits, jackets, and ties, very much in contrast to what was customary in Tel Aviv and Jerusalem in those days. They brought record players and radios (even though a Palestine broadcasting service did not yet exist).

The happiest among the newcomers were those who came with youth *aliyot* and those young men and women a few years older. Many of their letters (some signed only with first names, some only with initials) have been preserved, and it is difficult to imagine more enthusiastic descriptions. If there had been pain at leave taking, it was forgotten as their trains crossed Switzerland, and as they boarded the Gerusalemme and the Galilea in Trieste; the balmy summer nights of the Mediterranean overwhelmed them, as did the arrival, when they saw from a great distance a "small sliver of land with palms, the home of the Jews, our free Jewish country" (from a letter signed by Manfred and Uri).

Later the first nights in the kibbutz (Degania 1935), "more than a dance, a giddiness, an intoxication affecting those who come from darkness into light, who awake from a long heavy sleep to a new life, a storm of joy shared by everyone" (from a letter signed I. S.). The hot easterly wind with its sandstorms (the *chamsin*) did not affect the wonderful feeling: "We are driving through Jewish country!" Manfred says in a speech on behalf of his group—a long dream has suddenly become reality, but they have not yet fully grasped it. And Ben writes from Mishmar Ha'emeq that he was in Jerusalem, the most beautiful city he ever saw. Lisa was also in Jerusalem, and despite being accosted by strangers, found the old city wonderful with all the haggling, the beggars, and the poverty.

A young member of a kibbutz describes the arrival of a grand piano in Karkur and how from early morning to midnight one could listen to music from Scarlatti to Kurt Weill. In another letter, E. has only good things to report from her kibbutz at the Dead Sea, despite 47 degrees centigrade in the shade: Baron Rothschild visited them and also Wauchope, the British High Commissioner. Lisa (now called Aviva) writes from Merchavia that they work hard but like it tremendously, even though they have to get up at five in the morning.

The night sky is infinitely clearer than in Europe (in his letter, R. even reported that he spotted a rainbow in the moonlight) and they have only good things to say about even the heavy work on a building site (Karkur) or in the great heat of the bakery in Nahalal. They went to Tiberias to swim in the lake at night; they marveled at the beauties of Haifa; but, as Pnina wrote from Ein Harod, there was nothing more wonderful than living in a rural settlement together with like-minded people. Or as someone else put it, "we are no longer curious here to have the latest news from Europe."

Tel Aviv provoked mixed reactions: "It is not as bad as I thought but it isn't really Palestine." Ben who comes from a kibbutz is more favorably impressed and finds that Tel Aviv is more European than Europe, adding: "The city is very nice but not for longer than two weeks." Another youngster reports that Allenby, then the main road, and the beach promenade are always full, like Kurfuerstendamm and Tauentzienstrasse, "which for this reason we always shunned, and the beach is full on a Sabbath morning like the Wannsee."

From the very beginning Hebrew words appear in these letters to Germany. Letter writers no longer go to the shower but to the *miklachat*, not to the dining hall but to the *chader ochel*, they work not in the vineyard but in the *kerem*. And it is not only their language that is changing. Achim writes his mother from Ein Charod that he has the feeling that she and "Germany and everything that I loved there slowly disappear and that there is no way to stop this process, the new elements are growing stronger all the time, and sometimes I feel I have lost the language to talk to you. Sometimes I feel I am a new human being." There were no such letters from Shanghai, or La Paz, or London, or New York.

These young people who went to Palestine in 1934–1936 were an elite. They had been selected from among the Jewish youth movements, they had been dreaming about Palestine even back in Germany. We do not know what they thought and felt at the end of three or four years; there are no letters for the later period. For those who came alone, the difficulties of arriving and finding their feet in this new and strange land were infinitely greater.

The culture shock began with their arrival in port, which in the early days, up to the Arab riots of 1936, was Arab Jaffa; Tel Aviv harbor was as yet under construction and Haifa harbor was small. The noises, the smells, the whole spectacle was oriental (or Levantine or Asiatic as some of them wrote), very different from what they had been prepared for. It was loud, people were pushy, and one had to be careful that one's belongings did not get lost or stolen. A newcomer would usually spend the first few days or weeks with relations or acquaintances; people had small apartments but they were hospitable. For the many who had no Hebrew, the initial period of confusion would, of course, last much longer. Or they would spend their early days in one of the *bate olim* (immigrant homes) that had been established. Just before Hitler came to power an association of Jews from Germany was founded (in February 1932), initially in order to provide information for a growing stream of tourists; after 1933 this association, Hitachdut Olei Germania, was to play an increasingly important role in the life of the new immigrants. It was neither labor exchange nor hostel but it could provide valuable advice and contacts.

These initiatives were necessary because the Jewish residents of Palestine did not receive the German immigrants with open arms. The newcomers were thought responsible for a substantial rise in rents as well as a general increase in prices. The new immigrants were criticized for establishing their own schools and newspapers and thus endangering the as yet precarious position of the Hebrew language. If the new immigrants expressed dissatisfaction with the way they were treated, they were encouraged to return to Nazi Germany. Some demanded that the German immigrants not be allowed to congregate in certain regions, but be dispersed all over the country so as to minimize the various dangers. In brief, with all the frequent invocations of Jewish solidarity, the immigrants were disliked and suspected for the same reasons that all immigrants are resented at all times in all places. But there was an additional animus against new immigrants from Germany and Austria that did not exist with regard to newcomers from Eastern Europe. Their way of life, it was claimed, did not fit Eretz Israel, their customs and their speech were derided in the media, in the cabarets, and in Palestinian folklore. On the other hand, hundreds of articles in the Hebrew press, not counting letters to the editors, complained that the newcomers were systematically exploited and discriminated against. The old-timers in the Palestine of the 1930s were unwilling to accept anything that did not fit their established social and cultural patterns and the new immigrants were equally unwilling to make concessions to a way of life they regarded, at best, as primitive. It was not a happy encounter, and it did not change until the war years.

Much less complicated in the early days was the lot of the many young people arriving to join one of the existing kibbutzim or members of an organized group in the framework of youth *aliya*. The reception was rough but cordial. The luggage was thrown on the kibbutz truck waiting in the harbor, boys and girls climbed aboard, and within an hour or two or three (for the state of the roads, particularly in winter, was not up to European standards), they would arrive at their destination. For the young people it was great fun; it reminded them of the summer camps of their youth movement in Europe.

Those whom no one had come to welcome often felt at a total loss. Some would say it aloud, others would only think it: perhaps their trip had been a huge mistake, perhaps they should take the next ship back home? Few if any did take the next ship back, but there was depression, as well as sleepless nights and tears.

In later years, some of them described their early steps in the new country. Clara Bartnitzki had the additional misfortune to arrive in driving rain in Jaffa in November 1933; her husband was not a Zionist and far from kissing the soil of the Holy Land upon arrival, he said that if he had a return ticket he would now use it. Hugo Mendelssohn's reactions, also in Jaffa harbor, were similar, but then a distant cousin appeared out of nowhere, the problems were sorted out and the temptation to go back vanished. For Jenny Aloni, who had belonged to one of the Zionist youth groups in Germany and arrived only after the outbreak of the war, the doubts arose on board ship; had it been the right decision? She knew, of course, that she could not go back, rather it was fear of the unknown that made her consider jumping overboard to drown in the sea. Jehuda Steinbach began his stay with a tour of the country and went to visit the young kibbutz near Ein Harod, which he had intended to join. But the first impression was depressing, everything was too loud, "too Asiatic," and his wife did not like it at all. So they decided to join another kibbutz, Givat Brenner, where a sister of his wife lived—the presence of a relation or a friend often played a decisive role.

Naomi Koch (Laqueur) was just sixteen when she arrived in Haifa harbor in November 1936. Her sister was to welcome her but somehow missed her. She later wrote,

> I had just 75 centesimi in my pocket, but I remembered an address of friends of my family and convinced an Arab taxi driver to take me there.

I do not remember what language I used to make myself understood. Unfortunately, there was a lot of building going on in Haifa and the names of new streets were not known to the public or even the police. My taxi driver managed to drive for more than four hours through Hadar Hakarmel. At last we found the address we were looking for. The very first thing I had to do was to ask our friends to pay the fare. It was a rather big sum and I should not have been taken aback that they were not overjoyed to see me. Moreover, I must have been a pitiful sight, I had stood about an hour in the pouring rain, dressed in a flimsy summer dress and sandals. Of course, they let me stay the night, it would have been unthinkable at that time in Palestine to do otherwise.

Eventually, Naomi reached Ben Shemen, the children's village, where she joined a group of recent arrivals from Germany. The Haifa friends had given her the money for the bus fare, but not graciously. "I learned that people of whom I had been convinced back home in Frankfurt that they would share their last shirt with me behaved differently once I was far away from home without family and without money."

Meta Frank (Koenigsthal) was twenty when she arrived. Born in Karlshafen near Hofgeismar, a tiny place in the center of Germany, she came with a new husband and twenty pieces of luggage. It was hot and dusty, she did not know a word of Hebrew and people refused to speak German. She had been weeping already on board ship, she was now weeping even more. We are lost, she told herself, but was firmly admonished not to say this in public. Everything they had brought with them had been wrong—the furniture, the clothes. They did not know anything about agriculture or animal husbandry and these were the only jobs available. She did not want to go to a kibbutz because people were kept there as in a prison—for a year they were not permitted to travel to see friends and acquaintances. Her mother arrived from Germany for a visit and she was shocked and deeply disappointed by the horrible conditions in which her daughter had to live. It was not that this had been a particularly wealthy family and their daughter particularly spoiled, the problem was that everything was so different from what they had been accustomed to.

The Franks wandered about in the country, having the greatest difficulty finding a place to stay and work. In the end Meta got a position as a domestic with the owner of a big orange grove, but this was far away from any settlement and dangerous as the riots broke out in

1936. But then, very slowly, their luck began to turn. She picked up a few words of Hebrew, and the others did talk to her, and taught her more; they built a little house and had a little piece of land to cultivate, there was a child and then a second child, the parents arrived from Germany at the very last moment before the outbreak of the war. Meta Frank lived to a ripe old age and we shall encounter her again in the course of our narrative.

What a difference from the welcome extended to someone like Ehud Avriel, who did know Hebrew, his mother having been the head of a Hebrew school in Vienna. He was offered an interesting job even before reaching Palestine. On a visit to London in 1936, having just graduated from school, he met emissaries from Palestine who were interested in a newcomer from the Zionist youth movement in Austria who spoke Hebrew and was at a turning point in his life. Avriel became one of the central figures in illegal immigration and later in the purchase of arms for the state to be established, he undertook key missions on behalf of Israeli intelligence and later the foreign ministry

Martin Hauser was twenty when he arrived in late May of 1933 from Berlin, a committed, ardent Zionist. One week later he wrote in his diary that his arrival meant so much to him that he was sometimes afraid that he would wake up in the morning and find himself back in Berlin—all his longings had become reality, hundreds, thousands, even millions would envy him. He liked everything he saw. But later entries deal with the hardships of daily life. He lived in a cellar, which he shared with two other newcomers. There was no work in his field as a dental technician, nor could he find other permanent work for months. Sometimes he slept during the day so that he would not have to pay for lunch. He got part-time work cleaning shoes, giving Hebrew lessons to children, doing heavy work in great heat on a building site. He was put off by the disdain shown by Jewish authorities toward the new immigrants from Germany. "Life gets more prosaic by the day." The little money he had brought was rapidly melting away. But during the end of the year he found an apprenticeship as a locksmith and things were looking up a bit. Hauser was not among those who lost hope, and we shall encounter him again during the war years looking for and trying to help Jews who had survived in Italy.

Those who arrived alone, unprepared, and without even a smattering of the language felt lonely and bewildered. But others, who arrived in groups to join an existing kibbutz or establish a new one, also suffered and had to pass their apprenticeships in difficult conditions. And yet being in a group gave them psychological, and not only psychological, protection. One of these groups consisted of members of a German youth movement called *Werkleute*, the section of the *Kameraden* mentioned earlier that had, under the influence of the ideas of Martin Buber, embraced Zionism and decided to settle in Palestine. The first of them arrived in 1933 and went for agricultural training to already existing kibbutzim such as Givat Haim and Mishmar Haemeq. They did not learn much professionally but they were taught a lot about life in Palestine, usually the hard way. One of them had arrived with a thousand pounds sterling on a so-called capitalist certificate of immigration. He deposited it with the secretary of Givat Haim in the mistaken assumption that he would get the money back once his group would move on to its own place of settlement. They had brought a truck from Germany and tried to earn a little money by undertaking outside jobs. Some of them could even drive a truck, but they were not accustomed to working in a country without real roads, where their machine got stuck in the sand, or, in the rainy season, in the mud.

The Kibbutz

Jews from Germany, including the younger ones among them, had the reputation of being disciplined, orderly, and law abiding, and the *Werkleute* could never quite shed this image. But it did not take long for them to realize that nice guys finish last, that on occasion elbows were needed in their new homeland. When the municipality of Hadera where they had a transitional working camp stopped the water supply so that they could neither drink nor wash, they staged a violent demonstration against the head of the local council, which ended with arrests and the intervention of the British police. They had to pay a fine but they also earned respect as people not to be trifled with. In the meantime more than 150 members of the *Werkleute* continued to arrive in Palestine, and in 1935, after long negotiations and much prodding, they were allocated a piece of land near Yokneam, southeast of the Carmel mountains, to establish a kibbutz of their own.

For a year they lived in an old and dilapidated Arab building, a *khan*, then they put up tents and blockhouses; they sowed wheat on a small piece of land and bought a herd of sheep. The shepherds all had doctorates from German universities and the kibbutz lost money on the venture; while sheep were certainly part of the traditional image of an agricultural settlement, their role in modern agriculture was problematic. The kibbutzniks were a little more successful at acquiring a herd of cows, but agriculture remained a problem because they did not have sufficient land, and what they had was divided into thirty tiny pieces among fields belonging to neighboring Arab villages. Keeping Arab cows out of the kibbutz fields became a major, time-consuming problem. They made all the mistakes of the early kibbutzim in their desire to produce everything themselves, to bake their own bread, to make their own shoes. It was touching but it was not very productive.

When war broke out, Kibbutz Hazorea counted 120 members, and some of the parents had also arrived. They had moved far from the days of Martin Buber, facing the realities of work and life in Palestine. After long deliberations they had joined the Kibbutz Artzi, one of the three roof associations of kibbutzim, which imposed on them a fairly rigid ideological framework of Marxist Zionism.

So many had come in the years before the war that a second kibbutz of younger members had been founded, which merged with a group of pioneers from Romania. But this merger did not go well; there were constant quarrels on ethnic lines ranging from the quality of the food to the choice of members to serve in the British army. In the middle of the war this kibbutz split and the German members joined Hazorea. When Kibbutz Hazorea was first established in 1935/36 on its own land, it had some admirers among its neighbors and in the central Zionist institutions in Jerusalem, but few gave them a real chance to succeed because, it was thought, their idealism was so much stronger than their experience. But they defied the prophets of doom and over the years they became one of the biggest and most successful settlements in the country, with 550 members and almost 1,000 residents altogether. For years the furniture they produced was famous all over the country, with outlets in all the major cities. Today they have one of the biggest plastic factories; they also specialized in the breeding of tropical fish, and have a big gardening center. They were bequeathed a substantial collection of Far Eastern art, which became the basis of a museum. They absorbed new groups of settlers in the years after the war from countries such as Bulgaria. Of course, they were also affected by the various crises, financial, social, and political, that beset the kibbutz movement in general. Some of their members and more of the second generation were killed in the wars Israel fought beginning in 1948.

In brief, Hazorea became a name to conjure with, but this was not always the case. In 1935 at the nineteenth Zionist Congress, Berl Katznelson, the chief ideologist of the Labor party, made a programmatic speech on the absorption of the *aliya* from Germany. He could hardly have been more negative. These people were uprooted refugees, he said, who had been ejected from their homeland, they were burnt out cases without any knowledge of Hebrew and Hebrew culture. How can we build a people with individuals like these who have no culture; how can we prevent them from becoming a burden for us? Berl Katznelson died during World War II; he did not live to witness the immigration waves from Morocco, Romania, and the Soviet Union. One can only speculate how he would have judged these newcomers in terms of their Jewishness, their uprootedness, and their ability to build a new country.

Jeckes Distrusted

Berl Katznelson expressed views that were shared by many leaders on the left and of the kibbutz movement. The Chalutzim from Germany were thought incapable of establishing kibbutzim of their own; for years they were compelled to join existing settlements where they would be a minority among pioneers from Eastern Europe. As a result hundreds left the kibbutz and in the end the United Kibbutz Movement (Kibbutz Meuhad) was compelled to agree that the wishes of the immigrants from Germany should be taken into account. As a result kibbutzim were founded such as Kfar Blum, Galed, and others, that were largely German Jewish in character. The mentality of German Jews, including the Zionists among them, was different from that of East European Jewry, and this caused problems not only (and not mainly) in the kibbutzim. The level of Jewish education and of the language among the newcomers was considerably lower than among those from Eastern Europe. On the other hand, the former had a better general education and they looked down on people whose cultural interests were limited to Sholem Aleichem, Mendele, and I. L. Peretz, who were not familiar with world literature, who had no grounding in classical music, painting, and the other plastic arts. German Jews

were suspected of lacking idealism and the spirit of sacrifice; they had
come to Palestine because they were expelled, whereas the early
members of the kibbutzim had come from Russia and Poland of their
own free will.

Subsequent events have shown that these suspicions were largely un-
founded. True, it would have been desirable not to establish kibbutzim
along ethnic lines, but this aim could not be attained by fiat. The aesthetic sense of many German Jews, to give but one example, was more
developed than that of their brethren from further east who had no
time for such trivial considerations. The mixing of immigrants disre-
garding their ethnic origins was a laudable aim as far as the kibbutzim
were concerned, but it would have to wait for the second and third
generation. Jews from Germany and Austria were inclined to be more
critical in outlook, whereas in the old kibbutzim the attitude of members to some of their leaders was not that different from the reverence
in which certain local rabbis in the shtetl were held by their followers,
who attributed to them magical qualities.

Haim Seligman, who worked in the department for the absorption
of immigrants from Central Europe in the United Kibbutz, wrote
many years later that the leaders of this movement neither knew nor
understood the mentality of German Jews, who had other feelings and
values, another way of life, other cultural interests. Their attitude toward these immigrants was *a priori* one of disdain. Nor was it fair to
doubt the courage and steadfastness of the German *aliya*; a kibbutz
like Tirat Zvi in the Beisan valley, consisting mainly of religious pioneers from Central Europe, was to suffer more fatalities than most
from disease and outside attacks. But it did not disappear from the
map, and though many kibbutz members left in later years, especially
from among the second and third generation, this was true as much for
kibbutzim of Eastern European as of German-Austrian origin.

Those who had been so critical of the German Jewish sector in the
kibbutz movement did not take into account that within one generation the ignorance of the Hebrew language, which had bothered them
so much, would disappear. And they failed to understand at the time
that it would not be easy to pass on to the next generation the sterling
qualities of the early kibbutzim of which they were justly so proud. As
subsequent events were to show, it was much easier to acquire a good
knowledge of the Hebrew language than to keep alive the flame of
idealism and sacrifice that had inspired the early kibbutz settlers.

How quickly could a young girl from Germany turn into a *sabra* (a native Israeli), and in one case a national hero! One of the youngest to arrive alone in Haifa harbor was a girl from Berlin named Barbara Fuld. She came in June 1939, having attended a well-known private school in her native city of Berlin (Kaliski), and was a promising swimmer and athlete. Her mother was waiting for her at the pier, her father, a German patriot, had committed suicide after Kristallnacht. Babs, as she was called, was an unproblematical girl; she was quickly accepted by her contemporaries at the Balfour school in Tel Aviv. She joined one of the youth movements, she danced with them and went on hikes and fell in love. After graduation she joined the Palmach military units stationed in kibbutzim and was sent to an officers' course. She saw action first on "Wingate night" in June 1947, when a ship with illegal immigrants tried to land near Tel Aviv. She was killed in an ambush that night. Half of Tel Aviv went to her funeral, poems were written in her memory, a street was named in her honor, and six months later a ship with more illegal immigrants named *Bracha Fuld* arrived on the shores of Palestine. She was one of the first to be killed in the struggle for Israeli statehood and the first woman victim. She was nineteen when she died and perhaps one in a thousand knew that she was a recent arrival from Germany.

Young settlers from Germany found themselves in many kibbutzim, including those recently founded like Dalya in the Carmel mountains or Ein Gev on the eastern shore of Lake Tiberias, Dorot in the Negev, and Gvar Am south of Askelon. Some of these young settlers would have spectacular careers: Teddy Kollek of Vienna and Ein Gev became the legendary mayor of Jerusalem; Avraham Ben Menahem of Giessen, having been mukhtar (village headman) of his home kibbutz (Gvar Am) and acting as mediator and peacemaker in conflicts with Arab shepherds, subsequently became secretary of all Jewish settlements in the Negev and ended his career as mayor of Netanya. Ben Menahem's kibbutzic career had led him to Sdom at the southern end of the Dead Sea, arguably the hottest place in Palestine and one of the hottest on earth, where many young settlers from Germany worked for the Potash company extracting various much needed minerals, and where Gad Granach could at long last realize a childhood dream—to run a little railway. Born in Berlin, the son of Alexander Granach, a famous actor of stage and screen in the 1930s first in Berlin, later in Hollywood (of, among others, *Ninotchka* fame), he had not been an ardent Zionist

when he prepared himself for life in Palestine and subsequently joined
a kibbutz. He had always been quite critical, kept his distance, and
eventually left the kibbutz. But with all his criticism he did not dream
of leaving Rehavia, the part of Jerusalem that became his second home.
In his seventies, in the footsteps of his father, he had a new career on
German television as a born storyteller and entertainer.

Lawyers into Farmers

Not all refugees joined the kibbutzim. Thousands of the older ones
who had arrived with some money bought a little land and built a
small house, keeping a cow or two or becoming poultry farmers in
Kfar Yedidya, Sdeh Warburg, Ramot Hashavim, and the many other
settlements founded in the coastal plain. They had little orange groves
in Kfar Shmaryahu, today part of Herzliyah and one of the poshest
neighborhoods in the whole country, at that time a sandy hamlet in the
middle of nowhere. They founded Nahariya north of Haifa, today a
center of tourism, and a whole village from southern Germany emigrated and settled near Nahariya calling their place Shave Zion (returning to Zion).

Sometimes these enterprises succeeded; when they did not, the settlers and their children had to rely on outside work. Gershom Monar,
who had come at the age of eighteen (he would have to wait seven
years until his girlfriend could join him from England), became a
driver with Egged, one of the big bus cooperatives, then and now a
most desirable job. Eventually he became a multilingual guide for
Christian pilgrims to the Holy Land and the author of a guide book.

Life in these small agricultural settlements was difficult and the
new settlers were often abysmally ignorant of things agricultural. Meta
Frank almost got herself killed while trying to milk a cow in an emergency. She noted without envy that a great deal of idealism was
needed, of which her neighbors from Bulgaria had more than her family. But years of work led to a certain attachment to a place they had
once hated and to identification with the community of which she had
once written that "for us German Jews it is exceedingly difficult to get
along with this mixture of people from all parts of the globe." Her children, like the Monar children, went to school and joined the army;
many became officers and some war heroes. As Monar wrote, even the

parents who had come to Palestine kicking and screaming developed something like *Bauernstolz*, pride in their work as peasants; they helped as well as they could. Perhaps these elderly Jews from villages in Southern Germany remembered from their childhood that their own parents, before the turn of the last century, had cultivated their own piece of land and kept some animals, and that urbanization was a recent development.

Most of those who had bought land, however little, in the 1930s, could not possibly lose in the long run. Land prices rose sharply in the years after the establishment of the state, and even more thereafter, especially if the land was located not far from greater Tel Aviv, Herzliya, or Netanya. Some landowners became millionaires without even realizing it. And so, after many years of suffering and sometimes even despair, it was often a story with a happy ending. The first generation of these "middle class" settlers is long gone, but those who came as children can now be seen at family reunions on a Saturday afternoon on the veranda of their spacious modern houses, telling their grandchildren about the early, heroic days when no one had a car, when the next shop was miles away and, when Arab bandits came and stole their only cow.

Youth Aliya

One group's story remains to be told, a sizable group known as Youth Aliya (youth immigration). Historians have been divided about its origins. For a long time it was believed to have been founded by Henrietta Szold, a distinguished member of a well-known American Zionist family. But while it is true that Szold, who had moved to Jerusalem, made an enormous contribution and was for years the head of this institution, the original idea had not been hers. The founder was Recha Freier, the wife of a Berlin rabbi (and the mother of the future head of the Israeli nuclear program). Recha Freier was, to put it cautiously, not an easy woman, but she had the energy and determination to push through what might have seemed initially a hopeless task, thus saving thousands of young people. She suggested that young people in Germany, between roughly fourteen and sixteen years old, should be sent in groups to Palestine without their parents, to agricultural school but above all to kibbutzim, because these were best equipped to deal with such groups.

The first small such group went to Palestine even before the Nazis came to power; the first big group of about sixty, went to Kibbutz Ein Harod in February 1934. Altogether, more than six thousand from Germany and Austria followed up to 1940, some fifteen to twenty thousand more were sent out of Germany in 1938/39 to Britain and other countries because the British mandatory government had closed the gates of Palestine. Recha Freier stayed on in Berlin until after the outbreak of the war organizing the transports. On the Jerusalem end much of the work was done by Henrietta Szold, who through her American connections could enlist financial help, and above all her assistants, two young German Jews named Hans Beyth and later Chanoch Rinot (Reinhold).

The following routine developed: Groups of twenty-five to thirty-five boys and girls would assemble in Germany and travel with a youth leader to the institution in Palestine that would be their home for the next two years. They would be housed at least as comfortably as the members of the kibbutz; they would work half days, and the other half would be devoted to studies of the language, of the country, and general education. A qualified man and woman teacher of the kibbutz would be responsible for the group. What was to happen after the two years was left open. The members of the group could join the kibbutz if they wanted, or establish their own group and build a new settlement, or join their family if they had relations in the country, or make their own way in Palestine as they saw fit. In the early period it had been the rule that the parents would make a sizeable contribution toward the upkeep of their children during the two years. But as German Jewry became more and more impoverished this was impossible in most cases. The kibbutzim were poor and could not extend much help. As a result living conditions deteriorated as youth *aliya* became an instrument of rescue in a race against time. The organizers could no longer pick and choose their candidates, they had to take almost everyone.

The idea was brilliant and, though the execution was not always equally outstanding, it was the only way to induce parents to part with their offspring and thus to save young people who otherwise would have perished.

How did these young people fare, transplanted into a strange country, far away from their homes, families, and friends? It is next to impossible to generalize, for so much depended on local conditions and also the constitution of the groups. Some had been members of a Zionist youth movement abroad, knew more or less what conditions would be like, perhaps even had a smattering of Hebrew. There were others, especially in the later years, who came from small towns in Germany, had not been in a youth group, had perhaps never been away from home, for whom the new experience was not an adventure in the sun but a trauma. Some loved the new life, the work in the vineyards, riding on a horse (or at least a donkey), the companionship; they fell in love and were so busy that their teachers had to press them to write home at least once a month. Others were unhappy, hated the boring work and their roommates, complained of a lack of privacy, suffered from homesickness, and wrote long letters home complaining about the food and about everything else under the sun. Reports in the archives of the Zionist institutions mention an "an oppositionist spirit" among many of the new arrivals. And how could it be otherwise? Boys and girls transplanted to settlements far from home were very much in need of a little warmth and instead they were faced with the rigid code of behavior of the early kibbutzim: no private property, no pocket money, no private books, no sweets, no stamps—everything was to be shared. They had not been educated towards life in such a society. Shimon Sachs, who came with youth *aliya*, reported many years later that he wanted to be like the members of the kibbutz, but it was of no use— classical music attracted him more.

They did not, as a rule, find it easy to get along with their Israeli contemporaries, the kibbutz children, the future generation of 1948 and the Palmach (the elite troops), who were clannish, arrogant, kept to themselves, and had no interest in young Jews from abroad. These *sabras* were not deeply imbued by Jewish culture in the way Berl Katznelson had envisaged. In fact, the very language they were speaking, their slang, was liberally interspersed with Arabic phrases of *ya allah* and *wallahi*; this was the language of *Ahlen ya sahibi* (welcome my friend) and *Yakhri betak* (may your house be destroyed). The *sabras* were provincial, anti-intellectual, even anti-cultural; their ideal was the extroverted, courageous new type of farmer and soldier, the gregarious "chevreman," more or less the opposite of the Jewish intellectual abroad. They were deeply imbued with a love of nature and their country; they had been told a hundred times that they were the new elite, and they behaved accordingly—they had little time for Jews from abroad. With traditional features of Jews and Judaism they had even less in common than an assimilated young boy or girl from one of the western suburbs of Berlin.

Some of the young newcomers were deeply impressed by their Palestinian contemporaries and their way of life, tried to imitate them, sometimes very successfully, and were in the end accepted in their charmed circle. They were impressed by their fearlessness, their straightforwardness, and even their foolhardiness. Those newcomers who had already been exposed to some extent to European civilization were more critical of what seemed to them rude people and loud-mouths and stayed aloof. The meeting between these two very different worlds was fascinating and full of tension. The young German Jews insisted that one should be able to read a book, and play an instrument (other than an accordion) without being considered a "potz" (a yiddish term borrowed from the Slavic languages and referring to the penis) and a "degenerat."

It is difficult to generalize about the experience of the youth *aliya* not only because each case was different but because the attitude of young people changed over time. Those who had been initially enthusiastic became critical or negative later on, and vice versa. Ernst Loewy, a youngster from Krefeld in western Germany, arrived in Kiryat Anavim, a kibbutz near Jerusalem, aged sixteen in 1936. His first impressions (as conveyed in letters to the parents) were tremendous. He had been well integrated, and the country had made a great impression on him: "I felt like a human being who returned to his real homeland for the first time." But a few weeks later there was outspoken criticism. He was deeply disappointed by the spiritual life of the kibbutz, or rather its absence: "The people who live here are truly proletarian, who know nothing but work, eat, and sleep and who have no cultural interests." They have no interest, he said, in history and tradition, including their own. In addition they were miserly, only once a year one was permitted to go to the cinema. He conceded that the members of the youth *aliya* group were living better than the members of the kibbutz but this was of little comfort to him. Coming from a home in which Jewish rituals were observed he did not like the lack of religion, the fact that on Sabbath there was no kiddush, no havdala (two of the essential rituals). When the kibbutz children heard that some of the youth *aliya* were fasting on the high holidays, they merely laughed about such strange behavior.

The members of the kibbutz engaged in a kind of politics that Loewy profoundly disliked: On May 1, a big banner was displayed in the dining hall stating "Workers of the world, unite!" Loewy was later to change his views as he came to sympathize with the local Communist party. But what is of interest in this context are his impressions at the time. Naomi Koch (Laqueur), also in 1936, went with youth *aliya* to Ben Shemen, a children's village about midway between Tel Aviv and Jerusalem. She wrote many years later in a memoir, "The primitive character of daily life and the unaccustomed food I accepted not only as unavoidable but as self-evident; the youth movement had prepared me for it. However, I felt in Ben Shemen a spirit of pretentiousness and remoteness from real life." This referred to the educational ideals of Dr. Siegfried Lehmann, a Jewish educator from Germany, personally beloved, who had developed a doctrine of "village culture" by which German-speaking city children were to be turned into Hebrew-speaking, highly cultured agricultural workers. Lehmann's enthusiasm (Naomi writes) merely generated cynicism among the students. There was a huge and growing gap between the grand ideas (of village and culture and Hebrew humanism) floating in the air and the realities of life, hard manual labor in an agriculture that had not yet been mechanized.

Difficulties of Integration: Some Case Stories

Such an approach might have worked with an elite, highly motivated student body that knew Hebrew, but such a student body did not exist. Naomi also resented the cultural narrowmindedness that expressed itself, for instance, in the *Twelfth Night* scandal. The group that, in theory, was running the children's village had decided to perform the Shakespeare play, using every free moment for weeks to study their roles, to prepare costumes, and to rehearse. Instead of welcoming such an initiative those responsible recoiled in horror, and our amateur actors were not permitted to perform because they wanted to do it in German rather than Hebrew, which, needless to say, caused deep disappointment.

Tuvia Ruebner was born in Bratislava in 1924; he came to Palestine via Hungary with virtually the last legal transport in 1941. His first language was German, he went to a German school, he wrote poems in German, and as a precocious child he had not only read "Malte Laurids Brigge" but made his father do the same. He belonged to a group that was sent to Merhavia, one of the oldest kibbutzim, but their reception, in his words, was unfriendly. "The kibbutz was not prepared, we had to sleep in the beginning on straw on the floor of a big room." They were offended by the cold manner in which they were received and in order to annoy the kibbutz members they were singing Nazi songs, which did not endear them to Merhavia. They were given unpleasant work. True, they worked half days only, but the teaching was deficient, since their teacher was more interested in drawing maps showing the strategic position on the eastern front than in teaching his pupils Hebrew. At the end of two years Tuvia Ruebner's Hebrew was not good at all. A youth *aliya* inspector arrived in Merhavia, and complaints were voiced about the boy from Bratislava who continued to write poems in German. But the broadminded inspector told Tuvia that she had a neighbor in Jerusalem named Werner Kraft who also wrote poems in German. The two of them met, and Kraft and Ludwig Strauss (another neighbor and also a poet) became friends and teachers. Ruebner continued to write in German up to 1953 and to speak it all his life to family and friends.

Ernst Loewy returned to Germany after the war and worked there as a writer and historian of German exile literature. Tuvia Ruebner became a professor of comparative literature at Haifa University and a well-known poet, and, *mirabile dictu*, stayed on to live in unfriendly Merhavia. Naomi Koch lived much of her life in England and America but went back to Israel every year and is buried according to her wish in a cemetery at the entrance to Jerusalem.

Are these typical lives? No one has studied systematically the subsequent fates of the graduates of youth *aliya*. Perhaps a third, perhaps slightly more, of those who had gone through this experience stayed in a kibbutz, but most left, and most never used in later life their training in agriculture. Many joined the army during World War II, and more than a few were killed in that war or the Israeli war of independence in 1948, Some rejoined their families, who in the meantime had emigrated from Germany. One, named Shimon Perski, later Peres, a contemporary of Naomi Koch in Ben Shemen, became prime minister of Israel. Others could be found in virtually every walk of life and profession in Israel as well as in many other countries. Those who have survived are now in their late seventies or eighties, but only a few have written about these formative years in their lives. Was it, all things considered, a success? It is in many ways an irrelevant question, for conditions were far from ideal, the whole scheme was based largely on improvisation, and all that mattered was that thousands of young people survived who would otherwise have perished.

Tel Aviv and Jerusalem

Not all young Jews from Germany went to kibbutzim and youth *aliya*. Many went with their parents, and in some cases alone, to the cities, above all to Tel Aviv, Haifa, and Jerusalem. In these cities the better off congregated in and helped to develop certain neighborhoods. This was, above all, Rehavia in Jerusalem, which had been founded in the 1920s but tripled in size between 1933 and 1936 following the immigrations from Germany, Har Hacarmel, and Ahusa in Haifa. A map of the German Jewish settlement in Palestine would show that the side streets of Ben Yehuda and Dizengoff in northern Tel Aviv, particularly north of Mendele Mocher Sefarim, were Jeckeland, where a lot of German was spoken. There new shops and coffeehouses offering Viennese pastry opened, and even the shopkeepers, the milkmen, and the postmen learned a few words of German to accommodate their new clients. There was the famous Max Cohen delicatessen in Allenby, where ham, good coffee, and Limburger cheese could be purchased, the Kapulski coffee and konditorei (also called Jud Suess), and similar shops in Haifa and Jerusalem (such as the one run by the Futter family in upper Ben Yehuda Street). German Jews had their own reform synagogues, Yeshurun and Ichud Shivat Zion in Tel Aviv, Emet veEmunah in Jerusalem.

The architecture changed, and cultural life got a tremendous uplift with the creation of the philharmonic orchestra and other such institutions. A British travel writer (James Morris) wrote decades later that while Tel Aviv had been founded in 1909, its real birth as a city with its own character dates back to the 1930s, the years of the fifth immigration wave, which mainly came from Germany. Those who arrived as children with their parents grew up in relatively comfortable conditions. But they had to face difficulties of another order, school and the contact with their contemporaries. They wanted to be like the others, sunburned, with a daring lock of hair in the face, short trousers and sandals, and with their voices a few decibels louder than customary in Europe. Some newcomers made it easily. Avraham Frank, born in 1923, relates that he had no difficulty learning Hebrew and being accepted, but he went to school in Tiberias, where the cult of sabra-ism was not yet widespread. Yehuda Amichai went to school in Petah Tiqvah, and while he knew the language, he was shocked by the lack of discipline. How could one be so impertinent to the teachers, refuse to carry out orders, come to class barefoot? He later went to a Jerusalem school where some of the teachers came from Germany and where the level of education was higher. Chaim Haller's impressions of a Tel Aviv school were similar, and he also remembers that the formal attire of the boys and girls from Germany seemed singularly out of place in the Palestinian surroundings. Esther Herlitz went to a well-known Jerusalem school and her experiences were less positive. She came from a Zionist home and was eager to adapt herself to the new circumstances, but the native boys and girls called her and the other children from Germany "Nazis," and boycotted them socially: "I did not weep and did not show that I was offended, but in my heart I was very, very angry. I told my father and he went to school to talk to the headmaster and his deputy. There was a special enquiry, but the situation continued as before." Eventually a new school was opened in Talpiot, another Jerusalem suburb, and she and her friends from Germany transferred to the new place to everyone's satisfaction. Her early experiences caused no lasting harm; she became a member of parliament, an ambassador, and a leading figure in Mapai, the Labor party. Dalia Grossman in Tel Aviv attended an early version of an *ulpan*, an intensive language school, and adjusted herself once she was invited to join a local youth movement. Emanuel Strauss, who got his education in Ben Shemen in the late thirties, also reports about reservations on the part of the sabras against children from German-peaking countries.

But as far as the young were concerned, these were passing difficulties; within a year or two they had acquired a good knowledge of the language. In school they were as successful, if not more so than the sabras; their social integration, to be sure, took considerably longer. In comparison with the difficulties the older generation had to experience, the troubles facing the young were not very traumatic.

Hebrew lesson, school at Caputh, 1934. Courtesy Berlin Jewish Museum, Sonnenfeld collection.

Anita Lasker Wallfisch, ca. 1928, playing the cello. Fifteen years later, she was the cellist of the Auschwitz orchestra. She was liberated in Bergen Belsen. Courtesy Anita Lasker Wallfisch, London.

Gut Winkel, ca. 1936, a farm near Berlin where prospective young immigrants to Palestine received their agricultural training. Courtesy CZA (Central Zionist Archives), Jerusalem.

United States of America

UNITED STATES LINES
Affidavit of Support

County of **De Kalb**
State of **Missouri**   S.S.

Prepaid Ticket No._____

I, **Moritz Herz**_____ residing at _____
(Name)   (Street Address)

Maysville,_____ **Missouri**_____ being duly sworn depose and say:
City   State

1. (a) *That I was born a citizen of the United States on:*

   _____In the
   Date

   City of_____
   County of_____
   State of_____

   (b) *That I was naturalized a citizen of the United States on:*

   Date_____In the
   (City)   (County)

   _____(State) of my certificate being_____number

   issued by_____
   (Court)

   (c) *That I declared my intention of becoming a citizen of the United States on:*

   Date **August 3,1937**__In the
   St. Joseph, Buchanan
   (City)   (County)
   Missouri 1874 ____number
   (State)
   of my certificate being_____

   issued by **U.S. District Court, Western District**_____ **2/24/37 of Missouri**

2. That I am **32**_____ years of age and have resided in the United States since_____

3. That the undermentioned alien(s) desire(s) to come to the United States because **To make home with cousin**_____
   (State reasons fully)

4. That the financial status of the alien(s) is_____
   (State whether or not the applicant is dependent on you for support)

5. That my regular occupation is **General Retail Merchant**_____
   (Name and address of firm)
   _____My average weekly earnings amount to $ **50.00**

6. My other assets are as follows:
   (a) Bank account $ **1,300.00**_____ (b) Insurance: Total cash surrender value of policy(ies) $ **2,000.00**_____
   (c) Real Estate $ **1,775.00**
   Yearly income from rentals of Real Estate $ **X**_____ and that the encumbrance on said property, if any, amounts to $ **X**_____
   (d) Stocks and bonds $ **none. Stock of merchandise, invoice $18,159.00**

7. That my present dependents consist of **Wife, aged 27 years, Daughter,Sonja,aged 5 years, Fred. my son, aged four years**_____
   (Names and ages)

8. That it is my intention and desire to have my relatives whose names appear below, at present residing at:

   Sinzennich, Germany_____
   (Give complete address)

   come and remain with me in the United States until such time as they may become self-supporting.

Name of Alien(s)	Sex	Date of Birth	Country of Birth	Occupation	Relationship to Deponent
Jacob Scheuer	male	Oct.4,18__	Germany	Farmer	Cousin
Helene Daniel Scheuer	female	Nov.6/98	Germany	Housewife	Cousin
Ernest Scheuer	Male	Feb.17/23	Germany	None	Second Cousin
Ilse Scheuer	Female	Feb.20/94	Germany	None	Second Cousin
Ruth Scheuer	Female	April22,27	Germany	None	Second Cousin

REMARKS: **I have ample accommodations in my home and am financially able am willing to provided for my said relatives until such time as they are able to provied for themselves**

That I am willing and able to receive, maintain, support and be responsible for the alien(s) mentioned above while they remain in the United States, and hereby assume such obligations, guaranteeing that none of them will at any time become a burden on the United States or on any State, County, City, Village or Municipality of the United States; and that any who are under sixteen years of age will be sent to day school at least until they are sixteen years old and will not be put to work unsuited to their years.

That the above mentioned relatives are in good health and physical condition and are mentally sound, to the best of my knowledge and belief.

That I am and always have been a law-abiding resident and have not at any time been threatened with or arrested for any crime or misdemeanor, that I do not belong to nor am I in anywise connected with any group or organization whose principles are contrary to organized government, nor do the above mentioned relatives, to the best of my knowledge and belief, belong to any such organization, nor have they ever been convicted of any crime involving moral turpitude.

Deponent Further States,   That this affidavit is made by him for the purpose of inducing the American Consul to issue visas to the above mentioned relatives and the Immigration Authorities to admit said relatives into the United States.

Moritz Herz
(Signature of Deponent)

Subscribed and sworn to before me, a Notary Public, in and for said County,

this **31st** day of **December** A.D. 19__

Mrs. D. Williams
Notary Public

My Commission expires **January 2, 1939**

Affidavit of support, the prerequisite for a U.S. immigration visa. Courtesy Wiener Library, London.

Reference No. H/3929/35/I   Haifa, **Nǒ** 882̇8   B
Serial

Category ....D........

GOVERNMENT OF PALESTINE.

Immigration Certificate.

To ...Mr. Meijer VAN SAXEN

     I am directed by the High Commissioner for Palestine to refer to your application of 15th July, 1935,   and to inform you that the person(s) full particulars of whom appear below has/have been approved as (an) immigrant(s) into Palestine. He/She/They should apply for a visa for Palestine not later than 23rd July, 1936, ... at the office of

The British Consul-General, Amsterdam,

taking with him/her/them in addition to this certificate his/her/their passport and any other document proving his/her/their identity and suitability as (an) immigrant(s) for Palestine.

     This certificate must be retained by the immigrant(s) named below until arrival in Palestine where it must be produced and surrendered to the Palestine Immigration authorities at the Port of arrival or Frontier Control.

     This certificate remains valid only until .....23rd October, 1936,   after which date the holder(s) will not be admitted to Palestine.

I am,

Your obedient servant,

Haifa,   ASSISTANT COMMISSIONER
xIxxxxxxxxx, ...24th July, 1935.   For Ag. Director, Department of Immiration.

Particulars of approved Immigrant

Name	Age	Sex	Occupation	Address
Sara Flora VAN SAXEN née Wagenaar	52	F	----	Hilversum, Holland.

1) In case where this form is presented in blank for completion by H.M.'s Consul or Passport Control Officer or Palestine Immigration Officers only the names of the immigrant's wife and children under 18 years of age may be entered here.	(1) Particulars of persons accompanying.			
	Name	Age	Sex	Relationship
		N	I	L

The certificate of the government of Palestine that permits the bearer to enter the country.
Courtesy Wiener Library, London.

Window cleaning in Tel Aviv by a group of young immigrants from Germany, ca. 1935. Courtesy CZA, Jerusalem.

Kibbutz Hasorea in 1936, the first year at Yokneam. Courtesy Kibbutz Hasorea.

Youth *aliya* 1936. New arrivals dance the hora at Kibbutz Ein Harod. Courtesy IGPO (Israel Government Press Office) photo archives. Photographer Zoltan Kluger, March 3, 1936.

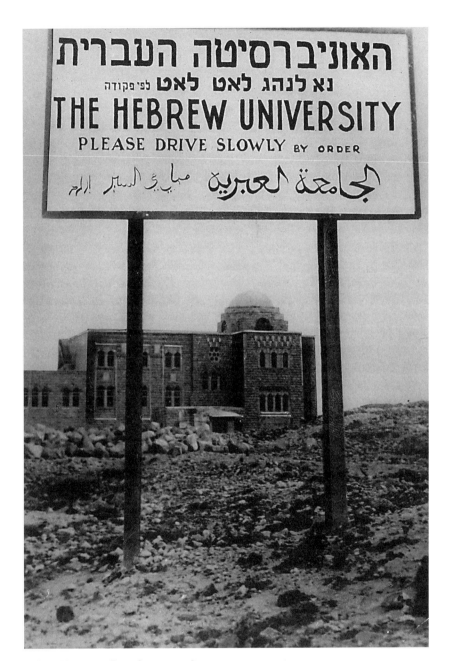

Hebrew University, Jerusalem, ca. 1938. Courtesy CZA, Jerusalem.

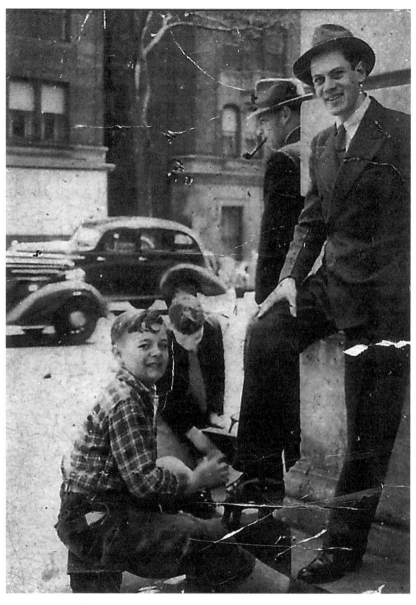

Shoe shining in Washington Heights, New York, ca. 1939. Courtesy Henry Marx, Dallas, Texas.

Kindertransport 1938/39. Dover Court Bay near Harwich, England. One of the main transit camps for children arriving from Germany and Austria. Courtesy Wiener Library, London.

Shanghai 1938/39. A class in a Jewish school. Courtesy www.rickshaw.org.

Karl Liebknecht School in Moscow (closed down in 1938). Its pupils included a generation of postwar East German leaders.

The author (on the left) on guard duty in Palestine, Sha'ar Hagolan, 1939.

Entering the internment camp, Isle of Man, 1940. Courtesy Imperial War Museum, London.

Amadeus Quartet, ca. 1950. One of the leading chamber music ensembles of its time, founded in the internment camp for enemy aliens, Isle of Man. Courtesy Suzanne Rozsa-Lovitt, London.

Those of the slightly older age group who attended the university, the technical university in Haifa, or one of the teacher's seminars, did not have major social difficulties, even though academically some had grave problems in the beginning. Paul Alsberg, a student at the Hebrew University, remembers that his professor failed him in an examination. He should have translated Sallust into Hebrew, but asked whether he could translate the text into German. The professor, himself a recent arrival from Germany, told him that this was the Hebrew University, and that he had failed. Those who lived in town alone as workers or students could not afford the rentals of Rehavia or northern Tel Aviv; they dispersed all over Jerusalem, Haifa, and Tel Aviv, and sometimes even found a room to rent in nearby Arab quarters where it was considerably cheaper. But this kind of peaceful coexistence came to an end with the riots that began in the summer of 1936 and lasted to early 1939. During the war years, life in the mixed neighborhoods such as the German Colony and Talbiye in Jerusalem was altogether normal.

For virtually all immigrants, old and young, life in Palestine meant a social and economic decline, and some were now at the bottom of the social ladder (as was the case in most other countries). The country was very poor, and life was quite difficult. Many of the amenities of Central European city life that had been taken for granted were not available. Gerda Paul was fifteen years old in 1935 and she vividly remembers the discomfort of the early years in Tel Aviv—it was horrible, she later wrote, "no refrigerators, only heavy blocks of ice that had to be carried long distances, no kitchen stoves but only primitive (and dangerous) Primus cookers, the insufferable heat, and the mosquitoes." She hated the Orient, and wanted instead the Tauentzienstrasse and the Kurfuerstendamm. And it was her tragedy, and that of some others, that the Kurfuerstendamm did not want her. The realization that this hot and inconvenient country lacking modern comfort had after all saved their lives came only after 1938 and beyond, when the news about first the pogroms and then the systematic killing reached Palestine.

Growing Roots

How many of the younger generation had come to Palestine as convinced Zionists with both idealism and a more or less realistic understanding of

what was expected of them, and how many had arrived simply because they had to leave Germany and the choice of destinations was
not great? No such statistics exist, and if they did they would be misleading. Some who came as Zionists lost their faith later on, and on the
other hand many who had not been committed one way or another
turned after a few years into staunch patriots. There were, of course,
disgruntled people, who came to regard their stay in Palestine as temporary and who dreamed of the day of return. Some joined the Communist party or one of its front organizations; others had no interest in
politics.

But if there are no statistics with regard to the motivation of those
who came to Palestine in the thirties, we do know how many stayed on
and how many left in the years after the war. Their number was
greater than those who returned to Europe from the United States, but
considerably lower than the young refugees who left Britain after 1945
for other countries. In other words, there was a process of growing
identification with the country even among those who had not initially
come as ardent Zionists. Opinion polls carried out many years later
show that those who visited Europe from among this age group very
much stressed their identity as Israelis while abroad. And whereas they
loved the European climate, the richness of cultural life, and the general cleanliness, they thought that in their new home there was more
warmth in human relations, less loneliness, more solidarity than they
found in Europe.

In the thirties and forties, the new immigrants reacted against the
absolute domination of the Hebrew language. This was regarded by
some as an Eastern European aberration, even Herzl in his utopian
novel *Altneuland* had taken it for granted that German would be the
official language spoken in the new Jewish homeland. There were
small circles in Palestine that met even during the war years to promote progressive German culture and among them there were not only
prominent members of the older generation like Arnold Zweig but also
younger men and women, usually from the fringe of the Communist
party. They were deeply interested in this specific cultural tradition
and regarded with dismay what they considered a cultural chauvinism
recognizing only Hebrew culture. One of them was Walter Grab, born
1918 in Vienna. For many years he had to work for a living selling
gloves in the old commercial center of Tel Aviv. Like many of his generation, he was a man of wide reading and intellectual curiosity, but

did not have the opportunity to study until the late fifties. He was almost forty when he obtained his doctorate in Hamburg, returned to Israel, and eventually became a professor at Tel Aviv University, specializing in Jacobin influences in Germany.

Few young people had similar interests though, and for the most part, unlike Grab, they left Palestine after the end of the war. Such a reaction against the spirit of Hebrew cultural exclusivity was by no means limited to immigrants from Germany and Austria, however. Decades later, with the big immigration wave from the Soviet Union, Israeli schools faced a very similar problem with young people who argued that since Hebrew culture could not muster the likes of Pushkin and Gogol, Dostoevsky and Tolstoi, why should they make the effort to master a language that could offer them only second rate writers? And it is of some interest to recall that at the time, in the 1930s, even old-time Zionist leaders from Germany like Kurt Blumenfeld and Sammy Gronemann complained about the persecution of the German language.

War

When World War II broke out, it was obvious that young people in Palestine should volunteer for the armed struggle against those who wanted to destroy the Jewish people. But for political reasons the British authorities were not particularly interested in Jewish volunteers unless there was at least an equal number of Arab volunteers, which were difficult to find. Nor were they willing, prior to 1944, to establish Palestinian Jewish units in greater than company strength. Nevertheless, individual Jews from Palestine did volunteer, and some saw action in France prior to the disaster of 1940. Most of the 608th company of the Pioneers, consisting almost entirely of Jews from Central Europe, were taken prisoner in Greece at the time of the British defeat the same year; there was no ship to evacuate them in time from the Peloponnes. They were to spend the next five years in Stalag 8B in Upper Silesia and were made to work in agriculture and forestry not that far from Auschwitz. Jews from Palestine joined the Buffs (a British infantry regiment) and in 1944 the Jewish Brigade, which was set up in Egypt, saw action in Italy during the last months of the war. Jews from Germany and Austria found their way to many other units, including the Royal Air Force and the Royal Engineers, anti-aircraft units and the Royal Artillery. This included officers who later saw action in the war of independence.

Many German-speaking soldiers of the Jewish Brigade had taken part in the organization of illegal emigration out of Europe, helping the Displaced Persons make their way to Palestine. Altogether some twenty-six thousand men and four-thousand women from Palestine served in the British army, and the percentage of ATS (women's units) with a German and Austrian background was even higher than that among men soldiers. This was not an inconsiderable figure considering that many more thousands had joined units such as the Palmach serving in Palestine, outside the framework of the British army. For all these soldiers, airmen and seamen, as for soldiers everywhere, these years meant an interruption of their educations and professional careers. But it also meant that they saw more of the world than they would normally have seen. The army did not provide a formal education, but it certainly was also a school of sorts—of life, character, and experience. They received new ideas and impulses. Many of these young people in Palestine had been lacking direction when they volunteered for military service. When they left the army in 1945/46, they were far more mature and knew better what to make of their lives. Unlike American G.I.s and (to a lesser extent) British soldiers, no G.I. Bill of Rights was awaiting them to pay for their study. (There was a modest scheme helping those whose studies had been interrupted to continue; among the beneficiaries was the poet Jehuda Amichai.) They were returning to an uncertain future, except perhaps for the kibbutz members among them. In fact, for many there was only a short civilian interval (1946/47) until they were called up again for a shorter but much bloodier war than the one they had been through, the war for the establishment and survival of the state of Israel.

How did they experience the war years? Like soldiers everywhere, they were bored a great deal, what with unending exercises in Egypt and pointless assignments. They all learned English of sorts and the more capable and ambitious among them were sent to officer's courses. They missed their friends and families and sweethearts. For those looking for action and adventure, army existence was not adventurous enough, and in any case no one liked the army routine. There were not in this respect any significant differences between soldiers of German extraction and the others in their units.

In the meantime, as Rommel's tanks advanced toward Egypt in 1941, the Jewish authorities in Palestine decided to establish for the first time standing units, to be called Palmach. This was done with the knowledge of the British military, who for a certain period paid part of the expenses, since some recruits were to be used for special missions as parachutists inside occupied Europe. Within the framework of the Palmach there was a special "German" unit, consisting of immigrants from Central Europe whose command of the language was perfect and who looked more or less the part of German officers or soldiers. They were given courses in commando operations, acts of sabotage, and the usual military arts, but their training was in German and they were taught to behave as German officers and soldiers would. This unit was headed first by Shimon Koch (Avidan), later a general in the early Israeli army, and subsequently by Jehuda Ben Horin (Brieger) both members of a kibbutz, both natives of Silesia, both militant left-wingers in their youth who had later embraced Zionism. Only individual members of the German group saw action toward the end of the war, in contrast to other units consisting of Hungarian and Balkan immigrants who were parachuted over Europe in 1944.

This exclusively German unit quite apart, there were many young people in other Palmach units who had immigrated from Central Europe in the 1930s and who were now stationed in various kibbutzim, primarily in the north of the country. Since the budget was quite insufficient, they both received military training and worked in agriculture in very difficult conditions, a combination till then unknown in the history of warfare. The story of these years and the subsequent role of Palmach in the war of independence (it was dissolved in 1948) has become a legend; it belongs to the annals of the state of Israel. To paraphrase Winston Churchill in a tribute to the Royal Air Force in the House of Commons in 1940, never in the history of human conflict was so much owed by so many to so few.

It would be invidious to single out young immigrants from Germany and Austria who played a key role in the Palmach and related units because it would be at the expense of others, less well known, who fought equally bravely, but whose military career was cut short because they were killed in action or because they subsequently chose careers in a nonmilitary field.

Still, of some of the main figures, a few names ought to be mentioned. Among the many heroes of the Palmach were Haim Bar Lev, born in Vienna and educated in Yugoslavia, who became chief of staff of the Israeli army in the seventies; Uri ben Ari, born in Berlin, who worked at Ein Gev and became a general and one of the founders of the Israeli tank corps; Generals Dani Mat and Josef Geva; General Dan Lanner, who defended the Golan Heights in the war of 1973; General Shlomo Lahat ("Chich"), who became a popular mayor of Tel Aviv; Oded Messer, also a native of Vienna; Nahum Spiegel (Golan), commander of the Golani Brigade; and many others. Whatever criticism, just or unjust, there had been before 1948 of the immigrants from Germany and Austria, no one would thereafter charge them with a *galut* (diaspora) mentality, with cowardice or lack of patriotism. On occasion it would still be said about an officer that he was a real "Jecke" rather than a "balaganist" spreading disorder. But this meant no more than being a strict disciplinarian, believing in accurate planning of an operation, and leaving as little as possible to accident. It also meant that he would not demand and expect more from his subordinates than he would be ready to do himself.

Israel Society

How did the younger generation of German Jews fare in later years? We have to rely on impressions and personal knowledge rather than statistics. We do not know, for instance, how many married their own kind and how many married partners of different origin; it is my impression that Jewish girls from Germany frequently married a *sabra;* the case of Lea and Yizhak Rabin is just one of many. Nor are there statistics about their choice of profession, there are few professions in which they were not represented. Outside the kibbutzim few worked in manual labor, but this was the general trend as new immigration waves came to the country and as yesteryear's immigrants moved up the social scale. Among the shop owners more than a few inherited their parent's businesses and this is also true to a lesser degree with regard to craftsmen. There was a substantial number of pharmacists, musicians (even before the arrival of the Russian *aliya*), and of people employed in banking—many of the smaller private banks, such as Jafet and Ellern, had been set up by immigrants from Germany.

There were many lawyers but few physicians among the younger generation, simply because there was no medical faculty at the one university that existed at the time. To train in this profession one had in the years prior to 1948 to attend the American University in Beirut and then proceed for two or three years to a European university; Geneva was one of the most popular. Few chose this cumbersome path. German or German-speaking Jews established the Israeli pharmaceutical industry including Teva, the industry's largest company; they were prominent too in the food processing industry (Strauss) and in textiles (Ata). Some of these enterprises flourished; others did not. A wealthy German Jew (Salman Schocken) bought the largest daily newspaper in the country *(Ha'aretz)* and the only independent one; his son took over from him. One of the most innovative industrialists among the young generation was Steff Wertheimer, the first to develop an industrial park on the most advanced American lines in the north of the country. In this industrial park, named Tefen, there was a "Jecke museum" commemorating Jewish life in Germany and the contribution of the German Jews to the building of the state of Israel.

A young man, Jekutiel Federmann, came to Palestine via London shortly after the outbreak of the war. He joined Kibbutz Galed but later went to work as a waiter in Haifa's Café Nordau. He must have been a very enterprising waiter, for within a few years he became the chief supplier for the British Eastern Mediterranean fleet and within two decades he was the manager of and co-owner of the largest chains of hotels in Israel, including the Dan in Tel Aviv and the King David in Jerusalem. The very largest business conglomerate in Israel was owned by Shoul Eisenberg, a Jew born of Polish parents in Germany. He was stranded in Shanghai with his family when the war broke out and spent the war years in that country. As the war ended, Eisenberg, in his early twenties, had the good idea of buying up all the scrap iron available in Japan (of which there was a great deal) and thus put the cornerstone to a billion-dollar business. When he moved his enterprise to Israel, the parliament had to pass a special law, for the country was not accustomed to deal with giants of this order. When Eisenberg died in 1997, there was a battle among his many children and their spouses and the half-Japanese widow, reminiscent of scenes in Balzac, as to who should get what and how the business should be run.

The overwhelming majority of German Jews were not in this economic class; they had modest incomes and led modest lives. Their situation improved as the economic situation began to improve in the late 1950s and 1960s, and bigger apartments were built than in the early days of settlement, though few of them owned their own houses. There was some reparation money from Germany, but not much in the case of the younger immigrants, a few thousand dollars compensating them for the "interruption of their studies" which was enough for a couple of trips to Europe or America but not much more. More fortunate were those who had already began to work in their field in Germany or who had already obtained a first or second degree. They would receive a pension which, given the strength of the German mark, did make a difference as far as their standard of living was concerned.

Few German or Austrian Jews went into politics; those who did belonged to the older generation, like Pinhas Rosen, who was minister of justice for many years, or Josef Burg, minister of the interior for an even longer period. In the early decades after the establishment of the state many young Jews of German Jewish origin served in the ministry of justice and in particular in the foreign ministry. The first director general of this ministry, Walter Eitan (Ettinghausen), an erstwhile Oxford don, came from such a family, as did several of his successors, such as Gideon Rafael and Shlomo Avineri, a philosophy professor and leading Marxologist who for some years was active in government service. Of the early generation of department heads and ambassadors a great number were of German Jewish origin. Ya'akov Shimoni, a noted Arabist, had begun his career in a kibbutz, as had Gideon Rafael and Chanan Baron and Arthur ben Israel, and too many others to be mentioned.

Some of the outstanding names in Israeli literature have been mentioned but they were relatively few compared with painting and particularly music, because in these fields language played a less important role. Hanna Merom, perhaps the greatest Israeli actress of her period, was of German Jewish extraction and had begun her career as a small child in a memorable scene in Fritz Lang's famous *M*. The other great Israeli actress, Edna Porath, was a German who had converted to Judaism when she married an Israeli in 1945. They had, in fact, to marry three times, first under the auspices of the British army occupying Schleswig where Edna lived at the time, later registering a civilian marriage in Palestine, and after a few years a traditional Jewish marriage carried out by the rabbinate.

There were many German Jews in science and technology at the universities and the Weizmann Institute, including its first director. In politics, most German Jews tended toward left-of-center parties. Back in the forties there was a widespread feeling that the existing parties tended to ignore the German Jews and their specific concerns. As a result a new party, *Aliya Chadasha*, was founded, which for years was represented in government, usually in coalition with the Labor party. But this was a party of the older generation of German Jews and it disappeared in the 1960s as the generation that had founded it vanished from the scene. Another attempt to establish a new party was made by Uri Avneri, a classmate of Rudolf Augstein of *Spiegel* fame and later a protagonist of Arab-Jewish understanding. A talented journalist, he was less successful in politics even though he was elected to the Knesset for more than a decade.

The Politics of the German Immigrants

Zionism of a right-wing persuasion, the Revisionists inspired by Jabotinsky, had never been influential in Germany. But in Israel in later years a few of those who had come as children to Israel moved to the far right. They included Elyakim Ha'etzni, born in Kiel, who became one of the spokesmen of the settlers in the Israeli occupied territories. Intriguing in particular was the case of Naomi Frenkel, whose family had owned an ammunition factory in Germany, and whose parents had died when she was still a child. An orphan, she was sent to an agricultural school in Palestine, together with her sibling, and later joined left-wing kibbutzim, Mishmar Haemeq and Bet Alfa. She gained a certain reputation as a writer of family sagas based in part on her own recollections. In her seventies she broke all ties with her former friends and colleagues and found a new spiritual and physical home among the most extreme nationalists of Kiryat Arba, one of their main outposts. As for her Arab neighbors, she told an interviewer in 1998 that she did not hate them, "but I don't believe in the possibility of cooperation between the two people. What I have learned from life here is that they are very different. You might find common ground with some other nations, but not with the Palestinians. All their concepts are different."

Frenkel went to B'nei Braq to receive Orthodox religious instruction, adopted religious practice, and started covering her hair. She then moved to Hebron, where she associated with the most radical anti-Arab elements among the settlers, those who not only spoke about the need to remove Arabs but did something about it by booby-trapping

Arab buses. She felt what she found in Hebron was "what I had been looking for. I found my place, I found what it means to be a Jew." The case of Naomi Frenkel was a very rare one, but it shows that this wave of immigrants had truly produced a thousand different flowers.

Illusions and Reality: A Summing Up

As the surviving members of this generation in Israel approach the end of their road, two questions remain to be addressed: What, if anything, will remain of their heritage? And how do they feel now, what do they make of the developments in their country in their own lifetime? To take the second issue first: Different people react in different ways. Not all of those who came were ideologically motivated. Many opted for Palestine because their families, friends, or comrades went or because there was not a great choice at the time. But all of them, the enthusiasts, the skeptics, and those deeply apolitical, have grown new roots in their lifetime. For the overwhelming majority, this had become their home—Israel was not another waiting room, a Shanghai or Paraguay. The number of erstwhile German Jews who have emigrated to other countries once the state was established has not been greater proportionately than among other ethnic groups.

Looking back sixty years later they may feel a great deal of satisfaction, pride, and even wonder as to how much had been achieved in these decades. The Palestine they knew first in the 1930s was a primitive and backward country, in every respect much behind the Europe they had known. Today not only the mosquitoes have disappeared, but the insufferable heat—the humid heat of Tel Aviv and the dry heat of a Jerusalem *khamsin* (the eastern wind blowing from the desert)—has become tolerable owing to air conditioning. A rich cultural life has developed and in many respects Israel is as technically advanced as any European country and in some ways more so. The per capita income is as high as in southern European countries and if one disregards for a moment the ultra-Orthodox part of the population and the Arab sector, which distort the general picture because of their high birth rate and because most of the women do not work outside their homes, it is considerably higher.

At the same time there is disappointment and sometimes even despair in other respects. Some may express unhappiness with the general direction in which Israeli politics are moving, others may even complain about being strangers in their own country. If they had grave problems in getting along with East European Jews, what do they have in common with more recent immigration waves, from North Africa or the former Soviet Union? Or with the ultra-Orthodox who impose their presence and rule on Jerusalem? Those who built the kibbutzim feel doubly aggrieved, by the political and social developments in the country in general and by the fact that the younger generation has been opting out of the kibbutz, preferring life in the city with its great and growing differences in income, with materialism and a soulless lifestyle dominated by television.

There is a famous poem by Yeats beginning with the words "Was it for this the wild geese spread," which some think is also true with regard to Israel. Was it for this that all the blood was shed, the delirium of the brave, the sweat and tears and all the sacrifices? "Romantic Ireland's dead and gone, it's with O'Leary in the grave" Yeats ended his poem. Romantic Israel is gone (and perhaps more than just Romantic Israel), the Israel of the pioneering spirit, of the generation of 1948, is in the grave together with Rabin and those of his cohort who preceded him.

But is this not an inevitable process, the iron law of routinization and normalization? Perhaps so, but it is still a source of great disappointment to this generation, quite apart from the fact that normalization involves peace. Herzl wanted a Jewish state for two reasons: for the Jews to regain self respect and to live in safety. One part of the dream has been realized, but the other seems as yet distant.

What will survive of the values of the generation of German Jewish immigrants who were in their teens when they arrived in the 1930s? Again, there might be as many answers as there are families and groups. Some have shed their German roots and traditions except for some vague recollections of Grandfather and Grandmother who hardly spoke Hebrew at all and had brought all kind of heavy, old fashioned furniture from the old-country and many books in a funny language no one can read.

But there seem to be many other cases in which features believed to be specific for German Jewry have survived, as shown in a series of interviews made in the 1990s (with Usi Biran, Benjamin Kedar, Ada Brodsky, Ruth Tauber, Dalia Grossman, Paul Alsberg, and others). While few of the next generation spoke German well, they had a passive knowledge of the language, and there was much interest not only

in the history of their families but in what life had been like. German
poets of the nineteenth and twentieth century have been translated
into Hebrew and are read proportionately more widely than in most
other countries. The 250th anniversary of Goethe's birthday was featured more prominently in the literary pages of the Israeli press than in
any other non-German-speaking country. There is a deep and abiding
love of classical music in the next generation and the one after. This
new generation is certainly more pragmatic and materialistic, more Israeli, than the generation of the parents. But cultural interests as well
as certain features of character seem to have been inherited in some
unfathomable ways and it is too soon to say that this process has come
to an end.

UNITED STATES

Golden Country behind Paper Walls

——

Most Germans in the 1930s had a general idea what life was like in the neighboring European countries but knew very little about America except some stereotypes: cowboys and Indians and the tremendously popular books of Karl May with the nineteenth-century Wild West as a background, the skyscrapers, Hollywood (including jazz and the gangster movies), chewing gum, big cars, and cheap products sold in certain chain stores. Those of the left had read Upton Sinclair's *The Jungle* and were reluctant to eat canned meat. Few people had visited the United States, which was far away and the fare expensive. There had been a German Jewish emigration to America, but this was back in the nineteenth century, and contact between the families, more often than not, no longer existed.

As a country of emigration America did not figure very highly in the first years after the Nazi rise to power, partly because the refugees preferred a nearer, European country with which they were more familiar, but mainly because the gates of the country were nearly closed, even though, in theory at least, they should have been half open. Prior to the summer of 1938 the legal quota for immigrants for Germany and Austria was not even remotely exhausted. The number of immigrants up to 1938 was 45,000, whereas 150,000 could have come according to the existing regulations. But 80 percent of American public opinion according to the polls were against the immigration of refugees, the relevant committees in Congress were headed by southern Democrats who were violent opponents, and Roosevelt, who might have been somewhat more liberal, did not want to endanger his electoral chances.

American consulates in Europe (and Havana) had strict orders to make entry to the United States as difficult as humanly possible by asking for documents that could not be obtained, and by rejecting as unsatisfactory affidavits of support that had been provided by relations or friends of the applicants. The violent opponents of immigration, such as Martin Dies and Breckinridge Long, knew, of course, that the Jews were persecuted, but they could not have known that they were effectively sentencing to death those whose applications were rejected. Would they have acted differently if they had known it?

There were no children transports to the United States as there were to Britain and other European countries; laws to this effect were killed in Congress even before they reached the plenary session. The number of unaccompanied children (under sixteen) who reached the United States was seventy-six in 1936, ninety-two the year after, seventy-four in 1938, and thirty-two (!) in 1939. Altogether about one thousand unaccompanied children reached America between 1933 and 1941, including a few hundred who came from France where they had found refuge. They were helped by a Quaker organization and placed with foster families, all Jewish, because U.S. law required that children be placed with families of their own religion.

True, when the question of providing temporary shelter to British children came up in 1940 there were some dissenting voices, but they were overruled within a matter of days and legislation was pushed through. When the August/September issue of *Pets* magazine published the picture of a puppy entitled "I want a home," the editors received within a very short time thousands of applications to provide homes for the pure-bred dogs of England. The number of refugees in the somewhat older age group, between age sixteen and the early twenties, the G.I.s of World War II who came alone, was also relatively small. Those who did arrive came with their families, and it is with them that we shall deal in the main.

Arrival in America (even if it was only Ellis Island) meant security and freedom for those who had escaped from wartime Europe, but not everyone was full of joy about the miraculous rescue. Marianne Loring (Stampfer), who escaped with her family from occupied France, wrote later that "I feared the unknown America, which I thought cold, even icy. I don't know whether I had not wanted to return." She felt that part of her, including her heart, had remained in the Old World. There was nothing specifically anti-American in these apprehensions; it was the general fear of the unknown, of being uprooted from familiar conditions and being transplanted into uncertainties, and these syndromes were apparently more acutely felt if the country of emigration was overseas. In this pre-aviation age the ocean was both a geographical and a psychological divide. The older the refugees were, the greater the fears and ideological or aesthetic reservations. There was also the case of the young German Jewish film star who in disgust booked her passage back to Holland after one week in New York. She had the opportunity to reconsider the wisdom of her decision behind barbed wire in Nazi-occupied Europe during the following years.

Arriving in New York

The attitude of each newcomer who arrived with the *Rotterdam*, the *Volendam*, and the other ships plying between Europe and America was different, just as the circumstances were different. Some had transferred a little money to the United States, others, like Elsbeth Weichmann, arrived with $1.50 in their pockets. Some were received by friends and relations, some by veritable reception committees, others were totally alone. Max Frankel, who came after the outbreak of the war, was welcomed by a considerable number of uncles and cousins, known and unknown. Herbert Weichmann (a future mayor of Hamburg) and his wife were steered by a representative of the American Federation of Labor through the bureaucratic maze and was not even interrogated at Ellis Island.

Lucky refugees were met by a representative of the National League of Jewish Women who steered them to a respectable hotel off Broadway. For most it meant a home belonging to Hebrew Sheltering and Immigrant Aid Society (HIAS), the Jewish welfare organization, four or five people in a small room. They were permitted to stay there for a week, after which they were on their own. Conditions were not at all like fifty years later, when a plethora of aid organizations, federal, local, and private provided help, housing, food, jobs, and general guidance to everyone asking for it.

The first day on the new continent quite often seemed like a dream or like arriving on another planet. It may be no coincidence that dreams figure prominently in the novels describing the very first impressions: the feeling of freedom and security after having been chased from their native country and often all over Europe, the strange colors and noises and even smells, the masses of people in the streets, the pulsating life of a city that dwarfed even Berlin and Paris.

There was a considerable difference between the relatively few who had come early and the others who had left Germany at the very last moment or even after the war had broken out. For some of the late-comers, America was the second or third country of emigration, and they were not quite sure whether this was the end of their journey. Herbert and Elsbeth Weichmann, young Social Democratic militants, were among the lucky ones who had many friends and acquaintances and even relations; they had so many invitations that they began, somewhat rudely, to turn them down. Herbert found on one occasion that his host had put expensive cigars into the pockets of his coat, and he returned them one by one, offending, no doubt, a man who had meant well. Elsbeth relates meeting at the Times Square subway sta-tion Adrienne Thomas, a best-selling author back in Germany *(Die Katrin wird Soldat)*. Adrienne wept, "Take me away from this Baby-lon, the giant blocks of concrete, the herds of people wholly devoid of consideration, the loud streets and the idiotic and shrill advertise-ments. I perish here."

Thomas displayed the sensitivity of an artist, and must have found it difficult to believe that there were even more horrible places on earth such as, for instance, the ramp at the Auschwitz railway station. But Elsbeth reports similar reactions from a manual worker who said that the dimensions of this city were too gigantic and frightening, the strug-gle for standing room in the metro too nerve wracking. As she saw it, the first encounter with New York was for many a nightmare, which few dared to articulate for fear of appearing ungrateful, since their lives had been saved. The shock of New York was therefore seldom de-scribed in the memoirs, and in any case, the refugees tended to forget it in later years as they built for themselves a new existence and their material situation improved.

The Jewish organizations wanted the refugees to leave New York and some did so of their own volition. Henry Ries, a twenty-one-year-old photographer, moved on to Bridgeport, Connecticut, not because he was overwhelmed by New York but, on the contrary, because he found it provincial after cosmopolitan Berlin. With regard to the prevailing sexual mores, for instance, it seemed to him unheard of that a young man was not to address a young woman, let alone to invite her for coffee or a drink. But he also wanted to leave the refugee milieu: "I wanted to breathe a bit of fresh air, I did not want to speak German nor did I want to listen to the constant complaints and accusations. I wanted to live." He found people who accepted him, Jews and non-Jews, and encountered generosity such as he had not known before. His life improved and he felt that he gradually became a native.

Shortly after the war in Europe ended, a nonsectarian committee published a massive, interview-based study on recent immigration to America. It was an answer to the xenophobes who had prevented substantial immigration prior to the Holocaust. Refugees were asked, among other things, what they thought of America. It emerged that most refugees had been overwhelmed. Why had no one told them back in Europe that New York was the most wonderful city in the world? "Why did we believe that American products were all junk and humbug?" They were spellbound by the quantity and variety of food, but they were also shocked by the waste. They realized that what was commonplace in America was luxury in Europe; as one of them put it, "The parking lot at a factory could rival that of the Munich opera on the eve of a gala performance." They were impressed by the lack of regimentation, the fact that people were so friendly and openhearted, that a knock on the door at night did not mean a visit from the Gestapo. What aspects of American life were regarded as most satisfactory? Of those asked, 27 percent replied "democracy or political equality," 26 percent answered "freedom," the difference between those two categories probably not being absolutely clear except perhaps to professional political philosophers. Only 12 percent answered that the high standard of living was the most attractive feature and 8 percent said friendliness. True, many refugees were shocked by the extent of race prejudice, by the exaggerated value put on money as a measure of social prestige, by the language and content of the American media, by occasional discrimination against them as Jews. But as to whether they intended to return to Germany, the reply of a former businessman was typical: "It is a very silly question—to go back to what?" Or as a social work executive explained, "We have lived, or tried for more than eight years now to live, and think and feel as Americans. Our children are Americans all through

. . . Naturally we do not feel as deeply rooted in this country as we were in Germany, but we have tried from the very first to forget our former life, because that seemed to be the only way to be at home and happy here."

The survey, the most authoritative at the time and for years thereafter, paints a picture of a great success story, but it was still a little misleading. The study was made years after the refugees had arrived and did not reflect their early experiences; it came after a war that had been won against Nazi barbarism; it was carried out as the economic situation improved, in a general atmosphere of optimism as far as the future was concerned. It came after the full extent of the wartime horrors became known, and it is perhaps also true that those asked wanted to show that they were patriots and that their early difficulties were behind them.

But this was not the general mood of 1938/39 and not even of 1940 when despair and hopelessness could be found, when some refugees (and not only sensitive writers like Ernst Toller and Stefan Zweig) committed suicide, having lost the will to live and to make a new beginning.

The focus of our narrative is on the younger generation and their impressions and experiences were not necessarily those of their fathers and mothers. They did not suffer the disappointments of lawyers whose training and experience was now totally out of place, of physicians who, however experienced, had to study again for their license to practice; they were not German writers or actors who could not adjust to the English language. And yet, they, too, were influenced by the mood of their parents who faced all these difficulties, as well as poverty and deprivation. Georg Troller relates that he did not burst with happiness having been saved and having reached the United States. He ridiculed those instant Americans, the "allrightniks" who claimed that the Rockefeller Center was the grandest cathedral of the world and Grandma Moses the greatest painter since Leonardo, that, as Max Reinhardt put it, a new kind of man was created in California (even though Reinhardt did not find a proper job in Hollywood). "Outwardly each of us celebrated the new Heimat, whereas inwardly he felt a failure, an outsider, a horse in the age of the automobile." After the war Troller went back to Europe and for many years worked as a German television correspondent in Paris.

Lost in the Big City

It would be neither fair nor accurate to put all the blame on the hostility of others, on the negligence and the patronizing attitude of Jewish relief organizations. While some newcomers showed initiative, inventiveness, and a willingness to accept almost any work, others spent their time lamenting their misfortunes, talking of how rich they had been once upon a time and how wonderful everything had been at home. As the *Aufbau*, the weekly that was read by everyone, wrote, "It is an open secret that many immigrants in New York are disappointed and discouraged once the grey daily life takes over, after all the old friends and relations have been seen." Most of the refugees had thought that things would be quite different. During the years before the refugees had been wholly preoccupied getting their affidavits, tickets, and other documents. Nor had there been time to ponder the future when they still were in the countries of transition such as France or England. But now, having at long last reached their target, they found badly paid jobs only with great difficulty. It was intolerably hot in New York, the room in the boarding house could not be aired, they never ventured beyond Eightieth Street in the north and Fourteenth in the south (and this was about all they knew of America), the children were naughtier in the new country than ever before, and the food in the cafeteria looked much better than it tasted. They had tried so hard to acquire a working knowledge of English in the old country and now they did not understand a word they heard. Was this America, was this the country of their future?

This negative attitude, the lack of enterprise, adaptability, persistence, courage, the inclination to be overwhelmed by difficulties, was very much against the American grain, and it annoyed their hosts. As Miss S. Cohen of New Jersey wrote in the *Aufbau* in August 1940,

> They bothered the life out of us in their letters. We thought they were hounded to death. Now we know after a most hectic year [of trying to help a family of four of distant relations], denying our own families to help them, that we should have left them in Europe. I am beginning to think that this influx is entirely unnecessary . . . they should stay there and sit tight a few years and things will adjust themselves later.

It's just a gag to get money out of us. Let them know, we are not all money bags and unless it is a matter of life and death, they should stick tight. To hear my relatives talk, those left in Germany still have many chances of happiness among themselves, more than we impecunious Jews have here."

Miss Cohen could not have been more mistaken—it was indeed a matter of life and death, and there was no chance of happiness in Germany and Austria, only the prospect of almost certain death. But she had obviously been provoked beyond endurance by the stupidity and tactlessness of her guests, who should have known better. Not all refugees were saints and geniuses. The crime rate among the new arrivals was virtually nonexistent, but some were very foolish people, lacking elementary common sense.

Sweatshops, Cafeterias and Evening Classes

It is, of course, true that the refugees suffered, that some of the older people were broken, and that life for the young was hard, to say the least. There are many accounts of boys and girls working at sweatshops at a dollar or a $1.50 a day or even less, of long bus and subway rides, of returning home exhausted, too tired to go to English language classes. One of them wrote many years later,

> On a personal level America was not sympathetic, it did not want us. Here we came in substantial numbers at a time when jobs were scarce and we were accused of taking work away from Americans, that we were willing to work at anything, jobs Americans would not take. We were often reminded that our situation was better than that of earlier immigrants. We never had to sleep on park benches, and our stomachs were never empty. But we quickly learned the meaning of "dog eats dog."

There were frequent complaints of a bad attitude toward the refugees at work on the part of fellow Jewish workers from Poland. Robert Goldman reports the ill will he experienced while working as the only German Jew in a big tailor shop. His coworkers treated him as a snob because, as they saw it, the German Jews had different clothes and behaved in a different way, like non-Jews. They neglected their

Jewishness or were even ashamed of it. They lived in West End Avenue, not in the Lower East Side. Edith Liebenthal reports that "the real problem (at work) was a group of old men, they spoke Yiddish and hated us because we did not speak their language. They were mean and gave us a hard time referring to us as the 'Yiddishe Shikses.'" Similar complaints, paradoxically, came from Polish Jews, who had been expelled from Germany in October 1938, had to return to Poland, and were treated as "Jeckes" by their fellow Jews in Lodz and Radom.

For a long time the new arrivals lived in one room, not always with a kitchen or a bathroom of their own. The girls and the mothers were usually the first to find work, of course, at the bottom of the scale. In the words of Eva Neisser:

> The girls cleaned houses, watched infants in sleep-in jobs ($30–40 a month) tacking buttons to cards with wire threads, 40 cents an hour or piece work. If you did not produce fast enough, you were out. One such place had 24 machines running 24 hours a day in the East Bronx; my sister and I had the 4 A.M. to noon shift and left the West Bronx at 3 A.M. to take the IRT to Harlem 125th Street, then the Pelham Bay-East Bronx train up again. We did home work stringing beads, gluing soles on slippers, three women working for about $8 a week. To get a decent office job you had to know someone.

Another young woman, aged seventeen, had been on the ill-fated *St. Louis* (the famous "ship of the damned" which was forced to return to Europe), but was one of the few who had a second chance to reach America the day before Thanksgiving 1940. It had been an eventful trip, the passengers were ordered to carry lifebelts at all times and heavy boots in case they had to get into lifeboats. Within a week of their arrival in New York, she found a job in a small factory through an advertisement in the *Aufbau*. The factory made knitted gloves for the army and navy:

> We had bundles of wool gloves on our laps and steam presses behind us, pretty hot in summer . . . New Year's eve we moved into a small furnished apartment in the 80ths. My sister and I slept in the living room on a narrow couch head to toe.
> We had our own bath, kitchen, linen, gas and electricity for $10.00 a week. Every evening my sister and I would bring bundles of gloves home to be finished. Every morning we took the previous day's work

back. So we managed to make a living. Every week one or two dollars went to a savings account. We bought day-old bread and took lunch in a paper bag. My first dress was from Klein on the Square for $2.95. I saw my first movie after one year in New York. A big date included an ice-cream soda for two.

But according to another contemporary this was a splurge: "to go out with a girl, the boys spent 11 cents—ten for a subway ride downtown and back, then a free concert at the Metropolitan Museum or the Frick Gallery and a stick of gum as a one-cent treat."

Young men changed jobs more quickly than women. Putty Eichelbaum, who had reached America by way of Italy and Cuba, began his working career washing dishes in the Waldorf Astoria and then graduated to being an usher in uniform in the Radio City Music Hall. His Americanization proceeded quickly: he took out citizenship papers, changed his name to Richard Henry Essex, and through his Italian girlfriend received a job first as a stagehand, and later as a minor actor in an Italian-language religious gala, *The Life and Death of Christ*, touring the eastern seaboard. His salary was princely, twenty-five dollars a week, and when the tour ended, he became a bellhop in a Florida hotel, bringing ice water to newly arrived guests. Among them were a fair number of attractive young married women from New York, minus husbands, whose motherly (or other) instincts he provoked. By then he was earning thirty dollars a week with tips. But the season came to an end, and he returned to New York, where jobs were scarce. At last he found one, very unsatisfactory, in a shoe factory in New Jersey. After that, Pearl Harbor and the army.

Many young men worked as waiters in restaurants and cafeterias. There are no precise statistics about the employment of those who reached New York aged seventeen, eighteen, or nineteen, but it is instructive to scan the curricula of future academics. Siegmund Baum, later a professor of physiology, worked in a factory; Hermann Freudenberger, who was to become an economics professor, worked in a mattress factory and later produced shoe polish; Kurt Eisenmann, future professor of mathematics, was for three years an apprentice in a gift shop, but also distributed newspapers and bread; Walter Eppenstein, later professor of physics, was a plumber; Ernest Bergman, professor of plant physiology, did farmwork, as did the historian Werner Angress; Carl Amberg, professor of chemistry, worked in factories producing paper and aluminium; Helmuth Adler, professor of psychology, was a welder; Henry Abraham, before studying at Kenyon College and becoming a professor of political science, delivered newspapers; and Paul Moritz Cohn, professor of mathematics, started his working career in poultry farming and was later employed as a bench fitting assembler.

Gunther Stent, who was to be a leading figure in the field of molecular biology, had his first job washing dishes in the evening shift at Goldblatt Brothers, a department store in the Chicago loop. He then worked in a drugstore soda fountain at Fifty-third and Woodlawn in the Hyde Park area, and eventually was ready for the big time, as a short-order cook in one of the busiest fountains in town, Liggett's drugstore just north of the loop. He earned seventy cents an hour, but found the work physically and psychologically exhausting because of the constant pressure.

These are just eleven careers chosen at random. Their number could probably be multiplied by a hundred. Were these wasted years? Gibbon wrote that his experience as captain of the Hampshire Militia was of help to him as historian of the Roman Empire. Mao Tse-tung sent Chinese students to do agricultural work in the countryside during the Cultural Revolution. For the young Jewish refugees these years were something akin to a cultural revolution. Washing dishes was of dubious help to a budding physicist or mathematician, but exposure to real life outside the groves of academe might have broadened their horizons.

The Stronger Sex

There was an important difference between the prospects facing young men and women. The girls were, as often noted, the stronger sex in these difficult conditions. They found it easier to obtain work and became the main money earners, especially during the first months after arrival. They cleaned houses and did other menial jobs of any kind. But later on, the boys not only enjoyed a wider variety of somewhat better paid jobs, they also could go into the army and upon return to the United States benefit from the G.I. Bill of Rights, which made a college education possible and opened up careers of which they had been able only to dream. For the girls, as one of them later wrote, "to

enter high school would have set us back a couple of years, to enter
college we were required to take courses in American history and English composition, regardless whether we needed them or not. Most
importantly our parents in their late forties or fifties needed any dollar
we could earn." Or, as another wrote, "my work was war work and I
could not leave. The hours were too long to attend evening classes."

As the war ended, the women married and then their biological
clocks were ticking away; if they wanted a family, the fifties were the
time to have one. True, when the children had reached a certain age,
the mothers were free to go to college, but when they received their first
or second degree they were in their late thirties or early forties, and
while this was a source of great satisfaction it hardly enhanced their career prospects. As far as the early years were concerned, it was certainly
true as a New York refugee poet wrote, "Wir alle wissen es gut und
genau/Das starke Geschlecht ist die heutige Frau"—woman had become the strong sex.

We have been dealing with the young refugee generation as if it had
been a whole, but there was a fundamental dividing line more pronounced perhaps in America than in other countries, and more palpably felt at that time than at any other. Those born in 1922 or earlier,
that is to say those aged sixteen or older when they arrived, had to help
feed the family. Those in the younger age group had to attend school
following the law of the land. Getting into school at this age not only
greatly assisted integration, it also allowed them to qualify for scholarships and college admissions that were out of reach for the older ones.
Unless they were lacking drive or were unlucky, they were virtually as-
sured of a decent professional career.

Children and the American Way of Life

Surveys of the youngest refugees all stress that, however bewildered and
bemused these lost children of Europe were in the beginning, however
anxious about the fate of their parents left behind, however painful their
past experiences, they showed astonishing recuperative powers. The
overall impression was that the children accepted life in the new country with a healthy optimism. Arriving in America after an adventurous
trip over the ocean was the realization of a dream and a release from

hardships and humiliation. As one boy described the entrance of his ship into New York harbor: "Every one of us felt overjoyed and our eyes were wet with tears, thrilled at the sight of this land of liberty and justice for all." This account sounds almost too good to be true but there is no reason to disbelieve the little girl who, more to the point, shouted to a companion parting at the station: "I wish you lots of fun, lots of ice cream and lots of money" (Viel Spass, viel ice cream und viel Geld).

The separation from the parents was not, of course, easily overcome and the adjustment to foster homes was usually not that quick, and sometimes far from complete. But there was general agreement that in school and later in college the refugee children did very well. They received not only high marks and prizes but also mixed easily with other youngsters. Language was only a temporary hindrance, even though the older ones among them took longer to lose their accents. Unlike in England, they were not encouraged to leave school at fifteen and sixteen. Max Frankel, who went to school in Washington Heights, found that English was his poorest subject and his nemesis was a teacher named Elsie Herrmann. He was a poor and lazy reader and had fallen hopelessly behind comprehending Dickens' *Tale of Two Cities*. She made him attend an extra journalism course, and applied more than gentle pressure, as well as positive reinforcement, until working for her became fun. Eventually he was promoted to editor in chief of the school newspaper: "Propelled by her force and faith I entered the privileged guild of ink-stained busybodies."

More than a third of the refugee children showed outstanding work in school and were given special honors, awards, and scholarships. They became valedictorians of their classes, presidents of various honor societies, and they became students and teachers at Harvard and Yale. In New York a special study was conducted to find out the reasons for their superior records. Was it a matter of native intelligence, the good work habits instilled in them from early childhood, the intellectual environment of the refugee families, or perhaps the fact that those who had made it to America were an especially enterprising group? Whatever the reasons, the enthusiasm, persistence, and general helpfulness of the American teachers were also crucial.

To relate one more such story: fifteen-year-old Richard Schifter arrived alone from Vienna in 1938. He attended DeWitt Clinton High School in New York and soon was the best in his year. But he still had

the foreign accent and he recalls an extraordinary young teacher named
Israel Schuldenfrei who made him read a passage, then dissected his
speech by identifying the various sounds incorrectly pronounced. He
would then tackle one sound at a time and made him recite sentences in
which the corrected sound appeared frequently, for example, "Around
the rugged rock the ragged rascal ran." He recalls walking the streets of
New York carrying dry-cleaned and pressed clothes for a nearby tailor
to earn a few nickels and dimes and repeating that sentence over and
over again. He earned some more money tutoring a mathematical illiter-
ate, the result of which was a passing grade in intermediate algebra.
Thus he learned a lesson that was to be of great importance in his future
career as an American diplomat: "One must learn to distinguish
between tasks which are very, very difficult and those that are impossible. One should not hesitate to take on the former."

A study of the fates of the unaccompanied children made forty
years after their arrival found that most did not merely adjust to
America but fell in love with it. Those aged ten or younger became
Americans within weeks, and within months they had forgotten all
about Europe. But the older ones had difficulties and never quite over-
came the feeling that there were differences between them and their
non-refugee peers. One who later rose to the rank of major in the U.S.
army wrote that he still felt as an emotional outsider. Almost all of
them had done well in terms of career and income, but with age they
felt that something was missing—roots, the extended family, feeling of
complete integration, though they were comfortable and accepted in
America. Hence, for instance, the urge to have reunions of the class of
1940 even though they had been very young when they had arrived
and had not stayed together for any length of time.

Perhaps the Americanization of the very young went even too fast
and was sometimes too successful. Their desire to be like the others
was so great (and the pressures to conform were probably even greater
outside New York) that they no longer had any interest in their native
language. Cultural background, values, and customs were all rejected.

Washington Heights

Refugees from Germany, like immigrants from all countries, tended to
congregate in certain areas of their new homelands. It was Rehavia

and north Tel Aviv in Israel, Swiss Cottage, Hampstead, and Golders Green in London, Belgrano in Buenos Aires. Most German Jewish refugees in North America, perhaps two thirds of them, were concentrated in New York. Others went to New Jersey and Pennsylvania, to California and Ohio. There were few states in the union where refugees did not settle and in some major cities such as Chicago (the Hyde Park area) and Los Angeles and its suburbs, there were, as in New York, concentrations of immigrants from Central Europe. This general picture changed somewhat during and after the war, but in broad outline it remained true for several decades.

In New York those better off, the intellectuals, and many Viennese, settled in the Riverside Drive and West End Avenue area between 72nd and 96th streets. But the biggest single concentration was in Washington Heights, an uptown section of Manhattan between 160th and 180th Streets, west of Broadway. Why the refugees congregated there and not in other parts of New York is impossible to establish; it was as accidental as the choice of a certain region in London or Jerusalem. It might have been, as one reporter put it, the gentility of the neighborhood, the style of the buildings, the parks nearby and the proximity of the Hudson River. But most probably it was the fact that a few acquaintances who had arrived earlier on had settled there, and those who came later were attracted by a neighborhood in which they knew at least a few people, and which early on boasted a few shops such as bakeries and butcher shops in which their language was understood.

It was a relatively homogenous neighborhood, consisting mainly of Jews from southern Germany rather than Berlin and the north; refugees from other areas of Germany were more often found in certain parts of Queens such as Forest Hills and Kew Gardens. There was a preponderance of Jews from small communities in Washington Heights and there was an emphasis on orthodoxy, not as practiced in Eastern Europe, but still quite pronounced. Once a certain number of Jews had settled there, social clubs (such as the New World Club and the Prospect Unity Club) attracted members, as did sports clubs such as Maccabi, synagogues of every persuasion, and food shops catering German specialties, and even a cabaret came into being. In some respects the street scenes in Washington Heights resembled those in a small town in southern Germany.

A correspondent in the *Aufbau* writing in 1939 complained about "the small town habit of some of our countrymen of standing around in front of cafeterias and at street corners in little gossip groups." He called this a terrible habit, which provoked on the part of Americans at first surprise and then disgust. Perhaps there was nothing specifically *German*-Jewish about it; the daily street parliament at Shderot Rothschild in Tel Aviv at the time was Eastern European rather than German in composition. Whatever the origins of this habit, in New York it was felt to be un-American.

A certain way of German Jewish life developed in Washington Heights (sometimes also called the Fourth Reich) in the 1930s. There were, of course, constant concessions to the American milieu: first the clothing changed, the furniture, and later, as the refugees discovered America, many other things too. On the whole, the refugees felt at home in Washington Heights in the 1940s. "For my mother it was exhilarating," a refugee reported, "surrounded by friends, active in the synagogue as a volunteer in its many activities, including the Sunday clothing exchange, she was completely at home. There were constant get-togethers, roof parties and picnics at Interstate Park across the Hudson River, reached by ferry."

The young played soccer even though it was anything but an American sport at the time. Various clubs emerged, the New World Club (later to unite with Blue Star), the Prospect Unity Club, and Hakoah Vienna collaborated with the Brooklyn Wanderers. The New World Club had a promising young player in its forward line named Erwin Weilheimer, who later emigrated to Israel and as Aharon Doron became a general in the Israeli army. Henry Kissinger belonged to the Maccabi second team. These clubs lasted up to the 1950s and had a league of their own.

With all the difficulties there was a buoyancy in Washington Heights that was less common in later years. Among the refugees who arrived after the war, criticism and pessimism sometimes prevailed. Ilse Marcus wrote, "I am very unhappy to say that I lost one fatherland and I did not find a second one. When we needed America badly it was closed to us and that's why I lost our family." Marion Rosen, who moved to New York from Ohio after the war said in an interview: "Isn't it a horrible place?" In Ohio there were wonderful, nice people, whereas Washington Heights disappointed her. "They're very clannish, if you don't belong to a certain group, you're out. If you are a middle-aged woman like I am, and you wear dungarees, you are either an idiot or they think you want to be in your twenties. Or they are just jealous because you don't conform." Comparing the prewar immigrants with the Russian newcomers in the 1980s, Sary Lieber said that those who arrived in 1938/39 "did not ask anything from anybody, took all kinds of jobs no matter what. There was no job too low for them to accept." The Russian immigrants who came in the 1980s had a different attitude. "If you want to give them something, they will look at it ten times before accepting it [if] it's not good enough. We would not have dared to refuse something that was given to us though no one offered us anything."

Acculturation was slow in Washington Heights except for the younger generation, which went to public school rather than to Jewish day schools. It has been said that the world of Washington Heights lasted longer than it would have normally lasted because those young immigrants who were too old to go to high school and instead started work immediately found it hard to make social contacts among Americans. Most of them at one time or another made an attempt to break out of the social ghetto but did not quite succeed and then retreated. According to a survey made in the late 1940s, 62 percent of male German Jews married German Jewish refugee girls, a very high percentage, and only a minority married American Jewish girls.

The main exceptions were the veterans who had been to college owing to the G.I. Bill of Rights and whose subsequent careers led them away from Washington Heights. Those who stayed behind or returned after the war formed social clubs including hiking and soccer clubs. According to an observer, they felt uneasy about their isolation and made some efforts to widen their horizon by, for instance, opening local chapters of nationwide organizations. But it is difficult to believe that this concern figured topmost in their minds. All immigrant groups in America had stuck together for a long time and there was no good reason to assume that the Jews would be different.

The Kissinger Generation

It was in this milieu that a generation of young refugees grew up. The case of Henry Kissinger was in some ways typical. His family had arrived from Fuerth in Bavaria in September 1938 and, like so many others, he attended George Washington High School. He went to work at sixteen at the Leopold Ascher Brush Company, becoming a delivery boy and a shipping clerk. He went to evening classes and wanted to become an accountant. He received his draft notice at the age of nineteen, went for his training to Camp Croft, and the rest is history.

Max Frankel, a few years younger, briefly attended Edward W. Stitt Junior High School, which meant crossing Broadway and entering an alien and dangerous world. He was attacked by Irish kids and waylaid by blacks, and the situation changed only when he transferred to another school. He subsequently was admitted to and attended the High School of Music and Art as a student of visual arts. On the other hand, Louis Kampf related that he became a radical precisely because he witnessed how policemen beat up a black man in a local shop. Kampf was the son of Polish Jewish parents who had come from Vienna. He arrived in America in the middle of the war, studied, became prominently involved in Students for a Democratic Society (SDS), the radical student movement, and was later made president of the Modern Language Association, one of the main bastions of radical influence in the academic world. But in a community like Washington Heights revolutionaries like Kampf were the exception.

After the war, there was a new influx to Washington Heights, albeit a small one, consisting of those who had survived in Europe. One of them was a young woman named Carola Siegel who had left Frankfurt at age ten with a children's transport to Switzerland. She was never to see her parents again. The great majority of the children in her home left Switzerland after the war, of whom about half went to Israel, the other half to America. Carola's career was remarkable by any standard. She first went to a kibbutz and later worked in a kindergarten. But she wanted to study sociology and psychology even though she had nothing but an elementary education.

Somehow she worked her way through high school and college, first in Israel and then in France, and eventually she got a doctorate in New York. She worked for Planned Parenthood, and later, as Dr. Ruth Westheimer, became a TV personality and America's most popular sexologist. As a dissertation topic at the New School she had chosen the fate of the children, about a hundred, who had been with her in a home in Switzerland. She found, perhaps to her surprise, that all of them lived normal, well-adjusted lives, as businessmen, farmers, nurses, teachers, a baker, and a watch repairman who eventually owned many of the duty-free shops at Kennedy Airport.

The German Jewish Washington Heights continued to linger on until the 1980s. The economic situation of the first generation of refugees had greatly improved in the post war period. Some opened their own businesses, a fair percentage received restitution and pension payments from Germany, and as the quality of life in Washington Heights declined, they moved on to more desirable parts of New York. At the same time, the younger generation, those born in the 1920s and after, had moved out as their careers took them to other parts of town, or of America, but also because they felt uneasy in the confines of the world of their parents, which seemed somehow outside the real America and even outside American Jewry.

The clash, as one observer put it, was cultural rather than political, and it affected even the Orthodox religious communities, which had seemed immune to change. This refers to the Frankfurt secessionists of Agudat Israel, headed by Rabbi Breuer, a community founded in Germany, and anti-Zionist in inspiration. Whereas the older generation stuck to the rigid observation of the traditional liturgy, the younger Orthodox were influenced by the revival of Orthodox religion, which was often Hasidic, enthusiastic, and romantic, such as existed in sections of Eastern European Jewry in America.

A visitor to Washington Heights in the early twenty-first century would discover a Jewish presence only with effort and in certain enclaves in what had once been a predominantly German Jewish neighborhood, namely close to Fort Tryon Park and in the north of the region. The area has become Hispanic with a sprinkling of more recent Russian Jewish immigrants. A few old ladies and men can be seen on sunny days on benches near the Hudson Rriver. As one of the survivors complained, it has become difficult even to buy a newspaper in English rather than Spanish. The great majority of German Jewish inhabitants have passed away or are living in senior citizens homes in Florida or with their children outside New York.

Café Éclair: Berlin and Vienna in the New World

It was the same in other parts of America. When Catherine Stodolsky returned to the place where she had grown up in Chicago she found that the Hyde Park she had known no longer existed. Once upon a time she had believed that everyone on Fifty-third Street spoke German, but all the old landmarks had disappeared—Nachmann, the baker selling poppy seed cake, Kronberg's delicatessen where they bought the excellent liver sausage. The only survivors she found were in their late seventies and they lived in self-help homes for seniors in the north of Chicago.

In the 1990s, Ruth Wolman engaged in a search and an oral history project in Los Angeles. Her parents, together with some German and Austrian Jewish refugees, had formed a social and cultural society, closely knit and vibrant, very active and engaged in mutual help, called Die Gruppe. It had been a spontaneous development. One day a worker in a furniture factory noticed the leather attaché case from which another worker took his sandwiches. He went to talk to him, realizing that only a fellow European would use such a case. Out of this conversation the group developed. Fifty years later all this was nothing but a fond memory; the German Jewish community of yesteryear had ceased to exist as a group.

If Washington Heights was the center of lower-middle-class refugees from Germany, the center of the Viennese refugees was a coffeehouse called Éclair on Seventy-second Street between Broadway and Columbus Avenue. It had been established by Hans Seliger, a lawyer from Prague, but the coffee and pastries, not to mention the schnitzel and the atmosphere, were strictly Viennese. It was there that former businessmen in search of business, former lawyers in search of clients or a new profession met, but also members of a younger set, those who had belonged to the Vienna Jewish sports clubs such as Hakoah. After 1941 the young men appeared increasingly in uniform. Others preferred the nearby Coupole, and those who could afford it went to Rumpelmayer in Central Park South, at that time the ritziest neighborhood.

Even though German and Viennese refugees shared a (more or less) common language they lived largely in different worlds. The Austrians were less likely to attend synagogue, they had their own clubs and social gatherings, and it is probably fair to say that whereas most German Jews realized early on that America was their new homeland, some Austrians were less likely to rule out an eventual return to Vienna. This may appear somewhat paradoxical, because by and large German Jews had felt more strongly patriotic than the Viennese (often first- or second-generation Viennese from Galicia or Bukovina), who were generally not as tied emotionally to their homeland. But then the Viennese were often more adaptable than the German Jewish refugees, and generalizations in this as in other respects are risky.

The social and economic problems the Viennese faced were the same confronting the German refugees. Those better off among them chose to live in more expensive parts of Manhattan or even in the more distant suburbs such as Scarsdale, even though these were rare instances at the time. They bought themselves into existing American firms or unhurriedly prepared for a new career, while sending their children to some of the better schools.

American Politics and the Young Refugees

As for their politics, the overwhelming majority of the German-speaking Jewish refugees was Democrat in the 1940s and they adored Roosevelt, who at the time was regarded as a savior and a great friend of the Jews. This was only natural, since the Republicans had at best never shown much interest in the refugees—they were about as attractive to a new immigrant as the Tories in Britain. Neither the German nor the Austrian refugee community was very politically minded; to the extent that they were politically active they tended toward social democracy, but there was no such party in America and they found their home among the Democrats. There were a few Communists among the refugees, but the German Communists felt somewhat out of place in America, which was for them no more than a temporary shelter. They would have preferred to be in Mexico where some of the leading party officials and intellectuals had found asylum.

The Austrian Communists showed great activity under the cover of various social youth clubs (the Kreis) hiking and playing tennis and various ball games. What was their political message? They could not proclaim it openly because as refugees they had to be careful, and because their opposition to the "imperialist war" (prior to June 1941) would not have been very popular among the refugees. After Russia was attacked they were all out in favor of the war effort, but so was everyone else. The whole affair of Communist penetration would never have become known but for the revelation many years later that the leaders of the circle, Fritzl Waller, Freddy Porges, and Werner Graetz, having served in the OSS and later joined the CIA, were stationed in Vienna and failed to return to the United States.

Among the young German refugees, political radicalization was equally modest and came a little later. It manifested itself in the establishment of the Ernie Pyle chapter of the American Veterans Committee in Washington Heights. This chapter was militantly leftist, according to a contemporary observer and was excluded for this reason by the national leadership of the American Veterans Committee. In truth, only a minority had belonged to this trend, but, as so often, it had been the most militant and vociferous caucus and also the best organized. Whatever political successes it had were short-lived.

Nor was Zionism very strong prior to 1946/47 when the struggle for Israel began in earnest. The great majority of the refugees had not been Zionists at home, and while on the whole sympathetic to the endeavor, if only because of the presence of many relations and friends in Palestine, they had no wish to emigrate there. It was only in 1948, when the survival of the Jewish community in Palestine hung in the balance, and perhaps even more so in the 1950s and 1960s, culminating in the war of 1967, that a truly emotional relationship and something akin to identification with Israel developed. The number of German Jewish refugees emigrating to Israel was still exceedingly small, and even the number of tourists was tiny. In the forties and fifties there was a Theodor Herzl Society, mainly among intellectuals, but it did not last long.

In the late 1930s and especially in the years after the war the great ideal was to become as quickly as possible a real American, a true patriot, even though the term was seldom used. Inasmuch as the German Jewish refugees had an ideology it was that of the Central Verein, the major German Jewish association, which back in Germany had long preached integration into German society. Once the object of assimilation had been Germany, now it was America and the American way of life.

The comments of Leo Lania, a left-wing writer, and, until recently, a committed antimilitarist, were symptomatic. He had been an officer in World War I and now he accompanied his nineteen-year-old son to the draft board in the East Seventies. He was deeply impressed by the seriousness and the dignity of the proceedings and he wrote that it was a moving experience to see how quickly and how radically these young Europeans had become Americanized, "not by adopting slang and outward trappings but becoming Americans in spirit and in soul." And a few months later he wrote he was proud that his young son writing from camp had given him a few lessons in democracy. Perhaps these youngest Americans, who had only come recently, who had known only hatred, civil war, class struggle and terror had a specific mission to fulfil, not just to defend their new homeland, not only to destroy Hitlerism, but also to liberate their old country from the shackles of prejudices rooted in a history of centuries: "I think they are ideally prepared to be mediators between America and Europe." This then was the spirit among the refugee community, and it was genuinely felt. Many young German Jewish refugees had volunteered for military service even before they received their draft notice, but virtually all were initially rejected as enemy aliens. A few did not easily accept this and went to Canada, serving in the Canadian army or air force. But eventually the erstwhile enemy aliens were drafted and soon they were found in most units of the U.S. armed forces. Unlike in Britain they were not confined to the Pioneer Corps in the early years and the question of naturalization was also solved, usually within a few months. They saw action in North Africa, Europe, and the Pacific, and for thousands of those who had originally come from Germany and Austria the war ended in the country of their origin, sometimes not far from the place of their birth. Their experience in the war years has been related elsewhere in our narrative.

The G.I. Bill of Rights

As they were demobilized these soldiers were eligible for the benefits of the G.I. Bill of Rights, originally called the Servicemen's Readjustment Act, passed by Congress in 1944, which has been rightly called one of the most enlightened pieces of legislation in American history and one that caused something close to a social revolution. No other country had such a far-reaching scheme to prepare the veterans for life in the postwar world. All those who had served a minimum of ninety days were entitled to one full year of training plus a period equal to his (or her) time in the service up to a maximum entitlement of forty-eight months.

The Veterans Administration paid tuition and other school costs as well as a monthly stipend of fifty dollars for bachelors, later increased to sixty-five dollars and subsequently again increased with the rise in the cost of living. American colleges and universities were not prepared to absorb such an enormous influx of students; many colleges had to double their prewar enrollment. They expanded rapidly, and many new junior colleges and community colleges came into being, as well as special training and year-round courses. The total cost of the program up to 1948 was more than $15 billion, a staggering sum, but one for which the booming American economy could provide, making it possible for millions to receive a higher education and skills that otherwise would have been beyond their reach. Among those entitled were tens of thousands of refugees who prior to the war had been eager to study but had not been able to do so. The new law truly changed their lives.

One story should stand for many. Harold H. Greene had arrived in the United States with his family in 1943, in the middle of the war, after an odyssey through Western Europe that included long periods of hiding in Belgium and France and ultimately crossing Spain and waiting in Lisbon for a ship. Soon after his arrival in America, he was drafted and sent with the army to Europe. When he was demobilized he had no education or craft except a little dabbling in jewelry, which he had learned from his father. But the G.I. Bill of Rights gave him his chance. He opted for law school in Washington, and eventually became chief judge of the Superior Court of the District of Columbia, and the author of many landmark decisions in the field of human rights. When he died in January 2000 he was perhaps best remembered for the decision to break up AT&T, America's telephone monopoly.

Dispersal and Americanization

The postwar studies under the G.I. Bill of Rights caused an unprecedented geographical dispersal of the refugee community and makes it difficult to trace their subsequent fate. Earlier on young refugees had been concentrated in certain quarters of certain cities, in certain clubs and communities and congregations. Now much of this disintegrated, as many moved away, first to study and later to follow their careers. They changed not only their addresses but also their names—if not their family names, at least their first names. Otto Salomon became Peter Hunter, Froehlich became Gay, Cohn had become Coser. Another reluctant descendant of the priestly order of the Cohanim, Manfred Georg Cohn, for many years editor of *Aufbau*, became first Manfred Georg and later Manfred George.

The issue of name change is a fascinating one and has not been sufficiently explored. Some changed their names when they joined the
army in England as in America because there was good reason to do
so. Others were unhappy with the ugly names with which they had
been saddled by malevolent German officials 150 years earlier when
German and Austrian Jews, like everyone else, had to assume family
names. But others wanted to distance themselves from their Jewish
and/or German origins; changing their names was an act of assimilation or mimicry such as had happened in many countries in recent
Jewish history, but seldom in such a concentrated way as in England
and America in the 1940s. Each case was no doubt different—some
changed their names after long reflection; others on the spur of the
moment because others were doing it; some wanted to change (or
hide) their identity; others, whose roots in the past had been shallow,
were simply seeking convenience.

True, the old clubs and landsmannschaften did not disappear overnight, and probably a majority of refugees still continued to live in
New York and vicinity. The *Aufbau* continued to appear even though
its circulation declined; in Washington Heights, Breuer's Orthodox
synagogue, Adat Yeshurun, continued to exist, and Ruth Westheimer,
the famed sexologist, became president of the local YMHA. There were
new cultural activities such as the Leo Baeck Institute with its library,
archives, and year book, perhaps an unprecedented achievement in
the history of emigrant communities anywhere in the world. In fact,
during the 1970s and thereafter, there was a renewed interest in the
German Jewish heritage, more books and articles were written on the
subject than ever before, more conferences convened, more people
went on pilgrimages to show their children and grandchildren the
places where they had been born.

In an essay written in the 1980s, a distinguished Harvard historian
specializing in British nineteenth-century history, the late John Clive,
in discussing Malthus and the neo-Gothic splendors of the St. Pancras
railway station in London, suddenly revealed that his original name
was neither John nor Clive, that he had been born of Jewish parents in
Berlin; and he disclosed what happened to them under Hitler. It is unlikely that most of Clive's readers had known these facts, and while
this particular context was not an obvious one in which to make such
a revelation, the author evidently felt an urge to do so. It is unlikely
that he would have done it twenty years earlier.

Onward and Upward

The integration of the refugees into American life, which had been slow before the war, proceeded by leaps and bounds during the years after World War II, so much so that large sections began to disappear from view, just as the much larger German communities in America had disappeared during World War I and the Italian during and after World War II. There was a difference inasmuch as many (by no means all) German Jewish refugees found their way into the American Jewish community. If in the 1950s ethnicity was not yet fashionable and the search for identity and roots did not figure prominently, this began to change in the 1970s and 1980s.

It is exceedingly difficult to trace, for instance, the fate of the young refugees who went into business in the 1940s, working their way up the ladder. It is somewhat easier to follow the career of smaller, more clearly defined, groups—those who chose a university career, for instance, or who went after the war into the foreign service of the United States. (The advent of the Internet eventually made such tracing a little easier.) As for those who had begun but not completed their studies in Germany, scientists were in far greater demand than their colleagues in the humanities or social sciences. While leading historians and philosophers were washing dishes in American restaurants, few scientists, even among the young, did so.

The Road to Academe

The career of Konrad Bloch can serve as an example. Born in Upper Silesia, he was twenty-one when Hitler came to power. He was enrolled at the Munich Institute of Technology studying chemical engineering, and got his Ph.D. at Columbia in 1938, having emigrated to the United States two years earlier. He got his first academic job as an assistant professor of biochemistry in Chicago after the war. Later he became a professor at Harvard, where he stayed until his retirement. He received the Nobel Prize in physiology and medicine in 1964 for his pioneering studies of cholesterol.

True, the major influx of scientists did not take place until 1938 and even after, but there had been far closer international contacts among scientists than in other academic fields. Owing to Rockefeller fellow-ships and other awards, many Americans had visited German centers of learning before 1933, and were familiar with both the research that went on and the young, up-and-coming colleagues conducting it. Of the young refugee scientists, a majority went first to Britain, having left Germany, and only subsequently found their way to America, and the same is true for their older colleagues. To give but one example: of the twenty-nine leading refugees specializing in nuclear physics, only seven had originally gone (or had been admitted) to the United States and fourteen to Britain. After the war, only five were left in Britain, whereas the number of those in the United States had risen to eigh-teen. The ratio in other scientific fields was similar. This could be ex-plained in part as the result of the crucial importance of research in nuclear physics (but not only in this field) for the American war effort. But the great upswing in scientific research in American universities had taken place even earlier, in the 1930s, and hence the greater will-ingness to employ refugee scientists.

More young Jewish scientists in Germany and Austria had opted for chemistry and biochemistry for the simple reason that chemistry traditionally opened the door to many careers outside academia, in which there were relatively fewer openings. In America however, the prospects for Jewish scientists to find jobs in chemistry were less bril-liant at the time and this, among other things, may have been the rea-son for a substantial influx at a later period into biochemistry (and the life sciences).

As for the youngest members of our generation, those who *began* their studies in the United States, the main hurdle was usually entrance to a leading university. Once they had accomplished this and shown promise, their further careers did not constitute particular problems (even though there was always competition) in view of the great im-portance put on science during the war and in the postwar world.

Many of those who chose a career in science reached the top of their professions. Some had graduated just before their emigration, as had the physiologist Sir Bernard Katz, a Nobel Prize winner in medicine or Salome Waelsch. Others are outside the purview of our story because, though born in Germany, they left at an early age (such as Arno Pen-zias, a Nobel Prize winner in physics, and Sir Walter Bodmer, the Ox-ford geneticist). But the number of high achievers among the young scientists of the generation in between was still very impressive. Some came from leading German Jewish families. The historians George and Werner Mosse were second cousins, but they were also related to Konrad Bloch (Nobel Prize winner in medicine, 1964) and Wolfgang Panofsky, founder and for many years director of the Stanford Linear Acceleration Center; they shared the same great-grandfather, Mosse, who had founded one of the biggest German media empires in the nineteenth century. Some of them had arrived in America early on, such as Wolfgang Panofsky, who had immigrated while still a young boy with his father the art historian in 1934. Others arrived late, such as Walter Kohn, another Nobel Prize winner (chemistry, 1998), who had escaped from Vienna shortly before the war and reached the United States via Britain and Canada. In the pictures of the ill-fated refugee ship *St. Louis*, which was sent back by the American authorities to Europe in 1939, appears the face of a sixteen-year-old boy from Fischhausen, a little village in East Prussia. His name was Arno Motulsky and he was among the lucky ones who made it to America on his second attempt in 1941, well after the outbreak of war in Europe. After studying medicine and genetics, he became a leading figure in his field.

The position of the young refugees who had opted for a career in the humanities and the social sciences was more difficult. A few examples should suffice. Reinhard Bendix, Lewis Coser, Albert Hirschman, Kurt Wolff, and Hans Steinitz had all been born between 1912 and 1915 in Germany, and none of them had a degree (Wolff and Hirschman subsequently acquired doctorates in Italy). All of them but Wolff had been active in left-wing student politics. Wolff, while studying sociology with Karl Mannheim, began his career as a novelist. Bendix had been loosely involved in a Marxist-Zionist group but while preserving some vague sympathies in later life, did not join them on their road to a kibbutz. Coser belonged in Paris to what he in later years defined as a Trotskyite sect and began to dissociate himself from orthodox Marxism only during the later years of the war. Their interest in things Jewish was limited.

The prewar career of Albert Hirschman was the most eventful of this group. Having studied at a French high school in Berlin and later at a French university, his knowledge of the language was excellent and he became an aide of Varian Fry, the American Scarlet Pimpernel in Marseilles, helping to smuggle to Spain refugees who were in particular danger of arrest during the German occupation. An economist, he was also the first to be accepted by a major American university, the University of California at Los Angeles (later he went to Yale) and had a distinguished career. It took Kurt Wolff, who, because of an unconventional approach, was never quite in the mainstream of American sociology, twenty years to get a job commensurate with his talents, at Brandeis, where Coser was also teaching. Thus, two of these five found work at a Jewish university. Steinitz did not choose an academic career in America but became an editor of *Aufbau*.

As for those who had not even begun to study in Germany or Austria, their initial obstacle race has been described earlier on, in many cases the turning point in their life came with the G.I. Bill of Rights. Some of them used their knowledge of German and specialized in German literature or history (Klaus Eppstein, Gerhard Weinberg, George Mosse, Fritz Stern, and others), but most of them did not. They went into so many fields that generalizations are virtually impossible. Many of them regarded themselves as non-Jewish Jews, since they were neither Zionists nor practiced their religion. In works of reference a fairly high percentage of academics stated that they did not belong to any religious community, and the percentage of "mixed marriages" was also high, higher perhaps than in other professions. However, it is also true that many of them, after two or three decades of work in other fields, became interested in the Holocaust or some other aspect of recent Jewish history. This was probably a reflection of the zeitgeist because it applied to other professions as well. It was certainly not a return to roots, which in most cases barely existed, but a reawakening of interest that had been suppressed before. Peter Gay wrote in a memoir that in his work he had deliberately refused to dwell on the mass murder of Europe's Jews, avoiding documentaries on the subject as well as museums and places like Auschwitz. ("We all have our defenses to help us to get through life, and these happen to be mine," he wrote.) Some colleagues took a similar position, some went so far as to shun all preoccupation with things Jewish, not just the Holocaust. A majority reacted in a different way.

At Home in America

After the end of the war, a substantial number of refugee politicians, writers, and journalists, as well as some others whose work was closely connected with the German language and German culture, returned to Central Europe. The number of academics who returned was considerably smaller; they belonged almost entirely to the older generation who had not been able in exile to work in their professions or who had received only temporary and unsatisfactory employment. They included, perhaps most prominently, the Frankfurt (critical) school, as well as some historians, philosophers, professors of law, and some educators, often half Jewish or converted with strong ties to Germany.

Others who were more or less established in the United States went regularly to teach or engage in research in Germany but retained both their domicile and their citizenship in the United States. A certain number who could afford it moved to Switzerland either as a base for their activities or as a place for retirement, émigré colonies came into being, for instance in Ascona and vicinity. Those who remained in America had not all been fully integrated and did not all feel wholly at home in the new country. But whatever their reservations about the American way of life, their reservations about life in Germany and Austria were even stronger. Even among the older generation, the number of those who, like Hannah Arendt and her husband, played with the idea at one stage or another of returning to Europe (not necessarily Germany) was considerably higher than the number of those who actually did.

What about the younger generation of refugees? There was a tremendous difference between even the youngest of the older refugees, say those born around 1910 and those ten years younger. The case of Friedrich Torberg, the great Austrian satirist, was quite typical. Torberg was something of a wunderkind, who at age twenty-two had written a great novel about a boy driven to suicide by pressures at school, and a few years later came out with one of the great novels in world literature on sports, *Die Mannschaft* (The Crew). He arrived in New York in October 1940 via France and Portugal; and later, asked by *Aufbau* about his first impression, he had written an essay entitled "I don't believe it." Yet only two months later, writing a friend from Hollywood where he was paid a little salary for doing nothing, he expressed deep unhappiness, even though he also said that he knew perfectly well that the alternative was a concentration camp. He also wrote a ballad on American life in the style of Hugo von Hofmannsthal about children who watched television and nothing else, about refrigerators, highways, frozen food, noise, and boring cities. Torberg felt out of place, and he also understood that while his life had been saved, he would never feel comfortable in this country.

The situation, mood, and attitude of those ten years younger were altogether different. They had not yet written bestsellers but received their higher education in the United States and in any case felt more at home in a country in which they had arrived while their hearts and minds were still open to new experiences. They had a good knowledge of spoken German but few of them had been deeply immersed in German culture. They had made their career outside Germany and were not well known in their native country, where it was most unlikely that they would be offered a major position.

They had no reason to feel particularly attracted by Germany, either for personal reasons or in view of the fate of Jews in Nazi-occupied Europe. Nor should it be forgotten that for years after the end of the war, large sections of Germany were in ruins and there was little to attract people living in the relative comfort of the United States. Hence it should not come as a surprise that of the young generation only a handful returned to Germany permanently. Those who did return went in the fifties and sixties rather than immediately after the end of the war.

There are no statistics as to the professions they chose, but there is the impression that the general picture was similar to that of American Jewry. Many went into commerce, banking, and commodity dealing, and some into manufacture, either inheriting a family business and enlarging it or founding a new company. They were prominent among art dealers and owners of galleries, traditionally a "Jewish" profession. There were few physicians in that generation because the study took too long and they could not afford it, but many of their children practiced medicine and the law.

Some young refugees went into government by way of the army and the military government in Europe. Henry Grunwald, former editor of *Time*, became ambassador to his native Austria, and Madeline Kunin to Switzerland, where she was born. Arthur Burns, a somewhat older economist, born in what was then Austrian Galicia, was made ambassador to Bonn, and Felix Rohatyn represented the United States in France. Ambassadors of Central European origin could be found in the Middle East (Arnold Newman) as well as Scandinavia (Strauss Hupe), not to mention the many who joined the foreign service as a career. Helmuth Sonnenfeld and Richard Schifter served on special assignments in the Department of State and the National Security Council. Michael Blumenthal served as Secretary of the Treasury during the Carter administration. The best-known and most influential diplomat was, of course, Henry Kissinger, who served both as Secretary of State and National Security Adviser in one of the most difficult periods of American postwar history. America had not been an easy country for the refugees of the 1930s to enter and to start a new life, but once they had been accepted, few doors remained closed to them.

WORLD REVOLUTION,
OR THE DREAM THAT FAILED

—◦◦◦—

The rise of the Nazis hastened the development of the political awareness of young Jews in Germany. In other times a boy or girl aged fifteen or sixteen would have hardly opted for one political party or another with great passion, or spent her time reading political literature, or devoted most of his time to political activities. But the persecution of the Jews changed all this: young people, like their elders, were looking for an explanation for the events that were threatening and uprooting them. Zionism provided one such explanation, Communism another.

There had been an inclination toward the left and in particular the extreme left among young Jews in Europe even before Hitler. The parties of the right, more often than not, were antisemitic, whereas the left promised not only liberty but also equality and even fraternity. While the older generation gravitated more toward social democracy, there was little in that party to attract young people. It lacked the dynamic character, the élan, the militancy that had always fascinated young people.

Nevertheless, young Jews in their great majority did not turn to the extreme left before 1933, partly, no doubt, because the Communist party did not particularly want them. It had been different in earlier days, when the party had been small and welcomed almost every supporter and when antisemitism had not been such a handicap in political activity. When a group of young Jews organized in the youth movement called Schwarzer Haufen decided to throw in their lot with the Communists in the late twenties, they were welcomed with open arms and some of them quickly rose to positions of responsibility. One became the deputy head of the clandestine apparatus of the Communist party in Germany, another the editor of a leading party newspaper, a third was made a leading figure in the Communist youth organization (KJV). But these converts to the cause of the Russian revolution belonged to a somewhat older generation; they were all born before World War I and their tragic fate does not concern us in the framework of the present study.

By 1932/33 when another, smaller group of members of the Jewish youth movement (the Freie Deutsch-Juedische Jugend) decided to opt for Communism, the political situation had changed. The Communist party had grown in strength and become more selective in admitting and promoting new members. They were interested, above all, in class-conscious young workers, but few Jews worked in factories at the time. At the same time, young Jewish intellectuals were more attracted by small independent groups such as the SAP (a left-wing party that had split away from the Social Democrats), the Trotskyites, the KPO (an opposition group that had been ousted from the Communist party), and the ISK, founded by philosopher Leonard Nelson. Neu Beginnen was another radical group established by former Communists and Social Democrats after 1933.

The Appeal of Communism

The pattern did not change after the Nazis came to power, for a variety of reasons. To be active in a party of the left after January 1933 was dangerous, for they were illegal, the security forces were quite effective, and those arrested faced concentration camp or years in prison. Those arrested in 1933/34 and the years after included a substantial number of young Jews and this acted as a deterrent. More important yet, as the Jewish community was driven into a ghetto, the possibility of being politically active became more and more limited. An anti-Nazi German worker could conduct propaganda at his place of work, whereas a young Jew had no such contacts. And if he did meet Germans he would be suspect as a Jew; antisemitism, in one form or another, had affected wide sections of German society. From a Communist point of view Jewish militants who wanted to be active in the underground constituted a double security risk and were usually kept at arm's length.

In the 1920s and early 1930s the attraction of the Communist party and the Soviet Union was considerably greater for idealistic young people than in later years. The Stalin cult was as yet in its beginning, the Moscow show trials had not yet gotten underway, and the forced labor camps were few and far between. At the same time, the Communists seemed to be the most active opponents of the growing Nazi movement. Even so, the number of those former members of the Jewish youth movements who set out on the long road toward Communism was not great, perhaps two to three hundred, and not all of them reached their promised land. Some soon opted out of politics, others, critical of the Communist party line, joined dissident groups of the left, while others turned against Communism altogether.

Of those who had become members of the party or the Communist youth organization only the leading cadres received instruction (and help) as far as their escape from Germany was concerned. The party could not act as a travel agency and the rank and file were left to their own devices and were dispersed all over the globe. A few case studies will bear out our contention. Karl Kormes was eighteen in 1933. He came from a poor family of Polish origin living in Berlin and was training as a locksmith. Originally a member of a Zionist group he joined the Communist youth after reaching the conclusion that the presence of Palestinian Arabs made it impossible for Jews to settle in Palestine without causing a national conflict. Arrested in 1933, he was sentenced to eighteen months on a charge of high treason and deported to Poland after his release. He volunteered for the Spanish Civil War, and was captured by a unit of the Franco army. He was released to Gibraltar in 1943, made his way to North Africa, and worked as a civilian translator for the British and American forces. His subsequent fate, after his return to East Germany, was typical: all those who had spent the war years outside the Soviet Union automatically became suspect in Stalin's last years, and someone like Kormes who had actually been employed during the war by the Allies was doubly suspect.

Helmut Eschwege, born in Hanover in 1913, had also been politically active in 1933. He had to leave Germany rather quickly and by way of Denmark and Estonia reached Palestine in 1937. He joined a kibbutz but was thrown out because of membership in the local Communist party, which was at that time not just anti-Zionist but opposed the very idea of Jewish existence in Palestine. He too, made his way to

East Germany after the war by way of Prague and his unhappy fate will preoccupy us further on.

But Jews Not Wanted

Fritz Teppich, born in 1917, like Kormes had belonged to a Zionist group but subsequently joined the Communists and went to France where he worked as an apprentice cook (he belonged to the Kempinski family of hotel and restaurant fame). He fought in the Spanish Civil War and after the defeat of the Republicans escaped to France, where he was interned. Eventually he went to Portugal, where he spent the last war years before returning to Berlin. His autobiography describes the difficulties facing a young Communist who had not totally abdicated his critical faculties. Even though he had strong doubts about the Moscow trials and the friendship treaty with Nazi Germany, he could not say so openly for fear that he would lose the only support he had, that of the underground Communist party.

Erna Nelki grew up in Neukoelln, a working-class suburb of Berlin. Aged nineteen when Hitler came to power, she had attended the Karl Marx School in Berlin and initially belonged to the Communist party. She realized early on that a Jew could no longer be politically active in Nazi Germany and emigrated to Britain. There she resumed her political activity among the "homeless left," the ILP (Independent Labor Party). Initially she and her husband had wanted to return to Germany after the war, but the two of them had become more and more integrated into British life and more and more conscious of the disaster that had befallen the Jews. Hence their decision to stay in Britain after the war, which was shared by many former militants of the left.

So much then about some of the young soldiers of revolution. The decision whether to return to Germany after the war was highly personal, and depended on the extent to which the individual had grown roots in exile and become integrated. Eric Hobsbawm was the lucky holder of a British passport even though he had grown up in Vienna and Berlin. A Marxist since his school days he took to English political and academic life like a fish to water, even though he found it a little provincial and boring after the cultural excitement of Berlin. He pursued an academic career as a social historian and steadily rose in the hierarchy of the Communist party of Great Britain, being a member of the Central Committee for many years. He played at the same time the roles of insider and outsider; critical of Stalinism, he still stuck to the party through thick and thin. For someone like him the question of returning to Germany never arose. Nor does Wolfgang Ehrlich seem to have been tempted to move from Israel back to Germany. He had studied philosophy at a German university prior to 1933, joined the Palestinian Communist party, and rose to be a member of its politburo. The only intellectual in this body, he seems not to have felt at home culturally in Palestine/Israel. Perhaps the party opposed his return to East Germany. Whatever the reason, he stayed in Israel.

Stefan Heym would probably have remained in the United States where he had already made a name for himself as a writer but for an unfortunate and largely accidental complication. His political awakening began during his last year at school in Germany; he had published a poem in a local newspaper that became something of a scandal. As a result he was expelled from school and blacklisted by the Nazis. Hence the sensible decision to escape to Prague almost immediately after January 30, 1933. Eventually he found his way to America, joined the United States army, published two war novels, which were well received, and married an American. He was very active on behalf of the Communists, though it's not clear whether he ever formally joined the party. He decided to move to Europe rather than be called to give evidence to the House Un-American Activities Committee. Whether he was in any real danger is doubtful, but his decision is understandable in the hysteria (on both sides) of those years. He wanted to go to East Berlin, but he had waited too long with this decision, for in the heyday of the cold war the East Berlin rulers were in no hurry to admit yet another suspect Jewish emigrant from the West. As a result he had to cool his heels for many months in France, Switzerland, and Prague before being admitted. He faithfully followed the party line for a number of years but later on emerged as a literary dissident who went as far as he could with his criticism of the party line without endangering his existence and safety in the GDR.

The Spanish Civil War, which broke out in 1936, was the great challenge for the left in the 1930s; according to one of its chroniclers, some five hundred German-speaking young Jews volunteered to serve in the

International Brigade and other Republican units. If correct, this is an astonishingly high figure considering that few of them could possibly have had any military training. Some names of the war victims are remembered: Hermann Feld, former member of a Zionist youth movement, served in the Republican air force, was shot down and killed in 1937; Walter Katz fell at the front fighting. Kurt Goldstein, a native of Dortmund, had belonged to the nonpolitical Kameraden in Germany, survived the war in Spain, escaped to France, was interned like so many others in Gurs and later on in Drancy and Auschwitz, but lived to tell the story. He had another political career first in West Germany as a party secretary, later in East Germany working for the GDR broadcasting service, and was also involved in the special office in charge of financial transactions with West Germany. He had every reason to be grateful to the party, which had helped him to survive Auschwitz through its internal network in the camp. Like many old Communists he had some doubts about the policies of the Communist party even before the downfall of the GDR. But he still wrote in a memoir in the late eighties that in his youth he had decided to join the social democratic (rather than the Communist) youth organization because of the "anti-Sovietism and anti-Communism prevailing in my milieu." Another soldier in the International Brigade was Arthur London, who rose to prominence after the war. Born in 1914 in the German-speaking part of Czechoslovakia, he played a role of some notoriety in postwar Czechoslovakia. He was among those accused in the Slansky trial but was not sentenced to death and in his second French exile wrote a novel entitled *L'Aveu* about his life and the background to the trial, which was widely read and made into a film.

There were also young German Jews who were killed at the time not by Nazis and Fascists but by their comrades from the left. Kurt Landau and Erwin Wolf were members of the inner circle of the Trotskyites and they were among those "liquidated" by the Stalinists, for whom they were the worst and most dangerous enemies. Gerta Taro was a twenty-six-year-old photographer and a member of the SAP. She went to Spain to fight with her camera; her pictures were featured in many newspapers all over the world. In 1937 she was killed in circumstances that have remained mysterious to this day. Willy Brandt, who belonged to the same party and visited Spain at the time, suspected that she was shot by the Communists rather than by of Franco's soldiers.

These then, in briefest outline, were the fates of some of the young Communists of the 1930s. There had been burning idealism among them, a readiness to fight and to sacrifice. There were authentic heroes among them such as Rudi Arndt, a Communist youth leader who, after his arrest, continued to help others, younger and less experienced than himself, and paid for it with his life. But precisely because there had been such fervent, even fanatical belief, despair was bound to be all the greater as their cause failed and as many of them became victims of the god in which they had once believed.

Young Refugees in the Soviet Union

What of those who went to the Soviet Union? The Soviet Union was generally unwilling to absorb "racial refugees," except for a few young specialists, scientists or engineers, who went there in 1933/34. But most of them returned at the end of the Five Year Plan or were caught in the maelstrom of the purges. The other exception was a group of some sixty Jewish physicians from Nazi Germany who were admitted with their families. Some of them survived the war and the postwar purges, others fared less well. Lastly there was a group of more than a hundred children of socialist families (Schutzbund) in Vienna who were admitted after the suppression of the socialist revolt in 1933. Virtually all other refugees from Germany and Austria who found temporary shelter in the Soviet Union, perhaps five to six thousand or slightly more, were political emigrants, members of the Communist party of Germany and Austria and their families. Those of interest to us in the present context are the young who, almost without exception, arrived in the Soviet Union with their families; no one under eighteen was admitted unaccompanied but for the Vienna Schutzbund children already mentioned.

Once the purges and trials began in 1936, the fate of the refugees was far from enviable. It has been said that Stalin killed more Communists than Hitler, and as far as the leadership of the party is concerned this is certainly true. A large percentage was arrested, perhaps 70 percent of the total German and Austrian party membership, but the others too became suspect in a general climate of xenophobia. As a Moscow newspaper wrote in 1937 it had to be assumed that every Japanese or German citizen residing outside his homeland was active (that is to say spying) on behalf of his country.

Some refugee Communists (between eight hundred and one thousand among them Jews) were deported to Nazi Germany, others came under pressure to leave the country, and yet others were asked to accept Soviet citizenship and membership in the Communist party of the Soviet Union, which was not however a guarantee of exemption from arrest and execution. The frightening atmosphere in Moscow in those days, the nightly arrests and the great fear, have frequently been related, and need not be invoked again.

To what extent was the younger generation affected? Initially, hardly at all. Young people had always been treated well in the Soviet Union, all doors were open to them, at least in theory, as the builders of a new world, the defenders of justice and freedom. The years 1934 and 1935 bore out Stalin's announcement that life had become better in the Soviet Union. The young people from Germany shared the general enthusiasm, appreciated being permitted to participate in the great work of socialist construction, and celebrated with the rest of the Soviet people the industrial achievements of the 1930s, such as Valeri Chkalov flying over the North Pole. They sang the song about no other country in the world where people were breathing as freely as in the Soviet Union. The orchestra of the Karl Liebknecht school with its flutes and drums was marching through the streets of Moscow to the applause of the Moscovites.

The School of Our Dreams

The Karl Liebknecht school (Shkola Nashikh Mechtei—the school of our dreams, as it came to be called) was founded in Moscow in 1924 for the children of political refugees from Germany, but the sons and daughters of some Soviet citizens, such as David Bergelson, the noted Yiddish poet, also went there. Among those attending were the sons of daughters of leading Communists such as Peter Florin (later the head of the East German delegation to the United Nations), Marianne Weinert, daughter of the famous revolutionary song writer, Jan Vogeler, Gregor Kurella, Max Maddalena, and Werner Eberlein. During the early years the school followed the experimental fashions of Soviet education. History as a discipline was abolished, there were no tests or marks, and, in theory at least, the children were running the school according to the framework of shock brigades, a technique popular at the time in Soviet industry and agriculture. In 1935 the pendulum swung and these innovations were denounced as Trotskyite in inspiration. The school came under attack for allegedly catering to petty bourgeois elements alien to the working class. Eventually, in 1938, the conclusion was reached that the existence of "national schools" was contrary to the party line; the school was closed and the children were transferred to Russian schools.

The Liebknecht school was at the height of its fame in 1934/35 when 750 pupils attended it. It was headed by Helmuth Schinkel, a gifted educator. The next year, the first arrests took place, of four teachers, and forty pupils, and many more parents. Eventually some twenty-five teachers were to disappear, most of them forever. The new head of the school was a lady of Hungarian origin who was so afraid of losing her party book that she sewed a pocket to the inside of her dress, creating a considerable bulge much to the amusement of the children.

And yet, most of the pupils enjoyed the school greatly and later remembered those years as perhaps the most enjoyable experience of their lives. There was so much to do—skating in Gorky Park and other frozen sites in winter, amateur theatricals, camps and excursions in summer, political expeditions to the Mennonite settlements in the northern Caucasus to persuade them not to accept financial help and food deliveries from abroad. There were war games against the background of the Spanish Civil War, and the pupils joined paramilitary organizations such as the Voroshilov snipers and the Ossoviachim, the organization preparing young people for defense against chemical and biological warfare.

This was the time of great friendships and first love which has been described in the memoirs of Wolfgang Leonhard and the book devoted by Markus Wolf to the memory of his brother Konrad, who became a noted movie director in East Germany. It was remembered also in several memoirs published during the glasnost period written by former pupils who had survived the camps and exile in places far from Moscow. The children were happy in the middle of a world of fear and danger; "We did not know what it meant to be alone," one of them later wrote. Their parents might have disappeared, but they still found support and uplift in their comradeship. They felt they were serving a great cause, fighting fascism, oppression and exploitation. True, there were a few critical spirits, but according to some reports, one of the closet dissidents later became a Soviet army general.

For the children of parents who had been arrested, such as Wolf-gang Leonhard, space was found in a special home where the Austrian children were kept (and received infinitely better treatment than in the orphanages of the secret police for the children of the "enemies of the people"). The summer camps in the Crimea continued for the luckier ones, and, as Leonhard reports, he was accepted in 1939 as a member of the Komsomol, the Communist youth organization. Even one year earlier, with his mother arrested and in a camp, this would have been unthinkable.

Children of refugees outside Moscow attended local schools, and for those a little older there were various institutions of higher learn-ing, some sponsored by the Communist International, others provid-ing military training and courses in sabotage. There were the univer-sities and language institutes for translators. Leonhard, too, was permitted to study in 1940 in an institute which was part of Moscow University. For the sons and daughters of the supreme leadership, jobs were found in the party apparatus and the media, even though the number of such jobs decreased as various organs were closed down in the late thirties (including the daily *Deutsche Zentral Zei-tung*, the monthly literary periodical *Das Wort*, and most of the clubs and theaters for German workers). In fact, there was a trend to scale down refugee activities, and Wilhelm Pieck, the leader of the German party, is said to have played at one stage with the idea of reducing the number of refugees by two-thirds. Those further down in the party hierarchy were trained as skilled workers or engineers and employed in factories.

Purges and Persecution

At the height of the purges a significant part of the younger refugees were arrested and deported, and some were executed or perished in the Gulag. Exempt were the very young, those under seventeen, and many more males than females were affected by the purges following the general pattern in the Soviet Union.

The families of the German and Austrian supreme leadership were seldom affected unless their loyalty to the party and Stalin was dubi-ous. There were exceptions (Remmele, Eberlein, Heinz Neumann), but these had deviated in the past or were not on good terms with the present leadership of Pieck and Ulbricht. The middle echelons of the party workers were severely hit and so were those further down. There was no rhyme or reason as to who was arrested and who was not, the security organs were given a plan to fulfill, a certain number of people were to be arrested in a certain region, and from this stage on it was more or less a matter of accident at whose door the NKVD (the secret police) emissaries would knock in the early hours of the morning. Demoralizing in particular was the widespread, almost universal incidence of informing on friends and comrades. This was based on the mistaken belief that people could save their own skin if they collaborated with the security organs and informed on their close friends. Since the security organs were purged themselves more than once, informing provided no insurance whatsoever.

The accusations against young people were to some extent different from those brought against older Communists. For it made no sense to charge a young person who had not been outside the Soviet Union since childhood with being a Japanese or French secret agent. Instead quite a few were accused of having belonged to the Hitler Youth in the Soviet Union. Such charges were of course totally false, and made no political sense after the friendship treaty with Nazi Germany in 1939, but the security organs were free to press charges however absurd and the attempts by the accused to prove their innocence were both pathetic and ineffective.

The idea of charging a group of young people in the Soviet Union with belonging to the Hitler Youth first occurred to the local security organs in Leningrad in 1930/31, but those arrested got relatively light sentences and most were released from the camps even before the great purges began. A far more ambitious enterprise was the case of the Hitler Jugend of January–March 1938. The commissar for internal affairs had given instructions to the organs to find and arrest a group of young people who had allegedly established a local branch of the Hitler Youth, praised Hitler in their meetings, and prepared various sabotage actions including an attempt to assassinate the French ambassador in Moscow. About seventy of them aged between seventeen and the late twenties were arrested. Some had been in the Karl Liebknecht school, others worked in various Moscow factories (such as the car plant or the ball bearing factory), or studied at universities. Some of the seventy arrested were employed in the Club of Foreign Workers or the theater group Kolonne Links. Among them were the children of

several well-known Communists like Max Maddalena or fellow travelers (both sons of Max Seydewitz, a former Social Democrat and later a
leader in East Germany). Many of them had come as children to the
Soviet Union, and many had accepted Soviet citizenship in 1936.

Among those who had escaped to the Soviet Union there were
members of the German Jewish youth movement who in the course of
political radicalization had joined the German Communist youth organization individually or in groups (Schwarzer Haufen, originally a
component of the nonpolitical Kameraden). Ironically, the Soviet
Union's reluctance to accept even Communists as refugees saved many
a life, for the majority of those who went to Moscow after 1933 perished
in the Stalinist purges, as did Leo Roth and Sammy Giesel, to name
but two. A few survived after many years in forced labor camps and
after the war returned to East Germany (Nathan Steinberger, Rubin
Rosenfeld). A few continued to believe to the very end that their own
fate and that of their murdered comrades had been an unfortunate accident and, in the final analysis, probably Hitler's, rather than Stalin's
fault. Others, like Steinberger, had learned their lesson, wholly or in
part, and refused to keep silent after their return from Russia, as the
party demanded from them, about their own fate and that of the cause
in which they had once so fervently believed.

These young Communists reacted like their elders: They thought at
first that there had been a horrible mistake or that enemies of the party
had caused a provocation as the result of which they had been wrong-
fully arrested; if only Stalin and the other leading comrades knew the
truth . . . Hence the millions of letters sent to Stalin at the time requesting that he take a personal interest. But as the months passed, as
the accusations became more and more grotesque, as the beatings and
tortures became more severe, such illusions became more and more
tenuous. Gustav Sobotka, son of a Communist leader, wrote after
twenty-six months in prison that he had lost all hope that his torment
would end and that the truth would be established. Only his faith in
the party had not been undermined, but if this faith too were taken
from him, it would be worse than any verdict and would lead to his
mental and physical collapse. Copies of many such letters were found
years later; their effect had been nil. Helmut Domerius was a close
friend of the son of Wilhelm Pieck, the leader of the German Communists, who decided for once to intervene with the Soviet authorities,
but without any success.

Of the seventy arrested in connection with the Hitler Youth affair, forty were executed, some immediately, others in 1938/39. Six were released, twenty received sentences of between five and ten years. Two were handed over to the Gestapo under the friendship pact of August 1939; Sobotka, whom we mentioned earlier, died in prison. In the days of de-Stalinization in the 1950s the case of the Hitler Youth was rein-vestigated, the accusations were proved baseless, and the survivors were released from prison and camps in 1954/55. Some remained in the Soviet Union, others went to East Germany. Some proudly declared at the time of their release that despite all the tribulations their faith in Communism had never been shaken, others (writing decades later) admitted that they had lost their faith.

However, the Hitler Youth affair was just one case among many. There are no precise figures regarding those who suffered "repression" to use the official term of the de-Stalinization era. Up to April 1938 about 840 German Communists had been arrested, about 70 percent of the KPD membership, but these figures did not include the Austrian Communists, or the many German Communists who had in the mean-time become members of the Communist party of the Soviet Union.

How did the fortunate react who had been bypassed by the Stalinist terror? Doubts must have occurred to them—everyone had close friends who were persecuted though they were not enemies of the So-viet Union. But they persuaded themselves that these were the excep-tions, that the party was always right, that Stalin knew more than they did, and that whatever mistakes and even crimes had been committed, this did not make it any less urgent to fight for the cause of Commu-nism and especially against Hitler and the Nazis.

Joining the Red Army

When war broke out, those who had come to the Soviet Union when they were quite young and who spoke Russian with hardly an accent were accepted as volunteers to the Soviet army, and quite a few of them became officers. Konrad Wolf ended the war as a decorated first lieutenant, as did Moritz Mebel, who had come to Moscow at age ten with his parents in 1933 and attended the Liebknecht school. He said in an interview fifty years later that he had known about the trials but repressed unpleasant news. When Stalin died in 1953 he had wept, he

said, but added that his wife had hated Stalin. In retrospect he regarded
the crimes that had been committed in the thirties not as Communist
crimes but crimes against Communism. But this was a little too facile,
for the crimes had been committed after all by the then Communist
leadership. Mebel studied medicine (urology) in Moscow after the war,
returned to East Germany in the late fifties, became a central figure in
the health service, and late in the day (in 1986) a member of the central committee. The brothers Markus and Konrad Wolf reacted in a
similar way and so probably did most others; they must have known
the truth all along, but believed that despite all the deviations and
grievous mistakes, everything would turn out right in the end. With
the German invasion of the Soviet Union in June 1941, most young
Germans, like their elders, were deported to the eastern regions of the
Soviet Union, to Chistopol and the Kama district, to Tomsk and Central Asia. It did not matter in the least whether they had meanwhile
become members of the Komsomol or the Russian Communist party.
Some were permitted to return to Moscow in 1942/43, many had to stay
behind in very poor conditions, often starving, in the eastern regions
until the end of the war.

Of the young, relatively few were taken by the army, though there
was a growing demand for translators on every level. Some were
drafted into the labor army to do hard manual labor in coal mines
and other such places. Some of the young people who had been in disfavor for one reason or another were now recalled for military and
political training and new assignments during the war and postwar
period. Some were trained as parachutists to infiltrate Germany, a
project that ended in disaster. Only one out of seventy parachutists
dispatched to Germany was not caught more or less immediately by
the Gestapo; the one who got away was a Polish-speaking worker
from Upper Silesia who arrived only toward the end of the war, hid
among fellow Poles, and abstained from any political and military activity. Of the parachutists who survived in Nazi camps, ten were sent
to Soviet labor camps after the war, like most others who had been
German prisoners of war. A few had been sent during the war to fight
with Soviet partisan units and there the chances of survival were
greater.

The training center of the Communist International was reactivated
in the neighborhood of Ufa; there were seven young Germans in the
first course and twenty-nine in the second. Among them were the sons

and daughters of well-known Communist families (Dahlem, Florin, Weinert) who had known each other from the days of the Karl Lieb-knecht school or other common activities in the prewar years. However, upon entering the Ufa school, each was given a new identity and name; they had to pretend they did not know each other and were for-bidden to refer to their earlier life. Jan Vogeler (the son of the painter Heinrich Vogeler who disappeared in the purges) became "Danilov," and Stefan Doernberg was called "Adler." After graduation most of them were sent to conduct propaganda work in Moscow or in prisoner-of-war camps or at the front, and after the war they were among the first to return to Berlin to help to build a new Germany.

The Return to East Germany

Even before Germany had capitulated, three groups of German Com-munists left for Germany, one for Saxony, another for Pomerania, and the third and most important one under the leadership of Walter Ul-bricht for Berlin. Altogether 83 German refugees arrived back in East Germany in 1945, 197 the year after, and 207 in 1947. These are very small figures considering that there had been thousands of refugees in the Soviet Union and only another 150 were to follow in the years up to 1954. Many had perished in the purges; their exact number will never be known.

But many of those who had survived were not wanted in East Ger-many by the Ulbricht leadership, which insisted that only those needed for party work should be given permission to leave the Soviet Union. Excluded were those, the majority, who for one reason or an-other had been arrested even if they had been fully rehabilitated. There were about thirty exceptions, among them individuals with good connections, such as the brothers Seydewitz, whose father had been made prime minister of Saxony under the new Communist re-gime, or Susanne Leonhard, the mother of Wolfgang who had been a member of the Ulbricht group in Berlin. The new Communist estab-lishment argued, no doubt, that those who had experienced Soviet prisons and camps for any length of time could not be trusted to forget or suppress their experiences, and were potential defectors.

This fear was not entirely groundless as the case of Susanne Leon-hard showed. After her return she promptly wrote a book about what had happened to her during the purges (*Gestohlenes Leben*, 1956). Furthermore, Ulbricht and his comrades must have felt uncomfortable in the presence of the victims, for in many cases these arrests had been the result of informers from among the Communist party establishment. At the very least the leaders had done little or nothing to help get them out of prison, even though they knew full well that they were innocent. On the other hand, the Soviet Communists, in particular the Central Committee and the organs of state security, had also no interest in permitting former inmates of Soviet prisons and camps to emigrate. Soviet spokesmen had argued all along, in particular after the Kravchenko trial in Paris in 1946, that there was no Gulag, that these were malevolent inventions by professional anti-Soviet inciters. Seen from their point of view, the release of dozens, perhaps hundreds, of survivors of these camps was asking for trouble, even though those permitted to leave the Soviet Union had to sign a solemn declaration that they would never reveal their experiences. Once these people were out of the hands of the Soviet organs, no one could guarantee that they would remain silent. Like Ulbricht, the Soviet leadership was willing to release only those who were truly needed for specific assignments in East Germany.

Of the Austrian children who had been taken to the Soviet Union in 1934, many had been arrested and some were executed. Other survived in camps in Central Asia and the Far East. But those who were still alive in 1945 found it easier to return to Austria, since they had to overcome only the one hurdle of Soviet party bureaucracy, rather than two, as did the German refugees. In March 1953, the month Stalin died, the East German embassy in Moscow was informed by its bosses in Berlin that all political refugees had by then returned to East Germany and that the issue therefore no longer existed. But requests and applications continued to be received by the East German leadership in Berlin, submitted in part by members of split families, and the KGB in Moscow also received more and more requests. In the thaw after Stalin's death, there was a growing willingness in Moscow to let people go, and East German policy also became somewhat more liberal. Altogether some three hundred refugees were repatriated between Stalin's death and the year 1956. The East Berlin leadership hoped, that with this the return would finally end. But it was a vain hope, for in the years that followed another three hundred former refugees arrived from the Soviet Union.

This was connected with the process of de-Stalinization in Moscow after Khruschev's speech in 1956 but also with the agreement between Konrad Adenauer, the West German chancellor, and the Soviet authorities in April 1956, according to which Germans on Soviet territory who wanted to be repatriated were to be permitted to do so. While this covered above all prisoners of war, others could also apply to the (West) German embassy in Moscow. This compelled the East Germans, however reluctantly, to liberalize their policy. All in all, while it had been exceedingly difficult for anyone but a leading Communist to enter the Soviet Union in the 1930s, it proved for many even more difficult to leave it.

Building a New Germany

How did the young refugees fare who returned to East Germany after 1945?

As in other Communist regimes lip service was paid to the crucial importance of young people, but in fact, Ulbricht and his colleagues (like Stalin, Khrushchev, and Brezhnev) believed in the wisdom of age rather than the impetuosity of youth. Pieck and Ulbricht remained in office to a ripe old age and their politburo consisted of old, trusted Communists. Young people were promoted, but not to the very top positions.

Markus Wolf, head of East German foreign espionage, was one of the few exceptions, but even he never became the head of state security. His superiors were Zaisser, Wollweber, and eventually Erich Mielke, who served as head of the Stasi well into his eighties. His brother Konrad, the former Red Army officer, received many honors, including the presidency of the Academy of Arts, but the political key positions in the cultural field were given to men like Johannes R. Becher and Alfred Kurella, who belonged to the old guard. Peter Florin became deputy foreign minister but never attained the top position.

By the time the erstwhile young refugees from Moscow were in their fifties and sixties and, as far as their age was concerned, qualified for the top positions, a new generation of native German Communists had grown up and thus the graduates of the Karl Liebknecht school never got their chance. Perhaps they were lucky not to have to bear responsibility for an experiment that failed.

But by no means all the young enthusiasts of the Karl Liebknecht school were given important political assignments after the war, or indeed aspired to have such assignments. It all depended on whether they had been trained in one of the party schools during their years in the Soviet Union, whether they had personally been known to the leadership of the party. While it did not matter as far as their careers were concerned whether their parents had been arrested, most of those who themselves had been in prison or a camp were disbarred even if they had been rehabilitated later on.

What was the balance sheet drawn by this generation after the GDR had ceased to exist? Those who had been professional ideologists, teachers of Marxism-Leninism, or leading party historians such as Stefan Doernberg (another product of the Karl Liebknecht school), found it virtually impossible to admit that they might have been mistaken. Few would argue that the system had been altogether without fault. Even stalwart Communists would admit that it had been wrong to argue that the party was always right, and that the leadership, to put it cautiously, had not been outstanding. But many would still claim that the basic ideas underlying the GDR system had been right, and that the ideals for which they had fought had not been disproved even though capitalism had outproduced the Communist system. They also thought that these ideas and the fight for them would not vanish from the world, in other words; that at some future date socialism (as envisaged in East Germany) would get a second chance.

At a conference in the 1950s I met an Austrian-Polish-Jewish scientist who, as a young man, had been arrested in the Soviet purges and was handed over to the Gestapo in 1939. When I asked him whether the Communist idea had been good and only the execution defective, Alexander Weissberg Cybulski said without a moment's hesitation that while the Communist practice had been atrocious, the basic idea underlying it had not been sound either. This point of view was not shared, however, by most of the young refugees who spent the thirties and forties in the Soviet Union. Their belief in the cause they had faithfully served all their lives was shaken only by the events of the 1980s that brought about the final downfall of the Communist regime.

A few young Communists from among the refugees returned to Germany and Austria after the war from Palestine (more of Austrian than of German origin) as well as a few from Latin America, but hardly any from the United States. Their subsequent careers will preoccupy us later on. But two organized groups of Communist repatriates, from Britain and from Shanghai, are of special interest.

Free German Youth in Britain

Communists had founded German refugee youth organizations in Paris (1934) and Prague (1936), which were sponsored by the party but outwardly appeared as nonpartisan, "antifascist" groups. They never amounted to very much despite the considerable effort invested, largely no doubt because the number of young refugees in France and Czechoslovakia was small and most of them were in transit. The number of those stranded in Britain, partly as the result of the children transports, was considerably larger, about twenty-five thousand under age twenty-five. Among them the Free German Youth (FDJ) was founded in June 1939. Its members established communal homes, and went on excursions and camps in the neighborhood of London (there were only a few branches outside London). Not long after the outbreak of the war, all refugees had to appear in front of tribunals and many were subsequently interned in camps on the Isle of Man; thousands were shipped to camps in Canada and Australia. Thus the activities of the FDJ were interrupted early in its history, but this was a blessing in disguise.

It saved them from confronting an unpleasant political situation, namely having to explain the Nazi-Soviet pact in terms of antifascist ideology. On the other hand, many young people underwent political training in the internment camps. There were only a few Communists in these camps, but they stuck together, followed the party line, and were better at indoctrinating young people than liberals and democrats.

As they were released from internment in 1941, and as many of those shipped to Canada and Australia returned, the FDJ resumed its activities on a much larger scale. Most of them worked in war industries but in the evening the communal homes provided both a home and much entertainment. "One never felt lonely," one of them said in later years. They were reading and debating, staging amateur theatrical performances, singing and dreaming about life in postwar Germany. Friendships developed, and quite a few of them later married people they had first met in their home in Belsize Park. Psychologically, such togetherness was important for uprooted young people, inasmuch as it provided stability. Some joined the army, a few were parachuted in U.S. uniforms over Germany during the last days of the war. As so often happened, these amateurish exploits ended in disaster—Werner Fischer, for instance, was caught and shot by a Soviet patrol despite his fervent declarations that he was a Communist.

The great majority of the members of the FDJ were Jewish, but the Communist organizers of the FDJ did not recommend that they join the youth organization of the Communist party of Great Britain, partly because of "class reasons"—young people of mainly bourgeois origin were not particularly wanted in the British party—but also because the Communist leaders of the FDJ "always observing the rules of conspiracy" (according to Horst Brie) rightly assumed that the ideological discipline imposed by the party would antagonize young people not accustomed to it.

The FDJ cooperated on occasion with other youth organizations, even some Zionist ones, collecting money for the Soviet war effort, demonstrating for a second front, and other good causes. A few did join the Communist party, but the majority did not. They had been given a Marxist schooling, but life in Britain had a corrosive ideological influence: they came to respect British democratic institutions and the tradition of free speech, and many came to regard Britain as their new home. Thus, at the end of the war, only about a third of them returned to Germany (and not all of them to East Germany), another third stayed on in Britain, and the rest joined their families in the United States and elsewhere. There were some minor tragedies, as the girlfriends of some militants refused to return to Germany, and as the feeling of duty and party discipline got the better of friendship and love.

Those who returned to East Germany were at first warmly welcomed. Horst Brie was told that "we are glad about everyone who comes back, we badly lack trustworthy cadres." He was sent to Schwerin, a provincial center, to head the local Communist youth association, which also happened to be called Free German Youth (FDJ). Horst Brasch, another leader of the London group, was also dispatched to be active among young Germans. Others became journalists or were in demand in various ministries as English translators.

All went well for a few years, but as the cold war became more intense the "West Emigranten" almost without exception became suspect and were demoted. Unlike older leading Communists who had spent the war years in Mexico, Switzerland, and other such places, they were not arrested, but merely given less important assignments. Horst Brie, for instance, was sent to a machine tractor station somewhere in the country. Karl Kormes, who after his flight from Spain had worked for a short time for OSS, the American intelligence service in North Africa, was exiled to a factory producing tires and soon after thrown out of the party altogether. Alice Zadek was dismissed from her post in the ministry of foreign trade, her husband Gerhard was sacked from his newspaper. They were also told that they had to move out of Berlin. However, by and large these young Jewish refugees who had returned from the West were not treated worse than the non-Jews, many of whom had been in senior positions and were given lengthy prison sentences or in some cases driven to suicide. According to party instructions at the time, never published, every Communist who had returned from exile in the West was a potential imperialist agent.

Most of them were rehabilitated within two or three years. Brie was eventually appointed East German ambassador to North Korea, Japan, and Greece, one of his sons became in the nineties the chief ideologist of the PDS, the successor of the East German Communist party, advocating a sharply anti-Stalinist line. Horst Brasch was made deputy minister of culture in the 1980s but lost his job when his son Thomas, a poet and dissenter, was arrested and subsequently opted for life in West Germany. Another member of the FDJ (Ursula Herzberg) became translator at the World Peace Council, another became head of Radio Berlin International, and a third, representative of East German media in Bonn.

Franz Loeser was lucky inasmuch as he had arrived in East Germany after the campaign against the "cosmopolitans" was already over. He had come to England as a boy from Breslau just before the war, enlisted in the army, and joined the Royal Army Medical Corps serving in North Africa. He then decided to study philosophy at the University of Minnesota, but the MacCarthy years were not a good time in the United States for writing an uncritical dissertation on Marxism-Leninism. So he went back to England, but the British Communist party did not want to have him either because he was not a citizen and there was also a slight suspicion of his being a CIA agent. Following the intervention of the secretary general of the British party, Loeser was permitted to settle in East Germany and there, initially at least, everything went well. His dissertation about subjectivism in the ethical concepts of Bertrand Russell was approved and eventually he became a professor of historical materialism. He was even delegated to represent his country at the World Peace Council, but took his mission a little too seriously and gained the reputation of being a bourgeois pacifist, rejecting nuclear weapons not only in the imperialist West but all over the globe. There were also some philosophical deviations, and in the end Loeser had difficulty placing his publications and was no longer permitted to attend international philosophical congresses. In 1983 he went to the West, not to return while the East German regime was in power. He was still in many ways a Communist at heart, but he could no longer identify with the society that had been built under Ulbricht and Honecker.

Jewish Communists in East Germany: The Second Generation

After they had overcome the shocks of the 1950s, the former FDJ militants felt reasonably happy in East Germany. They did not, of course, agree with everything that went on, but their criticism of government policies was voiced only in a small circle of like-minded friends. They were convinced that the system they had helped to build was infinitely better than the West German and that it was eventually likely to prevail in most other countries. They were politically and psychologically unprepared for the shock that came with the breakdown of the system in 1989 and the reunification of Germany. But even if most of them did not have much contact with the rest of the population and its mood, they should have been prepared for the ferment because there were danger signs in their own families. Their own children, those born in England or soon after their return to East Germany, were dissenters in their great majority, despite (or because of) the relentless indoctrination they had been given in school and in the party youth organization. They supported Wolf Biermann and other rebellious young artists and intellectuals, they associated with the Russian dissenters, they were severely critical of their own parents (What kind of socialism have you helped build? Why don't you admit that there is a great and growing discrepancy between the official doctrine and the realities in the GDR? Why have you been hiding your Jewish origin?). Perhaps they thought that this was no more than the usual storm and stress of a younger, utopian, and romantic generation, and that in due time their offspring would accept reality and make the compromises their parents had made—would conform to the party line. If these were their assumptions, they could not have been more mistaken.

There was a basic difference between the members of the FDJ who returned to East Germany after World War II and the 295 Shanghailanders (as they called themselves) who arrived in August 1947 at the Goerlitz railway station in Berlin by way of Naples. While the young Communists could have stayed on in Britain, the refugees from Shanghai were under immediate pressure to leave and they had few options. True, those who had organized the transport talked about collaborating in the reconstruction of the Russian zone in Germany, of participating in the democratization and socialization of Germany. But in fact the transport consisted mainly of middle-aged and elderly people who wanted to return to a country whose language they spoke and where they could spend the rest of their days in peace, if not necessarily in comfort. There had been 695 refugee passengers on "Marine Lynx," the ship that had taken them to Naples. But less than half continued to Berlin. Of those who reached the German capital not all chose to settle in the Russian sector. We shall deal elsewhere with the fate of the other Jewish refugees in Shanghai; there had been a small Communist (antifascist) circle among them, but the number of those who chose to emigrate after the war to the United States and other countries was considerably larger.

Among the leading spirits of the Shanghai Communists were Genia and Guenter Nobel. She hailed from a Russian Jewish family that had settled in Berlin in the twenties, he was the son of a rabbi. They met as students at Berlin University and joined the Communist party. Arrested by the Gestapo in 1936 they were released a few weeks before the outbreak of the war on condition of leaving the country immediately. They went to Shanghai, where Genia worked for TASS, the Soviet news agency, and Guenter was active establishing a Communist cell among the refugees. After their return, Genia worked for the Communist party newspaper *Neues Deutschland*, whereas Guenter found work in the party apparatus in West Berlin. Like most other West Emigranten, he lost his job in 1952 (even though Shanghai could hardly have been regarded a Western city) but was eventually rehabilitated and found work in the state planning commission, and in the East German diplomatic service, and even became a member of the editorial committee of *Einheit*, the theoretical organ of the party.

As Guenter Nobel later wrote, the decision to return to Germany had not been easy; they knew that not only the country had been destroyed but that many of their friends were no longer alive, and that everything would depend on whether they found people they knew and on whom they could rely. Guenter Nobel found such a person in Bruno Baum, whom he had known in the German prison in the thirties.

Most returning Shanghailanders were not, however, militant members of the Communist party, and they chose careers in nonpolitical fields, such as trade and administration. Some subsequently joined the party, others did not, and quite a few later settled in West Germany. These refugees from Shanghai stuck together for decades after their return, feeling that their common experience during the war had somehow marked them. But as a group their impact on developments in East Germany was minimal, certainly smaller than that of the repatriates of the FDJ from Britain.

Lastly we ought to mention a group of young Communists and fellow travelers that returned from Palestine to East Germany after the war. In October 1946, a list of forty-eight people was sent from Tel Aviv to the East German party leadership requesting entrance permits. They had a number of hurdles to overcome. First the Israeli party had to give its blessing, which in some cases it did reluctantly. (Guenter Stillmann, for instance, who was among the forty-eight, had been organizational secretary of the party in Tel Aviv, and the Palestinian party did not want to lose him. He later worked as a journalist in East Berlin.) Nor was the East Berlin leadership too enthusiastic, though it must have felt a certain obligation to its old comrades. Lastly, the occupying power, namely the Russians, had to be consulted; they were even less eager to have more West Emigranten (refugees to the West) in their occupation zone. Only a famous writer like Arnold Zweig belonging to the older generation could proceed directly to East Berlin, the others had to cool their heels in places like Czechoslovakia for as much as a year or even more. But this did not dampen their desire to return to their native country, and eventually most of them made it.

Looking Back with Sorrow

Several of the refugees who had returned to East Berlin tried to summarize their experiences in books, articles, and interviews after the fall of the GDR, when free speech again became possible. Most were of two minds with regard to the overall balance. Ursula Herzberg wrote that if she had known how the experiment would end, she would hardly have returned to Germany. But she still thought that trying to build socialism in East Germany was an "objective necessity," and that the four decades were not entirely in vain. Schalscha and Eberhard Zamory, two former members of the FDJ, did not look back in anger despite the dogmatism with which they had been indoctrinated (the deification of the working class, the belief that the party was always right), the balance of the war years had been positive overall. Though Zamory had left the Communist party in 1968 following the invasion of Czechoslovakia, he had remained "antifascist" at heart.

Often the charges against the refugees who had spent the war years in the West had been quite preposterous. Hans Jacobus had gone to England with the children's transport. A few years after his return to East Germany, he was arrested, not just for political deviations but because of allegedly having raped a colleague and also for criminal activities abroad. He had been a journalist before his arrest but was sent to work in a factory after his release from prison. And yet, even those victimized by the party had an infinite ability to find, in retrospect, mitigating circumstances for the measures taken by the authorities. Writing in 1993 Jacobus said that he felt the old fear (of neo-Nazism) in Eastern Germany but remained a critic of capitalism and had grave reservations with regard to the reunification of Germany. Horst Brie, who had belonged to the East German nomenklatura, would go no further than saying that the gap between vision and reality had become ever wider in the GDR, whereas the Zadeks complained that de-Stalinization in the GDR had been quite imperfect and that they had mistakenly assumed that antisemitism and racialism had been uprooted in the country. But "the idea to leave the DDR never occurred to us. We had known the bourgeois capitalist order in the past, and to live under such conditions was not an acceptable alternative for us."

Sadder were the conclusions of Helmut Eschwege, who had returned from Palestine in 1946. He was a good Communist, but after having declared in a census that his nationality was Jewish rather than German, he was expelled from the party as a nationalist deviationist, and not even permitted to attend the funeral of his mother abroad. He was employed in a lowly position in some archives and not permitted to publish the books he had written because they dealt with the role of Jews in antifascist resistance. He led a marginal existence: whenever East Germany was eager to improve relations with America and Israel, small concessions were made to him, such as a trip abroad or the publication of an article or book, but on the whole the title of his autobiography published in the nineties reflects his deep disappointment—*Fremd unter meinesgleichen* (A stranger among my own people). His daughter (Sonja Schmidt) became actively involved in Jewish affairs, quite independently of the views of her father, and applied for release from Communist party membership in 1982 when this involved the loss of her job. But she wrote of the GDR after it had ceased to exist that not everything had been bad, and "that we had more time for each other." Her children, however, showed little interest in Jewish affairs.

Even more negative was the conclusion drawn by Salomea Genin, born in Berlin in 1932, who grew up in Australia. She became a member of the Australian Communist youth organization, but her fondest dream was to move to the GDR, which she did in 1963. She worked as a translator for Radio Berlin International, became a citizen of the GDR and a member of the SED (the Communist party). She concluded, "I tried to become a German Communist, I became a mother and experienced daily life. After twenty years of attempts to work politically I realized that I lived in a banal police state which in many respects was worse than the capitalism I had given up."

Ingeborg Rapoport reached diametrically opposed conclusions. Born in 1912 in Hamburg she had trained as a pediatrician and married a Viennese biochemist in the United States. They were asked to appear as witnesses before the Unamerican Activities Committee, but the party advised them not to get arrested but to escape to a socialist country. They had a certain weakness for Israel, but felt that it would have been unethical for them as non-Zionists to live there, nor did they want their children to grow up as "nationalist Jews." And so they went first to Austria and later to East Germany, their application to settle in the Soviet Union having been turned down. They became members of the party and were given interesting jobs. Ingeborg Rapoport believes that the GDR did not collapse because it was an immoral state, and that it was a calumny to compare the Stasi with the Gestapo. True, she thought that the party had too much interfered, there had been no inner party democracy, but she still regarded the workers' rebellion of June 1953 as wrong, and she continued to be very angry about all the traitors and those spreading slander who had appeared after the fall of the GDR. She attributed crucial importance to personality and leadership, and believed Pieck, Ulbricht, and Honecker had all been deficient in one respect or another, and things might have turned out better "if we only had had leaders like Castro or Ho Chi Minh."

Eva Brueck, aged twenty-two at the time, had returned to Berlin by bike from Oxford in 1949 full of illusions. More than four decades later she wrote with bitterness how she and her friends had continued in the 1950s to find an explanation for everything that was wrong even though they had been humiliated and discriminated against as "Western agents" and "cosmopolitans." And yet, having had so much to criticize in later years in East Germany, was there not a need to continue fighting after reunification against the dictatorship of money, against a society in which only those with the stronger elbows would prosper?

The last word should perhaps go to a person of the left who did not return to Germany, Erna Nelki, whom we have mentioned earlier. She writes that "the idealism of our youth has been gravely disappointed. The socialism which we dreamed about in those days, the dictatorship of the proletariat which should have been a temporary phenomenon to be replaced by socialism, how can we still hope for it?"

Reading the life stories of people such as Genin and Rapoport, it is difficult to accept that they lived and were writing about the same country, walked the same streets, belonged to the same party. How to explain these widely divergent opinions? It goes without saying that the fall of the GDR was a shock for every party member. True, much depended how well they had felt in that society, whether they had satisfactory work, whether they belonged to the privileged class; much depended on personal factors such as the willingness to toe the party line, whether their critical faculties were under- or overdeveloped. Older people usually found it more difficult to engage in radical self-examination and self-criticism than younger people, for so much of their life had been spent in a society that in the end had failed, for whatever reasons.

In the final analysis these questions, why one person totally negated the GDR experience and regarded it as an unmitigated disaster, while another would defend it to the very end, is unanswerable, just as there is no explanation for why one person opted for the left, another for the right, and a third had no interest whatsoever in politics. In any case, these questions lead us well beyond the subject of our investigation, which is the specific fate of a generation of refugees. But though the question might be unanswerable, the issues continued to bother even in their old age those who had gone to East Germany full of enthusiasm to help build a new society after 1945. Had they chosen, after all, the right side, but the attempt had failed merely owing to unhappy and unforeseen accidents. Or was the disaster bound to happen for deeper, systemic reasons?

BRITAIN

Forever Refugees?

—◦◦◦—

Very few young people from Germany and Austria found asylum in Britain prior to 1938, far fewer than in France, Holland, or Belgium. The doors were almost hermetically sealed, except to people in transit, to factory owners with enough capital to establish industries that would employ British citizens, and also to a few scientists (but not physicians) of world renown. Since Nobel Prize winners or wealthy industrialists could not be found among teenagers, those who did reach the British shores were usually children of well-to-do families abroad who attended British schools and universities.

The reasons for this restrictive policy are well known and need not be reiterated in detail. These were above all, of course, the consequences of the world economic crisis with its millions of unemployed, but also the general conviction that Britain was a densely populated country, not suitable for immigration, as well as a mixture of xenophobia and social antisemitism. The attitude of the major commonwealth countries was, if possible, even more restrictive (even though Canada and Australia were hardly densely populated countries) and it was perhaps worst in the United States.

A change took place in British immigration policy only after the Anschluss (of Austria) in 1938 and in particular after the Czech crisis and Kristallnacht. There were a variety of reasons: the number of Jews who had to leave Nazi-occupied Europe suddenly multiplied; having effectively closed the gates of Palestine after 1936 and having tried (together with the United States) to stop Jewish immigration even to Shanghai, virtually the only remaining escape route, the British government found itself compelled to liberalize somewhat its policy vis-à-vis the refugees. As a result some sixty to eighty thousand refugees from Germany, Austria, Czechoslovakia, and a few from Poland entered Britain during the last twelve months before the outbreak of the war. Most were Jewish, many were young people arriving alone. Having turned down the proposal of the small Jewish community in Palestine to absorb all remaining Jewish children in Germany, Britain was now willing to accept ten thousand unaccompanied children, the so-called Kindertransports. This was hailed as an act of unprecedented generosity, and, measured by the humanitarian standards of other countries among rulers and ruled alike prevailing at the time, it was indeed such an act. To give but one example, the United States at the time refused to admit a much smaller number of refugee children. At the same time, British regulations were loosened with regard to certain other categories such as domestic servants (and butlers) as well as agricultural laborers, if employers made a specific application for a prospective employee.

And so the refugees began to arrive, committees were formed to receive them, and arrangements were made to find shelter and work (or education) for them. By and large the ignorance about the refugees and why they should be in such a hurry to leave their native country was immense. Lord Weidenfeld reports that he was asked in high society whether his family was socializing with the Goerings, and there are many reports from schoolboys as well as from soldiers according to which it was quite hopeless to try to explain to their mates why they should be with them rather than fighting with the Germans.

Naftali Wertheim, then a pupil at Parmiters Secondary School in Bethnal Green, London, tells the story of Mr. Dudlyke, his Welsh geography master, who hated all things German. Having committed some misdemeanor, Wertheim was ordered to "Come out here you Prussian swine," ignoring the fact that Wertheim was a South German rather than a Prussian. "I received six stripes of the cane, three of the best on each palm, and was sent back to my desk with the admonition: 'You think this is Nazi Germany, with a lot of Jerries doing what they bloody well like. Well, let me tell you this is a democracy and you do as you're bloody well told.'"

Nor was the urgency of the situation fully understood among all British Jews, including highly placed people. Dr. Josef Hertz, the then chief rabbi, complained that the children arriving with the transports were not always given kosher food and worse yet, the Sabbath was desecrated, because some of the transports left Berlin and Vienna on a Sabbath. Since it is unlikely that the rabbi had never heard of *pikuah nefesh* (the religious commandment which says that saving human lives was a duty overriding all others), it must be taken that he thought that the transports were not a matter of great urgency. Herz also published a letter which was handed to every arriving child wishing him happiness and telling him be at his best behavior, to show his gratitude, and not crowd together and talk noisily in public places.

When Lords Bearsted and Rothschild, leaders of Anglo Jewry, cabled Lewis Strauss of the American JDC (Joint Distribution Committee) with a request for American financial help to cope with the needs of the refugees, Strauss prevaricated as long as he could, thinking of all kinds of unlikely reasons why American Jews should not contribute, including the argument that such help could be of indirect help to the cause of Zionism, which they detested. In the end Strauss offered a fifty-thousand-pound contribution and the same amount again as a loan, a risible sum considering the magnitude of the emergency. During World War II, Lewis Strauss, who never heard a shot fired in anger, was appointed a rear admiral, and he ended his political career as the chairman of the Atomic Energy Committee.

Kindertransport

The transports were put together in record time. Sometimes the trains departed with only twenty-four hours notice, an astonishing logistical achievement considering that none of the organizers had any previous experience and that children and young people from dozens of smaller towns were also included in the scheme. The trains left Vienna, Prague, and Berlin (usually the Anhalter Bahnhof) and by way of Hoek van Holland (less frequently via Hamburg) reached Liverpool Street station in London.

The departure was painful. Parents took leave from their young children, who, in most cases, had never been out of their homes for more than a day. In many instances it was leave-taking forever. The youngest among them, with their dolls and toys in their hands, probably did not understand what was happening. The older boys and girls, aged fifteen and sixteen, may have regarded it as a great adventure—soon they would be reunited with their families and in the meantime they would enjoy unprecedented freedom. But those in between suffered most from the separation, and when in the subsequent weeks and months the full implications dawned on them, homesickness became worse. Mention should be made, at least in passing, of the brave young men and women, the German Jewish youth leaders, who accompanied these transports during the months and weeks prior to the war, who could have stayed abroad but went back to do their duty. A few of them survived, such as Norbert Wollheim at Auschwitz, and Kurt Reilinger underground in France and later in Buchenwald.

If departure had been sad, arrival was often chaotic. An organization had been established in Britain to find foster homes for the children. But not all of these arrangements worked out and for many, particularly for the older children, other provisions had to be made, concentrating them in temporary shelters, frequently holiday camps such as Dovercourt Bay. Particularly helpful in the process of refugee absorption were some of the nonconformist churches such as the Quakers, the Christadelphians, and the Plymouth Brethren. The assistance by the Church of England and the Catholic Church was more modest and mostly confined to Jews who had been converted.

Nor was the readiness of the Jewish community always admirable. Some members of the Jewish aristocracy, including Viscount Samuel, the former leader of the Liberal party, were extremely active, and among the Jewish working class there were splendid manifestations of solidarity and a willingness to share even in conditions of poverty. But the Jewish middle class was as yet small and its tradition of helping coreligionists in need was not yet well developed. In 1999, sixty years after the event, when the arrival of the Kindertransports was commemorated, a great many criticized the failure of Anglo Jewry to help.

Marion Harston, born in Tilsit, arrived in London at age thirteen. She went to a wealthy Jewish family in Wandsworth in south London but felt treated like Cinderella. After a little while her foster parents got rid of her altogether. A great many families had refused to accept refugee children in the first place. Socially and culturally Anglo Jewry, always excepting a tiny stratum on top, was a generation or two behind German Jewry at the time. It was quite poor and a higher education was as yet the exception. This caused difficulties with regard to the absorption of young refugees of middle-class background.

What were the first (and second) impressions of the young arrivals? They differed enormously. The very young very often adjusted quickly to their new surroundings, their recollections of home dimmed, and their foster parents became their beloved real parents. When their biological parents turned up (which happened occasionally after a year or more) they were strangers talking a funny language or at least with a strange accent. One of the youngsters wrote that the people of Selkirk in Scotland showered him with kindness. R. Brunnell related that her foster parents treated her like their own child. Steffi Schwarz found love and kindness, the simplicity of a good family relationship. England left on Jehudit (Judith) Segal an indelible, beneficial mark: "I liked English people and adjusted to English mentality easily."

One of these young refugees of 1938/39 wrote many years later that another reason for her unworried mood was

> our love and admiration for England, a refreshing spirit that is hard to
> describe reigned in England. The atmosphere was wonderfully different
> from what we had experienced before that, our admiration was bound
> less. The whole life style opened up entirely new vistas for us. The quiet
> courtesy, the freedom to express any opinion, the sincerity and honesty
> of the people, the ability to live undisturbed in whatever eccentric man
> ner one preferred. We, as many others, became Anglophiles.

Between these fortunate youngsters and their foster parents and their families lifelong ties of affection and love were forged and they stayed in touch even if they lived continents apart. But many children were not as lucky as Bea, who was met at the railway station by the sponsor's daughter and was driven in a limousine to a manor in Kent. She was greeted with a formal kiss by her sponsor. The billiard room had been converted into a suite of rooms for Bea. She was conducted there by the chambermaid who addressed her as "Miss." "For a girl from a middle-class Jewish Austrian home, this was heady stuff," she said in an interview. The less fortunate were walked to a slum in East London or some miserable provincial backwater and had to put in a few hours of work before being given their first meal.

Culture Shock in England

For many, the first meeting with England, apart from the trauma of separation and homesickness, was a culture shock. They had been accustomed at home to some elementary comforts that were not yet

known in middle-class (let alone working-class) Britain, such as central heating. Nor were indoor toilets frequently found in working-
class quarters. Furthermore, the winter of 1938/39 was the severest
in years. They had no suitable clothing and it seemed to rain almost
without interruption; long periods of sunshine were almost unknown. They found the food virtually inedible (except Cadbury
chocolate, which they preferred to the German brands). But what
passed for bread at the time in Britain tasted horrible and they
thought Marmite and macaroni sandwiches unfit for consumption
even by animals.

But it was not just the fact that they were hungry and cold much of
the time. They did not like the bullying in the schools, and the educational ideal of becoming nice English boys and girls did not appeal to
them. Many complained about exploitation and a few about sexual
harrassment and, more frequently, about beating, but these malcon-
tents were dismissed as troublemakers. Bertha Leverton relates that
up to the age of twenty-one she had to hand over to her foster parents
her whole pay packet even though they received a (small) sum for her
upkeep. Another witness reported that at school she and the other refugee children were treated as outcasts, that the headmistress was mentally unbalanced, wanted to convert all Jews, and made church attendance compulsory.

Susan Graham remembers that she went to a small boarding school
that consisted of fourteen children and an equal number of dogs, the
latter receiving preferential treatment. It was her impression that the
five elderly spinster sisters running the school positively disliked children. Lilian Furst reports from Manchester that the local Jews resented the secular culture of the Jewish children from Central Europe,
and the fact that because of their educational background they were
more readily accepted into good schools and by middle-class English
neighbors, whereas they, Jews from Eastern Europe, faced a hard economic struggle. Even years later the German Jewish refugees felt like
"foreigners with British passports."

Those attending school often reported social ostracism irrespective
of whether they attended a working-class or private school. Sylvia
Rodgers (who later became the wife of a Labour cabinet minister) felt
distinctly unhappy at Henrietta Barnett School in northwest London:
The Jewish girls were standoffish and entirely ignored her. They never
addressed her or expressed curiosity about her. She was not invited for

a walk, a game, a party, let alone for a visit to their homes. These were the daughters of Jewish middle-class families from Golders Green, who might have been apprehensive that their tenuous acceptance in Britain was endangered by refugees speaking broken English. Charles Hannan (born Karl Hartland) was lucky inasmuch as he progressed from an approved school (for young delinquents) to a minor public school (Elmfield), where eventually he became a prefect. But there was antisemitism and he found it prudent to hide the fact that he was a Jew and subsequently invented for himself a different "legend" altogether.

More often than not refugee schoolchildren made a deliberate effort never to speak German except on occasion to their parents. Judith Kerr, the daughter of Alfred Kerr, one of Weimar Germany's leading literary critics, was such a case, and her brother (who later became a judge) was even more determined in this respect. Some members of this generation who became famous in later years suppressed the place of their birth in works of reference, such as *Who's Who;* they had been educated at good schools and at Oxford, but (as Isaiah Berlin once noted) had apparently never been born.

The Kerr children had the good fortune to grow up in a family, but those who came alone and were adopted were more likely to face emotional problems. Many of them had been accustomed to warmth and caring in family life and they were saddened by the coldness often prevailing in the attitude of their foster parents toward them—but also toward each other. True, as the children grew up, as they began their working life or joined the army, these became less vital issues, but they had been important in their formative years.

A former pupil at Stoatley Rough School, at Haslemere, Surrey, related the story of a classmate named Hans who, at age eleven, realized that he would never become "English" at a school of refugee children and persuaded his guardian to transfer him to an English school. The writer notes that "nothing would have made me give up voluntarily the warmth, the feeling of comfort and home, that Stoatley Rough meant to us." He kept a lifelong accent when speaking English but he had a home at a crucial time in his development and, looking back, he wrote: "I think I got the better end of the bargain." There can be no doubt that a price had to be paid for suppressing one's identity and roots, German and Jewish. Sometimes the roots had been shallow and were easy to ignore, but at other times the psychological consequences of denying one's origins were lasting. These young people of no known background became, as it were, young Englishmen and women on the basis of false pretences.

It would be unfair to blame all the psychological difficulties on the foster parents and the teachers. It should always be remembered that without the change in attitude of the British government, many of the thousands would not have survived. Whatever the torments of British food, weather, and family relations, they can hardly be compared to Auschwitz. Nor should it be overlooked that many of the refugee children were bound to be difficult. They were not necessarily spoiled but they had grown up in very different surroundings and found the transition painful. In contrast to the older generation (which often faced even more difficult problems), they did not even understand why they should be transplanted to a foreign country. Why not return to Daddy and Mummy and the comforts of home from which they had been rudely extricated?

It cannot have been easy for foster parents to deal with children deeply afflicted with homesickness, weeping in bed for hours every evening. The emotional ties with home were deeper than many had thought even among young children. Judith Segal, whom we have mentioned and who said that she easily adjusted to English ways, also relates that she developed a secret ritual, of pretending to go for a walk in the streets of Vienna, where she used to go shopping with her mother, committing the names of shops and street names firmly to memory: "I rehearsed silently Viennese songs and operas I had learned at school and was afraid that one day I would no longer be able to visualize the small details." Young Helmuth Stern, a violinist in his Charbin, Manchurian, exile, reports engaging in similar fantasies about walking in Berlin streets when returning on foot at night from a concert. Some children thought of their gardens and pet animals, others about walking in forests or along a river.

The educated Jewish middle class in Germany had not been particularly interested in Britain, let alone in America; they admired France and went to Italy and Switzerland for their holidays. English was never the first foreign language taught, and in many parts of Germany it was not taught at all at the time. Hence the small number of young (and older) refugees who had a working knowledge of English when they arrived. But by and large they were better educated and had wider cultural interests than their British contemporaries, they were reading more books and had a deeper interest in music and the arts.

Perhaps that difference stemmed from the fact that even the best British schools emphasized the development of character and leadership more than intellectual qualities. The refugees were also, quite often, more deeply motivated to learn.

Refugee Children, Problem Children?

Whatever the reasons, the fact that the refugee children excelled in many fields did not pass unnoticed, and since teachers and headmasters were, on the whole, a fair lot, their achievements were rewarded. There were more than a few cases in which the young refugees after a year or two walked away with awards and prizes, including those for English. Peter Frankel, who emigrated from Breslau to Bulawayo, Rhodesia, relates that his headmaster made him sit for the Sir Alfred Beyth fellowship, Beyth having been a German Jew who became one of the South African goldmine magnates. In the very last moment before the exams it appeared that Frankel had to be disqualified for some technicality. The headmaster did not reveal this to the boy, but made him compete anyway, and when Frankel came out on top, the headmaster fought like a lion for his best pupil to get a state fellowship.

In Britain this was not so easy because the authorities had decided that refugee children should be given, like English children, free education only up to the age of fourteen, at which age they should go out and work in the factories or some other such place; girls should learn shorthand and typing so that they could be secretaries if they did not want to be waitresses or shopgirls. They were discouraged from even thinking about a career in the liberal professions, except perhaps in cases of exceptional brilliance. When a refugee boy told a social worker he intended to be a doctor, she said that she could not put this down since he was a refugee. Of the seven Nobel Prize winners who were to emerge from this age group, two came from among those who had escaped to Britain, but both had already graduated (just) from continental universities when they arrived.

The foster parents of the young refugees were on the whole unwilling and unable to pay for higher education; universities, after all, were not free in those days, and why should they provide for their adopted children something they could not give their own? But a lady named Greta Burkill in Cambridge kept a watchful eye on the academically gifted among the Kindertransport graduates, and she did a great deal to get loans and scholarships from a variety of institutions. And so it came to pass that some of them not only became professors in due time (albeit often outside England), but one even rose to be vice chancellor of a university.

What became of the roughly ten thousand who had come with the Kindertransport? Those who wanted to become naturalized after the war could do so without great difficulty unless they had been in collision with the law, even if the issue at stake was only a metro ticket that had not been paid for. Nevertheless, only about half stayed in Britain, the others emigrated to the United States, Israel (about one thousand), and other countries. There was a fair amount of intermarriage with the English; some of these marriages lasted, others did not. The choice of profession was largely accidental and varied widely. The boy who had been showered with kindness in Selkirk was later in charge of a herd of six thousand (Canadian) reindeer in the Arctic Circle. Gerd Ledermann of Berlin served in the Israeli army, ran a health ranch in Mexico, walked through the Gobi Desert, ran Buddhist meditation courses in Australia, and now lives near Katmandu, Nepal, in a twelve-by-twelve-foot mud and rock house. Most of the others opted for more humdrum careers as teachers, businessmen, engineers, and housewives.

Where Do We Belong?

To what extent do those who remained in Britain regard themselves as British? On a superficial level they integrated well, were successful in their professional lives, married, and brought up children. But few believe that they have been truly integrated in British society even if they have a rich social life or are active in politics. They say that they do not truly feel at home in Britain but they feel even less at home elsewhere. As one of them put it, after much travel and reflection he concluded that the British are one of the nicest and most decent people on earth, but that one will forever remain an alien for them unless one was born among them.

The question of identity will preoccupy us again. Why should it be so crucial for so many people? Obviously, it corresponds with a deep urge to belong. For people who have this longing it was a tragedy that they came to Britain before the multicultural age had dawned in Britain as well as other countries, before the arrival of millions from overseas with cultures, religions, and traditions far more remote from the British than those of the German Jews. The postwar immigrants made little effort to conform but, on the contrary, did everything to maintain their cultural legacy, and consequently faced no identity crisis.

The issue of homelessness was seldom as acutely felt as among refugees from Germany who went to Britain, where complaints (or the sad resignation) that "I am nowhere really at home" or that "my identity is really that of a refugee" were particularly frequent. Such problems would hardly be of paramount importance for a Zionist or a religious Jew, nor for those who went to traditional countries of immigration such as the United States, Canada, or Australia. But Britain at the time was not such a country and its society was relatively homogenous. The young refugees had not yet been deeply imbued by the cultural values of their community at home. They loved the German (and Austrian) landscape and their mother tongue, but they had no particular reason to love those who had expelled them so cruelly. They were impressionable and their critical faculties were not as yet very developed. Most of them very much wanted to be British, or at least like the British. They were not fully aware of the negative aspects of life in Britain, but quite simply wanted not to stand out as (bloody) foreigners, once they had overcome their initial culture shock. Britain in the 1930s was living through the Indian summer of its imperial history, when it had been the center of the universe. It was still supremely confident that the British way of life was the best in the world and that, as an earlier generation had put it somewhat crudely, one Englishman was as good as six foreigners. World War II was Britain's finest hour, so it is no wonder that the young refugees were deeply impressed and wanted to be like the British, to whom, all other things apart, they owed their very survival.

But the Britain they had admired and wanted to be part of came to an end after 1945. Its political and economic standing declined; its demographic composition changed. British society itself went through a crisis of identity. For those who felt deprived because of feeling that they had no real home, that after all these years they still could not always make out what the greengrocer was telling them, that despite elocution lessons they stuck out as aliens, it seemed a great misfortune that they had arrived twenty or thirty years too early.

It is one of the ironies of history that the Germans, who could not live with a few hundreds of thousands of Jews, a people who wanted nothing more fervently than to be like them, had to confront a few decades later millions of Muslims and other foreigners who had not the slightest intention of assimilating. In a similar way Britain, which had found it so difficult to absorb some tens of thousands of admirers from continental Europe, had to live soon after with millions of immigrants from overseas, of whom a variety of race relations acts made it a crime to utter a critical remark. A few hundred Jewish physicians from Germany and Austria, however proficient in their profession, were virtually barred from practicing in 1930s Britain. Fifty years later almost half of the medical students and most of the nurses training in some British universities and hospitals were of African and Asian origin.

The refugees who attended British universities in the late thirties were few, and were usually children of well-to-do families. The number of universities was small at the time and the number of students limited. As noted earlier, the Anglo Jewish community was poor in its majority and with the exception of some students of law and medicine, there were far fewer bent on an academic career than in continental Europe. Virtually all of the Nobel Prize winners living in Britain during World War II were of foreign origin, and the same is true of the Nobel Prize winners of the next generation, from Hans Krebs to Boris Chain, from Max Perutz to Aaron Klug.

The picture was not very different as far as membership (or corresponding membership) in the Royal Society was concerned. It was equally true for most of the leading lights in the humanities, from Sir Isaiah Berlin to Sir Ernst Gombrich, from Nicholas Pevsner to the historian Sir Lewis Namier (even though he never got the Oxford professorship to which he aspired). The genius of Anglo Jewry was more in business than in academia. It is difficult to generalize about the fate of academic refugees: some, like the sociologist Karl Mannheim and the philosopher Ludwig Wittgenstein, who arrived in Britain relatively early, received appointments commensurate with their talents, but Norbert Elias never got a tenured job at all and Sir Karl Popper had to spend years in New Zealand before he received a call back to London. Merit seems to have counted more in the sciences than the humanities, perhaps because of the outbreak of war and the new priorities.

When George Mosse went to Cambridge to study history in 1938 he did not find much encouragement: George Macaulay Trevelyan, one of the leading historians at this time, told him to proceed to America rather than stay in Britain because "Britain was finished." The warden of his own college noted in passing that "you people become journalists rather than historians." But Mosse also observed that there was no hostility to foreigners or race prejudice in Cambridge at this time, and the subsequent stellar career of Geoffrey Elton (Ehrenberg), another young refugee, tends to show that a German-Jewish background was no hindrance to a very successful academic career and even member- ship in the House of Lords. True, the family had converted earlier this century, but in the eyes of most non-Jews it was still German-Jewish. As far as the majority of the younger generation of refugees was con- cerned, their studies came to a halt with the outbreak of the war, and those who continued to study after the war quite frequently emigrated and went to overseas universities.

No Ideal Domestic Servants

If about ten thousand refugee children came with the transports of 1938/39, the number of domestic servants, predominantly female, was perhaps larger. There was a demand for domestics in Britain (because few wanted these jobs) and for many young Jewish women in Ger- many this was the only way to leave the country. It did not work out very well, as some British officials had predicted, because the young women applying for these jobs had not been trained for such positions, did not know how to make tea and scones the British way, and were likely to look for employment elsewhere within a short time. Working conditions in this field were bad all the world over, with very little money and long hours (often twelve hours a day, six and a half days a week).

Those willing to do such work on the continent were usually the less bright girls from rural villages, except, of course, if pay was good and working conditions superior. Jewish middle-class girls, even if impov- erished, were not accustomed to being treated as socially inferior, as was bound to happen in a society in which class counted for as much as it did in prewar Britain. Very often they had been of a higher social standing and better educated than those they were working for in Brit- ain. They felt that they were cleverer than their mistresses and when upbraided they were likely to talk back. They forgot that they had been hired to wash dishes, not to play the piano. When told that they would never become good maids, they were likely to reply that this was not their ambition in life in the first place. Lore Segall, a schoolgirl at the time, in a best-selling account (*Other People's Houses*, 1964), has described well the psychological problems facing those ill-prepared to work in such conditions.

They were, of course, not ideal domestics. Even if they knew how to cook, they could not prepare toast or kippers or haddock or Yorkshire pudding the right (English or Scottish) way, they had difficulty making a fire or preparing high tea or cooking venison or pork, which were not kosher.

Some of these domestics had understanding mistresses, but these were the minority. As for the rest, even if we ignore cases of crass exploitation, those who came as domestics were treated as such. The experience of the Schneiders, a husband and wife from Vienna who went to a remote castle in Scotland with twenty-two rooms and twelve bathrooms was not atypical. Their mistress was reasonable and fair but she had been accustomed in the past to experienced domestics and Indian servants, and the newcomers, whose English was very poor, who did not know the difference between a larder and a scullery, must have caused her considerable aggravation. Thus when she asked Mr. Schneider to give a hand to the gardener, the man went into a state of panic because, much as he wanted to please his employers, he was not willing to accept amputation. And so it was without hard feelings on either side that this arrangement came to an end when the war began.

Since most employers of the domestics had never been quite aware of the difference between Nazis and German Jews, and since their country was now at war with Germany, the great majority of alien domestic servants was dismissed within a few weeks of the outbreak of the war. As Viscount Eliband had warned in the House of Lords, thousands of female spies were about in England, each more dangerous than any male spy, and was it not a national duty to get rid of these Mata Haris as quickly as possible? This dismissal brought temporary hardship to thousands but in the long run it was a blessing. Many were interned for a while, and then went to work in factories or hospitals, but most of them felt that anything was better than returning to domestic service.

Hostels and Camps

The older boys and girls were housed at first in hostels and camps in the East End of London, in a Ramsgate hostel, near Ipswich, on the grounds of the estate of Baron James de Rothschild, and other places. These were intended to be provisional places (though some of them lasted until after the war) and at first the inhabitants were not kept very busy. Later they were sent to school or work, until they were detained in 1940 and later drafted into the army or work in factories engaged in the war effort. It was not an ideal existence, but they had a roof over their heads and received food more or less regularly. Those who had belonged to Zionist youth movements in Germany were dispatched either to *hachshara* (agricultural work on farms) or, if under seventeen, to youth *aliya* groups. There were initially almost a thousand of them and they were sent to twenty such centers all over England, Scotland, and Wales. One of the biggest farms was Great Engeham, where up to two hundred were housed temporarily. Living conditions were abysmal, the children slept in tents on muddy ground, there was neither water nor toilets, and food was quite insufficient. The children complained in letters to their parents (this was before the outbreak of the war) and there were irate calls from Berlin and Vienna that their children should not be abused in such a way.

But the institutions dealing with these groups were poor and though there was a gradual improvement in living conditions, they remained bad throughout the war—low wages, long hours, harassment by the authorities. Whereas the hostels and farms for the younger ones were initially led by teachers or social workers, former army officers stepped in after the outbreak of the war to try to introduce military discipline. Among some of the boys there was open rebellion, a few defied their leaders and tried to escape to the bigger cities such as London. There seem to have been a few asocial characters among them, for on at least one occasion there was an appeal signed by all group leaders demanding the removal of a few of the troublemakers.

To establish something akin to a kibbutz in these conditions was unthinkable. In 1940 many were temporarily detained, but released after a while because agricultural work was considered an essential

part of the war effort. Most of the older ones stayed the course, working in nurseries, vegetable gardens, and forestry, and after the war, in
1946/47, emigrated as a group to Palestine. But the situation of the
youth *aliya* was more complicated. Their motivation to live and work
in Palestine had not been as deep and, upon reaching the age of eighteen, some joined the army, and others found their way to work in the
cities.

    Lastly, there were the relatively fortunate ones who had arrived in
England with their families. They lived a more or less normal life, inasmuch as this was possible in their very straitened circumstances.
They depended heavily on the advice and the financial help of the refugee aid organizations, such as Woburn House and the Central British
Fund (CBF). Some went to school, and the older ones tried to find a
job somewhere. At this time certain territorial refugee concentrations
developed for instance in Swiss Cottage in London, behind the department store then known as John Barnes. If they had money, and many
did not, they could frequent the continental restaurants and coffee
houses that had opened in this neighborhood. Many were trying to
help their relations left behind in Germany receive a permit to enter
England, others were contemplating emigration to the United States or
other countries. And then war broke out and everything changed:
many were detained for a year or longer, thousands were shipped to
Canada and Australia, and thousands joined the armed forces. Thus a
new chapter began in the history of the young refugees, who had the
good fortune to reach Britain just in time.

Internment of Young "Enemy Aliens"

When the war broke out, more than a hundred tribunals were set up
according to a plan prepared earlier on, to find out whether individual
refugees could be trusted or whether they constituted a reservoir of
spies and saboteurs. These measures were directed not only against
Jews, even though they constituted about 90 percent of those affected.
Eventually even Italian waiters who had been born in Britain but
never bothered to take out British citizenship were included. Altogether, some 73,000 aliens between ages sixteen and sixty were interrogated and divided into three categories. The great majority, 63,000,
were considered no security risk (class C), some 6,700 (class B) were

thought to be doubtful cases, and 569 were thought to be high security risks (class A) and immediately arrested.

One cannot fairly blame the British government for these measures, which were more or less normal practice among belligerents in wartime. The execution of the Home Office orders was open to criticism—people were put into the "doubtful" category when there was no doubt about their anti-Nazi credentials, and, on the other hand, dubious elements resident in Britain escaped the high security risk category mainly because they had good contacts among highly placed friends in British society. What happened in early summer of 1940 is more difficult to explain: the indiscriminate arrest of tens of thousands of refugees beginning May 15, 1940, and their detention on the Isle of Man and other places on the British mainland. Among those arrested were not only leading anti-Nazis, but also scientists who could have been of considerable value to the British war effort, also hundreds of children who could not possibly endanger the British empire or the allied cause.

It would be fruitless to look for rhyme and reason in these measures. The scientists who were not arrested, for instance, were not permitted to work on the development of radar, but they could pursue their studies on nuclear physics and the construction of an atomic bomb. The arrests were the results of a wave of hysteria sweeping Britain (and subsequently also the United States and Canada). It was hysteria rooted in the belief that the Nazi victory in Western Europe had been so sudden and complete that some secret weapon must have been involved, namely the famous fifth column, the secret army of Nazi helpers. This belief was shared not only by an ignorant popular press (which only a short time before had been among the main appeasers of Hitler) eager to boost its circulation, but by highly placed diplomats such as the British ambassador to the Netherlands. Subsequent investigations were to show that the fifth column had been a figment of imagination, but at the time it was an article of faith shared by many. It was not so much a matter of racial prejudice but of deep ignorance, a failure of both intelligence and common sense.

Among those arrested were most of the young people who had reached Britain prior to the outbreak of the war, especially the males among them. Excepted were those who had volunteered for the Pioneer Corps of the army at the outbreak of the war, some of those engaged in work deemed important for the war effort such as agriculture, and the not inconsiderable number of young people who were simply overlooked by an administration that was far from perfect.

Our concern is with the young among the internees, and there are many personal accounts of the circumstances of their arrest—in their chambers at a Cambridge college, the dining room of a girls' school, coming home from work in the fields or factories, confronted by two policemen who told them that they were under arrest. Reverend Sommerville was arrested straight from the pulpit. He had a German mother and the fact that his three sons were serving in the Royal Air Force was deemed irrelevant. Circumstances of the arrest greatly varied. Bern Brent was given a few days to take leave from his mother, friends, girlfriends, bosses, and colleagues. He was also told to take his tennis racket. Renate at her school in Kent, on the other hand, was taken in school uniform to Holloway Prison and was not even permitted to phone her mother. Being half Jewish she had been brought up in Germany as an Aryan and later in Britain as a potential member of the British upper class and found it difficult to understand, let alone to accept, what happened to her.

Once inside the camp, the lot of women was easier than that of men. Still, life was tolerable, as Josef Eisinger aged seventeen recalls.

> Once a day we lined up for our skimpy food rations, mostly bread, powdered milk, sugar and rice from which we prepared rice pudding in our kitchen. The island must have had a bumper crop of rhubarb for I remember rhubarb being issued with unusual largesse. We were taken on escorted walks through the lovely countryside of the island and were even allowed to swim from the nearby beach albeit with a Bren gun prominently positioned to discourage would be long-distance swimmers.

Walter Foster, who celebrated his seventeenth birthday on the island, remembers the barbed wire, elderly soldiers, and a neurotic major in command. He also relates that considerable moral pressure was applied on the younger, single internees by older married men to volunteer for shipment to Canada so that they should not be separated from their families. Yakov Friedler has fonder memories of the camp: Not yet sixteen he lived in the camp of young women separated from their menfolk. While formal schooling was not extensive, his education as far as bridge and sex were concerned was of a high order.

Those arrested were usually advised to take a toothbrush with them and they were also given to understand that they would be back soon. In fact, after a short time in concentration points on the British mainland they were shipped to the Isle of Man, where hotels and boarding houses had been taken over by the authorities. Since a considerable number of those detained had previously been inmates of German concentration camps, and since the difference between these two experiences could not be overlooked by anyone in his right mind, internees reacted with restraint, even though they considered their arrest a matter of criminal stupidity.

They were concerned about the fact that they were not permitted to fight Nazism and they were equally concerned about their own security—if Hitler invaded Britain, they would have no chance to hide. By the end of 1940, after thousands had been shipped to Canada and Australia, there were still nineteen thousand internees on the Isle of Man, including about four thousand women, and no great attempt was made to differentiate between German refugees and Nazi activists. As the camp commander said, it was not easy to know who was who.

In the camps of the Isle of Man and later also in the Canadian and Australian camps, there were outstanding academic experts in almost every academic field, and musicians and artists of world renown. Within a few days of their internment they began to teach, to perform, and to give master classes, and eventually a university of liberal arts as well as a technical school came into being. The world famous Amadeus Quartet was conceived among a small group of young musicians in the barracks of the detention camps on the Isle of Man. There were seminars and debating societies on subjects ranging from Greek philosophy to physical chemistry. There were theatricals and concerts. Not everyone availed himself of these opportunities, but for young people with intellectual curiosity but unfinished education, these were unique opportunities to acquire an education. This continued in the Canadian and Australian camps. Josef Eisinger, who became a distinguished scientist, recalls that after only a week in Camp B a school was organized, and that he took courses in English, Latin, physics, and mathematics to prepare himself for the McGill (university) Junior Matriculation exam. As an enrolled student he was released from work three mornings a week. In Australia similar arrangements were made with the Victoria department of education and Melbourne University.

These courses led to a bachelor's degree. To write their exams the students in Canada were sent to Montreal, where they had the additional benefit of being taken by friends and well-wishers to real restaurants and clubs in the city. The studies were frequently interrupted by army service, but subsequently credit was given, and in not a few cases students went on to distinguished academic careers, including one Nobel prize.

In addition, the younger inmates received a political education in the camps. The Communists were few but they were the most active and most experienced in indoctrination. True, this was not an easy period for believers in Lenin and Stalin. On the one hand they claimed to be the only consistent antifascists, but on the other they had to explain the inconvenient fact that between September 1939 and June 1941 Western imperialism rather than Nazism was the main enemy of all progressive mankind and that, as Molotov had solemnly declared, Soviet-German friendship had been cemented in blood.

An experienced dialectician could overcome these handicaps, but he still faced an uphill struggle. He could appeal to the considerable resentment against the British and the other Western powers for having detained them among his prospective proselytes. After June 1941, when Hitler attacked the Soviet Union, the task of the Communists in the camps became easier, since Russia was now an ally. But by and large the Communists made few converts and even their leaders, having returned after the war to East Germany, did not have spectacular careers, since all emigrants were deemed unreliable. In this respect there was little difference between Churchill and Stalin.

Churchill announced soon after becoming prime minister that he wanted all the detainees out of Britain. And thus the ships began to leave Liverpool for Canada and Australia. Some twenty-five thousand were sent to Australia, mainly on SS *Dunera*; while its designation as a floating concentration camp was probably exaggerated, the unwilling passengers were certainly maltreated and their belongings were systematically pilfered. This led subsequently to court-martials and some of the belongings were returned. The fate of some of those shipped to Canada was worse. The *Arandora Star* was torpedoed off the coast of Ireland with heavy loss of life. Among those shipped out to camps like Sherbrooke near Montreal and Tatura not far from Melbourne, many hundreds had come with the Kindertransports and others were of the same age. In any case, the great majority of those interned were people who had been registered by the tribunals as constituting no security risk whatsoever.

The British government realized almost as soon as the decision to deport had been made that it had been a mistake. But governments, even more than individuals, are reluctant to admit mistakes. In addition, shipping space to bring them back to the United Kingdom was at a premium at the time. Eventually, the mistakes were admitted also by the Canadian and Australian governments, and by late 1942 the detained were informed that they were considered from now on "friendly aliens." By that time only some 350 refugees were still detained in Canada.

The situation in Australia was different partly because of lack of transport. Life in the Australian camps did not constitute particular hardships. As one young detainee reported, "the guards were good to us: We had everything there, football teams, lectures, entertainment." The nearby Jewish communities provided books and other help. Some studied for exams, others languages such as Spanish and Hebrew. Some 130 young "pioneers" actually made their way from Australia to Palestine during the war. Several hundred who had opted for enlisting in the British army returned to the United Kingdom in 1942. Some 970 preferred to stay in Canada, which was made possible following a Canadian government decree in 1942; an unknown number stayed on in Australia. These were usually young, unattached males, or those with families in Canada or the United States.

Those who had been detained on the Isle of Man and subsequently deported to Australia and Canada looked back in later years on their misfortunes with some detachment. True, the case of the *Dunera* had been a scandal, they had been shabbily treated and robbed of their belongings, and the authorities had shown both stupidity and heartlessness. But they also understood that stupidity in wartime is often the rule rather than the exception, that the enforced arrest had given many of them an opportunity to study and to lay the foundations for a career that otherwise might have been impossible. They were spared the London Blitz and were perhaps fed slightly better than they would have been in England. Some were willing to understand, if not to forgive, the hysteria that had caused the detentions; others, such as future Nobel Prize winner, Max Perutz, did not.

When the refugees were released from the camps on the Isle of Man and returned from Canada and Australia, many joined the army, which in the early days meant the lowest form of (non-fighting) units, the Pioneer Corps. We have already discussed their fate during the war, and their contribution to the war effort. After the war the majority of those who had come to Britain in the 1930s decided to stay, but a significant minority, perhaps 20 to 30 percent left for the United States, Palestine/Israel, and other countries. Among the young people the percentage was apparently even higher, at 30 to 40 percent. More left in the 1950s and 1960s, either to be reunited with their families or for professional reasons. In certain fields, such as in Jewish thought, there simply was little demand in Britain. Alexander Altmann, Nahum Glatzer, Leo Strauss, Abraham Heschel, and Simon Rawidowicz, leading people in this field, were all in Britain at one time but not one stayed—America offered so many more opportunities—and it was the same in many other fields. Hundreds returned to the continent, more to Austria and Czechoslovakia than to Germany, because of the cultural ties they still felt, because they thought that they might find some of their family still alive, or because they wanted to believe that somehow the old homes they had left as children still existed. There were not a few perpetual wanderers, people leaving Britain once, twice, three times, returning after a few years, and deciding where to make their permanent home only after a decade or two.

Professionally, the younger generation did not do badly. They learned a craft, opened small businesses, and if they did not study at a university, their children certainly did. Some had spectacular careers, most led modest suburban existences. It had been easier for German Jews to engage in a political career in Britain in the century before. (One of them did become a member of Parliament, but one would look in vain for details about his origin in works of reference.) Others became famous film producers and stage designers, a few went into journalism and publishing and rose high in their professions, and several were highly successful businesspeople.

Almost Englishmen and Englishwomen

Conditions for those aspiring to a career in the professions became easier after the war, as they could now practice law and medicine. It is tempting to relate the story of the refugees in terms of a social success story, how some became rich and famous, or at least moderately well off and useful citizens. But this would be only one aspect of a complex story.

To what extent did they grow roots in the new country, to what degree were they accepted? This, needless to say, is not a specifically British problem, it existed in one way or another in every country. But there were some specific British difficulties that ought to be mentioned at least in passing. The attitude of refugees who chose to stay in Britain was ambiguous just as attitudes toward them were. On the one hand, there was great pride in having been admitted as a member of a superior club and the desire not just to prove that they were worthy of this honor but to show gratitude. Hence the "Thank You Britain" initiative in the 1970s, in which a considerable sum of money was collected and put at the disposal of the British Academy. On the other hand, such Anglophilia was not, however, shared by all, there was the realization that the once great club was in decline, that they were perhaps regarded as second-rate members after all, and that any debts of gratitude had been amply repaid. As one woman said in response to the "Thank You Britain" initiative, "they let us in the last moment to do some miserable chores. They have opened their doors for me but I have enriched them." Nevertheless, the feeling among most was not one of great bitterness; other countries, after all, had not even opened their doors for domestics.

But there was yet another deeper issue, the problematical character of their national identity. They might be holders of British passports, or even local councilors and justices of the peace, but were they accepted as full-fledged Englishmen? Interviewers interrogating refugees in the 1970s and 1980s often found a certain resignation, the feeling that, having tried to be wholly like the British in their younger years, they had given it up, even if they had no linguistic or other problems, simply because there were differences in mentality and culture. They tremendously liked the British but felt at the same time that there were differences that could not be overcome, that, whatever their achievements, they were not quite considered part of British society. But it could be argued that the same was true for Anglo-Jewry in general, including its third or fourth generation. In any case, these issues lost much of their acuteness in the age of multicultural society.

Refugees had felt more intense about the question of identity and the need for roots when they first came. But in later years these issues seldom were the cause of deep unhappiness, constant preoccupation, or sleepless nights. In other words, as time went by, they approached the issue with a greater measure of detachment or even indifference. Most of the refugees felt less of a need for approval and had established for themselves a little world of their own, in their family, and among neighbors and colleagues. Their children, after all, spoke English without an accent and had accepted English ways, in fact knew no others. It was with these surroundings that the refugees had to deal in daily life rather than with abstractions such as Britain and the English way of life. There were exceptions, namely those who felt a deep urge to eradicate their origins to the extent of denying them, inventing a new identity for themselves and their offspring, obliterating all traces of a past they loathed or were ashamed of. This is an intriguing psychological problem and could be found in other countries as well, but perhaps nowhere as acutely as in Britain.

German Jews and Anglo-Jewry

The first and the second generation of refugees had problems not only with British society but also with Anglo-Jewry. There was gratitude for what members of the Anglo-Jewish community had done during the weeks and months after the arrival of the refugees in Britain, but integration into the existing community was another proposition altogether. There was no place for the refugees among the old families that constituted the aristocracy in the community and there was not much in common with the mainly Eastern European elements in the community (the great majority), their religious practices and social and cultural life. Soon after the arrival of the refugees there were complaints that the German and Austrian Jews were standoffish. On the other hand, the Anglo-Jewish community made no great effort to integrate the refugees into its institutions, though they constituted a numerically significant part of the community. And so the refugees came to establish their own social organizations, such as the AJR (Association of Jewish Refugees), the Leo Baeck Lodge, and even their own religious communities such as the New Liberal Congregation at Belsize Square.

This had to do in part with the old tensions between Eastern European and German Jews, but also with their different religious orientations (most of the latter were liberal whereas the majority United Synagogue was more traditional), and different cultural interests. As for the German Jewish intelligentsia among the refugees, both the first and the second generation, their interest in things Jewish was limited, and the community showed no particular wish to establish closer relationships with them, except at a much later date with the establishment of Hillel branches at the universities.

The lack of interest in things Jewish is reflected, for instance, in a survey of refugee historians, all of whom belonged to the younger generation; a significant proportion converted, or was converted, and had no interest in Judaism. As one of them noted, it was not until the 1970s that he reflected on the price that had to be paid in psychological terms for suppressing his origins. Another (H. Koenigsberger) related that he only realized at school in Newport that he was not English when the geography master asked him whether they kept dogs and cats in his country. Werner Mosse felt a strong involvement in the fight of the Palestinian Jews for statehood but no close emotional identification. Even though he felt that he was wholly at home in Britain, Sidney Pollard, who had come from Austria at age thirteen, realized that he was never quite like those born there. However, he said, "any feeling of Jewishness had long since dropped away." Similar feelings of somehow being different from their non-Jewish colleagues could be found among many others, not necessarily on the left. There was a growing tendency to dismiss the importance of these differences (their Jewish origins) and it is impossible to say what psychological price had to be paid in each individual case. For some it was crucial, for others it did not matter.

At least some of them discovered in later life a new interest in certain aspects of Jewish history, such as the Holocaust and Israel. Perhaps it was because they had become less self-conscious about their origins, or because the general mood around them had changed. There was a similar trend among French and American academics of Jewish origin, though perhaps not quite as palpably felt.

Some of the cultural institutions that had been founded by the first generation of continental refugees ceased to exist as the generation of the founders passed away, but others, such as the AJR, the religious communities, and the lodges, continued to function. Some of the second generation of refugees turned their backs altogether on the community from which they had come. Others of the second generation of refugees found their place among Anglo-Jewry; one of the younger refugees, after all, became an influential chief rabbi (Immanuel Jakobovitz, born in Koenigsberg in 1921). It is also true that in many fields there was cooperation, for instance, with regard to Israel. But the differences, for whatever reasons, continued to exist.

THE GREAT DISPERSAL

Hotel Bolivia and Hotel Shanghai

———∽∿∽———

After the war in Europe had broken out, during the last weeks of 1939, the youth *aliya* group in Givat Brenner, one of the largest kibbutzim located in the south of Palestine, prepared an exhibition, open to the public. One of the graphics showed that the twenty-five members of the group, all from what was then known as Greater Germany, had parents, brothers, and sisters in thirteen countries. The fact is worth mentioning, not because it was in any way extraordinary, but, on the contrary, because it was quite typical. The persecutions in Germany had caused a dispersal of communities and families unprecedented in Jewish history and probably in the history of any other people.

The fate of the apprentices of the Gross Breesen farm in Silesia provides another example. This, as mentioned earlier on, was the non-Zionist answer to the Zionist agricultural training centers; about three hundred young people passed through this farm. They had no clear plans for settlement outside Germany as a group, at one time the state of Virginia was mentioned, at another, Paraguay and Australia, but in the end only small groups went to these places. The majority left after the November pogroms of 1938 as quickly as it could to whatever country was still willing to accept the occasional immigrant.

When Professor Curt Bondy, who had been the director of Gross Breesen, published an information letter in June 1946, he entitled it quite appropriately "Gross Breesen all over the world"; his former students were now found on all five continents. Several were writing from

Kenya, others from Australia and Chile, not to mention such obvious places as Holland and Scotland, Italy, France, Austria, Argentina, and so on. Quite a few had gone to the United States, where the men were now mostly out of the army and studying; similar reports were received from the Gross Breesen veterans of the British army. There was even a report entitled "physician in the jungle" (in Bolivia) dealing with Indian folk medicine, and perhaps, even more surprising, some enthusiastic letters from Palestine (soon to become Israel), a country to which the young people of Gross Breesen originally had not wanted to go. One such letter expressed admiration about the successes of dairy production in the Palestinian settlements. Titi Sander wrote from Jerusalem that some people had gone to America from Palestine but were now homesick (home being Palestine), and Alisa Tworoger said that while she was against terrorism, the gates of Palestine had to be kept open for immigrants by any means, including violence. The prewar quarrels and antagonisms about where to go from Germany were largely forgotten.

The choice of profession was as varied as the choice of country. One of the former members of the group had been ordained as a rabbi and become an Australian citizen, another worked in a sausage factory in Buenos Aires. One, working on a farm in England, had been asked to become an instructor for displaced children in Europe; a man in New York was working as a machinist, having been released from the army (but he, too, was eventually to become a professor); a couple lived on their farm in North Carolina; another couple in Chile was preparing for emigration to Palestine. The bulletin also included much information on those who had not emigrated in time, the great majority of whom had perished. Professor Bondy in Virginia (but about to regain his professorship in Hamburg) had made a great effort to reach as many former apprentices as possible, but he had failed to contact all of them, especially those who had gone to the more exotic places. It appeared that those who had once been working on a medium-sized farm in Silesia were found at the end of the war in more than twenty countries.

This then was the fate of the members of just one group. Altogether, looking back sixty years after the event, it appears that young refugees from Central Europe had gone to almost a hundred countries, which is far more than the total number of independent, sovereign states at the time. Some had been hiding in Albania during the war, others were living in Rhodesia, Bechuanaland, and what was then known as Nyassa and the Belgian Congo. They had gone to every South and Central American country and most Asian countries.

Probably the last book by a Jew published in Nazi Germany (it came out on the eve of the November pogrom of 1938) was a little encyclopedia for would-be emigrants issued by the Philo publishing house. It contained practical information about countries, climates, visas, possibilities of work and other practical information, and virtually every entry ended with the words, "prospects are poor." This, in most cases, had been an understatement, because prospects were not just poor, they were virtually nonexistent. But the young refugees had to ignore these dire facts, just as they had to ignore letters received from abroad saying "that the climate here is wholly unsuited for Europeans, a temperature of 45 degrees centigrade, tropical rains and tropical diseases." They had to escape from Nazi Germany however inclement the weather and dismal the prospects of finding work of any sort.

The question was asked after the war why even greater numbers of German Jews had not left the country, especially in the early years after the Nazi takeover. While it is true, as Anneliese Borinski wrote many years later, "that we thought it was five to twelve whereas in reality it was already past twelve," the entries to the Philo lexikon provide the answer. (Borinski, a leader of a Zionist youth group, was deported to Auschwitz, survived, and later became a member of a kibbutz in Israel.) To this one should add certain obvious demographic and social facts; of those who remained, many were old and sick or they were so poor that they could not afford the price of a visa and a ticket to their destination.

Emigration from Germany during the first three or four years was mainly to Western Europe and Palestine. From 1937 to 1939, Britain and the United States were in first place. But after the November pogroms of 1938, when pressure to leave the country became overwhelming, the great dispersal began, above all, to Latin America, Shanghai, and many small and unlikely places, from the newly established Japanese puppet state, Manchukuo, to the Dominican Republic, of which most, including the would-be immigrants, had not heard until a few weeks earlier.

Flight to Latin America

More than 3,500 went to Argentina and about the same number to Brazil and Chile, about 2,500 to Bolivia, about 1,000 to Uruguay, 600 to Ecuador, and 3,000 to Central America. These were the official figures at the time but there is reason to believe that the real numbers were higher, probably considerably higher, certainly with regard to some countries. It can be taken for granted that more than 230 refugees (the official figure) went to Peru, and more than 2,500 to Bolivia. According to estimates made after World War II, about 40,000 refugees from Central Europe went to Argentina, 17,000 to Brazil, and 15,000 to Chile. Registration at the borders was less than complete, and furthermore the borders of most Latin American countries are very long and not well guarded, and it was not too difficult to enter a country illegally. Altogether, close to 80,000 refugees may have gone to South and Central America, but this figure includes many thousands who did not stay there, not to mention those who went to Cuba and other Central American countries waiting for their North American visas. It became increasingly more difficult in the late 1930s to reach Latin America from Europe. The case of the *St. Louis*, which belonged to the German Hapag Lloyd company, is well known: the "ship of the damned" with more than 900 passengers was turned down by every American country and had to make its way back to Europe, where eventually many of the passengers found their death. Franklin D. Roosevelt played an inglorious role in this affair; he was worried about his third term as president, assuming, rightly perhaps, that admitting the refugees would be unpopular.

It is less well known that at the same time, in 1939, at least a dozen similar ships were trying to make their way to Latin American harbors, but were refused entry because most of the would-be immigrants had invalid visas, or, to be precise, bought from corrupt Latin American consuls in Germany or elsewhere in Europe and recognized by every country in the world except those for which they had been issued. (There were also some consuls, including the Brazilian consul in Hamburg, who issued visas not to enrich themselves but because they genuinely sympathized with the plight of the unfortunate refugees.) Twelve ships included the German *Koenigstein*, *Karibia*, *Erika*, and *Iberia*, the British *Cap Arcona* and *Okinia*, the Portuguese *Horazio*, the French *Flandres*, and others. Their story resembles in some ways that of Wagner's opera *The Flying Dutchman*, of a ghost ship that cannot find safe haven, except that the basic theme of the opera is salvation through love, at least at the end, whereas very little love confronted the refugees on these ships. True, most were eventually permitted to land somewhere but not because of humanitarian reasons, only after long negotiations and after Jewish organizations such as the Joint Distribution Committee (and in a few cases also the shipping company) had made additional payments to strategically placed local officials. The one ship that was not permitted to land, the *Okinia*, returned to Gibraltar. In one specific case ninety refugees from Central Europe were fifteen months at sea. They left Europe in January 1941, were refused entry in Argentina, Brazil, Trinidad, Jamaica, and other countries until at long last the Dutch government in exile gave them permission to land in Curaçao in April 1942.

With all of these difficulties, tens of thousands of refugees went to Latin America during the years after 1938; together with Shanghai, this had become a haven of last resort. The difficulties were enormous. Without a working knowledge of the language, the refugees could not hope to find employment, yet Spanish and Portuguese were virtually unknown in Central Europe. According to postwar estimates, only 5 percent of the emigrants who had come to Argentina had a good knowledge of Spanish, and even this could be an exaggeration. The climatic conditions were often wholly unsuitable for newcomers from Europe, the altitude of the urban centers of Bolivia was too high, and other parts of the continent had a tropical climate and lacked elementary services, including roads.

Many refugees had taken vocational courses in Germany and Austria, usually in crafts, which were thought necessary in the country of absorption. But these were often not the professions that were needed and the skilled newcomers were regarded as competitors and rivals by the local specialists. That physicians, lawyers, and other members of the professions could not practice goes without saying, but merchants too could not operate without at least some starting capital, which no one was ready to give them.

The Latin American governments were willing to absorb a limited number of farmers, but hardly anyone among the refugees had such experience. A few settled in certain regions of Brazil, such as Rolandia, but the second generation of immigrants usually left. Koch Weser, who had been a member of the German Reichstag, went to Brazil to grow coffee; his grandson became a high official of the World Bank, and later a top official in the German government. The Jewish institutions in Argentina maintained from the very beginning that farming was possible only in groups and with a reasonable knowledge of language, customs, and living conditions. To prepare oneself for such a life, at least two years in town were needed. But having lived in a city for two years, hardly anyone was willing to move to some desolate, faraway place.

Governments more often than not were unfriendly or even hostile; there was a strong antisemitic tradition in Latin America, mainly nurtured by the Catholic Church; most governments were neutral in the conflict between Nazi Germany and its Allies; and even if, as in the case of Brazil, they reluctantly joined the anti-Nazi coalition, this in no way affected domestic policies such as Vargas' protofascist "New State." Argentina was the country with the largest Jewish community but also with the most active antisemites. There were sizeable German, often pro-Nazi, communities in Latin America, and they too contributed to the anti-refugee, anti-Jewish propaganda.

Lastly, and most important, there were the psychological difficulties the refugees had with the local population, which, especially in the case of the less developed countries, struck them at best as exotic and inscrutable, at worst as wholly unsympathetic, uncultured, unreliable, devoid of almost any positive characteristics (though at least they did not kill Jews, as the Nazis did). Whereas in almost every European country (and in Palestine and North America) refugees tried to assimilate as quickly and as thoroughly as possible, such integration seemed altogether impossible in many Latin American countries, not just as far as the Indios were concerned, but also the white population.

True, the situation was better in some countries than in others, for instance, in the urban centers of Brazil, in Argentina, Uruguay, and Chile. But even there assimilation seemed very difficult. The white underclass was deeply xenophobic and regarded the new refugees with suspicion. The upper class disdained them as penniless erstwhile lawyers and doctors, now roaming the streets as peddlers, and kept them at arm's length. For the small middle class, they were both aliens and rivals. Nor were the few intellectuals greatly interested, as their traditional orientation was toward Paris rather than Berlin.

Relations were not close either with the existing Jewish communities. For the local Jews of Eastern European origin, the Germans and Austrians were "Jeckes"; the Sephardi communities did not want any dealings with the "Germans," fearing that they would endanger their precarious political and social status in the country. These fears were not entirely without foundation: in the middle of the war, for example, the Bolivian government began to register all Jews, including those who had converted to Christianity, which seemed a bad omen to those who had escaped from Europe.

Nor did the refugees always show always the tact necessary to escape undue attention and hostility; they would, for instance, congregate on the central square of La Paz and discuss politics, a kind of little parliament in exile that immediately attracted unfavorable attention. In the end, the only Jewish institutions that helped were North American, such as the Joint, which mediated with the local governments and offered some material help during the first weeks and months after the refugees' arrival.

Success and Failure

These, in broadest outline, were the seemingly insurmountable difficulties facing the new arrivals. And yet, even in these inauspicious conditions, there were enterprising people who succeeded right from the beginning, at least in material terms. Some had connections with foreign banks or corporations, or got themselves attached to local firms and rapidly rose up the professional ladder in view of their knowledge of languages and other experience. Those few who knew Spanish and had the right personality (extroverted and quick to adjust to local manners and customs) had invaluable advantages over the others. One example was Benno Weiser Varon, a refugee from Vienna who had dropped out from medical school just before the final examination. He arrived in Quito, Ecuador, and had the good luck to be invited to write for local newspapers. Within a short time he not only made a name for himself but also came to know influential people in various walks of life, including politics and business.

Another interesting case was Gunter Holzmann, a native of Breslau, who in the tradition of the German youth movement craved adventure. With some knowledge of mineralogy he volunteered to live for years in mining settlements high up in the Andes among Indios and thus made a small fortune. His politics were eccentric, to say the least. Having begun on the extreme right (he had published an advertisement in German newspapers just before Hitler's rise to power to say that he had nothing to do with the Jewish community), he became an extreme anti-American populist, bequeathing much of his money to left-wing publications in Europe. He also devoted much of his time to a search for cures for rheumatism developed by Indian tribes, which unfortunately ended in failure, curing neither him nor anyone else. Yet another success story in an unlikely place and in adverse conditions was that of Werner Guttentag, who arrived in Bolivia at age nineteen in 1939. He had no profession that could be of possible use to him in La Paz and Cochabamba, but he shrewdly realized that there was a demand for books both Spanish and foreign. The tiny shop he established spread over the years, he pioneered both the national Bolivian bibliography and the Bolivian encyclopedia, and he lived to see in the 1990s his picture on a postage stamp of his adoptive country as a pillar of the development of Bolivian culture.

Generally speaking, many refugees did show more initiative than the locals, and those who one way or another managed to go into business quite frequently established firms that succeeded. But in most cases the next generation did not want to continue in the family business, and while the names remained, the shops changed hands and the sons and daughters moved on to other fields and often to other countries.

The lucky ones arrived young enough to attend school in the new countries so that they soon acquired fluency in Spanish and Portuguese. Some of the schools were excellent, such as the famous, liberal Pestalozzi School in Buenos Aires. Elsewhere American and missionary schools provided a reasonable education. But even in Chile parents faced problems unless they lived in the capital. True, there were Catholic and German schools, but refugee children were often not admitted and there were reports about humiliating experiences even where the non-Jewish German element was absent, such as in Peru. A German lady who had lived in Peru since 1938 remembered in her old age the school days of her daughter in an English language school (the Cambridge House) and in a school run by the order of the Ursulines. In some ways these had been the happiest years for her daughter: her classmates, who belonged to the local aristocracy, had frequently invited her home and everyone had been nice to her. But they would never have dreamed of visiting the home of the refugee child, and the moment their ways parted, they lost any interest in her. The friends, male and female, had been very lively, likeable, but wholly unreliable and superficial. It took the refugees years to understand that "mi casa—su casa" (my house is your house) meant even less than the American "You must come and see us one day." And so the daughter, like many others, had married a North American and moved to the United States.

The mother who related this story was particularly harsh in her assessment of the Peruvians. With a very few exceptions she had met with no loyalty or gratitude, only mendacity, falsehood, and great ignorance, which often turned into colossal conceit. Perhaps the lady in question was oversensitive, perhaps she measured by impossible high standards. K.M., who lived in Chile for many years and who later came to divide her time between Israel and Germany, remembers the years in Santiago as happy ones. She would not have left the country but for the fact that her sons went to study abroad, and stayed abroad. But then so many went abroad and did not return.

There is much evidence that the great majority of refugees were never integrated into this society. Egon Schwarz relates that in all his years in Latin America he was never invited to the home of a local family in Bolivia. When Leo Spitzer, U.S. historian born in La Paz, asked them in later years about their first impressions, the refugees mentioned the horrible smell in the streets and the fact that men and women were all dressed in black. But again, many of those who left Bolivia after the war said that they were eternally grateful to the country that had let them in, and that they would like to see the country again and eat the delicious saltenas (a midmorning spicy snack). Liesl Lipczenko, who had left La Paz in 1951, said she still felt a strong connection and even longing for La Paz where everything still seemed familiar. She had no such longing for Vienna from which she had come.

In later years, in the 1960s and 1970s, the old traditions and colonial lifestyle began to change, and customs and manners became freer all over Latin America among the local upper and middle classes. But by that time the young generation of refugees of the thirties had reached middle age; for them the changes came too late and hardly affected their social life.

Few of those who arrived in the 1930s could afford to study at a university and so they went into businesses of various kinds. Most were moderately successful, but only by the low local standards; a minority became destitute, and disappeared from sight, and an even smaller minority did very well but even they were seldom integrated in local society. There were mixed marriages but not very many in the Andes states. The young generation did not go into politics; a few made a career on the local level, but they were not wanted on the national level, and in the light of their experience in Europe they were not particularly eager to try their luck in this field.

There were, as always, a few exceptions, such as Ernesto Kroch in Uruguay, but their experience, more often than not, was painful. Kroch had to absent himself from his adopted country for years and his son was in prison for an even longer period. Boris Goldenberg, one of the youngest militants of the Socialist SAP in its Paris exile, went to Cuba and played a minor role on the legal left in Cuban politics. But he, too, left Havana in the sixties and returned to Germany where his old comrade in arms, Willy Brandt, had risen in the meantime to a position of great influence. But not all were left-wing militants: Ulli Neisser in Arequipa, Peru, married into the local aristocracy, converted, and twice became mayor of the city. Several bishops officiated at his funeral.

Others, in addition to men and women of the left, returned to Europe, none perhaps stranger than Pater Paulus Gordan, born in Berlin, who had studied philosophy and theology in Berlin, Breslau, and Paris. Following a sudden spiritual revelation before his twentieth year (and perhaps under the influence of his friend George Bernanos) he had converted to Catholicism and become a Benedictine monk. After Hitler had taken over, his abbot had sent him to a monastery in Brazil. He returned in 1948 to the Beuron monastery, became chief editor of the internal journal of the Benedictines *Erbe und Auftrag*. He ended his career as head of the order in Rome and died in 1998 in his Bavarian abbey.

If the younger refugees committed themselves politically, they did so, more likely than not, among the various Free German and Austrian movements during the war, Communist and non-Communist. A few returned to Germany after 1945, but the great majority lost interest in Germany, and if they had a political commitment it was more often toward Israel.

The refugees tried to have closer social contacts with their associates and neighbors, but it was an uphill struggle that seldom led to great success. Eventually they established their own religious communities and synagogues, social clubs, old age homes, sport clubs, Sunday schools, Masonic lodges (such as the Spinoza lodge in Mexico), even German-language journals and theaters, and a Boy Scout organization in Sao Paulo. Relations with the East European and Sephardi Jewish communities were still not close, except under pressure; those who had come earlier (to give but one example) had a monopoly as far as burial societies and cemeteries were concerned, and the newcomers had to cooperate with them.

For some of the younger generation of refugees, Latin America became a new home. This is true, above all, with regard to those who had gone to the more developed countries. For others, Latin America had been only a temporary asylum and as the war ended and traveling became possible again, there was a new migration wave, or, to be precise, several such waves. The great majority of refugees who had lived during the war in Bolivia, Paraguay, Peru, and Colombia disappeared. Less than a thousand Jews were left in Paraguay, Bolivia, and Ecuador, which had been home during the war to many thousands. They felt that there was no economic future for them; culturally and socially, they were isolated. Most of them went to Argentina, but some, those who could, went to the United States. A few hundred, mostly elderly people or political emigrants, returned to Germany; thousands, mainly young people, went to Israel.

At one time there had been flourishing German Jewish communities in Rio, Sao Paulo, and Porto Allegre, as well as in Buenos Aires, Montevideo, and Santiago. In Brazil the German-language community bulletins could not be published during the war because Brazil was part of the anti-Axis coalition. (Argentina came into the war only a few months before its end.) Furthermore, the leading rabbis in Rio and Sao Paulo welcomed the trend toward "Brazilianization." After the war the German language bulletins reappeared, but their readership declined to the point that 95 percent of the text of the Sao Paulo news bulletin was in Portuguese and only a tiny part in German; the younger generation was more at home in Portuguese and the communities had been joined by new members not of German Jewish origin. While the community bulletins in La Paz (*Mitteilungsblatt*, for example) and Bogota kept their German names for a long time, the contents were preponderantly in Spanish.

In the 1950s, CENTRA was founded. An umbrella organization of German Jewish communities in all major South American countries, it convened conferences and seminars, arranged summer camps for the younger generation, and generally promoted Jewish culture and traditions. It even participated in the establishment of a rabbinical seminar in Buenos Aires. However, within twenty years, by the 1970s, CENTRA had virtually ceased activity because of the increasing integration of the German Jews into these countries.

In the 1990s the two countries with sizeable Jewish communities were Argentina and Brazil, especially, because of the Sao Paulo conurbation. But of the German Jewish element not many traces were left. At one time there had been not only new religious communities, especially in Belgrano, the part of Buenos Aires where about half of them had settled, but also cultural and philanthropic societies—a Theodor Herzl Society and a religious-cultural group called Lamrot Hakol, not to mention sport clubs such as Bar Kochba. The religious communities still existed decades later, but most of the clubs and other organizations had disappeared or changed their character. The second generation of refugees had opted frequently for a university career and the free professions, but now they were found as often in the United States and even Israel as in the cities of Latin America Both the older and the younger refugees sometimes looked back with nostalgia to the colorful life they had once witnessed in Latin America. But these feelings of nostalgia were not strong enough to make them consider a return to these places. Argentina and Brazil were the exceptions.

The refugees from Central Europe had not done badly in these two countries; when the younger ones among them in Argentina were asked about their economic situation in the 1980s, some 78 percent said that it was good or very good and only 3 percent that it was bad. Restitution payments from Germany had had a greater impact in Latin America than in Europe or the United States but, as argued earlier on, the younger generation of refugees benefited only to a limited extent. When asked whether they felt themselves attached to Argentina, only a tiny fraction replied in the negative, while more than 90 percent said "yes" or "yes, in part." But when asked whether they were holding Argentinian passports, it appeared that some 40 percent were never naturalized and did not have Argentine nationality. When asked for an explanation, one of the refugees said that naturalization did not imply equality before the law. The passport made it clear that the holder was not Argentinian by birth and for this reason the higher echelons of the administration were closed to him either by law or by tradition.

Shanghai, the Last Shelter

If some of the Latin American countries were mainly a shelter for the duration of the war, then Shanghai was not even a shelter but a dubious waiting room with few facilities. Nevertheless, it was the only place on earth for which no visa was needed: as the result of the Japanese invasion of China it had become a legal vacuum, a no man's land. The Japanese were the real masters, but they preferred, especially until Pearl Harbor, not to become too closely involved in the running of Shanghai affairs. At the same time, particularly after the November pogroms of 1938, this unlikely haven for European refugees became the last hope for many of them. Tens of thousands had been detained in concentration camps in November 1938, and the Gestapo made it known that they would be released only if they would leave Germany within a number of days, or at most weeks. Since it was virtually impossible to obtain a visa in so short a period, Shanghai became the main destination for many families. Whereas emigration to Britain and France, but to many neutral countries as well, had become impossible with the outbreak of war in Europe in September 1939, it was still possible to travel to the Far East, by way of the Italian shipping line Lloyd Triestino through the Suez Canal, and, after Italy had entered the war, through the Soviet Union, by way of the Trans-Siberian Railroad.

And so almost twenty thousand refugees went to the Far East during the months just before and after the outbreak of the war; a few stayed in places like Charbin in Manchuria, and Tientsin, but the great majority settled in Shanghai. To say that they left for the Far East with great misgivings is an understatement—very often it was an act of despair. This was not so for the young, who did not worry about money and sources of income. Thus Michael Blumenthal, age thirteen at the time, described many years later the deep crisis facing his parents on the road to Shanghai; they were not comfortable being Jews, and they were confused about having been Germans. They remained wedded to German culture and felt nostalgia for the comfortable ways they left behind. But for him it was the beginning of a great adventure, new experiences, and unfamiliar, exotic sights.

Inge Nussbaum relates that after her father had been taken to a concentration camp, her mother sold their house and their other belongings and from the proceeds bought tickets for eleven members of their family, even though many of their friends told them that this was madness.

The refugees' Shanghai consisted at the time of three sectors. Frenchtown, the French concession, was the nicest, the most elegant and expensive, and only the few people who had arrived with some means could afford to live there. Next came the International Settlement. But for most of the refugees Hongkew (Neu Kurfuerstendamm) became their new quarters. This was a lower-class area which had further suffered as the result of the fighting during the war. And yet, within a short time, Chusan road, once a typical Chinese lane, came to look (in the words of Laura Margolin, a representative of Joint, the American aid organization) like a little street in Vienna with its delicatessens and sidewalk coffee houses. There were German language newspapers, such as *Die gelbe Post*, *Shanghai Woche*, and *Shanghai Morgenpost*, theater performances, and even a Miss Shanghai contest. Among the refugees were eighty actors, thirty-three singers, and scores of dancers and other professional theater people. But who could pay for the delicatessen and the newspapers, and the tickets for the theater and the performances of the Shanghai municipal symphony orchestra? Who would pay the salaries of the teachers, actors, and rabbis?

This is one of the great mysteries in the annals of emigration, for the refugees were mainly interacting with each other and the great majority were destitute. Three-quarters needed financial assistance, about a quarter lived in so-called homes that were paid for by the American aid organizations. Living conditions were crowded and miserable, food limited to the bare necessities. Above all, after Pearl Harbor, the representatives of the American aid organizations were detained and no more money was forthcoming. And yet, while people were starving at times, no one actually died of hunger.

The Shanghailanders, as they came to be called, showed incredible ingenuity in earning a little money; there was after all the foreign (non-Jewish) colony counting tens of thousands and some of them did have money. Others were dealing with Japanese and Chinese firms and eked out a living of sorts. Ernest Heppner, who had arrived in 1939 as young man of eighteen, worked first as a salesman in a toy shop, then as a bookseller. He found that (prior to Pearl Harbor) American sailors were his best customers, buying up textbooks and other serious literature, so that after each visit by a group of sailors, his stock had to be replenished. Later yet, Heppner went to work for a firm selling and servicing typewriters, an occupation that was to help him with his first steps in the United States. Illo, his girlfriend and later his wife, was from Berlin and two years younger. She knew English and French and shorthand and was in demand as a secretary.

The younger refugees of school age attended the Horace Kadoorie schools, which had been built and were maintained by the Baghdadi Jewish multimillionaire whose family had lived in Shanghai for more than a century and provided a good deal of help to their fellow Jews from Europe. The main school was later ousted from its building and tuition interrupted for a year or longer. But while it lasted, it provided an education from which the pupils greatly benefited; many became professionals in later years.

The situation dramatically deteriorated in May 1943 when the Japanese herded the refugees into a ghetto of about a square mile in Hongkew, which they could leave only with a special pass. This caused obvious additional hardships, and on top of it all U.S. bombers aiming at a nearby Japanese airfield bombed the ghetto instead, killing some, including the head of the Jewish community.

Liberation came with the armistice in August 1945, but most refugees had to stay on in Shanghai for another three years or even longer. Chiang Kai-shek announced that he would deport all German and Austrian refugees and the policy of the Communists was no different. The American army and navy stationed in Shanghai became a major employer of refugees, but this did not mean that the refugees were wanted in the United States. Those who had close relations in America could apply for a visa, and the young Orthodox Jews and their rabbis who had the strongest lobby in Washington were among the first to leave.

A considerable number of refugees went to Australia and some to Israel, though the number of Russian Jews among those who went to Israel was larger than those from Central Europe. Most of them had not been Zionists in the first place. There was great joy when the state of Israel was proclaimed, but it was also clear that there was trouble ahead in the Middle East, and the majority of Shanghailanders wanted, at long last, only peace and quiet. Many hundreds returned to Germany and Austria, but the destination of the majority was still America. But America, despite all that had happened during World War II, was most reluctant to liberalize its immigration policy. There were new laws spearheaded by Pat McCarran, head of the Senate judiciary committee, which allowed Displaced Persons to enter the United States but discriminated against the Jews among them. Some could not come because they had been born in Poland, and the Polish quota was tiny, others because their health problems prevented the issuance of a visa. By 1948 half of the remaining refugee community was still, or again, on cash relief. Some of those who had reached the United States on the *General Gordon* were again expelled for a year, which they had to spend in refugee camps in Germany before being readmitted.

By 1952 the Jewish community of Shanghai had ceased to exist—somehow, somewhere a place had been found even for the hardest cases. Of those who went to the United States many, perhaps most, settled on the West Coast. In the 1980s, when China opened up for tourists, and when sufficient time had elapsed to forget the hardships, the humiliations, and the disasters, former Shanghailanders began to return for sentimental visits in Shanghai. Documentaries were produced and novels written about the city that during World War II had given them a shelter, however miserable. The old-timers met for annual conventions, reminiscing about the old days, which no one called good old days, but which had provided a common bond that was to last for the lifetime of even the youngest among them.

Oriental Hospitality

There were several other countries that served as temporary shelters for Jewish refugees escaping from Nazism. One of them was Turkey, which was in a category apart because the Turkish government actually invited a selected number of refugees. These invitees were almost exclusively teachers, physicians, scientists, and a few others with special qualifications, such as Ernst Reuter, who became after the war the famous Social Democratic mayor of Berlin resisting the Soviet takeover. Strictly speaking, many of those who went to Turkey were not Jews but Christian non-Aryans, half Jews according to the Nuremberg laws, Jews who had converted, or Germans married to Jewish women.

Turkish academic life had traditionally been oriented toward Germany. The Turks thought more highly of German science than that of any other country and they were happy to use the opportunity to invite some researchers and teachers of world renown to help build up the Turkish universities and also provide guidance in other fields. And so about three hundred refugee academics arrived with their families to teach or work in Istanbul and Ankara. Working and living conditions were far from ideal but at least those concerned could pursue work in their field of specialization, which was rarely true in most other countries as far as refugees were concerned. While elsewhere hundreds of thousands of Jews were persecuted, Erich Auerbach could write unmolested his *Mimesis*, hampered only by primitive library facilities.

The Turkish authorities wanted the foreign guests to train "native cadres," which were gradually to replace them; they were invited by contract for a few years only. But the authorities need not have worried, because with all their gratitude to Turkey, virtually no refugee intended to stay in the country permanently. Some emigrated to the United States or other parts of the world even before the outbreak of World War II, others left Turkey as soon as feasible after its end. Not all their memories were entirely happy; most of those who had lost their German citizenship during the war were deported by the Turkish authorities to deepest Anatolia, where living conditions were just barely tolerable.

For the younger refugees Turkey was not an easy country either because the Turks had accepted them only because of their parents. Training and work options were limited. Some young refugees, such as Dankwart Ruestow, became Turkish experts on the basis of their knowledge of the language; Edzard Reuter, the son of Ernst, had a spectacular management career (he became chief manager of Mercedes Benz); and Kurt Laqueur went into the German diplomatic service as soon as it was set up after the war. By 1960, only a few of the refugees were still left and in the years after, virtually all of them disappeared.

In India, Jewish refugees, however distinguished, were not made honored guests. The authorities in New Delhi did not want them; the

Congress party expressed their sympathy on a few occasions but did not want them either because they were anti-Zionist, or to be precise they feared that the arrival of even a small number of refugees would provoke the Muslim politicians. Nehru, to be sure, persuaded the Indian Medical Council to recognize European medical qualifications so that the refugee doctors could practice in India. Ali Jinnah, head of the Muslim League, objected to the presence of refugees because of the Zionist aim to establish a state of their own in Palestine. Gandhi, in a famous letter to Martin Buber, advised the German Jews to sit quietly and to resist nonviolently in accordance with his doctrine of *satyagraha*. Gandhi had some German Jewish pupils who had joined him in India and who tried to explain to him that the situation in Germany was not quite similar to that in India, that the Jews did not number hundreds of millions, but this was all in vain.

It is difficult to fathom why the entrance of a few refugees should have been rejected because of Zionism and Palestine, for those who wanted to come to India were not, after all, Zionists. On the contrary, giving them shelter would have reduced the pressure to set up a Jewish state. But there was little logic in Indian attitudes; whatever the reason, Jewish refugees were not wanted.

However, the country was so big that in the end the entrance of a thousand refugees was hardly noticed. Physicians, dentists, a few scientists, technicians, and some others found a temporary shelter in India. They had come with their families and they stayed for the war years. A branch of the Jewish Relief Organization was set up in Bombay, and as did such bodies in other parts of the world, admonished the refugees to avoid "loud conduct." Even avoiding loud conduct, they were not particularly well treated: soon after the outbreak of the war most of them were detained at Ahmednagar together with real Nazis. Max Born, a future Nobel Prize winner, was told by a British resident (whose name has unfortunately not been preserved for posterity) that a second-rate scientist who had been chased from his own country was not worthy of employment at the Indian science institute at Bangalore.

There were the usual tragicomic situations with the authorities at cross purposes. A young lawyer from Berlin, who was supervising road work in Burma at the beginning of the war, was taken over by the army and made a lieutenant. At the time of the retreat from the advancing Japanese he was arrested in Calcutta as an enemy alien, but

Helmut Hirsch, the young Jew who tried to kill Hitler. Arrested, sentenced to death, and executed in 1936. He had German and U.S. citizenship. Courtesy Mrs. Sugarman.

The Chug Chalutzi, a Zionist youth group, underground in wartime Berlin. Second from the left, bottom row, Gad Beck. Second from the left, second row, Joachim (Jizchak) Schwersenz. Courtesy Jizchak Schwersenz *(Die versteckte Gruppe)*.

Ernest Fontheim spent the war years in Berlin, first as a forced laborer, later in hiding. He arrived in the U.S. in 1946, studied physics, and eventually joined the staff of NASA. Courtesy Ernest Fontheim.

Home of FDJ (Free German Youth), Belsize Park, London, ca. 1943. Courtesy Alfred Fleisch-hacker (*Das war unser Leben*, Berlin, 1996).

FREIE DEUTSCHE JUGEND
IN GROSSBRITANNIEN

(Affiliated to the International Youth Council)

Mitgliedskarte No. 252

Name WOLFF, Liselotte

Adresse 6 Cunningham Rd.

Ort Manchester

Mitglied Seit Nov 1939

Unterschrift.

F.D.J. Leitung.

Membership card, Free German Youth, London, ca. 1944. Courtesy Liselotte Wolf, Berlin.

The team that never won. Soccer in Kibbutz Haelsinggarden, Sweden, ca. 1943. The players are young Jewish refugees. Courtesy Mrs. Judith Rothschild, Stockholm.

The German Squad of the Palmach, Palestine, ca. 1943. This was an elite unit of young German speakers scheduled to be parachuted behind German lines in occupied Europe. Courtesy Givat Haviva.

Esther Herlitz, in command of a unit of Palestinian Jewish women soldiers stationed in Egypt, ca. 1943. Herlitz later became a member of the Israeli parliament and a diplomat. Courtesy Esther Herlitz.

Shimon Avidan (Koch), member of a kibbutz, commander of the German Squad of the Palmach, one of the first generals of the Israeli army. Courtesy IGPO photo archives.

Edith Kurzweil escaped in wartime, at the age of fourteen, from Vienna, to Belgium, to France, to Spain, to New York. She later became editor of *Partisan Review*. Courtesy Edith Kurzweil.

Arms for Israel. Ehud Avriel (Ueberall), born in Vienna, an Israeli diplomat and member of a kibbutz, played a crucial role in the race against time in 1948 obtaining weapons for the newly founded Jewish state. Courtesy IGPO photo archives.

Werner Guttentag arrived in Bolivia at age twenty. Fifty years later, the Bolivian government issued a stamp commemorating his services to Bolivian culture as publisher and editor. Courtesy Werner Guttentag.

Michael Blumenthal went from Berlin, to Shanghai, to the U.S., to Berlin. He became an ambassador, Secretary of the Treasury in the Carter administration, and head of the Jewish Museum in Berlin. Courtesy Michael Blumenthal.

Back to the city of his birth. Gunther Stent in front of the ruins of the Adlon Hotel, Berlin, 1945/46. Courtesy Gunther Stent.

Teddy Kollek, born in Vienna, aide of Ben Gurion and legendary mayor of Jerusalem. Courtesy IGPO photo archives.

PFC Henry Kissinger in Germany, 1945. To his right is Fritz Kraemer. Courtesy Henry Kissinger.

Fifty years after. A reunion of the Kindertransport, London, 1989.

Shanghailander Rickshaw Reunion, Philadelphia, 1999.

soon after released and given the Burma Cross, first class. Moving on to Bombay he was again detained, but when the authorities saw his Burma Cross (of which at the time there were but a few holders), he was again set free.

As the war ended, the refugee families left the country. Max Born went to Britain, where he was not considered a second-rate scientist; Alex Aronson, who had left Germany as a student, continued his studies in Cambridge and had stayed during the war at Tagore's college in Bengal, rejoined his family in Palestine, where he went to teach at the Hebrew University. A few eccentrics remained behind after the war; Anita Desai describes the fate of one of these unfortunates in one of her novels. He was accepted by his neighbors as a harmless madman but was killed by a German hippie, to whom he had offered shelter.

Mauritius, Island Paradise

The strangest waiting room by far was the island of Mauritius. The saga of the Mauritius refugees goes back to the months after the outbreak of the war, and involves German Jewish organizations, a Viennese freewheeling merchant named Storfer, and the Gestapo department dealing with Jewish emigration headed by Eichmann. All of them, albeit for different reasons, had a vital interest in Jews' leaving Germany and Austria, even though emigration had become infinitely more difficult. The transport, as planned, was to consist of thirty-six hundred people. Many of them had visas for Latin America, some genuine, most bogus, but it was understood that the real destination was Palestine. Groups of people from Berlin (about five hundred), Danzig, Vienna, Prague, and some Jews from Poland were to assemble near Vienna, in the Bratislava region, to be shipped down the Danube to the Black Sea, and eventually transported to the shores of Palestine.

There were endless delays—during the winter months the ships that had been acquired could not sail down the Danube; later it was discovered that extensive repairs were needed. Eventually, on August 28, 1940, four relatively small steamers took the passengers to Tulcea, a Black Sea harbor, where they were transferred to slightly larger, seagoing ships, the *Atlantic*, the *Pacific*, and the *Milos*. On all three ships, which were grossly overloaded, there was not enough water, the sailors were drunk almost every evening, the only radio did not function, and every few days the coal ran out and there was no money to replace it in Turkish or Greek ports. Still, the passengers survived, and on November 1, the *Pacific* reached Haifa, the *Atlantic* arrived three weeks later, and after another two days came the *Milos*.

The British had eighteen hundred passengers transferred to a much bigger ship, the *Patria*, without explaining the purpose of the maneuver. The British authorities in Palestine had in the meantime asked London for permission to deport the illegal immigrants to Australia. Their main argument was that there might be enemy agents on board these ships. London turned the Australia plan down and suggested Mauritius instead. But the Jewish organizations in Jerusalem had heard of these plans and decided to prevent the departure by carrying out an act of sabotage in Haifa harbor. A mine was smuggled on board the *Patria*, and it was, as soon became apparent, far too powerful for the purpose. The mine exploded on November 25, at a time when most passengers were on the upper deck,with the resulting loss of more than 220 lives. Following much adverse publicity the British government decided that the survivors of the *Patria* were to be permitted to stay in Palestine. But the deportation of the others went ahead on December 9 against fairly heavy resistance—many passengers had to be carried naked on board the ships that were to take them to Port Louis, Mauritius. These were 1,581 refugees, including 635 women and 71 small children. Having arrived on the island they were taken to a detention camp surrounded by barbed wire and heavily guarded. There was hardly any need to do so because the nearest inhabited place on earth, other than a few small islands, was Madagascar, at a distance of eight hundred kilometers.

Mauritius is a beautiful island and its shores became a major tourist attraction in the last third of the twentieth century. However, this is not how the unwilling travelers saw it at the time; they had no eyes for the marvels of nature, the blue ocean, and the luxurious vegetation. But in the end they had to accept that this island would become their home for an indefinite period. It was a very heterogenous community: The majority were members of Zionist youth movements, idealistic young people eager to go to Palestine and work in a kibbutz. They came from educated middle-class families. Others were anything but idealists and had simply bought themselves into the transport as the only possible means to escape death in Europe. There were tensions between groups of people of different backgrounds and the whole atmosphere became increasingly more depressing because the inmates of the camp had been told that their fates would be decided only after the war ended. No one in 1940/41 could even begin to speculate when this would be.

As the years passed, tensions and irritation in the camp grew, there were manifestations of claustrophobia and even signs of mass hysteria. One of the inmates later wrote that imprisonment caused mental deformation ("It became a real madhouse, no rumor was too stupid to be disbelieved"). Civilized behavior was no longer the norm, and people became inconsiderate and depressive, but there were only two cases of suicide.

The treatment of the inmates was not deliberately cruel, but conditions were very primitive. There was, for instance, no electricity in the camp, and while the commanders of the camp were not hostile (the deputy commander was in fact well disposed toward Zionism, as was the Anglican bishop of Mauritius), many of the regulations were exceedingly stupid. For a long time the inmates were forbidden to read the local newspapers and to listen to the BBC in Czech and Polish but permitted to listen to the German-language programs. When a Japanese submarine was sighted not far from the island, searches for hidden arms in the camp were made. Only in the summer of 1942 were families permitted to meet and stay together. Food was poor, as were sanitary conditions, malaria was common, and more than fifty people died in a typhoid epidemic in 1941. At any given time more than 10 percent of the population was hospitalized.

There was a rich cultural life in the camps, since the refugees included experts on almost any subject, and there was a school for the young and language courses for adults. For most children the school became their real home. There was a camp library and a camp newspaper as well as exhibitions and musical performances. One of the inmates wrote a novel, which was published after the war.

During the last two years of the war, several dozen volunteered for the Jewish Brigade and also for Czech and Polish units, but not all were accepted. Finally, in February 1945, the governor of the island invited a delegation from the camp and told them about the decision of the British government to let those who wanted to proceed to Palestine once the necessary conditions had been created. This caused great jubilation in the camp, the regime became much more liberal, and the

long awaited departure took place in August 1945 when 1310 refugees
boarded SS *Franconia*. It was the first major transport of refugees to
reach Palestine after the war.

What became of the Mauritius detainees in later years? According
to a poll taken in the camp during the war, 61 percent had opted for
Palestine, 10 percent wanted to return to their countries of origin (but
none to Germany), the rest wanted to proceed to the United States,
Australia, and other countries. In the end, as far as can be established,
more than 80 percent did go to Palestine, though some left for other
destinations after a year or two, but others who had gone elsewhere
eventually went to Israel. Thus ended one of the strangest and most
frustrating episodes of the Jewish dispersal. Considering what happened to those who had been left behind in Europe it was a happy ending of sorts; those who were sent to Mauritius lost five years of their
lives, but they lived to tell their story.

Australia, Canada, South Africa: Refugees Need Not Apply

Mauritius was part of the British commonwealth, which consisted of
large, underpopulated countries such as Canada, Australia, and South
Africa, seemingly obvious places for immigrants. Yet the refugees from
Central Europe were not wanted there. All of the dominions taken together took in fewer than the single city of Shanghai. About a thousand refugees landed in South Africa between 1933 and 1935, and almost a thousand in 1936, of whom half came on a single ship, the
Stuttgart. But this number was sufficient to set off a major political
storm, demonstrations, and violent protests. The relatively liberal
government of the day introduced a new Aliens Bill, which virtually
closed the doors of the country. The three Jewish members of the
South African parliament voted for the bill. After 1936 only several
hundred relations of lawful residents of South Africa and some independently wealthy persons were permitted to enter.

The number of those permitted to enter Canada up to the outbreak
of the war was about four thousand and they were almost exclusively
people with means. Australia admitted some seven thousand refugees,
among them two thousand from Austria. To these figures one should
add the refugees who had been detained in Britain, shipped to camps
in Canada and Australia and at the end of the war, when the political

climate and also the economic situation had changed, chose to stay rather than return. The reasons for the rejection of refugees were more or less the same in all three dominions. All three had suffered from the world economic depression and there was the fear that the refugees would steal jobs from the native population. But this explanation accounts more for the early thirties than for 1938/39, when the situation had improved. There was, perhaps most important, the wish to preserve the Anglo-Saxon, Christian character of these countries and not to admit people who might be difficult to assimilate.

The term "race" was seldom used, but there certainly was a feeling that Jews were not the most desirable elements to build the country. There were Nazi and pro-Nazi parties in all three dominions, strongest in South Africa, least influential perhaps in Australia, but there too, there was an antisemitic tradition, though it was social rather than political. Certain professionals, for instance doctors, feared competition by equally or more qualified newcomers. Strong parochialism prevailed in all three dominions, which accounts, in part, for the lack of charity shown by the churches (always with a few exceptions). They simply were not interested in events in faraway Europe. The religious injunction to love thy neighbor, to act as their brothers' keepers did not apparently extend beyond the waterfront.

The Jewish community in Canada was weak and could not exert much pressure even if it had wanted to. In Australia the communities were dominated by the "Anglo" element, which while not in principle averse to helping, was deeply apprehensive that the newcomers would not behave well, antagonize the locals, and thus generate a new wave of antisemitism. Thus Abraham Boas, one of the leaders among Australian Jewry, gave an interview to a leading newspaper in which he argued that there must be no mass immigration to Australia, and this followed a report that two thousand Jews were seeking entry into Australia, each of them with two thousand pounds, which was a great deal of money at the time. As Susan Rutland, an Australian political scientist, wrote many years after: "The Australian Jewish leaders were concerned primarily with maintaining their high social and economic status and feared any change in the status quo. They were not prepared to agitate for the right of entry of their less fortunate coreligionists." The South African Jewish community was more numerous and wealthier, but its leaders too feared a nativist blacklash. This fear paralyzed them.

The experiences of the young refugees varied. Eugen Kamenka, who was to become a leading political philosopher in later years, remembered that

> those who came young were not especially made to feel foreigners in Australia, even less feel rejected. They were far more readily accepted in the state schools by children and teachers alike than in any country I had been in before or have been since. The Melbourne Club and the Royal Sidney Yacht Club were outside my experience—the antisemitism I met as a child came spontaneously from below rather than above.

Kamenka had the good fortune to come with his family and led a somewhat sheltered life (the sins of the parents, he wrote, were on the whole not visited on the children—referring to the manners and accent of the older generation). Those who had come unaccompanied and were housed in hostels such as Larino felt less comfortable. They were isolated and later had fewer educational and career opportunities. Many boys were forced into careers not of their choosing, but a determined minority went on to night classes and even pursued tertiary studies. As a sympathetic matron later wrote about how the girls felt at a particularly sensitive period in their life: "We stood out in a crowd and we did not stand out as fashion models. We stood out as orphanage children. We were in second hand clothes that looked it and had to go to synagogue looking drab." With all this, years later most young refugees had fond recollections of and even felt a certain closeness to Australia, which, as one of them put it, had given them an education and a sense of fairness and freedom that they could not have had elsewhere at the time.

Some young men went to work on farms where they could earn good money and even save. Among them was a group of trainees from the Gross Breesen farm center in east Germany, which has been mentioned. At the outbreak of war, all those over the age of sixteen had to register with the police as enemy aliens, and at eighteen they were drafted into the army, unless they worked in a protected industry, one that was vital to the war effort. Many volunteered for fighting units and saw combat in New Guinea and elsewhere. But the majority, especially those in the detention camps, were taken to "employment units," even though they had been reclassified meanwhile as friendly aliens. This was something akin to the Pioneer Corps in Britain, and involved loading and unloading trains and trucks, building roads,

digging latrines, and doing similar necessary but uninspiring work. As
the war ended, several hundred moved on to Israel or in some cases rejoined their surviving families in America and Europe. Most stayed in
Australia. Their economic situation greatly improved, many established their own businesses, and they became part of Australia and of
the Jewish community in Australia. There was a fair amount of intermarriage, but also a renewed interest in Jewish affairs and support for
Israel even among quarters that had been anti-Zionist in Germany
earlier on. Many visited Israel, some went back to Germany to revisit
the sites of their youth. Most German Jews joined Reform synagogues
such as Temple Emanuel in Sydney, headed for many years by Rabbi
Brasch, originally of Berlin, who had arrived, like some others, via
South Africa.

Forgotten in Calabria

The fates of young refugees from Central Europe trying to escape
during World War II varied enormously. One of the illegal transports
from Vienna got stuck in Kladovo in Yugoslavia and the unfortunate
travelers were shot by the Germans following the occupation of the
country in 1941. Those who were interned in southern Italy, paradoxically, fared better. This is the story of the two thousand inmates of a
camp in Ferramonti, Calabria, in the southeast of Italy, not far from
the city of Cosenza. The internees came from many countries, including Germany, Austria, Yugoslavia, Greece, Czechoslovakia, and even
Albania. The biggest single group were the five hundred survivors of
an illegal ship from Czechoslovakia, the *Pentcho*, which had been
shipwrecked in the Aegean. Among the inmates were some professional painters who had been living in Italy and a leading Jungian analytical psychologist.

The camp had been established when Italy entered the war in June
1940. Mussolini wanted to have concentration camps of his own, and
the original inmates were Jews from Germany and Austria who had
somehow managed to stay on after the racial laws of 1938. The
grounds were bad, the area was marshy and malaria-infested, but the
camp commander behaved humanely, even sympathetically. He
understood the predicament of the refugees better than some of the
camp commanders in Allied countries.

There was a gentleman's agreement between the commander, who believed in self-management, and the inmates, mostly Jewish, about 60 percent German speaking. The Vatican also took a benevolent interest because there were Catholics among the inmates. They had, in short, a great deal of freedom. And so the war bypassed the camp in this desolate area, and when the Allies landed in Sicily and southern Italy in the late summer of 1943, the German divisions on their retreat had neither the inclination nor the time to hunt down the inmates of the camps, who had been permitted by the Italian authorities to escape into the nearby mountains.

The camp continued to function as a transit station under the Allied forces until well after the end of the war. The refugees dispersed; some, especially the Czechs, the Yugoslavs, and the Greeks, made their way back to their homelands; the Jews went to Palestine or the Americas. Thirty and forty years later elderly people from faraway countries were seen from time to time in this distant part of Italy showing their families the site of the camp in which they had the good fortune to survive when the world around them was in flames. These were the ones protected by a guardian angel at a time when angels' visits were few and far between.

RETURNING TO GERMANY

A s the war ended many young Jewish refugees in Allied uniform found themselves back in their native country, often near their places of birth. Corporal Walter Hellendal returned to Moenchen Gladbach on March 15, 1945. The center of the city was destroyed, but some famliar sites, such as the statue of Bismarck, were still intact. On one side a big sign had been affixed: "Welcome to Moenchen Glad- bach, courtesy of the 29th division," with a famous sentence from a Hitler speech in 1940, "Germans, I promise you will not recognize Ger- many in another five years." He went immediately to Regentenstrasse 99, the house where he was born and had grown up, and found it in- tact but not inhabited. In what had been their dining room he cut a lit- tle piece out of their carpet to send home to the United States.

These scenes have been described many dozens of times—often the houses had been destroyed or strangers lived in the apartments. Some- times the soldiers met acquaintances who were greatly astonished to see them again and were, or pretended to be, even overjoyed, telling them how much they had suffered from the Allied air raids and how happy they were that it was all over. Sometimes, albeit rarely, there was a happy ending to the search for family, as in the story related ear- lier of the lieutenant in British uniform who went by jeep to Theresien- stadt and found his parents alive.

Arno Hamburger had gone with youth *aliya* to Palestine in 1939 and had not heard from his parents after that day. In early 1945 he was stationed in Bologna with the Jewish Brigade and hitchhiked in late March to his native Nuremberg. He arrived on a Sunday, did not rec- ognize the city, which was in ruins, and did not find a single acquain- tance. Eventually he went to the Jewish cemetery where he met Mr. Baruch, the keeper, who had belonged to the same Jewish sports group as Arno. ("He went as pale as a ghost.") Were his parents alive? Yes, they lived in a back room in the morgue. He asked Baruch to call the father to come out. The father recognized the son only when he had removed his cap: "He shrieked and embraced me. Then my mother came, saw us embracing and immediately fainted." Arno Hamburger stayed on in Nuremberg and became chairman of the local Jewish community, but only after violent discussions with his father, who told him that he was neither physically nor emotionally capable of starting all over again somewhere else. Arno Hamburger was the only son and he considered it his duty to support his parents, who were at the end of their tether.

Jews in Germany, 1945

Of the Jews living today in Germany, less than a quarter were born in that country and less than 10 percent are of German Jewish origin. True, when the war ended, some two hundred thousand Jews were temporarily on German soil, but these in their great majority were Displaced Persons from Eastern Europe. By the end of the 1940s, all but fifteen thousand had left Germany and migrated overseas, primarily to Israel and the United States. There was some remigration of German Jews in the years that followed, but by and large the Jewish community was aging, the birth rate was low, and between 1950 and 1990 the number of Jews in Germany did not exceed thirty thousand, to which perhaps another ten thousand who were not registered as Jews should be added, and perhaps another two thousand registered in the East German Jewish communities. About a third of them lived in Berlin, six thousand in Frankfurt, and four thousand in Munich. Public opinion polls showed that when asked the great majority of Germans vastly exaggerated the number of Jews they thought were living in their midst. They thought the number of Jews was at least a million if not more.

The number of Jews in Germany increased in the 1990s, with the great exodus from the Soviet Union. However, a third of those who came, probably more, were not Jews but the non-Jewish partners of Jewish immigrants or non-Jews who pretended to be Jews knowing that as such they would be given asylum in Germany. Asked why they chose Germany of all countries, some mentioned Russian antisemitism as the main factor, others said that they did not like the climate of Israel or the danger of war, or the fact that their children would have to serve in the Israeli army, and some mentioned their great love of German culture as distinct from their Jewish heritage. Two other pertinent factors were seldom mentioned: the fact that the Israeli authorities under pressure by the ultra-Orthodox made life very difficult for mixed marriages, and the fact that social benefits for new immigrants were considerably higher in Germany than in Israel, let alone in the United States.

Nevertheless, despite the fact that since World War II the Jewish community in Germany has been overwhelmingly Polish Jewish, German Jews long played a leading role in the communal hierarchy. The reasons are obvious: German citizens by birth, with German as their native language, they could negotiate with the German authorities with greater authority than the new arrivals.

Among the first to return from their British exile were Karl Marx and Henrik van Dam, the former a journalist, the latter a lawyer. Marx, in the words of his widow, belonged to a generation that had been deeply rooted in Germany and for this reason he quickly felt at home. She said that he had originally come to help those few who had survived and that the decision to stay was made only later on when the full extent of the disaster dawned on him. He helped to found the Central Council of Jews in Germany and also a weekly named *Allgemeine Juedische Wochenzeitung*, which in the beginning was independent but later became the official organ of the Central Council. Marx' office was in Duesseldorf, not by accident, because the majority of the emerging Jewish communities in South Germany were predominantly Eastern European in character and preferred Yiddish- to German-language periodicals. The weekly edited by Marx had a circulation of more than forty thousand, more than twice the total number of Jews in Germany, which is to say that the readership was largely not Jewish. During the early years the attitude of Jewish organizations outside Germany toward these initiatives were entirely hostile—they did not agree with Marx and van Dam that there should be communities and Jewish life in Germany after all that had happened. It took a long time for the Central Council to be recognized by Jewish organizations abroad. Marx and van Dam were later replaced by two younger men, Werner Nachmann and Heinz Galinski. Nachmann's star began to rise in the 1970s but after his death in 1987 it transpired that this colorless

individual had embezzled more than thirty million marks of reparations money. Galinski, who succeeded him, was Prussian both by birth
(he hailed from western Prussia) and in his authoritarian style of management. Born in 1912, he was a survivor of Auschwitz, where he had
lost his young family. A dour man and a model of rectitude, he ran the
affairs of the biggest community, Berlin, from its beginnings in 1949 to
his death in 1992.

It was only after Galinski, with the rise of Ignaz Bubis, that a new
type of Jewish leader came to the fore. He was born in Breslau, then
Germany, in 1927, into a Polish Jewish family, which returned to its
homeland in 1935. While Bubis got his primary education at the Erich
Ludendorff school (*sic*) in Breslau, he retained a slight accent, which
in no way impaired his business and political career. He lost his whole
family, survived several ghettos and camps, and reemerged in East
Germany after the war. At age eighteen he showed considerable apti-
tude as a trader on the black market, which was the only market then
in existence in East Germany; later he moved to Frankfurt, where he
made a fortune in real estate. His business career became the subject
of an antisemitic play by Rainer Werner Fassbinder—antisemitic not
because it was factually untrue but because it singled out the Jew from
among many non-Jews who had engaged in the very same activities.
Bubis was a popular and dynamic figure, very much in contrast to his
somewhat stiff and reserved German Jewish predecessors. He became
well known nationwide and was either loved or hated by the Germans;
he left few of them indifferent. His wealth gave him an independent
status that other Jewish leaders had not had. He died in 1999; in his
last interview he stated that his life's work had been in vain.

The number of young refugees who returned to Germany for good
was small; some of their motives have been mentioned earlier. Most of
them had left families and friends behind in Germany, but these were
no longer alive, leaving only the memories of persecution and death.
German Jewry no longer existed. Twelve years or more had passed
since their emigration, in which time new roots had been grown, new
languages been learned. Their educations and the first steps in their
careers had been taken in the new homelands. Even if there had been
great difficulties in the process of transition, the hardest years were
now behind them, whereas Germany was still in ruins. Their situation
was quite different from that of the older generation, whose memories
reached further back and who had been more deeply rooted in the old

country. The generation of the parents had usually faced far greater obstacles in the process of integration abroad, and this was true with regard to mastering the new language and finding employment more or less in line with their past experience. As Henry Kissinger's father wrote in his will in 1946 on the eve of an operation from which he was not expected to recover: "I know the different conditions in this country which gave a man of my age so little hope for future life [and this] made it impossible for me to be a guide for you both as I would have been in normal times." Some of the older refugees never made it. They had lost their homeland and not acquired a new one, they had become estranged from the place they had come from and they did not feel familiar and comfortable in their new surroundings. They felt a longing for the places where they had been born and grown up even if it had been explained to them many times that the Germany they had known no longer existed. This was true in particular with regard to those who had spent the war years in places like Shanghai, which, quite obviously, had been only a temporary haven.

Young Remigrants

And yet, remigration to Germany even from these places remained small. True, the occupying powers made remigration very difficult, often impossible, and while the East Germans made it known early on that "progressive, antifascist" refugees willing to cooperate in the rebuilding of a new Germany would be most welcome, the political implications were obvious from the beginning. Walter Ulbricht, the Communist leader, reprimanded the writers in East Germany in 1948 for their unhealthy preoccupation with the past, including the experience of exile. What was this good for? It belonged to the past and was no longer of topical interest. If the writers still felt a personal urge to do so, they should not be prevented, but "why should we give them paper for this purpose?" Unfortunately, paper or no paper, for many of those who returned, or wanted to return, the Nazi years were not so easy to forget.

As for West Germany, there were no appeals directed to the refugees to return, except by some individual Social Democrat politicians in later years. As Henrik van Dam, the first general secretary of the Council of German Jews, wrote in the late fifties, no one had waited for the refugees to return and this was true as much for the immediate postwar period as for the later years. The public attitude was at best one of indifference but there was also a considerable amount of anti-emigrant feeling, not exclusively anti-Jewish, as politicians such as Willy Brandt and Herbert Wehner were to experience. Nor was this limited to politicians, as Marlene Dietrich witnessed during her first postwar visit in Berlin in 1960.

There were certain categories of people more likely to return than others, including refugees who continued to be involved in German politics, scientists and artists of renown before 1933 who had not found suitable employment and who were personally invited to return, and German writers and actors who had no public except in the German-speaking countries. Furthermore, there were men and women who had suffered badly from a tropical or subtropical climate, as well as some who had lost their property in Germany and Austria, and hoped to get at least some of it back if they pursued their claims on the spot.

There were a few other categories, such as refugees who were only partly Jewish by origin and who had family left in Germany. But altogether there were very few young people among those who even considered going back. There are only estimates with regard to the number of refugees who returned, but some 2,000 came back between the end of the war and 1952, about a third of them to Berlin. Between 1953 and 1960 some 6,000 more arrived, more than 60 percent from Israel and again, about one third settled in Berlin, more than 800 in Frankfurt, some 350 in Duesseldorf. The number of remigrants might in fact have been higher because not all would register with the Jewish communities. On the other hand many of those who did register did not stay for long. In any case, the majority of those who returned were well over fifty years old, and their children often did not remain in Germany but returned to Israel or went on to other countries. As Zvi Azaryah, the Cologne rabbi, wrote: "The children of the remigrants experienced in their young hearts the deepest disappointment, and the parents had to listen to the bitterest complaints." Among these children was one born in Haifa, whose protest against his transplantation was strenuous, and who had to change school four times in three years. In later years, Jehuda Reinharz became president of Brandeis University.

Why Did They Return?

With all the misgivings and the enormous potential problems, some young people did return and some of them stayed. Why did they go back in the first place? Their stories are quite similar. Alfred Moos, a young Jew from Ulm, had found work in Palestine but he felt that in view of his lack of knowledge of Hebrew and his apparent inability to learn the language, he was never really integrated, whereas in his home town he again became a respected citizen after his return. Alfred Goodman and Helmuth Stern were both musicians. Goodman had emigrated to Britain and later to America, but never found suitable work in his profession. He says that in 1961 he was more or less by accident in Germany and told himself, "Let's try it." He subsequently worked as a musician first in Munich and later in Berlin.

The story of Helmuth Stern is more complicated. He had tried his luck as a violinist first in Charbin, Manchuria, and later in Israel and the United States. When he went back to Berlin he found that their old house was still standing, and he stayed and became a leading member of the Berlin Philharmonic Orchestra. In his own words, he had not become a German patriot; his attachment was to the city of his birth rather than to the country. A similar comment came from Ruth Bratu, a native of Darmstadt, who said, "Strictly speaking I have no German identity, only one of Darmstadt." Kurt Hagen, who had been hiding during the war in Belgium, went back to Germany by accident (his own words); he had a sister who survived in Hamburg. He did not accept German citizenship either. Ernest and Renate Lenart were actors who failed to get a foothold in Hollywood. They tried their luck as photographers, but without much success. Renate Lenart's father (the economist and sociologist Franz Oppenheimer) had been a well-known academic in Weimar Germany. His friends and students, of whom Prime Minister Ludwig Erhard had been one, provided connections that allowed the Lenarts to return.

Among those asked for the motives of their return, the answers "practical reasons only" or "for professional reasons" figured most prominently. Some did not want to go to Israel because they preferred a quiet life to one of war and tension. H.M. had married a German woman abroad who wanted to be reunited with her family, and

Ruth K. had been taken from Hagen in Westfalia as a ten-year-old to Eastbourne, England, with the Kindertransport. She was half Jewish and was informed after the war that her father had returned home. She went to meet her parents, even though she had totally forgotten her German. ("What I told them had to be translated.") But she stayed on.

The scientist Henry Gruen also mentions the emotional link he felt with his hometown (Cologne), even though he had left as a child; his parents, like so many others, had been killed. He went first to England, then to America to study, graduated, and in 1959 revisited Cologne. In 1971 he accepted an offer to work in the Max Planck Institute in his home town, even though he had not spoken German for twenty-five years. Asked whether he had kept his American passport, he replied, "Yes, I do not think much of dual nationality. They took away my German citizenship; if they want to return it, they should come to me and do so."

Peter Max Blank's father, who had been a physician in Cologne, emigrated with his family to France. Peter, who became a Communist, was detained in various French camps and later in Auschwitz. After the liberation he returned first to Paris and later to Germany. As a Communist he had never considered Palestine: "It makes a great difference whether one experienced the cruelties of the Nazi regime as a [class] conscious antifascist or as a Jew." Had he felt like a Jew he would have stayed in the United States as some of his relations did. Did he regret his erstwhile Stalinist convictions? There was no clear answer—Blank does not believe in hindsight, and without the Red Army he would not have been liberated. But it was also true that he had to make compromises after the war; idealism was a beautiful thing but he had a family to feed.

Friedel Schoenfeld had lived in Palestine and mentioned her asthmatic condition as the main reason for her return: "But I know that this condition is frequently psychosomatic in origin. And it could well be that subconsciously I had a longing for Cologne." Once she returned to Cologne her illness did not recur, but the moment she went for a visit to Israel she again fell ill. She had to take antibiotics for half a year after revisiting Israel. Schoenfeld and her friend Anneliese Stern had reapplied for German citizenship ("One has to have some passport, after all."), but another friend, Fridl Liebermann, had kept her British passport even though her husband had applied

for a German travel document. But this involved so many humiliating difficulties that he too desisted. Schoenfeld, Liebermann, and
other women interviewed in the 1990s about their reintegration into
postwar Germany, all agreed that one had to repress memories to live
in this country, and that there always remained a measure of distrust
with regards to members of their generation—what had they done
during the war? Liebermann said that she would on no account have
returned but for the insistence of her husband, who had argued that
they should go for a year or two only. But once they had settled in
Germany it had proved very difficult to take their son out of school
and get him into a school in Britain, and apartments in London were
very expensive, and so in the end they had become accustomed to life
in Germany.

The case of Malka Schmuckler is another illustration of the initiative of the husband in the decision to return to Germany. Born in Nuremberg in 1927, she was the youngest of three sisters. At age ten she
went with her parents to what was then Palestine, joined a kibbutz,
and later went to Jerusalem to study music. She had virtually become
a *sabra* when the war of independence broke out; she served as an officer during the siege of Jerusalem. At about this time she fell in love
with and later married a fellow musician who had also come from
Germany even earlier than she had. But he had strong emotional ties
to Europe, had never understood why his family should emigrate to
Palestine, and even on board ship had studied Italian rather than Hebrew. He became an accomplished soloist and also conducted a popular program on Israeli radio. But he still was not happy in Israel and
went to Germany in the 1950s to study his new field of interest, elec-
tronic music. While in Germany he was offered a position in television, which he accepted with enthusiasm, feeling at home and, unlike
his wife, free from scruples or guilt with regard to his stay in Germany. There followed years of indecision, of traveling to and fro, first
the wife returned to Israel, later the husband joined her and their two
sons, but he felt so unhappy there that he accepted a new offer of
work in Cologne. This pattern repeated itself a few times, and after
long periods of separation, with one son serving in the Israeli army,
Malka realized that unless she joined her husband with the younger
son, who was experiencing serious psychological problems, their marriage would not last. At age forty, she returned to what was for her an
alien country.

Uneasy Coexistence

True, among those who returned from abroad early on there were a few who developed something like a new German Jewish ideology, arguing that Jewish existence in postwar Germany was possible, perhaps even desirable. Among them was Hans Lamm, who returned from the United States first to interpret in the Nuremberg war crimes trial and later became head of the Munich Jewish community. But Lamm was an exception. The majority of Jews living in West Germany were either elderly people who wanted to be left in peace or younger Holocaust survivors who had established businesses in the booming German economy, made a comfortable living, but still felt apprehensive, fearing a revival of the extreme right and antisemitism, sitting on their proverbial packed luggage. They sent their sons and, especially, their daughters to Israel to find a nice Jewish wife or husband, and quite frequently the offspring stayed in Israel. The major German Jewish cultural periodical was called *Babylon* and young Jewish authors wrote books with titles such as *This Is Not My Country*.

The Jewish communities had no rabbis in the beginning; this function was fulfilled in the early days by American military chaplains. Later several refugee rabbis returned: Heinz Gruenewald from Jerusalem to Munich; Zvi Azarya to Cologne, also from Israel; Nathan Peter Levinson from the United States, first to Berlin, and later to south West Germany. Levinson had been among the last Jews to leave Germany legally in 1941, and had studied for the rabbinate first with Leo Baeck and later in the United States.

In East Germany there was no ordained rabbi. Martin Riesenburger, who was made chief rabbi by the Communist government, had survived the Third Reich as a grave digger because he had a non-Jewish wife and was exempt from deportation. He was somewhat shabbily treated by the new authorities, who gave him a car that broke down every few miles and had to be pushed. When the archives were opened, after the Wall had come down, many letters of complaints were found, written by Riesenburger to the Communist authorities, stating that this treatment was unbecoming considering the dignity of his office. After Riensenburger's death, a Hungarian rabbi or at least a cantor *(chazan)* would come for the High Holidays to East Berlin to conduct services.

Not much need be said about the Jewish community in Vienna, which had little, if anything in common with Viennese Jewry before World War II. True, some ten thousand Jews, belonging and not belonging to the Jewish community, live now in Vienna, but the majority are recent arrivals from Poland and the former Soviet Union, with a sizeable number of immigrants from Persia and Georgia who keep very much to themselves and do not mix with their Ashkenazi coreligionists.

Reunification and the Second Generation

Jewish life in Germany continued inside and outside these "liquidation communities," as they were often called, for no one saw much of a future for them. Then, in the 1980s, as the old leadership in which the refugee generation had still played a leading role began to disappear and the gerontocracy was replaced by a younger leadership, something like a renaissance took place in Jewish life in Germany, above all in Berlin. There were a variety of reasons for these new impulses. The number of Jews in Germany increased by leaps and bounds and reached about one hundred thousand in 2000. The budget of the Berlin community alone was forty-seven million marks for education, social work, and other purposes.

As the result of the reunification of Germany, there were new cultural impulses, new synagogues and museums opened in Berlin and elsewhere, new rabbis appeared—Reform, Orthodox, and female—Jewish bookshops opened in Berlin and Munich that were bigger than any that had existed before 1933, and new periodicals started, such as *Berlin Umschau* and *Das juedische Berlin.* The cultural calendar registered several events of Jewish interest for every day, ranging from a performance by Isaac Stern to the most recent klezmer ensemble. There were lectures about any conceivable topic, meetings of Jewish doctors and psychologists, meetings of Jachad (Jewish homosexuals and lesbians), meetings of Kesher, an organization of ex-Israelis, and many more such organizations. If there was a common denominator to all these initiatives it was the belief that they would look forward rather than back. The new president of the Berlin Jewish communities, Andreas Nachama, was the son of a Saloniki Jewish cantor who had survived Auschwitz and moved on to Berlin. Nachama, a man in his forties, had a doctorate from a German university, but he did not have the blue Auschwitz number tattooed on his arm.

What have these activities to do with what was once German Jewry? At first look, little, if anything, except that some of the old names have been preserved and that they take place in the same cities and sometimes streets. But there is, in a curious way, a direct connection, because the leading members of this new generation, especially in the cultural field, are often the sons and daughters of the generation on which our investigation has been focusing. Furthermore, they were among the first to ask some of the questions that go right to the center of our narrative, the question of Jewish secular existence in the modern world and the issue of the heritage of the German Jewish world that has disappeared.

Among the leading spirits of this erstwhile East German group were Peter and Barbara Honigmann, Irene Runge, Jalda Rebling, Annetta Kahana, and Helga Kurzchalia. Peter Honigmann had worked for the Central Committee of the party in East Germany but underwent a religious conversion, left for the West, and became head of the Central Archive for the Study of German Jewish History; Barbara is a novelist; Irene Runge, born in New York, is a key figure in Berlin Jewish cultural life; Jalda Rebling is the daughter of a famous singer. They all have in common that their parents were faithful, even doctrinaire Communists, Jewish or part Jewish in origin, who returned from their exile in or after 1945.

The second generation was educated to be good Communists and in many respects were privileged to belong to the East German establishment. The fact that they were of Jewish origin was seldom if ever mentioned by the parents. In the words of Irene Runge:

> I did not know what Jews are . . . After all that had happened those who returned from abroad did not want to be Jews anymore nor burden their children with this. In our circles it was said that this was a question of religion and we were, of course, internationalists . . . However, in the street this was interpreted in a different way."

Rediscovering a Jewish Identity

During the 1970s and 1980s, these party children began to stray from the party line and discovered an interest in Jewish affairs and traditions. To understand these developments, reference has to be made, however briefly, to the general political background. The policy of the East German Communists toward Jews and Judaism had always been contradictory. Individual Jews were not persecuted, except during the last years of Stalin, and Jewish communities were never banned. Jews were recognized as victims of fascism, but they were considered to belong to a lower species, because only Communists could be true antifascists, and the Jews had been mere passive victims. The fact that there had been Jewish antifascism was kept quiet or at least played down. Furthermore, everything was done to expedite the end of any organized Jewish activity in East Germany. The number of members of Jewish communities in East Germany was initially about two thousand but gradually dwindled. It was perhaps symptomatic that the heads of all East German Jewish communities escaped in one night to West Germany in the early fifties.

The total number of Jews who did not belong to East German Jewish communities was considerably higher, perhaps ten to twelve thousand and, it is doubtful whether even the Stasi (the secret police) knew their exact number. During the last years of its existence, the East German leadership made great efforts to be recognized by Washington, and to that end the good will of American Jews was considered essential. As a result, the Jewish policy of the regime became intermittently somewhat more liberal, and honorary doctorates (to give but one example) were bestowed on leaders of the World Jewish Congress. Nevertheless, in East German propaganda, Israel was still one of the chief enemies, whereas the Arabs, irrespective of their politics, belonged to the camp of progress and peace. The young rebels in East Germany did not become Zionists, they simply advocated greater objectivity in the media. But far more important was their rediscovery of Judaism, an inevitable result of the poverty of the official East German ideology, as well as a vague feeling that they were somehow different from their fellow Communists. Some of them began to attend religious services on the High Holidays, if possible under the cover of darkness, but it is doubtful whether the religious factor was paramount. The Jewish rituals often bored or even antagonized them. They were rather looking for like-minded young people who were dissatisfied with the mendacity of the official party line and, like them, interested in their roots.

Wir Fuer Uns

A circle of friends developed (It was called "Wir Fuer Uns," we for ourselves, which implied a certain common identity.) and, though they engaged in cultural activities together, most remained members of the party, some rejoined the Jewish community, some became religious, others remained secular. As Vincent von Wroblewsky, born in French exile and partly of Jewish origin put it, "We were citizens of Jewish origin, but not of Jewish faith." This belief was common to the East German government and the official Jewish communities. Wroblewsky says, "It was not a matter of religion, but we were conscious of a difference between us and citizens of non-Jewish descent. This issue was important in our life." To the extent that the identification with the East German state became weaker, it led quite a few of the second generation toward a preoccupation with the question of Jewish identity. It also implied a rebellion against their parents, the majority of whom had done all they could to distance themselves from their Jewish origins, which they regarded as an embarrassment. While young Germans often asked their parents, "What did you do in the Third Reich?" the young Jewish rebels asked their parents, "What did you do after 1945? What became of socialism in your time, why did you fail to reveal your identity?"

These critics believed that Judaism was more than the synagogue liturgy, more than a single-minded preoccupation with the Holocaust, more than klezmer music, folklore, and a nostalgic glorification of the Eastern European shtetl, and that, at the very least, one should explore the heritage of Judaism with regard to the present world and the future. This they did with considerable energy, and if a fresh impetus was given to Jewish life in postwar Germany through discussions and study groups, it came from the East rather than the West. Wir Fuer Uns became in 1990 the Berlin Juedischer Kulturverein, in contradistinction to both the official Jewish communities in both West Berlin and East Berlin, which the founders considered both bureaucratic and sterile.

The Kulturverein was secular but it revealed an interest in Jewish religion. Thus the members of the predominantly Eastern European Jewish communities in West Germany were primarily interested in their business affairs and professions with little more than a traditional, perfunctory interest in Jewish activities, whereas the erstwhile young Communists from the East, mainly of German Jewish origin and mainly intellectuals, showed considerably more genuine interest in their heritage. Their searches may not lead anywhere beyond the vague feeling that is difficult to explain that they have a certain mentality in common. It is certainly too early to speak about a genuine Jewish renaissance in Germany. Figures mean little, especially since the Russian immigrants have swelled the membership in the communities, but they keep largely apart, have a culture (or at least way of life) of their own, and have little interest in the soul searching of the young ex-Communists. These Russians are far more Russian than Jewish, just as most German Jews before 1933 were more German than Jewish. If they want to assimilate, it is to German culture (or the German way of life); their Jewish roots are largely meaningless beyond vague childhood reminiscences of their grandparents and the reading of quaint Sholem Aleichem stories, which belong, as they see it, to a Russian subculture rather than a specific Jewish tradition.

With all this it is too early to write off the spiritual searches of the East German ex-Communists for Jewish traditions and values. If these searches for a third (secular) way fail, they will fail everywhere—outside Israel, that is. The fact that they are few is not of decisive importance: new spiritual impulses are seldom generated by masses of people; the Jewish cultural renaissance after World War I, for instance, was the work of a handful of people in and near Frankfurt who established the famous *Lehrhaus.* The intellectual interests of most Russian refugees of the 1990s might be limited, but they have children, many of whom will acquire a higher education, and some of whom, in due time, will ask questions similar to those that were raised by the rebels of 1990, the second and last GDR generation.

German Jewish Writers: The Postwar Experience

So much, then, for those who returned to Germany after World War II, and the curious fate of their offspring. But there was yet another category, the refugee German writers, many of whom returned to the country of their birth. The situation of German writers in exile, like all writers cut off from their reading public, was desperate, with the

exception of a very few of world fame, such as Thomas Mann and
Lion Feuchtwanger (whose books were widely read in America), or a
few of the younger ones who made the transition to English (Arthur
Koestler) or French (Manes Sperber, Ernst Erich Noth). It is therefore
more remarkable that some writers did not return, rather than that so
many did. But the return of the older generation, with a few exceptions like that of a "classic" such as Thomas Mann, was not a success,
and in many cases it turned into a disaster. True, the East German
government had invited some of the bigger names and treated them
royally, at least by the standards of the GDR. But it is difficult to think
of a single one among those who returned who did his or her best
work after 1945, and they must have been aware of this. In other
words, those who returned to East Germany, such as Arnold Zweig,
served mainly as ornaments, useful for signing political manifestos
for peace and against war and in praise of a government that treated
them so well.

The fate of those who went to West Germany was worse, materially
if not morally. The authorities had no particular interest in literature
and the arts, and the public was preoccupied with the economic mira-
cle. Literary fashions had changed since the twenties and early thirties, and writers once popular had lost their reading public. The
largely Jewish readership in old Berlin West had disappeared, and so
had their publishing houses and journals in which they were published. Perhaps they had forgotten that the German (not left-wing, not
Jewish) public had always preferred Carossa to Alfred Doeblin, and
Agnes Miegel to Arnold Zweig or Ernst Toller.

The refugees of the older generation were bitter following their exile
experience, and over the years, when they were largely ignored, they
became even more bitter. They had hoped that West Germany would
be a country that had radically broken with Nazism, a strange delu-
sion, for quite obviously the German people that had lived through the
Nazi years was still largely the same, and remained the same until a
new generation appeared on the scene—only the leading figures of the
Nazi era had been removed. Many of those who returned expressed
deep disappointment, feeling that this was not their state, no one
needed them. A few, such as Alfred Doeblin, left Germany for a second
time. Some of them had delusions about East Germany, where, they
thought, a truly free society had come into being, and where sometimes their old books were reprinted. In fact, not a few refugees who

had settled in East Germany voted with their feet (including Ernst Bloch, Hans Mayer, and Alfred Kantorowicz), as did the intellectual dissidents of the seventies and eighties, whereas no one moved from West to East.

A new, younger literary establishment came to the fore in West Germany, Group 47, which was at least as critical of the political and social order as the returning refugees. But this was a new generation with a different style and different literary preoccupations, and they, too, ignored the literary refugees who had returned.

What of those who were too young to have published before their emigration, who began to write only after the war? None of these writers was older than twenty when Hitler came to power, and some were considerably younger, and the question immediately arises: why should they have become *German* poets, writers, or playwrights? Some had no doubt from the beginning that this was their avocation. When Erich Fried arrived in London at age seventeen and was asked by the interviewer of the rescue committeee what career he wanted to pursue, he replied that he wanted to be a German poet. He was advised not to mention this again and went to work as a factory worker and glass blower before finding employment at the British Broadcasting Corporation. Obviously these aspiring writers must have had a good grounding in the German language, an attraction to German literature, and a belief in their ability to express themselves, not just precisely and clearly, but elegantly and profoundly. In other words they felt that they had not only something to say but also the talent to do so.

Age was of decisive importance. Jenny Aloni was a mere five years older than Yehuda Amichai, yet Aloni remained wholly unknown in Israel, even though she wrote on Israeli subjects, while Amichai became something close to an Israeli national poet and writer. Mascha Kaleko was less than ten years older than Jenny Aloni, but she had become a famous figure in the last years of the Weimar Republic; she never mastered English or Hebrew, and her life in America, and later Jerusalem, ended in tragedy. Many of the young wrote their first works in languages other than German (Peter Weiss in Swedish, Marcel Reich-Ranicki in Polish, Paul Celan in Rumanian, Wolfgang Hildesheimer in English, Maxim Biller in Czech).

Beyond this, it is not easy to find common features in their work or its reception. Some wrote about their experience in Nazi Germany, about emigration and the Holocaust; others essentially ignored these themes. Many of them preferred to publish in Germany but to live in other countries, Weiss in Sweden, Hildesheimer in Switzerland, Amery in Belgium, Erich Fried in London, Celan in Paris. Hildesheimer explained this with reference to the asthma from which he suffered. Weiss played for many years with the idea of returning (to East Germany) but never did. Erich Fried held readings each year for mass audiences in Germany rather than his native Austria, but also preferred a foreign domicile. Some of those who did not return to Germany would have agreed with Ilse Blumenthal that her *Heimat* (her home) remained in the German language, but that she had eradicated Germany.

Some of these writers were broken people, as Michael Hamburger (his translator) wrote of Celan, the greatest of this group; he survived the Holocaust in body but not in spirit. (Celan committed suicide, as did Jean Amery and Peter Szondi.) Others, like Reich-Ranicki, were people of tremendous vitality whose experiences during the war in no way affected their zest for life in the years after. Some of these writers were, first and foremost, Communists (such as Stefan Hermlin, who joined the party while still at school) or at least ardent revolutionaries, while others did not believe in political engagement (Celan). Hildesheimer regarded himself a liberal and a believer in social and political reform, but did not think that literature was the right medium to achieve this. As for the reception of the younger writers, they all found their admirers and detractors, but on the whole the reaction was friendly. The poems of Hilde Domin were printed in many thousands of copies; few German poets reached such a wide public. Erich Fried was for a while a cult figure. After an uncertain start, Reich-Ranicki became the most influential literary critic in Germany, even though he had been born in Poland, where he spent most of his formative years. But as far as the reach of his knowledge was concerned he had few equals in his time.

The work of others was overrated because they were politically correct, this is true in part for Peter Weiss and in particular for Erich Fried. The poems of Fried on Vietnam and the German terrorists, his relentless perseverance in a posture of protest was clearly in line with the zeitgeist of the late sixties and seventies, but it was bound to go out of fashion after a number of years. This is not to deny his literary talent; his translations of more than twenty Shakespeare plays attracted much praise. His political verse, so often quoted at the time of the great demonstrations, were virtually forgotten even in his own lifetime.

The case of Peter Weiss is more complex. Born near Berlin in 1916, he lived in Stockholm from 1940 to his death in 1982. He began his career as a painter and wrote as a sideline, with limited success, in Swedish. Some of his plays were powerful and attracted much attention in the post-Brecht period. His semi-autobiographical trilogy with the quaint title *Aesthetik des Widerstandes* (Aesthetics of Resistance) found more interest among the professional Germanists than among a wider public. His politics were somewhat confused. In 1967 he thought he had found a spiritual home among the New Left, but at the same time negotiated with the East German leadership about a possible move to East Berlin. Then in 1968 he wrote a play on Trotsky, which, of course, spoiled his chances in East Germany; the Communists wanted him to dissociate himself, which he was not willing to do.

Did any of these writers consider himself primarily a Jewish writer? Certainly not the Communists or the sympathizers with the New Left, even though Jewish themes can be found even in Stefan Hermlin, in the later work of Stefan Heym, and of course in Peter Weiss. The most Jewish (and the most famous) of these writers was Paul Celan, born in Czernowitz, who came from a much less assimilated background than those from Germany proper; his German was perfect, but his Hebrew was also excellent. He had been in the camps, and the Holocaust and murder of his parents had been a central event in his life (the other turning point was "Jerusalem"). His "Death Fugue" (originally called "Death Tango") is one of the great poems of our time and was translated more than twenty times into English. He said in an interview that he thought his poetry was not only Jewish thematically but also in spirit. But he added, "I grew up in and with this culture [German], Rilke was very important to me and afterwards Kafka." Seen in this light there was a universalism in Celan's work, as in all great writing, transcending language and theme.

The most influential literary figure in postwar Germany was Marcel Reich-Ranicki, born in Poland in 1920. Later on, his family moved to Berlin, where Reich-Ranicki went to a German school and developed an an abiding interest in German literature, theater,and music. His family was expelled from Germany as were all Polish Jews in 1938, and Marcel spent the war years first as a minor employee of the Warsaw Jewish Council and later in hiding with his young wife. Again, like other Polish Jews of this generation liberated by the Soviet army, he

joined the Communist party, and then served as a junior diplomat in
London, and also briefly as an official of the Polish secret police. However, he fell into disfavor, was excluded from the party, and earned his
living as a translator from the German and commentator on recent
German literature. His literary beginnings were more or less within the
obligatory Communist parameters but, after his defection to West Germany he developed an approach of his own and became Germany's
most respected but also most feared and most embattled critic. Unique
perhaps in German literature in the twentieth century, he also became
a critic known to millions, thanks to television—showing, even at an
advanced age, a temperament uncommon in literary circles, but one
highly conducive to success in this medium. In brief, Reich-Ranicki
was a phenomenon, combining solid knowledge and judgment with a
high degree of showmanship.

To what extent was Reich-Ranicki a Jewish or refugee phenomenon? He would not deny his origins nor ignore writers of Jewish descent. He thought highly of many of them and called them disturbers
of the peace, the title of one of his collections of essays. But his interest
in things Jewish was minimal. He did not think of himself as a rootless
person, he believed in a portable homeland. A *Heimat* that could be
transported was, as he saw it, not the worst kind of home. And, "literature, or to be precise, German literature" was for him a *Heimat*.
Whether literature (or arts or science) can replace a home is an interesting and probably unanswerable question. All that matters is that for
some in Germany and elsewhere, literature and the arts served this
function. For this reason Reich-Ranicki is of interest not just as a formidable figure but as a symptom.

The story of his life is similar in some respects to the career of another well-known writer in postwar Germany, Jurek Becker. He too
was born in Poland in 1935, but his father had earlier lived in Bavaria,
and the two of them returned to East Berlin in 1945. Jurek had survived as a young boy in a camp, his father in Auschwitz. The novel
that made him famous, *Jakob the Liar*, is the story of a Jew in a ghetto
who, in order to encourage his fellow Jews, spreads stories that the advancing Russians are much nearer than they really are. His authority
rests on listening to a radio that he allegedly kept in a secret place in
violation of the strict Nazi ban.

Whether the story bears any resemblance to life and behavior in the
ghetto is a moot point; Jurek's father refused to talk to his son for a

year after the publication of his book. It was an original and powerful
story, and Becker returned in passing to Jewish topics in his later
works. But he certainly did not consider himself a Jewish writer; when
asked about his attitude to things Jewish, he always replied, "My parents were Jewish." The attitude toward him in East Germany was ambiguous: *Jakob the Liar* should have been a movie sooner, but was not
passed by the censors for many years; on the other hand, he received
the National Prize of East Germany, the highest award, though that
did not prevent the suppression of his later books. He eventually left
East Germany and settled in the West, but more for reasons of personal loyalty to some of the other dissidents who had been expelled
than of deep ideological commitment. He observed on more than one
occasion that he would have stayed in East Germany if his books had
been published there. He died in 1997.

Reich-Ranicki belonged to the generation that came of age under
Hitler, whereas Becker's earliest recollections are of life in the camps.
What of the generation born even later, during or after the war, which
produces what is now known as German Jewish writing? They are a
motley crowd: some were born in Israel (Rafael Seligmann); others
were born in hiding during the war in Eastern Europe (Robert Schin-
del) and in America (Irene Dische, Peter Jungk); and some after the
war in Germany and Austria (Hans [Chaim] Noll, Esther Dischereit,
Barbara Honigmann, and Robert Menasse). Some do not write in German but in English (Irene Dische) yet are considered German writers
because they reside in Germany. They are relevant in this context only
because their books are published in Germany, and because some of
them are the children of the younger refugee generation.

Most of their readers are bound to be German, but why should German readers be interested in what is at most a subculture or a "minor
culture" (postmodern literary theory, Deleuze and Guattari are quoted
in this context)? Interest in things Jewish did not exist in the 1950s and
1960s, when there was, in fact, considerable resistance against a preoccupation with the recent fate of European Jewry and Jewish topics in
general. This was the case, by the way, not only in Germany; Primo
Levi had to look for many years for a major publisher for his books.
Such interest was awakened only in the late 1970s; and what exactly
caused it is not quite clear but it followed the television coverage, both
documentaries and feature films, of the persecution of the Jews. Jewish
topics became interesting at almost every level of sophistication, partly

because of the realization that they belonged to a past that had not yet been mastered, but perhaps even more because they were considered exotic, yet somehow familiar. It is likely that there will be similar interest if Sinti and Roma, Turks and Kurds one day produce their own young writers, born in Germany and educated in the German literature seminars of the universities. In fact, the process has already begun.

Generalizing about this young German and Austrian Jewish writing is bound to be unfair, since generalizations cover both serious, talented writers and other, to put it cautiously, more ephemeral figures. Beyond an inchoate and free-floating anger, it is difficult to find what message they wish to convey. They are angry with their parents who brought them to Germany (and Austria) from exile, but they would probably have been equally angry if they had not returned. They are angry with present-day German society and individuals. They are angry with their fellow Jews, with Israel, and with the media. These angry young people, now in their forties and fifties, want to get away from the dead and the Holocaust ("the whole Holocaust shit," in Biller's words), but they are obsessed with what happened to their parents and grandparents. Fed up with both Germans and Jews, some writers have moved to other countries (Honigmann, Jungk, and Korn to France, Noll to Italy, and so on). But they still are not interested in France and Italy, and Israel interests only a few as an abstract place in search of religion or identity. Their repertory is limited: they want to shock by attacking a philistine Jewish establishment interested only in money making and a German society distinguished mainly by xenophobia, arrogance, a false philosemitism, and a lack of tact.

The reasons for their heavy preoccupation with Jewish affairs and German Jewish relations is not always obvious. Irene Dische and Esther Dischereit, two of the leading female writers, were children of mixed marriages, and the former was brought up a Catholic in the United States. Some of the male writers have been called the children (or grandchildren) of *Portnoy's Complaint* on a lower level of intellectual sophistication. But while Philip Roth at least succeeded in annoying a fair number of people, his German pupils, in trying to be sarcastic for the better part of their work, mainly generate boredom. It is difficult for someone not belonging to this generation to judge whether they express a mood not only of their own but of a broader stratum.

In contrast to the activities of the second generation in the former East Germany, of Wir Fuer Uns and the Kulturverein, the new German

Jewish writing is of no visible relevance for the understanding of the refugees of the 1930s and their subsequent fate. Only some of the young Jews now writing in German are of German origin; more hail from an Eastern European background. Even if their parents were German Jewish by origin, they did not live in a German Jewish milieu, and their knowledge of and interest in the German Jewish heritage is limited. Just as the Jewish communities at present in Germany can in no way be regarded as the successors of the communities that once existed, just as Ignaz Bubis could hardly be considered the heir of Leo Baeck, it is pointless to look for the origins of Rafael Seligmann or Irene Dische in Paul Celan and Peter Weiss, let alone in Kafka and the German Jewish writers of the 1920s. There is such a relationship, not just a biological one, between the young refugees of the thirties and forties and their children's generation in the former East Germany. This is an issue we will confront at the end of our story, where we will ask whether there is a heritage and of what it consists.

We have described the first encounter of the young refugees from Germany and Austria with their native country in 1945, when soldiers and officers entered German cities and villages with their units, in American, English, French, and even Palestinian uniform. Many were in fighting units, others came and stayed for a while as translators and public relations officers. Then, during the fifties and sixties, there was a certain amount of remigration, limited in number but still of interest in view of the motives that led refugees to return to a country from which they had been expelled and in which so many of their families and friends had perished. But there was yet another kind of encounter, the visits in later years to Germany and Austria, motivated by an urge to see again the places of their childhood and the graves of their ancestors. Some of those who had escaped Germany resolved firmly never to set foot again on German soil and kept their resolution to the end of their days. Others who had been equally averse changed their views in time, as new generations came to the fore in Germany and the one that had been involved actively or passively in the Nazi era disappeared. A person aged sixty in 1990 could not possibly have served in the army during World War II, let alone have been a member of the Nazi party. This consideration as well as others brought about a change in attitude. Hermann Broch wrote to a friend in 1947 that after the expulsion from Spain in 1492, Jews had not set foot on Spanish soil for centuries, and how could one react differently after the horrors of World War II? Manes Sperber wrote in his autobiography that one day during the war he decided never to go back. On this day he had heard what had happened in Auschwitz and Treblinka, in the Baltic countries and Russia. "I ceased to be an emigrant even before the time had come to look for a new Heimat." This was the reason that he was now at home in France.

But Sperber did not mind returning for visits nor, in all probability, would Broch have minded in later years. The first to visit Germany to accept a literary award, the Hamburg Goethe award, was Martin Buber. The prize had been awarded in 1949, and when Buber went, only two years later, to the German city to accept it, there was much criticism in Israel where Buber then lived. During the early years after the war, there was an unofficial ban on German language and literature in Israel, Israeli passports were stamped with a special note that said "valid for all countries except Germany," and, when the issue of reparations became topical, there were not a few individuals who refused to accept pensions from the German government. However, as the years passed, the majority of those who had left under Hitler did not hesitate to return for a visit.

Fifty Years After: Revisiting the Places of Their Birth

Up to about 1960 such tourism was rare, and few could afford it except perhaps for professional reasons. Almost all these visits were private in character, but from the 1970s, many German towns began to invite groups to visit as the guests of the municipality of the place in which they had once lived. According to an inquiry made in 1994, at least 120 cities in West Germany had such schemes, and the total number may well have been even larger. Altogether thousands of former German Jews, most belonging to the younger generation of refugees, revisited the place of their birth in the framework of these schemes. Some cities, such as Frankfurt, also published occasional circular letters for the benefit of former citizens, and many hundreds of books were published in the 1970s and 1980s dealing with the history of Jewish communities in even very small places—including communities that no longer existed.

The reactions, in interviews, of those who participated in these group visits are of interest, because they reflect the feeling of individuals who were not professionals, writers, or journalists. Reactions ranged from bitterness, arguing that the invitations had come too late, that those invited were too old and too frail to come for a visit, to an expression of profound gratitude that the person invited was given the opportunity to perform toward the end of his life in the very city in which he had been born and made his first steps as a musician (Horst Prentki, born in 1922, who had emigrated to Uruguay). Another native of Berlin, born the same year and then a resident of London, took exception to the frequent emphasis on Berlin as *Heimat.* How could one consider as *Heimat* a place in which there had been so much persecution and suffering? The phrase "place of birth" would be appropriate, but not *Heimat.* When asked about their attitude toward Germany, many mentioned a love-hate relationship—love for the language, the landscape, and the culture, but also hate (Eva Herrmann). Another visitor, Ursula Neville, born Ursula Levy in 1920 and later a resident of Dundee, Scotland, said that hatred was perhaps too harsh a word. Still, she said, "When I open my mouth, people think I am a German, but I am not."

At the same time, many visitors took a positive view as far as the initiative was concerned. In particular, they mentioned the productive discussions with young people, in schools and elsewhere. They visited the houses where they had lived, the streets in which they had played, the schools they had attended, and found it moving. But quite often the houses, streets, and schools no longer existed; the face of Germany had changed. The visitors were glad that they had come, and equally glad to leave again. For some it had been psychologically necessary to lay certain ghosts to rest. As a woman returning with her daughter to her native Vienna put it, "I had one last urge to stand once more at the railing of the bridge and look at the Vienna woods. I had yearned for this lovely, unspoiled view of the hills for many years." But seeing it again made it possible for her to separate herself from it, retaining it as a symbol of a happy childhood: "As I stood on the bridge, the yearning for a memory faded, to be replaced by a strong desire to go home, my real home, America."

Where Is My Home?

The question "Where is my home?" did of course preoccupy young refugees after the war. Ruth Bondy, born in Prague, was sixteen when the war broke out. She was bilingual, but the poems she wrote as a girl were mostly in German. She survived Theresienstadt, Auschwitz, and typhoid fever in Bergen Belsen. In June 1945 she was repatriated to Czechoslovakia, and she relates in her autobiography how upon reaching the Czech border they left the truck for a few minutes singing "Kde domov muj," ("Where Is My Home," the Czech national anthem). It was very moving, but she felt, at that very moment, that Czechoslovakia was no longer her country. Three years later she went to Israel and has had a respectable career as a journalist, a radio personality, and a biographer. She felt content in Israel; to be a secular Jew there was no problem as it was in other places. Did she ever fully belong as a native-born Israeli did? Of course not. But this was only to be expected, and this problem, if a problem it was, would no longer confront her daughter.

The young Germans who interviewed the young refugees of the 1930s returning for a visit and the professional Germanists researching the problems of exile tended to exaggerate the psychological consequences of being uprooted. Or, to be precise, they failed to see the difference in the psychology of the older and the younger generations. The older, who had been far more deeply rooted, were bound to experience the separation strongly, to feel a longing for a world they had known, which no longer existed. The younger ones among them, asked fifty years after the event how it felt to have lost their *Heimat*, were much less nostalgic and often failed even to understand the question. As one of those asked, a woman from Vienna, put it, she had gained a new home, Israel, which was very dear to her, and for this reason she was not living in exile, and requested to be exempted from investigations into the mentality of rootless refugees. This was true not only for those who had found a new home in Israel, but also for many others, who, however interested they were in their origins and the familiar sites of childhood, did not devote much thought to Germany, and if they did, unlike Heine, did not spend sleepless nights as a result. Furthermore, the historians and psychologists of the German Jewish emigration exaggerated the consequences of uprootedness, partly perhaps because they sought to interpret it in the light of a past age, when the lack of *Heimat* meant (to quote a famous Nietzsche poem), "Weh dem, der keine Heimat hat," soon winter will come, woe to him who has no home. True, for some of the refugees, especially those who had gone to countries that, unlike Israel or America, had not been built by immigrants, getting accepted constituted major cultural and psychological problems. Thus Ms. Neville of Dundee, who was mentioned earlier on, noted with some obvious sadness that "if I open my mouth at home [in Dundee] people recognize that I am a foreigner. Thus I am a stranger everywhere."

Similar testimony can be found elsewhere, and some people may have felt it more acutely than others. But it is also true that an Englishman, too, would be considered a foreigner in Dundee, as would, probably, a Sassenach (a lowland Scot). The importance of the urge for *Heimat* and belonging and roots should not be dismissed, but it has certainly declined in importance in the age of the airplane, with millions of people moving from country to country, when enormous new migration waves have taken place even in Europe, when countries have become far less homogenous than they used to be, when not only a common market but a common passport has emerged in Europe, when a true Englishman may no longer feel at home on a London bus, nor a Frenchman in the Paris metro, when for many of those uprooted, forcibly or by their own choice, the issue of being accepted has ceased to be of paramount importance. In the Middle Ages, the figure of Ahasver, the eternal Jew, cursed to wander from country to country and finding nowhere to rest, did figure prominently. More recently the traces of Ahasver seem to have been lost, even though there are still complaints about being nowhere at home. But there is no certainty that those feeling this pain acutely would have been at home anywhere in a world that has become so fragmented and restless, even if they had never left the place where they were born.

PORTRAIT OF A GENERATION

———◦∾◦———

It has now been over sixty years since the young refugees left Germany and Austria. Of those who had the good fortune to get out in time, probably a majority is no longer alive, and the survivors, in their seventies and eighties, are approaching the end of their lives. For those who have survived it is a time of remembrance. In June 1999, twelve hundred who came to England with the children's transports of 1939 had a reunion in London. There had been earlier reunions in London in 1989 and in Jerusalem in 1994. Another such meeting by members of this group, who subsequently settled in America, took place in New York, and a documentary movie was made on the occasion. In July 1999, four hundred former residents of the twin cities of Nuremberg and Fuerth and their descendants met in Monticello in the Catskills. Those who came with youth *aliya* to what was then Palestine had their reunions and the younger Shanghailanders meet almost yearly in New York, Philadelphia, Los Angeles, Las Vegas, and Israel.

Reunions and Remembrance

The *halutzim* (pioneers) who hid in Holland or tried to reach Spain during the war have their annual conventions. And the graduates of various schools such as the Berlin Waldschule Kaliski and the Haifa technical school, class of 1940, also meet. The group of Gross Breesen agricultural trainees had several meetings, including one in Shavei Zion, Israel; those who went to Australia meet yearly. Among the arrivals in 1938 was a young man named Kurt Danziger, who later changed his name to Denby; for years he had misgivings about their future in Australia and doubts about whether they would ever be truly integrated. He need not have worried; had he lived another few years, he would have been able to listen to the maiden speech of his son, a representative of the Labor party in the Australian federal parliament. There were many dozens, probably hundreds of similar reunions all over the world.

Why should people who came from a certain region or town and shared for a little while a certain experience meet so many years after the event? The answer is not readily obvious. Many of them did not think of themselves at the time as a distinct group. And it is even less obvious why there should be so much enthusiasm invested in the preparations for these meetings. They walked the same streets as children and attended the same schools; they belonged to the same youth and sports clubs; but is this really of such significance after the many years that have passed since their ways have parted? Or did they come mainly out of curiosity to know what has been the fate of their companions of many years ago? Or was it, as one of them put it, a great process of catharsis, of exorcising the ghosts? Or could it be that those who had gone with youth *aliya* to Palestine felt less of an urge to meet again after so many years than the Kindertransport because the former had, by and large, been more fully integrated in their society?

There was laughter and smiling at the London meeting but it was not an entirely joyous occasion. As one of those attending an earlier reunion of the Kindertransport wrote: "On the second day we heard stories with deeply unhappy endings. One after another, speakers went up to the flower bedecked rostrum and told their harrowing tales [of having been abused and forced to slave in unloving households]. They told their stories with tears coursing down their cheeks. I left midway through the second day because I could not take any more."

True, there is a tradition, especially in Germany and also among the Jews of Central and Eastern Europe, of *Landsmannschaften*, of people hailing from the same village or town or region gathering for social events, at dances, in synagogues. But this was at a time when there was less mobility in the world and these associations often had an eminently practical purpose, of mutual help in the new country to find lodging and work. As these functions became less important over the years, the *Landsmannschaften* faded away. But in the case of the refugees of 1933 and after, such groups initially played much less of a role; the refugees were dispersed over the United States and Canada and Israel and the rest of the world, and there was much less cohesion among them. The urge to be together, at least for a little while, seems to be stronger now than decades ago. Very often contact was not kept and it proved very difficult to track down invitees for the reunions of the nineties.

But these reunions also attracted members of a younger generation. At the Monticello meeting mentioned earlier, a significant proportion of those present were born after World War II. The same is true with regard to the London reunion in 1999 of the Kindertransport. Why did they attend, coming, as many did, from afar? The answer most frequently given was that they really knew very little about their parents and grandparents and their lives. They said they found it difficult to live with this lack of history; the Holocaust was the proverbial elephant in the living room—everyone was aware of it, but no one talked about it. Were the reunions to replace their (missing) extended family?

A significant number of those who had left Germany when quite young and who had been fully integrated in their new homelands rediscovered in their later years an interest in their origins that they had not felt before. Michael Blumenthal had gone with his parents to Shanghai in 1939 and had risen to the top of the corporate world less than three decades after his arrival in America. He had also been a top-ranking member of President Carter's administration, a man wholly Americanized. But he volunteered to head the new Jewish museum in Berlin in the nineties. Josef Porath, a senior member of the Mossad, had been present at its creation and undertaken many delicate missions, such as representing it for years in Morocco. But, in his retirement, he became active in the association of Jews from Central Europe in Israel. There was the erstwhile Palmach officer thought to be a native-born Israeli by all but his close friends, who late in life became very involved in a group of contemporaries who had come to Israel from Koenigsberg in East Prussia, once a German city and now part of Russia. It was certainly not nostalgia that motivated these men and women, the wish to recapture a past that had disappeared long ago. If so, what drove them—a wish to know more about their origins?

No emigration wave has ever produced so many written accounts, published and unpublished. They cover their youth in Germany and Austria, the circumstances of leaving, their arrival in the new country, their subsequent fate in war and peace. There are several thousand such memoirs, some admittedly quite short, others full-length books, not to count the oral histories. There are circular letters and bulletins, some of which have been published at irregular intervals since the late 1930s.

Those who put their recollections on paper must have felt that something extraordinary had happened to them. They had the urge and perhaps a feeling of obligation to share what they remember with their families and friends and perhaps an even wider circle of people. They felt that they had been lucky not just to survive, unlike so many of their friends and contemporaries, but to build a new life in what were, initially at least, adverse circumstances. Many of them realized, some perhaps belatedly, that they owed their survival to a great measure of good luck. Some were fortunate: their families had money or close relations abroad, their parents were both farsighted and wealthy, they could leave fairly early or they were quite young when they departed and others took care of them. But a majority was less fortunate: they had only distant relations or acquaintances abroad, if any, and whether these would provide guarantees for them was doubtful, as was whether they would obtain in time all the necessary stamps, visas, police permissions and confirmations, results of medical examinations, and ship tickets.

Survival: The Role of Accident

The role of accident in survival was often crucial and it has not been sufficiently stressed in our account. The case of the young Italian partisan from Vienna has been mentioned; looking at the corpse of a close friend executed by Italian fascists a few hours before liberation, he thought how easily this might have been his fate too. Irene Kirkland, a native of Prague (and in later life the wife of Lane Kirkland, head of the AFL/CIO), relates that arriving on the railway ramp in Auschwitz she and her twin sister, though near sighted, had not been wearing their glasses out of vanity. They could not have known that this saved their lives. Zvi Aharoni, whose name has also come up earlier, has written a book about how he was nine or ten times close to death, escaping by inches or seconds. This does not refer to his experience in war and the Israeli secret service (in which he was a leading figure), but to perfectly ordinary conditions. Hans Rosenthal, one of the stars of German radio and television in the postwar period, was in hiding as a boy in wartime Berlin. He later wrote that on at least six occasions only accident saved him from certain death.

Many of the memoirs written in later years have titles such as *By a Silken Thread* or *Accidental Journey*. As I look at a photo of my class taken in 1935 or 1936, I find that about half survived the Second World War, and that no one could have possibly predicted who would be the lucky ones. The fact that I was able to leave Germany just in time (on the eve of Kristallnacht) depended on a number of paradoxical accidents, stranger than fiction.

Life, to be sure, is full of risks and threats, but this generation faced many more dangers than others, and some survived against overwhelming odds. This is particularly true with regard to those who went underground or managed to cross the borders in wartime to a neutral country. Quite often they owe their survival not just to one accident but to a whole series, a gesture, a word spoken, a meeting with a stranger who proved to be helpful but might equally have betrayed them.

Blind accident decided whether a young refugee in Moscow survived the years of the great purges unscathed or whether he would perish in a Gulag. Accident took one individual to the United States and to a brilliant academic career and his close friends from Berlin or Vienna to a kibbutz in Israel or some dead-end job in a provincial town in Britain. They were equally talented, perhaps equally ambitious. But when they met again forty years later, the new American, be he an academic or a businessman, might well be a great man, his name well known and his authority undisputed, widely traveled, equally at home in New York, Paris, and London, perhaps a little world-weary. He had become a man of the world, whereas his childhood friends, living in a small world of their own, had become provincial, preoccupied with the small problems of their small community, perhaps in awe of their erstwhile comrade and present visitor who had come so far in the world. Yet, in the final analysis, it had been a mere accident that the great man (or woman) had received an affidavit from an American relation in the thirties and later on, after serving in the army, a free college education from Uncle Sam. Otherwise he might have become a tradesman in a British provincial town or a plumber in a kibbutz, whereas the kibbutznik would have been the recipient of honorary doctorates. Without belittling the intellectual level of the academic world and unduly exaggerating the intellectual potential of those who did not have the same chances that were open to their American friend, it is still likely that the brain power assembled in a kibbutz (and not only there) would have been sufficient to staff several faculties in a university.

All this refers to prestige, reputation, and material success. It is another question altogether whether the person who had a great career led a happier life than his contemporary cutting the hedges in the front garden of his little house, whether the former found more satisfaction in life at a deeper level—with his family and colleagues and the world that surrounded him.

But there were also the sad, sometimes tragic, cases of people of this generation, people who got stuck in a backwater and hated it, yet could never get out, of those who never had an opportunity because they were not in the right place at the right time, who were struck by misfortune, be it physical, financial, or political. When asked what they regretted most, not a few members of this generation replied that it was the fact that they left Germany or Austria without a proper education, that all they got were some commercial or technical courses in Australia (or America or Israel or elsewhere) and that for this reason they could never realize their potential.

Gruenfeld and Koszyk-Schiftan, the Story of Two Neighbors

Gerhard Koszyk-Schiftan hailed from an old Silesian family. He lived in the part of Upper Silesia that had been German until World War I, became Polish after 1921, German again in World War II and Polish again after 1945. Many members of his family were deported and murdered, but others survived because there was also non-Jewish blood from his father's side. He was bilingual, as was virtually everyone in Ruda, a small coal-mining town near Katowice, and, somehow evading the attention of the authorities, he was permitted to keep a little shop until the last year of the war, when neighbors denounced him, claiming that it was intolerable that a Jew should continue to live among them.

He got an order to appear for deportation and went to the train station where the people were to assemble. Then and there he decided to disobey orders and went into hiding in a room in Katowice. None of the people in this transport returned. Then liberation came and also

Communism, and after a short while he was again denounced by
neighbors, this time as a collaborator with the Germans (for how had
he survived otherwise?) and also as a class enemy, namely a shop-
keeper. This took him first to prison and later to a marginal existence.
After being exposed to a quarter century of Communist rule (and lack
of medical care) Gerhard Koszyk-Schiftan drank himself to death. He
was a talented man with interests in literature and philosophy as well
as economics. He understood finance and was a good organizer. In
other circumstances, he could have been head of a major business enterprise or, perhaps, even a minister of trade or industry. But after all
these setbacks, he was a broken man, lacking initiative and ambition.
Perhaps there were too many ties of family and friendship, which kept
him in this miserable little town and prevented his escape to the West.
Being cut off, living in a small place in virtual isolation, he did not
know about the possibilities of emigration.

Walter Gruenfeld was born about the same year as Gerhard Koszyk-Schiftan, at a distance perhaps ten minutes by car. He too was bilingual, but studied in Germany, where he had a short political career
at age nineteen, as a leader of the Republican-Democratic Students
Association in Berlin. Like Koszyk-Schiftan he was interested in literature, philosophy, and economics. After Hitler came to power, he returned to his native Katowice and, after the outbreak of the war, following an perilous journey by way of Italy, Turkey, and Palestine,
which lasted some eighteen months, found employment in Mufulira in
the North Rhodesian copper belt. This was the beginning of a successful business career as a commodities dealer.

Accident had taken Gruenfeld to godforsaken Mufulira and had
taken his sister Marianne to Britain, seemingly a safe haven, even before
the war. It was accident again that made Marianne opt for the island of
Guernsey, one of the Channel Islands, which were occupied by the Germans in 1940. The local authorities collaborated with the Germans, and
Marianne Gruenfeld was one of four Jewish women deported from there
to Germany, or to be precise, to a place named Auschwitz, a few miles
from where she had been born. She did not return.

There were those whose lives were cut short by accident, just as others survived by sheer good luck. A young man named Klaus Lebeck, a
schoolmate of mine, was studying hotel management in Nice when the
war broke out. Having been interned by the French, he returned to his
native Germany because he feared that his Jewish mother would be

held hostage if he fled to England, as some of his friends did. This was his first mistake, but it might not have ended in tragedy, because as a *Mischling* who had been brought up as a Christian, he was exempt from deportation. However, during the winter of 1942/43 there were thickening rumors about the Jewish partners in mixed marriages being arrested and killed, and Klaus went to find ways to cross the Swiss border. He was apprehended at a railway station, and a compass and a map were found in his possession. He had been educated to tell the truth, and, instead of preparing a more or less plausible story as others did in similar circumstances, he revealed what his intentions had been. The consequence was Auschwitz. He succumbed within a few months. He might have lived, for he was delivered to Auschwitz as a political rather than a Jewish prisoner; his chances of survival would have been greater if he had belonged to the Communists or another mutual help group. But he was deeply apolitical, a young man trying to save his mother, and such lonely people had few chances to live.

Accident played a notable role in the subsequent fate of the individuals. True, those who went to Britain, not to mention Shanghai or Bolivia, had much greater difficulties acquiring a higher education than those who went to the United States. Some still succeeded because they were exceptionally talented or persistent, or simply lucky. They could still reach the top of their profession or become wealthy, but it is unlikely that one of them could become the foreign minister of his adopted country, as in the United States.

It was much easier to grow new roots in countries that had been built by immigrants, such as the United States or Israel, than elsewhere. Of course, the age of the refugees played an important role. If a Berlin-born American historian (Peter Gay) later wrote that he felt comfortable in America early on, whereas a Berlin-born sociologist (Reinhold Bendix) said in his old age that he never felt entirely at home in the United States, the reason might be not so much personality but the fact that the former was ten years younger than the latter when he first arrived.

Common Bonds

We have been dealing with the young generation of German Jews, those who left in time, the few who somehow survived underground or succeeded in escaping in wartime and also the very few who went back after the war. What did they have, what could they have in common? Was it, strictly speaking, a generation? Ortega y Gasset wrote that a generation consists of people living at the same time and in the same space. But the ways of our generation parted as they left their country of origin, they dispersed all over the world—what could they have in common under these conditions?

True, the element of distance matters less now than it did fifty or a hundred years ago, what with the spread of mass communications and mass tourism. The many reunions have been mentioned, those that brought together people who once shared a common experience. In addition there has been a great amount of intercontinental traveling to see old friends, relations, the sites of one's youth and adolescence, and, of course, the graves of one's parents. This would not have taken place unless there was an urge to do so, and perhaps even a common bond. Those who came with the children's transports to England, or traveled on the St. Louis, or came to Palestine with youth *aliya* still feel, after fifty or sixty years, that what happened to them at the time should be remembered, since it created a certain bond between them.

According to many accounts of these reunions, the participants found a common language quickly and easily, even though they had not seen each other for decades and, in many cases, did not at first even recognize each other. After all, they had not known each other that well at the time, and their life in common had lasted only a few weeks, months, or years. But as for war veterans, or for graduates from a British private school with their old school ties, these had been the most impressionable years of their life. They had been the time of rescue from almost certain death, and the first months in a new country in which everything was new and strange.

Their exchanges, joyous and sad, would not keep them busy and excited for more than a few hours. But there was still the feeling of a common experience to which outsiders had not been privy. It had been their St. Crispin's Day, when they had been present at a great and traumatic event, which made them, with only a little exaggeration, brothers and sisters forever.

The young refugees from Central Europe had a certain background in common. The majority was middle class, they had a common language and a similar education, they had watched the same movies at the time and the same soccer games, they had grown up with the same hit songs, and they understood the same allusions. The impact of Germany was stronger if they had spent at least some of their formative years there. Departure was less traumatic, or not traumatic at all, if all they remembered was kindergarten and a few years of primary school.

With emigration their ways parted. In the United States there was strong resistance against immigration in the 1930s and America took in proportionally fewer refugees than the other Western countries. But once the refugees had entered, they enjoyed rights equal to the natives', and few careers were closed to them in later life. In Palestine, they faced difficult years of adjustment in the beginning. There were social and cultural problems of integration, but those willing (and young) enough to make the effort usually did find their place in the new society. The transitional shelters have been mentioned, ranging from Shanghai to Bolivia; in between there were countries ranging from Britain to Argentina which accepted a certain number of refugees but expected a major effort on the part of the newcomers to assimilate themselves to their way of life.

This was not too difficult for the very young, who, within a short time, were speaking the new language without a trace of an accent and quite often forgot their native language. But for those who had not grown up with English nursery rhymes and cricket and fish and chips, integration was far more difficult. Many realized later in life that though they were holders of British (or French) passports they were still regarded as foreigners. This greatly bothered some of them, and for others it was largely a matter of indifference or even amusement. In any case, integration was much less of a problem for the next generation, for they would not stand out as alien elements. In the postwar period, children of the refugees would become business executives, presidents of universities and English public schools and even air commodores in the Royal Air Force. Eventually, even the head of the British Council, the organization scheduled to propagate British culture and its way of life abroad, was a man who had arrived as a little boy from Vienna.

Hiding the Origins

Little has been said so far about the attitude of the young refugees toward Judaism. In their overwhelming majority they were Jewish by origin, at least according to the interpretation of the Nuremberg laws, that is to say with at least one Jewish parent. But in its majority, German Jewry had been highly assimilated, and most families felt primarily German and only incidentally Jewish. A substantial number had tried hard to distance themselves from their Jewish origins, either by converting or simply by becoming lapsed, non-Jewish Jews. Some had deliberately suppressed his or her Jewish origin, keeping it secret, others had tried to ignore it as a matter of little consequence. This syndrome could be found among many of the young refugees who had returned to East Germany after the war from England and other Western countries. Annette Kahane, the child of such parents (good friends of the famous Viktor Klemperer), wrote that, in retrospect, her parents and their friends had certain features in common, but that these, for the better part, could not be articulated. This meant their Jewish origin and their persecution as Jews under the Nazis, and it also referred to their fear and distrust of the (East German) people and the authorities. But they still had their dream of a better world for which they were working and for which a price had to be paid. They also had the memory of the country of exile where (the children surmised over the years) everything had been freer and easier.

Chaim Noll and Barbara Honigmann were born in East Germany after the war; their parents were well-known Communists. Noll writes in his autobiography that he was told at home that only class origin mattered—as for Jews, "there is no such thing anymore." (Noll's father was a popular writer of non-Jewish origin, only his mother was Jewish.) And Barbara Honigmann said of her parents, "They had come to Berlin to build a new Germany, which was to be altogether different from the old Germany and therefore the Jews had better not be mentioned anymore."

This syndrome could be found as often on the right as on the left of the political spectrum. Readers of the memoirs of the great Austrian economist Ludwig Edler von Mises (to give but one example) will learn that he was born in Eastern Galicia but will not find a single reference to the fact that he was born a Jew. In the nineteenth century, German Jewry had lost most of its established upper class to conversion, including the entire Mendelssohn family. This provoked a great deal of criticism and contradiction within the community, and even the attitude of the most liberal Jewish leaders toward the converts was one of disdain. They were attacked as renegades, sacrificing honor and conviction in order to gain recognition. They were called cowards, who, through their action, justified the antisemitic allegations that Jews were unscrupulous opportunists.

These attacks were justified inasmuch as most apostates did not convert out of religious conviction. A Jewish intellectual (Fritz Mauthner) once noted that, while in theory it was possible that such people (converts out of religious conviction) existed, he had never come across such a case. Usually, people converted to pass, to remove obstacles to their career, to provide greater security for their children. But Edith Stein certainly converted out of conviction, and so did Paulus, the Benedictine monk, who has figured more than once in our narrative. Most converted for other motives, and yet it is not quite just to call them traitors and renegades, for the Jewish religion had become meaningless for them. They no longer believed in the Jewish traditions and certainly not in the existence of a Jewish people. To charge them with betrayal was simply not apposite, for how could one betray something in which one did not believe in the first place? They had remained Jews out of filial piety perhaps or because conversion was somehow aesthetically (and perhaps even morally) displeasing. Why continue to belong to a religion that had become meaningless and only brought disadvantage and danger? The converts' assumption that converting would safeguard them against persecution was erroneous, but, of course, they could not have known this at the time.

All this should have been a private affair, not a crucial issue in modern society. Ironically, it became a matter of major importance not for those who had remained Jews, practicing or not, but for those who had distanced themselves. Biographies of Henry Kissinger, U.S. Secretary of State, mention his Jewish origins in a few paragraphs; it was after all of little relevance to his policy in China, Vietnam, or the Soviet Union. He never hid the fact, did not change his name even in the army, and did not take elocution lessons. In the biography of Madeleine Albright, one of his successors, her Jewish origin figures as the main theme, and detailed tables account for her family tree, and even remote relations, precisely because an attempt was made to suppress these origins. She was born Madeleine Korbel, and her family converted to Catholicism in London during the war when she was a small child (she later became an Episcopalian). Her father worked at the time for the Czech government in exile and regarded the Jewish origins of his family as a hindrance to his career, and he also wanted to provide greater security for his children. Throughout his life and the first decades of his daughter's life, the Jewish skeletons in the closet were simply not mentioned. But this also meant that the fate of Madeleine's grandparents (who died at Auschwitz) was not mentioned. The moment Mrs. Albright became a public figure there was, of course, increased interest in her family, and the suppression of the truth became a major issue. The fact that she had denied existing family ties, that she could not mourn her grandparents nor keep in contact with her cousins, made a curious impression among Jews and non-Jews alike. Far from being of any help in her career, it raised questions concerning character and truthfulness. It would have been one thing to state the facts and maintain that they were of little consequence as far as she was concerned (which was perfectly true). It was another to stick to a "legend" that was manifestly untrue. She had been born into a certain situation not of her doing, but by perpetuating the legend she got involved in a maze of contradictions. Times had changed, and what had seemed to Professor Korbel a sensible step during World War II, appeared suspect and undignified fifty years later.

Such cases were not rare. They attracted painful public scrutiny only if the people involved were in the public eye, but they invariably created personal problems for the families involved. In some cases the children were simply not told by their parents about their true origins, in other cases something was vaguely known, but there was a tacit agreement not to discuss it. One of these cases was Henry Wallich, the economist, whose name has appeared earlier in these pages. His mother was a German Protestant, but his father was the last owner of a well-known Berlin Jewish banking house, which for two generations had tried to distance itself from its origins. Distancing, however, had not the least effect on the Nazis. Henry's father committed suicide after Kristallnacht by drowning himself in the Rhine. This was never mentioned in the Wallich family, because it would inevitably lead to questions about why he did it, and thus to the Jewish origins of the family.

A perusal of the biographical dictionary of the emigration from Central Europe shows that a significant percentage of those listed had been converted, some at birth or a very early age, others had become Lutheran or Catholic following the conversion of their parents (such as, for instance, Joseph Rovan, a leading French expert on Germany). Some became faithful churchgoers, such as Max Perutz, the Nobel

Prize winner, but this was clearly a small minority. Some listed themselves as nominal or non-practicing Jews, yet others stated that while they had belonged to a Christian denomination following their conversion, they had ceased to consider themselves Christian after World War II, perhaps because they had been hurt by the lack of support extended by the churches to these non-Aryan Christians.

But there were also some extreme cases—refugees, usually quite young at the time, who wanted to distance themselves to such a degree that they did not want to be included in works of reference of this kind in the first place. They did not want it to be known that they had not been born in the country in which they now lived. Such antagonism toward their origins clearly went deeper than the mere desire to remove an unpleasant stain on their record or enhance their chances of promotion, for a Jewish origin was no longer a hindrance in most fields.

It was not a specifically German Jewish phenomenon; stories similar to that of Henry Wallich could be found among Hungarians, Russians, and others. Why should people go to such lengths to deny their origins? The answer has been provided already: it seemed a prudent thing at a certain time to people who did not foresee that conversion would provide no protection against racial antisemitism. As Kurt Tucholsky wrote in a letter toward the end of his life, "In 1911 I tried to leave the Jewish community by converting to Protestantism not realizing that such a step would be ineffective." Nor was it anticipated by those who had their families converted that times would change, and that after the fall of Nazism being a Jew would usually not involve much of a stigma, and that in some strange ways, for instance in postwar Germany, it sometimes even became a slight advantage.

In some cases during the war a little blackmail was involved to convert people. Alfred Grosser, leading French expert on Germany, relates that he was in contact with a monastery at Valance near St. Raphael in Southern France after the German occupation in November 1942. He urgently needed help to hide, and the abbot made it clear to him: "Either baptism and help, or no baptism and no help." But Saul Friedlaender, who had been hidden by his parents (who soon after perished) in a monastery school and was not even aware of his Jewish identity, was told by the monks at the end of the war that he would have to decide whether to opt for one religion or the other. Grosser opted for Catholicism, Friedlaender for being a Jew. Few of the refugees whose families had converted found their way back formally to the Jewish community, but even fewer chose to make it known that they had converted. In later life, some of them showed interest in things Jewish or, as did some historians and political scientists, such as Fritz Stern and Peter Pulzer of Oxford, even made it one of the main topics of their professional careers.

Changing Names

Changing one's name was not as far-reaching a step as changing one's religion. But neither was it a lark as some of the very young soldiers thought when it was suggested to them by their officers early on in their army career. In Britain, there was the unwillingness to give British nationality to soldiers of foreign birth, and a name change was thought to be preferable, even though it did not, of course, provide protection if the soldiers fell into enemy hands. No one was obliged to change his name, and many did not. On the other hand, there was a considerable amount of name changing by civilians both before and after the war. Martin Goldberg (a very assimilated young Jew from Berlin and a descendant of a major Jewish sage of the sixteenth century), who had studied surgery before and during the war in London, was asked by Jewish colleagues in Manchester how he had managed to enter the profession without a name change. It amounted, after all, to a change of identity, to cutting oneself off from one's forefathers, and, in some cases, from one's relations. There are no figures showing how many changed their names during the war, how many reverted to their old names after the war (as did Helmuth Koenigsberger, a history professor living in Britain, after his service in the Royal Navy, in which his name had been Kingsley), and how many struck a compromise by combining their old and their new names (for example, Leighton-Langer). Changes of family names in Palestine among German Jewish immigrants were not frequent prior to the establishment of the state, whereas a change of the first name (which did not have to be officially sanctioned) was almost the rule. According to official statistics, the changes hardly ever exceeded a hundred a year, and not all the new names adopted were Hebrew. But statistics can be misleading for a number of reasons. A significant number of immigrants had names that were Hebrew in origin in the first place, and others could not apply because they were illegally in the country.

During World War II there were even fewer name changes; it could well be that the news about the mass murder in Europe inhibited them. But when the state of Israel came into being, diplomats had to hebraize their names, and the same was true with regard to the higher echelons of the army. Others followed suit. Generally speaking, young immigrants showed more willingness to change their family names, as this reflected their full integration in the new homeland.

Returning to Their Roots?

Following the Nazi rise to power, there had been a return to their roots among German Jews, and in particular among the younger generation, which manifested itself in the growth of Zionist organizations, greater synagogue attendance, and, generally speaking, an increased interest in things Jewish. Hebrew classes sprouted, and a new one-volume Jewish encyclopedia became a runaway bestseller. And historical novels and biographies about Jews ranging from the travels of Benjamin of Tudela, a thirteenth century Spanish Jewish traveller to Glueckel von Hameln, a formidable seventeenth century German Jewish mother, housewife, and businesswoman were widely read.

Having been told that they were not Germans and that there was no room for them in Germany, young German Jews were groping for a new identity, and in this endeavor began to rediscover a heritage that in many cases, had been discarded long ago. A century of assimilation was, of course, not undone in a week or a month, but it was also clear that the German Jewish symbiosis, such as it was, had come to an end. If, as Rabbi Leo Baeck sadly noted in 1933, the history of Jews in Germany had come to an end, their own lives continued, and they had to look for new substance and content. They had to become part of a new history.

The trend of re-Judaization was reinforced by the impact of the Sho'ah and the establishment of the state of Israel. Their impact varied in intensity. Some refugees did not have close relations and intimate friends among the victims of the Holocaust, but they were a minority, probably a small minority. Most had lost at least some of their nearest and dearest, and not a few had seen their parents, brothers, and sisters for the last time the day they left Germany. This trauma had consequences even for the staunchest believers in the essential goodness of humankind, for the inevitable progress of freedom and tolerance, and for international friendship and solidarity. Nor could the pain be easily suppressed. Quite often it took years, even decades, to comprehend fully the magnitude of the disaster which had befallen both individuals and the whole community. It was probably not by accident that the best known cases of suicide (Paul Celan, Peter Szondi, Primo Levi) took place not immediately after the war but two decades later. It was certainly not by accident that most of the memoirs were written only in the 1970s and 1980s, not in the first years after 1945 when other concerns prevailed. The same is true with regard to most of the literature about the Holocaust, its prehistory, and its aftermath. There was among many, and for many years, an understandable tendency to suppress the sad memories, to go on with one's life and try to forget about the irreparable losses suffered. This was true both on the individual level and on the study of this tragic period.

A British historian of German Jewish provenance wrote many years later about his reluctance to proclaim his origins, and that it was not until the seventies that he began to reflect on the price that had to be paid in psychological terms for such suppression. It might be argued, of course, that a certain amount of suppression was necessary to enable those who had gone through the horrors of Auschwitz to function. But, in the main, our narrative concerns not the survivors of the camps, but those who in their great majority had left before the outbreak of the war and never experienced in person the deadly forms of persecution. They were not marked men (as Marcel Reich-Ranicki put it) for the rest of their lives as were those who had been in the camps and the ghettos and had witnessed the deportations. For them the act of suppression, conscious or unconscious, must have been rooted in other motives.

While traditional Zionism did not appreciably gain support among the younger generation of refugees after 1945, Israelophilia certainly did. There were sometimes frequent visits to and considerable interest in developments in Israel. Many had family and friends in Israel, and, even those who had none, agreed that the Jews had as much a right to have a country of their own as any other people. They sympathized with Israel even if they preferred not to live there. There was an emotional link with Israel among most of this generation, even though they might bitterly criticize the Israeli government of the day or specific aspects of its policy. It was perhaps an atavistic link as some critics would claim, but nonetheless very real.

Those who attended synagogue in Germany went predominantly to Reform services, and this tradition was continued by the younger refugees once they settled abroad. Refugees established their Reform communities in Belsize Park, London, and other parts of the United Kingdom, and had their synagogues and coffee houses in New York, San Francisco, Buenos Aires, and elsewhere. A significant number of young Jews from Germany went to study for the rabbinate, some initially in Germany and later abroad, others began their studies in the United States.

They did astonishingly well—one of them even became chief rabbi of Britain (or, to be precise, of the United Synagogue, the biggest such federation in the country). The influence of this generation of young rabbis in the United States and Canada was considerable. As one of them wrote:

> In Los Angeles in 1983 at the annual convention of the Central Conference of American Rabbis, the German born president Hermann Schaalman was yielding the gavel to another president of like origin (Guenther Plaut); and at the same time the presidents of the other three reform movements were all German born as well; the Union of American Hebrew Congregations (Alexander Schindler), the Hebrew Union College-Jewish Institute of Religion (Alfred Gottschalk) and the World Union of Progressive Judaism (Gerard Daniel). Since that time the president of the Jewish Theological Seminary (Ismar Schorsch) has also joined this constellation of surprising German Jewish influence.

How to explain such German Jewish predominance? The writer refers to the superior education these young people had received in German high schools, which could be true. But it is also true that they all faced the considerable difficulties of having been uprooted, and in any case some of them left Germany after only a year or two of high school, or even before that. Nor did all of them proceed directly to rabbinical studies. For instance, Alex Schindler was born in Munich, went to a school where theology played only a minor role, and joined the U.S. army, where he served in a special skiing unit. He later combined a rabbinical career with other public functions, serving as president of the "president's committee," the leading U.S. Jewish political coordination committee, and became head of the Memorial Foundation, which had been founded by the Claims Conference to support Jewish culture. Whatever the reason for the prevalence of young German Jews in this field, it seems not to have been a mere accident.

Some German Jewish rabbis felt a special commitment to the remnant of German Jewry. Peter Levinson, born and educated in Berlin, went back to serve as rabbi in that city and later in Mannheim. Jacob Petuchovski, born in Danzig, who had been a mere thirteen when he had left, and who had sworn not to set foot again on German soil, changed his attitude fifteen years after the end of the war and became actively involved in Christian-Jewish dialogues.

But it was not only in the Reform movement that German Jews were so prominent. They had been leading in all religious trends and institutions in the preceding century, Conservative as well as Orthodox (Western-style), trying to combine strict adherence to the religious law with modern civilization *(derech eretz)*. Thus the largest synagogue and religious school (and also the longest lasting) was the very Orthodox institution established by Rabbi Breuer of the famous Frankfurt dynasty in Washington Heights.

There was one country in which German Jewish religious thought was singularly unsuccessful, and this was Israel. This happened despite the presence of major religious thinkers from Germany, ranging from Martin Buber to the ultra-Orthodox. German Jews had founded religious communities in Palestine, such as Emet veEmuna in Jerusalem, Bet Israel in Haifa, and Moria in Tel Aviv, and they had initiated the opening of the Horev religious school in Jerusalem. The religious kibbutzim, such as Tirat Zvi, Yavne, Rodges, and others were almost entirely German Jewish. But their influence, never very great, declined over the years. As an observer of the Israeli religious scene put it, the next religious generation retreated into extreme isolation from the outside world, a retreat based on the belief that the whole world was united in its hatred of the Jews.

A large section of the German Jewish refugees continued to be religiously indifferent. It appeared that the "return to their roots" that had taken place in the years after 1933 had not been a lasting one. For all one knows this might have happened even if the ultra-Orthodox had been less domineering, thereby antagonizing all the others. As the fundamentalists claimed a monopoly as far as the practice of their religion was concerned , the secular saw all the more reason to distance themselves from Judaism. This too was part of a worldwide trend—whatever the reason, the number of Jews was shrinking all over the world, except in Israel, and not only as the result of a declining birth rate and mixed marriages.

As the years passed, toward the 1980s and 1990s, diaspora links with Israel became somewhat weaker, even though tourism continued as before. Those who did visit were impressed by the great strides that had been made in a few years, and were overjoyed by meeting again old friends and relations. But there was also quite often a feeling of being strangers in a country that, in its ethnic composition, had moved far from what it had been in the 1930s and up to the establishment of the state. In the 1950s, the existence of the country could not yet be taken for granted, and in 1967 and 1973 its very survival seemed at stake. But as the country became economically and militarily stronger, there was no longer reason for passionate concern as there had been in earlier years. Interest in Israel did not vanish altogether, but it certainly became a little less intense. One could, after all, be proud of Israel and defend it privately and in public without making it the central concern of one's life.

Community of Fate

If religion no longer provided the common bond and if the belief of being one people declined, what could possibly take its place? It had been maintained in the postwar period that, all other considerations apart, the Jews were a "community of fate" *(Schicksalsgemeinschaft)*, but this had been more correct in the period of the Nazi persecutions, during the war and its immediate aftermath. In the years that followed outside pressures became much less palpably felt. Discrimination continued here and there in the Western world, but the Jews no longer lived in a beleaguered fortress, and it was no longer disgraceful to desert the community, as it was no longer subject to violent persecution.

From the eighties on, all polls showed identification with Judaism becoming more shallow, a trend that was even more manifest among those with a higher education. Assimilation had failed in Central Europe, but this did not mean that it was bound to fail always and everywhere. As the twentieth century drew to a close, there were predictions that European and probably also American Jewry would be

acculturated out of existence, leaving only Israel and the ultra Orthodox. During the war and its aftermath, young refugees had mainly
found their partners among the other sex in their community simply
because fate had kept them together, because their social contacts
were mainly with fellow Jews. But this, too, changed in the following
years, and hence the increase in mixed marriages. There were few who
proclaimed non-Jewish Judaism as a new ideology, but there certainly
was more indifference as time passed.

All this is not to proclaim the near end of Judaism in the Western
world, and, perhaps, also Israel as the character of the country profoundly changed. Some traditions as well as common bonds lingered
on. The many recent reunions of survivors showed that there was a
deep urge to remember, and a feeling of belonging to one great family
(this was the term used, for instance with regard to the German Jewish children who had shared a home in 1939/40 in Bradford, England). Accounts of the life of the German Jewish refugees in the
United States and Australia, in Britain, Israel, and elsewhere showed
that they stuck together, seeing each other quite often. Memoirs were
still published, some of the old organizational frameworks and bulletins continued to exist (not to mention their senior citizens' homes),
even though their number was shrinking year by year. But it was also
clear that, while the next generation might share an interest in the origins of their parents, this could not possibly be the central experience
in their lives.

Not all of those who had emigrated to Palestine had been Zionists,
but whether they wanted it or not, they had opted for a certain new
identity, one far less complicated than that of emigrants to other countries. They might be very patriotic or very critical Israelis, but they still
were members of one people. What was the identity of those who had
gone to the United States and Britain, to Argentina and Australia? The
German Jews in their majority had been Germans first and Jews second, and it was only natural that the same attitude would prevail in
their new homelands. But this feeling in Germany had developed over
several generations, and it was obvious that even in countries built by
generations of immigrants, as in the United States and Israel, such a
feeling of identification and loyalty could not develop in only a few
years.

The problems of acculturation have been mentioned more than
once in the course of our narrative, as has the fact that this was far

more acutely felt by the older refugees than the younger. The older generation suffered because America was not Europe (Australia or Argentina were even less so), but the younger refugees were less deeply rooted in Europe and more adaptable. True, even among the young members of the youth *aliya* there was the longing for the language and literature of which they had absorbed something even at an early age. Shimon Sachs related that he never read as much Thomas Mann, Kafka, and Rilke as in his days as a member of the youth *aliya* group in Ein Harod, when his teachers wanted him to study Hebrew and to read Bialik. He describes how a little later, in the war years, he saved every penny and even sold some essential belongings from home, in order to buy books in the German second-hand book shops in Allenby and Ben Jehuda Street in Tel Aviv. Sachs was not a political or cultural extremist, nor anti-Zionist; he did not leave the country after the war but became a professor of education at Tel Aviv University. The story simply shows that there were more than a few youngsters who believed, not without justification, that there was more to read in German than in Hebrew. Kurt Blumenfeld, the leader of the German Zionists, had once declared that he was a Zionist "von Goethe's Gnaden" (owing to Goethe). Yes, they would be told, but Goethe was not theirs, whereas Bialik was expressing the specific Jewish genius and tradition. This they found difficult to accept—it was part of the Eastern European tradition, not of their cultural heritage, and the ways of Eastern and Western Jewry had diverged for too long.

Language and Belonging

The issue of language was fundamental for most of the refugees. It was not crucial for musicians or engineers or others who could make themselves understood, regardless of the language. But for many professions, mastering the new language was a precondition for working in one's field. For many more, whether they would feel at home in the new country depended on mastering the language. And it was a problem that faced not just the older generation, the young too sometimes felt it acutely. Editha Koch (born 1917) wrote that "my roots are in the air." But she added that in Europe too (she had grown up in the German-speaking part of Czechoslovakia), she had not felt rooted and had been afraid to show openly that she was Jewish: "I am a cosmopolitan, a

citizen of the world, as such one is everywhere at home and nowhere."
But cosmopolitanism was a sentiment as difficult to maintain in the
first half of the century as in the second. Ilse Blumenthal, another
young writer domiciled in England, wrote that the German language
had remained her *Heimat*. And Hilde Domin (Palm), a noted poet,
stated that her native language *(Muttersprache)* had remained inalien-
able despite all the other losses. It was the last refuge, the last shelter
for the preservation of her identity. (She had adopted the family name
Domin when she emigrated to the Dominican Republic.) For her,
clinging to the use of the German language was an existential necessity: "I have come back [to Germany] because of the language."

But the great majority of refugees did not share this attitude. For
them, the German language was neither home nor emotional pillar.
They were by no means anti-German fanatics, they merely regarded
Germany as a closed chapter in their lives. Konrad Bloch, the scientist,
said in an interview that after he had been expelled from Munich University in 1935 he simply did not want to speak German any longer.
English and Spanish were relatively easy languages to master even
though pronunciation was difficult. Hebrew was infinitely more difficult; Hannah Arendt, seldom averse to exaggeration, thought it was
"unlearnable." But there was Reuven Meir, a physician in Jerusalem,
who had arrived right after graduating from medical school in Germany. Even though his Hebrew was far from perfect, when addressed
in German he would automatically answer in Hebrew. He did not want
to be impolite, nor was he a Hebrew language fanatic. He just did not
want to speak German any longer.

Hilde Domin was only in her thirties at the time, but she was either
not young enough or did not have the capacity for a new beginning in
another language. Aharon Appelfeld, her junior by more than a
decade, born in Bukovina, had been in school for one year only when
the war broke out. His native language was German (and his parents
had tried to keep his German pure) but he had to speak Yiddish with
his grandmother and Ukrainian with their servant. He spent years in
Romanian labor camps, and, after the death of his mother, having survived in the forests eating rotten apples, he surfaced at the end of the
war and began to write a diary in German. But the diary consisted only
of words, since he was incapable of writing sentences. He kept this up
for some time, but even on the ship from Italy to Israel the first Hebrew
words crept in, and in Israel, despite his desire to continue writing in

German, the native language quickly disappeared. Eventually, he became a leading Israeli writer.

Many refugees felt self-conscious about their accent, especially in countries such as Britain and France. True, even in later years, Nixon would tell Kissinger not to give too many press conferences because his accent would not play well in Peoria. But eventually Kissinger gave more press conferences than any other member of the admistration, without lasting harm to his reputation in Peoria. Some found his accent funny, others exotic, but in the final analysis what mattered was what he had to say, not the way he said it. As a leading British scientist charmingly put it on one occasion; "Up to Hitler German had been the language of science, after 1933 it was English with a German accent."

Much has been written on the emotional consequences of the Holocaust. But the great majority of young refugees left well before the mass murder began. The lucky ones went as a group with youth *aliya* to the land of youth and sun; they were, for a few years at least, sheltered and carefree. Those who went with the Kindertransport to England suffered and some of the wounds never healed. The accounts of the children (and not only of children) who had left Germany overnight are full of stories of bitterly weeping every night for years before falling asleep.

The separation from the parents, friends, and familiar surroundings was traumatic, and the intensity of the trauma varied from case to case. The cohesion of groups like the Kindertransport can perhaps in part be explained against the background of this trauma. As one of them wrote many years later,

> There is no doubt that when I meet people of my own background an immediate rapport is established because of our common experiences, no matter how different the details might have been. My closest friends in the truest sense of the word are all ex refugees. . . When we meet, usually once a year, distance and time seem to have made little difference in our relationship.

This phenomenon has been observed even among those who arrived at an early age. At least to some extent, this community has replaced the family that was lost. There was a need for close attachment, perhaps free-floating, and the peer group fulfilled this role. But there remains a paradox that has not sufficiently been studied and for which there perhaps are, finally, no answers: on the one hand, the resilience of youth, its ability to adjust to new conditions, its capacity to forget even the native language within a short time, and, on the other hand, the return, quite often in later years, of memories believed to be buried or discarded long ago.

Memories and Bad Dreams

We do not know how many of the young refugees were in deep psychological trouble during and after the war, how many of them needed medical attention. There were few cases of suicide (mainly, it would appear, among artists and writers), not surprisingly perhaps, because in time of war and immediate danger, emotional distress is often suppressed. In any case, most young refugees were too poor in the postwar years to afford lengthy analysis.

There were bad dreams (of having missed the last train and being caught in a trap) and attacks of sudden fear, claustrophobia, agoraphobia, which continued for years, but this was common after a major war, among not only refugees but also soldiers and civilians who had experienced heavy bombardment. Klaus Scheurenberg, a Berlin Jew born in 1925, has provided a vivid description of the fears that continued to haunt him and his fellow survivors of camps for many years after. While they were in mortal danger, they were among the bravest of the brave such as "Horst" who escaped from Birkenau (Auschwitz) with a SS watchdog named Rex, which helped him masquerade as a blind veteran in Berlin for the rest of the war. But the psychological consequences did not fail to appear in the years after.

Individuals tended to react in different ways. Lothar Martin, whose story has been told earlier, fled alone at age fifteen from Germany to France, escaped countless times from prison camps, made his way to Spain, and had a distinguished war record with the Free French army. As the war ended, he was an officer with many medals but with, as he put it, "no soul left." He could not sleep in a bed for years, and when anyone touched him accidentally in the street or the metro, he immediately hit back hard and was arrested by the Paris police countless times. Even ten years after the war he was hyperaggressive. He opened a shop but ruined it; he married and divorced soon after. He calmed down, after emigrating to Israel and marrying Zamira, his teacher at the *ulpan* (language school) for immigrants in Netanya. Only after having been married to Zamira for twenty-two years, did he begin to talk for the first time about his experiences since he left Germany.

Having survived several camps, Ruth Elias, born in Moravska Ostrava in Moravia, arrived in Israel and found a reasonably happy life in a kibbutz despite very primitive living conditions. Yet when her first child was born in a Hadera hospital, her reaction was psychotic. She shouted; "Give me my child back, it should live." After listening to her for a while, the doctor slapped her twice, a crude and cruel response, but in the circumstances, probably the only effective one. No one had been interested in her story before, nor had she been willing to talk about it. Now, following the trauma of childbirth, she told her doctor the whole story for the first time, and after doing so, she was able to settle down.

Ruth Klueger was fourteen when the war ended, a survivor of Auschwitz, Gross Rosen, and the death marches. She found herself in Bavaria, wrote poems, read hundreds of books, and within a year graduated from senior high school, and attended university. After two years, she arrived in New York, where she attended Hunter College. She then took a professorship in California. She was moody, arrogant, did not get along with her mother, and tended to have depressions. She saw a Viennese psychiatrist in New York and hated him, an interesting case of negative transference. Many years later she wrote a book about life during the years after the camps, which stood out both in its pitiless frankness and in its literary merits. Hers had not been a particularly happy and harmonious adolescence, but how could it have been different?

There was the issue of guilt, felt far more strongly by the survivors of camps than by the young refugees. Why had they survived and so many others had perished? They mourned their families who had perished but what could they have done at the time to save them? A psychologist investigating the subsequent fate of those who had arrived with the children's transport found few manifestations of guilt among them—it was not a major factor preventing them from leading a more or less normal life. Nor did their experience have the effect of frightening them for the rest of their lives. On the contrary, it strengthened, if anything, their resolution to resist, to hit back. This reaction could be found not only among those who had gone to Israel, where fighting back ("Never again") had become part of the national ethos; it could be found also in other parts of the world.

Mention has been made of the price paid by those who tried, successfully or not, to suppress the truth of their origins. Viktor Klemperer, the author of the famous diary accounting for every day of his life in Nazi Germany, relates a meeting years after the war with a nephew who had emigrated to America and was now back in Berlin for a visit. The nephew, whom Klemperer thought a splendid young man, told him proudly that he had been doing everything possibly to remove once and for all the stigma of their Jewish origin: under no circumstances would he have married a Jewish girl. This seems to reflect a person of slightly less than average intelligence and sensibility, and for all one knows, he might have been successful in his endeavor.

Others might have felt less comfortable with the new identity they had constructed, a one-dimensional identity without a past. The issue at stake was not the act of conversion but the suppression of their origins. The grandfather of the young man had been a rabbi, and by Viktor Klemperer's generation, he had already been renamed a "small town clergyman." One generation later the rabbi-clergyman had even ceased to exist. But there was always the danger that a still younger generation engaged in the search for roots would discover and even be proud of the hidden secret.

Common Features

Any discussion of the fate of a generation leads sooner or later to questions about the features, if any, that this generation had in common. They are legitimate questions but as impossible to answer as questions concerning "national character." Generalizations concerning national character are always dangerous and often misleading, and this goes *a fortiori* for a group of people who came from a certain country but later went to various parts of the globe, learned different languages, became part of different cultures, and, in the case of Israel, should not really be considered refugees in the first place.

Herbert Strauss, the sociologist of the German Jewish emigration, has rightly noted that German Jewry had never been monolithic in any aspect of its legal position, culture, religious orientation, politics, demographic composition, or any other area. It represented a plural world of differences. About a fifth were not German citizens but recent arrivals from Eastern Europe. A significant proportion did not belong to

Jewish religious communities, but had converted or simply opted out. German Jewry included Jewish professionals and businessmen from Berlin, Frankfurt, and Breslau, and rural Jews from Hesse and Bavaria, or those who were but one generation removed from the villages of these and other areas. It consisted of ardent Zionists and equally ardent assimilationists. All this also applied to the young generation.

And yet, with all these differences, many of the survivors believe that there are common features irrespective of the geographical distance between them, and of different cultures to which they now belong. They do feel a common bond, an instinctive understanding, difficult to explain but nonetheless quite real, however it was acquired. This does not apply to everyone of this generation. Some have made a deliberate effort to cut themselves off from their erstwhile companions, and, to some who were very young at the time, such cutting of the roots might have come naturally. They feel themselves entirely belonging to their new homes and do not want to be reminded of memories far away and long ago, either because they genuinely lack interest or because such remembrance would only be painful.

The generation that has been the subject of our narrative was not that of Einstein, the theorists of nuclear fission, the major writers of the 1920s who went into exile, the academics who brought to their new countries new disciplines ranging from art history to certain schools in psychology and sociology. But even if their education was unfinished they, like their parents, had the traditional German Jewish belief in the importance of *Bildung*, of higher education, and in their exile they tried very hard to catch up and to fill in what was missing. Such an urge was not entirely selfless, because a finished education opened gates to a more rewarding life and a higher living standard. But it is certainly true that, in contrast to other societies (including Jewish societies), even though wealth was not despised, *Bildung* still remained the ideal. Ostentatious consumption among German Jewry did exist but was still frowned upon and not only out of self-consciousness. (What would the others say? Would it not cause antisemitism?) Just as an Orthodox Jew would like his daughter to marry a promising student at a religious school rather than a wealthy trader, secular parents considered *a gute Partie* (a good marriage) in similar terms.

The eagerness among this generation, the thirst for knowledge, to continue their studies even in the most difficult circumstances, was certainly one of its outstanding features. There were, as it later appeared, excellent businessmen and entrepreneurs among them, but they were less numerous and less prominent than the professionals. On the other hand, the number of workaholics and high achievers was as great among one group as among the other. The young refugees knew that they were alone in the world, that no one owed them a living, that it was a question of sinking or swimming. This impetus would not have existed had they continued to lead a normal life in Germany.

Not a few rose above the station they would have attained in their homeland. Many became academics who in other circumstances would not have chosen such a career. This is true, above all, with regard to those who went to the United States; elsewhere conditions for such careers were more adverse, openings were fewer. There was a relatively large number of people, especially in the academic world, who held more than one job, sometimes on different continents at the same time. Was it only lack of security? Few retired from their jobs and cultivated their gardens upon reaching retirement. But it was not only ambition that drove them, since many continued to work as volunteers or consultants. They did not want to stop working, could not do so and this certainly had not been the case in previous generations.

Many of them had belonged to youth movements, and the essential feature of these groups had been their idealism. This meant among other things a modest lifestyle, working for a better world, and being active in their community. It implied selflessness and honesty in their own lives. It involved helping others, and creating a new spirit of community, a cultural and spiritual life. What became of these ideals in the harsh realities of exile? They were preserved to a certain extent in the kibbutzim, where the pioneering ethos continued to prevail for many years. Life in the kibbutzim was in some ways a continuation of life in the youth movement.

Ideals of Youth and the Search for Adventure

The ideals of the youth movement took some hard knocks during the difficult years of the fight for survival not only in Shanghai and Bolivia, but also in the United States and Britain. In any case, only a minority had belonged to the youth groups and it was not surprising that in later years the number of card players was possibly greater than the number of listeners to classical music and readers of serious literature.

But something of the essential nonmaterialistic values, the interest in the higher things in life, did survive, and in some instances one could detect it in the generation after, though less so in the third.

One of the ingredients of the youth movement was its romantic character and the thirst for adventure, physical and spiritual. Some thought such adventurism un-Jewish. But the record shows that some of the most noted explorers of the nineteenth century were Jews— Emin Pasha (originally Schnitzer) in Africa, Palgrave (better known for his anthologies of English poetry) in Arabia, and Vambery, the Hungarian, in Central Asia, of whom it was said that in his life he belonged consecutively to half a dozen religions and was a priest in four of them. When the generation of young German refugees left their native countries, there was less left to discover in faraway places, but some still made the most of it. David Shaltiel joined the Foreign Legion for five years and then became an arms smuggler. Others went to Nepal (not then a well-known tourist attraction), and to the jungles and mountains of Latin America, as well as to deepest Africa.

Life in the kibbutz was an adventure, although not everyone liked it, and so was race driving for the successful designer John Weitz. German Jews became pilots, daring to fly in conditions in which more prudent men would stay grounded. Mention has been made of Ulli Beier, who bcame a Yoruba chief and made Oshogbu art known all over the world. There was apparently an irresistible attraction to the exotic, as was the case for Ruth Prawer-Jhabwala. Born in Cologne of Polish Jewish parents, she went to school and studied literature in London, where she met a Farsi architect, married him, and moved to India. There she wrote a number of successful novels and became even better known as a screenplay writer (*Heat and Dust, Shakespeare Wallah*, and many others). She showed little interest in her German Jewish background, vowed not to return ever to the country of her birth, and the only short story in her considerable oeuvre dealing with the refugees describes a birthday party in Hendon, the then largely Jewish suburb in London in which she had lived. In this short story, few refugee clichés are omitted, including the inevitable apple strudel.

Perhaps she went to India to get away from the apple strudel and all that it stood for. But after two decades in India she felt a great longing for Europe and therefore settled in New York, where on the West side of Manhattan, she found the apartments with high ceilings, heavy furniture and the delicatessens she had known and loved in her youth.

And so in the end the apple strudel prevailed. Meanwhile, her brother became professor of German literature in Britain, which shows how difficult it is to account for the predilections of the one and the aversions of another, even within one family, let alone a larger group.

The lust for adventure was overwhelming as far as some were concerned; in other cases an exotic fate had resulted from accident rather than intention. Eva Hsiao, née Sandberg, the sister of the well-known conductor, had married a Chinese poet in Moscow, and so it seemed only natural that they would settle in her husband's homeland. Eva had been a Communist and later a Maoist; during the Cultural Revolution she spent seven years in prison. Eventually she found a spiritual home in Daoism, and when asked where her real home *(Heimat)* was, she answered that it was in nature, in forests, rivers, and meadows.

Others longed only for a permanent abode. Having been uprooted and sometimes lived through more than enough excitement, having had a hazardous escape or hidden underground, they wanted nothing better than to stay in one place, preferably a very peaceful place, for the rest of their lives.

One of the complaints about the German Jewish refugees concerned their arrogance, or, more accurately perhaps, their belief, real or imaginary, that they were somehow better, that they were culturally and/or morally on a higher level than the natives of the countries to which fate had dispersed them. That such a belief existed, more among the older than the younger refugees, can hardly be denied. But it often existed alongside an exaggerated respect for the upper class of the new country, their beautiful English (certainly in the case of Britain) or Castilian Spanish or French, their self-assurance, their exquisite (or rude but elegant) manners. There was on the part of some refugees a comic desire to ape them or at least to count a few of them among their acquaintances.

Cultural Superiority?

A feeling of cultural superiority went frequently hand in hand with a feeling of social inferiority. The *Jeckes* who came to Palestine were considered a laughing stock by the *sabras* and the earlier immigrants. But the recent arrivals, on the other hand, were shocked by the primitive character of the country and its inhabitants, their low cultural standards, their lack of honesty, reliability, and efficiency. This shock appears in virtually all accounts written by new immigrants at the time of their arrival or after. As they saw it, Tel Aviv was at best Lodz transplanted to the Levant, the mentality was that of the shtetl (or ghetto) once removed. Experts were horrified when they saw what was done in their fields of specialization.

Hermann Zondek, a well-known Berlin physician, was not a young man when he first came to Palestine and asked to see a hospital in Jerusalem. They showed him a building in which (he reports) fifteen pious people were studying the Talmud. When he observed that this was obviously a yeshiva, a religious school, he was told that he was quite mistaken, even though the lack of cleanliness and elementary order made it unlike any hospital he had ever seen. And he remembered the advice by a friend, Carl Prausnitz, given to him in Manchester: "Do not go to Palestine, it is too primitive for you." Zondek did not heed the advice, and, in his lifetime, modern medical institutions came into being in Jerusalem, and he was to play a leading role in the process. Younger people, less sophisticated or less spoiled, were similarly affected, but they knew that the country had yet to be built—and built by them. Nevertheless, they certainly did not take kindly to the suggestion that just because their Hebrew was less fluent, and their way of life and education removed a few more generations from the ghetto, they should somehow be considered second-class citizens.

Hence the reluctance even on the part of the youth *aliya* to accept that, as they saw it, Abraham Mapu and Smolenskin should replace Goethe, Shakespeare, and European culture. Refugees from Europe were appalled when they went to the more primitive countries of Latin America and they were appalled even in Western Europe, most notably in Britain. Young Eric Hobsbawm has been quoted as saying that London was far more boring than Berlin in the 1930s, and a similar reaction could be found even among the very young. Here is the dialogue between two Kindertransport children upon arrival in Britain, presumably translated from the German: "England is p-p-primitive," said Paula through chattering teeth. "S-S-Stone age," I agreed. The two little sisters had the misfortune to arrive in the middle of a severe winter.

To complain was of course unforgivable, like criticizing the quality of the food or the china and cutlery at a meal to which one has been invited. Not all refugees were tactful, and their behavior provoked sometimes violent resentment—who had asked them to come in the first place? But there is no denying that deep down there was a feeling of superiority expressed for instance in an interview given by Fred Lessing, who had arrived in the United States early in the war and was by the 1970s a well-to-do industrialist. When asked whether he thought that a Jew put higher moral demands on himself, he answered without hesitation that, while he could not prove it, he deeply believed that as a German Jew (especially one born in the city of Bamberg) he was something better. As far as his generation was concerned, he thought that German Jews were on a higher cultural (and moral) level than other Jews in America—"look at the public at concerts and the opera, twenty percent are our crowd."

Generalizations such as this are of course untenable. It is moreover unclear that attendance at concerts or the theater necessarily reflects on character; classical music was, after all, also well attended in the Third Reich. But there is no denying that such a conviction existed, that it was not always unjustified, and that German Jews were often aggrieved by the lack of sympathy and help during and after the war on the part of their coreligionists of Eastern European origin. Most of the friends of this generation were Central European. A German Jewish solidarity with East European Jewry came into being only in the camps, as Norbert Wollheim, a Berlin youth leader and a survivor of Auschwitz, observed on various occasions.

Politics of the Uprooted

Can one point to certain common features as far as the politics of this generation of refugees is concerned? Much depended on their subsequent fate, the surroundings into which they were transplanted. Psychologists who have studied hundreds of those who came with the children's transport have reached the conclusion that among many of them a darkened view of human nature has prevailed, and that terms like "disillusioned," "cynical," or at least "cautious" have frequently recurred in the answers they have volunteered. But such a grim view of humanity (and fears regarding the political future) did not preclude a longing for personal attachment. They might not trust mankind in general, but this did not affect their trust in individuals. Their experience produced a distrust of political extremes, of demagoguery, and the great majority has come to appreciate a free society such as they did not know in the Nazi age in their countries of origin. But this is true in large measure of all the victims of this age, irrespective of generation and ethnic origin. Since they suffered greatly, many tend to believe that a disaster that happened once could happen again, that a new Hitler could appear anywhere—in the United States, as well as in Israel. At the time of McCarthyism in America and the rise of the far right in Israel, even some of the more sophisticated members of the refugee community had apocalyptic forebodings and showed symptoms of political hysteria. One psychoanalytical school has coined the term "parataxic distortion," the instinctive belief of, for example, a cat having been burned on a hot stove, that all stoves are always hot and ought to be shunned.

But as time has passed, and as neither fascism nor a new Holocaust has taken place, at least not in the more advanced countries, these fears have certainly diminished in intensity. On the other hand, a substantial number of former refugees, to the extent that they have been active in politics at all, have been engaged in various groups fighting for human rights. Political militancy among them has been limited to certain specific groups, such as the young Communists who went to East Germany after World War II. But their revolutionary spirit gradually petered out, and we have mentioned the disillusionment of the second generation among them. Involvement in Israeli politics has been limited partly by linguistic difficulties, except for those who arrived when still very young. While immigrants from Central Europe can be found on all parts of the political spectrum in Israel, their main contribution has not been in the field of politics. In the United States there have been senators of German Jewish origin, but they either came as small children (Rudy Boschwitz) or belong to the generation of the sons and daughters (Senator Ron Wyden of Oregon). There have been very highly placed government officials, such as Kissinger and Michael Blumenthal, but they were appointed rather than elected.

In other Western countries, very few refugees chose a career in politics. Even in a liberal country like Sweden there was resistance against politicians not born in the country. The chief economic adviser of the Swedish trade unions was called a vagabond by his political enemies even though he came as a student from Germany to Sweden and had been identified with Sweden all his life. Denmark has been more tolerant in this respect, but one would look in vain for refugees in French politics, excepting only those belonging to the next generation, such as Cohn Bendit. Born in France, he turned his origins to good use ("we are all German Jews now") and later became something like a moderate elder statesman of the Green Party.

What of the misfits, or, to put it less harshly, those who have been of little or no credit to their community? There is an inclination, which should be resisted, to believe that the refugees in their great majority consisted of leading scientists, writers, artists, and prosperous businessmen, the kind of people to be found in a "Who's Who." There was an unusual percentage of such people among the older generation of refugees, but it was still a small minority, and it was, of course, even less true with regard to the younger generation, who had not even begun their studies, had not published books or launched businesses. The younger generation of refugees contained, like every generation, a mixture of humankind: good, bad, and indifferent people, clever and not so clever. It contained few if any violent criminals. One can think of a banker in Israel and a few in Britain whom greed brought into conflict with the law, and an American academic who had a similar fate and even wrote a book about it. A handful of traitors, on behalf of the Gestapo, hunted fellow Jews in the Berlin and Vienna underground during the war; unfortunately, such scoundrels can be found in all societies at all times.

But on the whole, Central European Jewry had been law-abiding and this tradition lingered on. Some of their reputations in the academic and artistic field were exaggerated, but this applies to every group of people. The refugee experience did not necessarily generate saints; arrogance, pomposity, and nastiness could be found among them, as among mankind in general.

There was occasionally an inclination, more often found among the older ones than among the younger, to blame their failure in life on others. One example should suffice. Sweden has been by tradition one of the most democratic countries, even though its attitude toward refugees has been mixed. There are about a dozen memoirs by members of the older and the younger generation of refugees who went to this country. Some highly praised the country that gave them shelter, whereas others were exceedingly bitter about Swedish society, its mediocrity, boredom, intrigues, and pettiness. There can be no doubt that both these perceptions are sincerely held. But who can say whether those who complain about their misfortune would have been happier and more successful elsewhere? Would they have been content and successful in Germany if Nazism had never come to power? Persecution can account for an interrupted education and material sufferings; it cannot account for talent or lack of talent, or for the capacity to lead a full and happy life.

The Next Generation

The last and most difficult question concerns the next generation. If there was a German Jewish legacy, a proposition that cannot be taken for granted, how much of it was transmitted to the sons and daughters of the young emigrants of 1933? We know only to a limited extent what became of the following generation. As we mentioned earlier, the first and second generations of Israeli diplomats were largely of German Jewish origin. A few of their children continued in the footsteps of their parents and are now employed by the foreign ministry; one served at one time as its director general (Uri Savir), another as its spokesman. A few were killed fighting in the wars of Israel. There are at least half a dozen professors among them, not all of them teaching in Israel. Perhaps one in four or five made their home outside Israel. One became ultra-Orthodox, another practices Buddhist meditation. There are lawyers and movie critics among them, insurance company executives, a supervisor of El Al, stewardesses, interior designers, microbiologists, students of the oceans and managers of hotels in Africa. Several disappeared from sight. Only one is a farmer, though, whereas many of their parents originally belonged to a kibbutz.

In brief, this breakdown looks like a cross section of the professional structure of middle-class children in modern society. Probably this group is not quite typical, because having received at least part of their education outside Israel, they mastered foreign languages and had greater opportunities to find employment outside Israel. Would a similar survey of the second generation in the United States or Britain show a distinct pattern? It goes without saying that the second generation feels itself primarily Israeli or American or American Jewish or Anglo Jewish, and that the German Jewish heritage is at most one factor among several in their lives. Did it manifest itself in their educations at home? We have it on the authority of some members of the second generation that it showed itself in certain taboos—one does not do certain things among our kind *(bei uns)*. These things included (in America) comic books, chewing gum, cartoons on television (in fact large parts of television programs), as well as shoes with pointy toes. In Israel there were fewer taboos.

The second generation was not at first particularly proud of the heritage their parents tried to imbue either consciously or simply by example. They were outside the mainstream of American (or British or Israeli society), their language was frequently accented, they stood out in a way that often caused embarrassment. This was the time when refugees were not yet welcome in America, even less in Britain, and when being a *Jecke* was anything but a source of pride in Israel.

But this changed with time. There is general agreement now that the refugees made a notable contribution to American society, and it is illuminating to what extent the image of the German Jewish parents in Israeli literature is different now from what is used to be a generation ago. In Yoram Kaniuk's novels not the *sabra* but the German Jewish father is the ideal figure; in Nathan Shaham's *Rosendorf Quartet*, the German Jewish immigrants with all their problems personify culture. This is equally true for the very youngest generation of Israeli writers including Joel Hoffman and David Shuetz. The traditional image of German Jews as problematical figures, rootless cosmopolitans, lacking interest and engagement in Jewish tradition, stiff and devoid of a sense of humor, has given way to something like a wave of nostalgia—if there had only been more of them . . . But there were not, and hence the limited impact they had beyond their lifetime.

It is impossible to generalize about the extent of knowledge of the German language among the children of the refugees. The majority has only a smattering, if that, but others speak it fluently because they heard it spoken at home. Thousands of refugees applied to obtain a German passport, mainly in Latin America but also in Israel (as a second passport), and many of their children followed suit. Israelis are great travelers, and, in this context, the German passport has advantages over the Israeli, quite apart from the fact that a German (now European) passport entitles the owner to reside and work without a special permit all over Europe. But this is a matter of convenience and does not reflect a sense of identification.

In politics, the attitude of the post-refugee generation was predictably a rebellion (though usually not extreme and not "personal") against their parents. Those in the United States participated in the

student revolts of the late sixties and were in the front ranks of opposi-
ton to Vietnam and similar causes. The second-generation academics
frequently belong to the feminist and postmodernist camp, but those
outside the groves of academe have hardly been affected by intellectual fashions and conform with the rest of American society. Those in
East Germany rebelled against the Communist state that their parents
had helped to found and maintain.

There has been in the United States, and even more in Europe and
Israel, a renewed interest among the young generation not only in the
Holocaust but in the Jewish tradition in general, as well as criticism of
their parents' generation for not having told them about it. Robert
Jungk, born in Berlin in 1913, well-known author of *Brighter Than a
Thousand Suns* and a leading ideologist of the Greens, has defined
himself not just as a cosmopolitan but as a "planetarian": "The whole
world is my Heimat, not a specific country. I was in Kibbutz Hazorea
and visited friends of my youth. They have built a wonderful Kibbutz,
but I would not like to live there." But Jungk's son Peter was less than
happy about his father's decision to settle in Austria; he visited Jerusalem and rediscovered his Judaism, equally impressed by Jewish orthodoxy and messianism. There has been two-way traffic away from and
toward Judaism, and it is too early to say whether overall the traffic
flow is stronger in one direction or the other.

Perhaps it is too early even to pose the question of whether something of the German Jewish legacy of the refugee generation lives on in
their children and grandchildren. Few generations have had a lasting
impact and generational conflict is more frequent than generational
conformity. But even if the common features that characterized the
young refugees of 1933 should disappear without a trace, the fate of
that generation, uprooted and transplanted, will be of abiding interest
for a long time, because it was so different from those who came before
and after.

GLOSSARY

———✺———

affidavit. A document needed by prospective immigrants to the United States from a sponsor, usually a relation, assuring the authorities that he (or she) would be responsible for the upkeep of the person applying for a visa.

aliya (Hebrew). Literally "ascent" to Palestine (Israel) as distinct from "immigrant" or "refugee." This is based on the Zionist assumption that Palestine is the ancient homeland and those entering it are returning, rather than moving to a new exile.

Aliya Chadasha. A political party in Palestine founded in the 1940s by immigrants from Central Europe.

aliya bet. This refers mainly to the illegal entry of new immigrants to Palestine under the British mandate after severe restrictions had been introduced. They came mainly by ship and their number is estimated at 120.000 or more.

Ben Shemen. A children's village near Lod, east of Tel Aviv, founded by Dr. Siegfried Lehmann in the 1920s.

Bund (German). In our context, the countrywide associations of German and Austrian youth, more or less on the lines of the German youth movement. Some were Zionist, others non-Zionist in character, they were socialist, religious, as well as nonpolitical. The Zionist groups usually aimed at establishing kibbutzim in Palestine.

Comintern (Communist International). Founded in 1919, and officially dissolved in 1943.

Kristallnacht (German). Known also as Reichskristallnacht, because of the mass of broken glass. This major pogrom was carried out by the Nazis in November 1938 and resulted in the destruction of many synagogues, the detention of some 30,000 Jews, the liquidation of most Jewish organizations and newspapers, and the seizure of Jewish property.

chalutzim (or halutzim) (Hebrew). Pioneers, usually referring to members of kibbutzim. The ideal figure of Zionist reconstruction in Palestine.

G.I. Bill of Rights. A series of laws passed by the U. S. Congress toward the end of the war aiming at the reintegration of veterans into civil life and providing for generous help in, among other things, further education and vocational training.

Gross Breesen. A farm in lower Silesia founded in 1935 for young Jews wishing to work in agriculture in countries other than Palestine. Most of the trainees succeeded in leaving Germany before the farm was liquidated in 1942. Those remaining were sent to the death camps.

halakha (Hebrew). Jewish religious law as distinct from the secular law of the state.

hachsharah (Hebrew). Literally, preparation. Training centers for young people mainly in agriculture, mainly in Germany, but later also abroad, preparing them for life in Palestine through work and also language courses.

Jecke (Yiddish). Derogatory term for German Jews. There are several etymological explanations but none is undisputed.

Jewish Brigade. A Jewish military unit of soldiers from Palestine, established within the framework of the British army in 1943/44 following long but inconclusive lobbying by the Zionist leadership. The Jewish Brigade saw action in Italy in 1945.

Jugendbewegung (German). "Youth movement." Beginning at the turn of the last century, groups of young people in Germany and Austria advocated and practiced something that in later years was called youth culture, and was without the interference of adults (in contrast to the Boy Scouts). There were scores of such *Buende* until their dissolution in 1933, and while some young Jews belonged to the German youth movement, a majority joined Jewish groups, sharing many of the ideals of the youth movement.

Kameraden. The biggest of the Jewish *Buende*, originally nonpolitical in character. It ceased to exist following a split, mainly between Zionists and non-Zionists, in 1932.

kibbutz. A collective agricultural settlement in Palestine. The first such settlements based on social equality came into being before World War I; their present number is about 270.

Kindertransport. Children's transports. This refers to the decision made by the British government and some other West European governments in late

1938 to allow the entrance of thousands of children under the age of eighteen from Germany, Austria and Czechoslovakia. These transports arrived betweeen December 1938 and the outbreak of World War II in September 1939.

Mischling (German). A person of "mixed race" according to the Nazi Nuremberg laws (1935). There were several degrees of *Mischlinge* depending on how many of the ancestors had been Jewish. *Mischlinge* were subject to persecution but were not normally sent to death camps.

Palmach (Hebrew). Elite units established by the Hagana, the unofficial Jewish defense forces, in 1941. They were originally based in kibbutzim. Palmach was dissolved in 1948 shortly after the regular Israeli army (Zahal) came into being. Many military commanders of the subsequent decades had originally served in the Palmach.

Reform Judaism. A trend in Jewish religion that originated in nineteenth-century Germany and later spread to other Western countries aiming at doing away with outdated elements in religious teaching and ritual. This was strongly opposed by the traditionalists.

Sho'ah (Hebrew). Literally "destruction," "catastrophe." Hebrew term for "Holocaust," a term that has gained general currency since World War II but is thought to be inappropriate and even misleading by a majority of scholars in the field of recent Jewish history.

youth aliya. An institution initiated in Berlin in 1932/33 aiming at the dispatch of children aged between fourteen and sixteen to study and work in Palestine. Most of them were educated at kibbutzim, a minority in other institutions. Some 5,000 came before the outbreak of the war, and 9,000 more during the war, but, among the latter, a majority hailed from countries other than Germany and Austria.

BIBLIOGRAPHICAL ESSAY

—⟨∿⟩—

Introduction: Growing Up between Weimar and Hitler

A comprehensive history of German Jewry remains to be written. The fullest existing accounts are Donald Niewyk, *The Jews in Weimar Germany* (Baton Rouge, 1980), and, more recently, volume 4 of *German Jewish History in Modern Times*, edited by Michael A. Meyer and Michael Brenner (New York, 1996–1998). Jewish cultural life and education are described in Michael Brenner, *The Renaissance of Jewish Culture in Weimar Germany* (New Haven, 1996); the social and economic situation after 1933 is analyzed in Abraham Barkai, *From Boycott to Annihilation* (London, 1989). Saul Friedlaender, *Nazi Germany and the Jews* (New York, 1997), volume 1, deals with the persecution of German Jewry after the Nazi rise to power.

About family life and growing up in the Weimar period, there is a wealth of literature, much of it unpublished. Accounts describing the life of families that were highly assimilated or were hiding the fact that they were Jewish are Katie Haffner, *The House at the Bridge* (New York, 1995), and Angelika Schrobsdorff, *Du bist nicht so wie andere Muetter* (Munich, 1994). George Mosse's *Confronting History* (Madison, Wis., 2000) relates the story of growing up as the scion of a very wealthy, liberal Jewish family. George Weidenfeld's *Remembering My Good Friends* (London, 1994) adds a Viennese perspective.

Life in other social strata was, needless to say, quite different. Marcel Reich-Ranicki and Ignaz Bubis hailed from Polish Jewish families who had recently settled in Germany; see M. Reich-Ranicki, *Mein Leben* (Stuttgart, 1999), and I. Bubis, *Damit bin ich noch laengst nicht fertig* (Frankfurt, 1994). Growing up in families that were traditionally Jewish or Zionist was also quite different, as shown in the accounts of Yehuda Amichai and Pnina Naveh in *Lebensgeschichten aus Israel* (Frankfurt, 1997), no editor given.

There is a great variety of sources on school life before and after 1933. Rita Meyhoefer, *Gaeste in Berlin?* (Berlin, 1996), focuses on Jewish pupils in the German capital, which also happened to be the biggest Jewish community by far. *Fuer ein Kind war das anders*, edited by Barbara Bauer and Waltraut Strickhausen (Berlin, 1999), consists of papers submitted to a conference dealing with the experience of young Jewish children in Nazi Germany. Of the individual accounts I have used, the following should be mentioned: Zvi Aharoni, *Operation Eichmann* (London, 1986), on Frankfurt/Oder; Georg Iggers, *Eine juedische Kindheit in Deutschland* (unpublished), on Hamburg; Nathan Peter Levinson, *Ein Ort ist mit wem du bist* (Berlin, 1996), on Berlin. Hilde Hoffmann (in *Lebengeschichten*) and Naomi Koch Laqueur (*A Memoir*, privately published, Washington, 1996) both grew up in Frankfurt, as did Alfred Grosser, *Mein Deutschland* (Hamburg, 1993). Esther Herlitz (*Esther, lean isha yehola lehagia* [Tel Aviv 1994]), Erwin Leiser (*Gott hat kein Kleingeld* [Cologne, 1993]), and Yohanan Meroz (*Jetzt wohin?* [Verein Aktives Museum, Berlin, 1995]) were natives of Berlin. Michael Wieck, *Zeugnis vom Untergang Koenigsbergs* (Heidelberg, 1988), describes conditions in the then capital of East Prussia, whereas Walter Laqueur, *Thursday's Child Has Far to Go* (New York, 1994), grew up and attended school in Breslau. For the fate of the last young Jews to graduate in Germany in 1940, see interviews with Ernest Fontheim (Ann Arbor, May–August 1999).

The great educational importance of the *Buende*, the autonomous youth organizations, has been stressed throughout the text. On the Zionist youth movements, see two recent studies: Elijahu Kuti Salinger, *Lamrot hakol* (Jerusalem, 1998), and Hannah Weiner, *Noar toses be'eda sha'anana*, volume 1 (Jerusalem, 1996). Interviews with former members of these groups in the period prior to 1933 are collected in Jutta Hetkamp, *Ausgewaehlte Interviews von ehemaligen . . .* (Muenster, 1994). Henry Kellermann was leader of a non-Zionist youth organization who became an American diplomat in later life; Henry J. Kellermann, "From Imperial to National Socialist Germany," *Leo Baeck Year Book*, volume 39 (1994). Guenter Holzmann, *On dit que j'ai survécu au dela des mers* (Paris, 1995), is the account of a youth leader of an extreme assimilationist group, whereas Froitz Teppich, *Der rote Pfadfinder* (Berlin, 1997), briefly describes life in a youth organization that was converted to Communism.

The problems facing the slightly older age group studying in universities at the time are related in Avraham Bar Menachem, *Bitterer Vergangenheit zu Trotz* (Frankfurt, 1992); their attempts to continue their studies abroad are described in Klaus Voigt, *Zuflucht auf Widerruf: Exil in Italien* (Stuttgart, 1995).

Many thousands went to agricultural training centers after 1933. Their experiences are related in Rudolf Melitz, *Das ist unser Weg: Junge Juden schildern Umschichtung und Hachschara* (Berlin, 1937), and in the circular letters *(Rundbriefe)* published by and for the graduates of Gross Breesen, a non-Zionist training farm in Silesia, that began to appear in the 1930s.

The obstacles facing refugees from Germany are detailed in Herbert A. Strauss, "Jewish Emigration from Germany" in *Leo Baeck Year Book*, volumes

25 and 26 (1980 and 1981), and in *Jewish Emigration from Germany*, edited by Norbert Kampe (Munich, n.d.). David Wyman, *Paper Walls* (New York, 1968), and Henry Feingold, *The Politics of Rescue* (New Brunswick, N.J., 1970), are the standard accounts on U.S. restrictions on immigration. Yehuda Bauer, *Flight and Rescue* (Tel Aviv, 1970), covers the story of the illegal emigration from Europe. I have referred in the text to the personal stories of John F. Baer (*Witness for a Generation*, Santa Barbara, 1997), Eva Neisser (personal communication, March 1999), and Werner Guttentag (La Paz, personal communication, summer 1999).

Escape

The history of how emigration from Germany proceeded is another story that remains to be written. For the last-minute attempts at flight and rescue, see *Proceedings of the Second Yad Vashem International Historical Conference* (Jerusalem, 1977). See also an interview with Max Zimmels, emissary from Palestine in Berlin up to the outbreak of the war (Jerusalem, April 1999). Among the witnesses quoted who left Germany after the outbreak of the war are Max Frankel (*The Times of My Life* [New York, 1999]) and Wolfgang Hadda (*Knapp davongekommen* [Konstanz, 1997]). On Jewish Communists in concentration camps, see Emil Carlebach, *Buchenwald* (Frankfurt, 1984), and the same author's *Tote auf Urlaub* (Bonn, 1995), as well as the semi-documentary novel by Bruno Apitz, *Nackt unter Woelfen* (East Berlin, 1960), which was also made into a movie. In the Communist accounts of the camps, Jews, other than party members, appear only on the margins, never as true heroes of the antifascist struggle.

The Zionist network in occupied Europe was coordinated by Natan Szwalb in Switzerland. The full extent of his work became known only when his papers were made accessible. See Shabtai Teveth, *Ha'aretz*, September 24, and October 3 and 6, 1995. See also the interview with Szwalb in *Juden im Widerstand*, edited by Karsten Borgmann (Berlin, 1993). Heini Bornstein, a Zionist youth leader in Switzerland during the war, is critical of certain aspects of Szwalb's work, viewing his style of working as that of a lone wolf. See H. Bornstein, *Ha'i Schweiz* (Tel Aviv, 1999).

For a general account of the work of the members of Zionist youth movements in Sweden and occupied Europe, see Perez Leshem, *Strasse zur Rettung* (Tel Aviv, 1973). The story of those who escaped to Sweden is related by Malin Thor, *Hechaluz I Sverige* (Lund, forthcoming), and Emil Glueck, *Pa raeg till Israel* (Stockholm, 1985). On German Jewish youngsters in Denmark under the German occupation, Joergen Hoestrup, *Dengang in Denmark* (Odense, 1983), and the memoirs of Melanie Oppenhejm, *Mennes Kefaelden* (Copenhagen, 1981), on the years in Theresienstadt.

On the underground in the Netherlands there is a rich literature, above all J. Benjamin, *Ne'emanim leazmam veledarkam* (Tel Aviv, 1998), and the same author's *They Were Our Friends* (Jerusalem, 1990), which is dedicated to their non-Jewish helpers.

There is no comprehensive study as yet covering the fate of the young Jews who survived the Third Reich underground, but there are many accounts of small groups and individuals. Among the most interesting is the Chug Chalutzi (Pioneering Circle) in Berlin headed by Jizchak Schwersenz and later by Gad Beck. This story was told first in J. Schwersenz, *Machteret Chaluzim begermaniya hanazit* (Tel Aviv, 1969), and later by the same author in *Die versteckte Gruppe* (Berlin, 1988). See also the recollections of Gad Beck, *Und Gad ging zu David* (Berlin, 1993).

Stories of individual survival include Edith Hahn Beer, *Ich will leben* (Muenster, 1996); Inge Deutschkron, *Outcast* (New York, 1989); Armin Schmid, et al., *Lost in a Labyrinth of Red Tape* (Evanston, Ill., 1996); Herbert Strauss, *Ueber dem Abgrund* (Berlin, 1998); Marianne Loring, *Flucht aus Frankreich* (Frankfurt, 1996); and the as yet unpublished memoirs of Edith Kurzweil, which describe her escape from France to America after the German invasion.

One of the earliest accounts published of survival underground was that of "David," Joel Koenig, *Den Netzen entronnen* (Goettingen, 1968), and one of the most widely read was Shlomo Perel, *Europa Europa* (New York, 1997), which became a movie produced by A. Holland. Two accounts by natives of Czernowitz describing escape (and internment) are Zvi Yawetz on Israeli television, *Ele hem chayecha* (This is your life, 1991), and Margot Bartfeld-Feller, *Dennoch Mensch geblieben* (Konstanz, 1996). The story of Ernest Fontheim in our text is based on interviews and personal communications throughout 1999. Fontheim survived, owing to the help of, among others, a German neighbor, Heinz Drossel, who also provided an account, *Die Zeit der Fuechse*, and published it privately (Bensheim, 1988). The story of Hans Rosenthal (the television personality) has been told in Leonard Gross, *The Last Jews in Berlin* (New York, 1982). Two other Hans Rosenthals also survived, one of whom subsequently became a biology professor in East Germany and belonged to those who rejoined the Jewish community even before the fall of the GDR. His story is told in Robin Ostow, *Juden in der DDR* (Berlin, 1996). The third Hans Rosenthal belonged to a somewhat older generation. The catalogue of an exhibition in Berlin entitled *Juden in Berlin 1938–45* (Berlin, 2000), sponsored by the Stiftung Neue Synagoge and edited by Hermann Simon, includes much of interest about the life of Jews surviving underground in Berlin.

Particularly adventurous stories are those of Larry Orbach, *Soaring Underground* (Washington, D.C., 1996), and Valentin Senger, *No. 12 Kaiserhofstrasse*

(New York, 1990). Senger, strictly speaking, did not hide; he lived under an assumed identity in Frankfurt throughout the Nazi era. A fascinating recent report by a Jewish youngster who became a well known actor in postwar Germany is Michael Degen, *Nicht alle waren Moerder* (Duesseldorf, 1999). The amazing story of Konrad Latte was told by Peter Schneider in the *New York Times*, February 13, 2000, and in a German television documentary shown in 1999. The equally incredible story of Guenter Gerson is in Eugen Herman-Friede, *Fuer Freudenspruenge keine Zeit* (Berlin, 1991).

Survival in Austria was more difficult than in Berlin. Some of the attempts are described in Gertrude Schneider, *Exile and Destruction* (Westport, Conn., 1995), as well as in Jonny Moser, *Die Judenverfolgung in Oesterreich* (Vienna, 1966), and Herbert Rosenkranz's magisterial work *Verfolgung und Selbstbehauptung* (Munich, 1978). See also Walter Foster, *All for the Best*, privately printed (Bournemouth, 1995).

Among the few young German Jews who survived Auschwitz or other death camps were Anita Lasker-Wallfisch, *Inherit the Truth 1939–45* (London, 1996), and several former trainees of the Gross Breesen farm, including Friedel Walheimer and Bernie Weinberg; their story is told in Gross Breesen *Rundbrief* 50 (1986/88).

Resistance

The most comprehensive general account so far of anti-Nazi resistance on the part of Jewish individuals and groups is Konrad Kwiet and Helmuth Eschwege, *Selbstbehauptung und Widerstand* (Hamburg, 1984). To a certain extent this has been overtaken by the volume edited by Loethken and Vathke mentioned below. There exist specialized studies on the smaller left-wing groups such as Neu Beginnen, the KPO, the SAP, the ISK (Nelson Bund), and others, in which Jews were heavily represented, but they are not of direct relevance in this present context. The case study of KPO (Communist party opposition) in Breslau is based on interviews of several surivors as well as Deposition Putzrath in Archiv der sozialen Demokratie, Bonn, and Ernesto Kroch, *Exil in der Heimat* (Frankfurt, 1990). The tragic story of Helga Beyer is based on interviews and on Antje Dertinger, *Weisse Moewe, gelber Stern* (Berlin, 1987).

The complicated attitude of the Communist party toward its Jewish members during the Nazi period is briefly discussed in Jeffrey Herf, *Divided Memory* (Cambridge, Mass., 1997). The activities of the Baum group in Berlin are related in the recollections of Margot Pikarski (a survivor), *Jugend im Widerstand* (East Berlin, 1978), and Lucien Steinberg, *Jews against Hitler* (Glasgow, 1978). More recent accounts include Wolfgang Wippermann, *Die Berliner*

Gruppe Baum und der juedische Widerstand (Berlin, 1982), and in greatest
detail and most authoritatively, Michael Kreutzer in Wilfred Loehken and
Werner Vathke, *Juden im Widerstand* (Berlin, 1993).

The activities of non-Communist groups and individuals have been neglected, by comparison. There is no biography so far of Hilda Monte, only
references to her in Max Fuerst (her brother-in-law), *Talisman Scheherezade* (Munich, 1976). There has been a German television documentary
about Helmut Hirsch, but no book-length study, only an article by J. Etzold,
"The American Jew in Germany," *Jewish Social Studies* 35 (1973). Very little
attention has been paid to the Society for Peace and Reconstruction except
for Eugen Herman-Friede, *Fuer Freudenspruenge keine Zeit* (Berlin, 1991),
and Barbara Samizadeh, in her paper in Loethken and Vathke, *Juden im
Widerstand*.

The life stories of Herbert Herz, Leo Weil, and Lothar Martin, three of
many more young German Jews who fought in the French Resistance are told
in Gernot Roemer, *Wir haben uns gewehrt* (Augsburg, 1995).

An early work on the German Jewish part in the British war effort Norman
Bentwich, *I Understand the Risks* (London, 1950), is full of interesting material but somewhat uncritical. John P. Fox, "German and Austrian Jewish Volunteers in Britain's Armed Forces 1938–45," in *Leo Baeck Year Book*, 1985,
contains an extensive bibliography. The most comprehensive account so far is
recent: Peter Leighton-Langer, *X steht fuer unbekannt* (Berlin, 1999). Wolfgang Muchisch, *Mit Spaten, Waffen und Worten* (Vienna, 1992), deals exclusively with the exploits of young Austrians of Jewish descent.

There is a plethora of personal wartime accounts, published and unpublished. On top of many interviews, I have drawn on the following: Peter Masters, *Striking Back* (Novato, Calif., 1998); Stephen Dale, *Spanglet*, privately
published (Hitchin, U.K., 1993); Ernest Goodman, unpublished manuscript;
Fred Pelican, *From Dachau to Dunkirk* (London, 1993); Mark Lynton, *Accidental Journey* (New York, 1995); and interview with Albert Lisbona, London, December 1998. Many young refugees joined elite commando units. Accounts of their wartime experiences include, in addition to Dale and Masters,
Ian Dear, *10 Commando* (New York, 1989), and Fred Warner, *Don't You
Know There Is a War On* (Hamburg, 1985). Michael Thomas (*Deutschland,
England ueber alles* [Berlin, n.d.]) was an officer during the war and in occupied Germany.

In comparison, perhaps as the result of the dispersal of young refugees in
the U.S. armed forces, there are fewer accounts of their military service in the
United States. There is no comprehensive review of refugees in the armed
forces, only some chapters in more general works such as Maurice Davie, *Refugees in America* (New York, 1947). Many were drafted into intelligence units,

on which see Guy Stern, "In the Service of American Intelligence," in *Leo Baeck Year Book*, 1992. Personal accounts include Ernst Beyer (unpublished manuscript, dealing in detail with his experience as a POW in German hands), John Weitz (interview), and Bernd Engelmann, *Die unfreiwilligen Reisen des Putti Eichelbaum* (Munich, 1986). Of interest with regard to the administration of occupied Germany are Heinz Kellermann, Gross Breesen *Rundbrief*, September 1945 (the writer was part of the U.S. team preparing the Nuremberg trial), and Gunther Stent, *Nazis, Women and Molecular Biology* (Kensington, Calif., 1998); the writer was a member of a scientific team stationed in Germany.

On the Jewish war effort in Mandatory Palestine, see, above all, Yoav Gelber, *Toldot hahitnadvut*, volume 3 (Jerusalem 1983), and the same author's *Moledet hadasha* (Tel Aviv, 1994), dealing specifically with the role of German and Austrian volunteers. For personal accounts, see, for instance, Martin Hauser, *Wege juedischer Selbstbehauptung* (Bonn, 1992), a diary. An early account of the Jewish Brigade was written by its chaplain/rabbi Bernard Kasper: *With the Jewish Brigade* (London, 1947). Esther Herlitz, *Esther*, is of particular interest with regard to refugee women in the army stationed in Egypt.

Israel: Immigration Jeckepotz

The standard work is Yoav Gelber, *Moledet hadasha* (Tel Aviv, 1994). See also Lilo Stone, "German Zionists in Palestine before 1933," in *Journal of Contemporary History* 2 (1997), a summary of her dissertation at Haifa University.

On the first encounter with Palestine—culture shock, enthusiasm, and disappointment—see Guy Meron's unpublished dissertation, *Mesham lekan* (Hebrew University, Jerusalem, September 1998), and Miryam Getter "Ha'aliya hagermanit beshanim 1933–39" in *Katedra* 12 (July 1979). For the early enthusiasm of members of youth *aliya*, see *Jerushalajim, den . . . Briefe junger Menschen schildern Erez Israel*, edited by Raanan Melitz (Berlin, 1936). Individual accounts include interviews in Anne Betten and Miryam Du-nour, *Wir sind die Letzten* (Gerlingen, 1996), as well as Jenny Aloni and Hartmut Steinecke, *Man muesste einer spaeteren Generation Bericht erstatten* (Paderborn, 1997); Naomi Koch Laqueur, *A Memoir* (Washington, D.C., privately published); Meta Frank, *Schalom meine Heimat* (Hofgeismar, 1994); Avraham Bar Menachem, *Bitterer Vergan genheit zu Trotz* (Frankfurt, 1992); and Gad Granach, *Heimatlos* (Berlin, 1997). About the early days of Kibbutz Hasorea and its history in general, see the massive *Ma'agale yehid veyahad* (n.p., 1997) published on the occasion of the sixtieth anniversary of its settlement in Yokneam; and also Asher Benari, *Chalutz me'aretz Ashkenas*

(Hasorea, ca. 1996). The author was one of the founding members of the kibbutz.

The difficulties encountered by the newcomers confronting the labor establishment are described in detail in the books of Shlomo Erel, *Die Jeckes* (Jerusalem, 1985) and also *Neue Wurzeln* (Tel Aviv, 1983). The following deal specifically with youth *aliya:* Recha Freier, *Let the Children Come* (London, 1963); Braha Chabas, *Sefer aliyat noar* (n.p., n.d.); Ernst Loewy, *Jugend in Palaestina* (Berlin, 1997); and the same author's *Zwischen den Stuehlen* (Hamburg, 1995). Tuvia Ruebner's story in *Lebensgeschichten aus Israel* edited by Ingrid Weltmann (Moehlin, 1998), and Naomi Koch Laqueur, *A Memoir.* In contrast see Oz Almog, *Hazaber, diokan* (Tel Aviv, 1997) about the uncomplicated generation of the native-born Israelis.

On middle-class immigration, see Gelber, *Moledet,* as well as Joachim Schloer, *Vom Traum zur Stadt* (Gerlingen, 1996), about life in Tel Aviv, and the much earlier books by Erich Gottgetreu, *Das Land der Soehne* (Vienna, 1934), and Gerda Luft, *Heimkehr ins Unbekannte* (Wuppertal, 1977). On German Jewish life in Jerusalem, see Amnon Ramon, *Rechavia, doktor mul doktor gar* (Jerusalem, 1998). The quotations from Gerda Paul is from Schloer, *Vom Traum;* that of Naomi Frenkel is from *Jerusalem Post,* December 18, 1998. Frank, Amichai, Brodsky, Tauber, and Grossman are quoted from Betten and Du-nour, *Wir sind die Letzten;* Walter Grab from *Europaeische Ideen* 47 (1980) and his autobiography *Meine vier Leben* (Cologne, 1999).

For the fate of young immigrants in military elite units, see *Sefer hapalmach* (n.p., n.d.). The privately published memoirs of Shimon Koch (Avidan) and Jehuda Brieger are of particular interest with regard to the "German Squad" of the Palmach. See also Uri Ben Ari, *Nua, nua, sof* (Tel Aviv, 1999). The Yeats quotation is from "September 1913."

United States: Golden Country behind Paper Walls

The study of the refugees of the 1930s by Maurice R. Davie, *Refugees in America* (New York, 1947), was written immediately after the war and deals lightly with the difficulties confronting the newcomers. Personal accounts of first impressions are Edith Liebenthal, unpublished manuscript; Robert Goldmann, *Flucht in die Welt* (Frankfurt 1996); Georg Troller *Selbst-beschreibung* (Munich, 1991); and the personal communications by Eva Neisser and Ruth Zellner. Sybille Quack, *Zuflucht Amerika* (Berlin, 1995), deals exclusively with the experience of women.

For the experiences of those who arrived at a younger age, sometimes unaccompanied, see Judith Tydor Baumel, *Unfulfilled Promise* (Juneau, Alaska, 1990); the unpublished memoir of Richard Schifter; and Max Frankel, *The Times of My Life.*

Life in Washington Heights is described in Steven M. Lowenstein, *Frankfurt on the Hudson* (Detroit, 1989), and in an early, vivid journalistic account, Ernest Stock, "Washington Heights Fourth Reich," *Commentary*, June 1951 . On the life of the young generation in Washington Heights, see Gloria Kirchheimer, *We Were So Beloved* (Pittsburgh, 1997). On sports in Washington Heights, Helmut Kuh in *Aufbau*, January 7, 1994. On the exodus from Washington Heights, Steven M. Lowenstein, "The German Jewish Community of Washington Heights," in *Leo Baeck Year Book* 30 (1985). Recollections of young people growing up in Washington Heights are given by Max Frankel, Ilse Marcus, Louis Kampf, and Sary Lieber in Kirchheimer's *We Were So Beloved*.

On the lack of gratitude and tact shown by some refugees, see *Aufbau*, August 2, 9, and 16, 1940. On concentrations of new refugees in other parts of the United States: *Das Exil der kleinen Leute*, edited by Wolfgang Benz, on Hyde Park, Chicago (Munich, 1991); Abraham Peck and Uri D. Herscher, *Queen City Refuge*, on Cincinnati (Cincinnati, 1989). On a Darmstadt Landsmannschaft, see Moritz Neumann, *Das zweite Leben* (Darmstadt, 1993). On refugees from Mannheim in the United States, see Robert B. Kahn, *Reflections by Jewish Survivors from Mannheim* (New York, 1990). I am grateful to Dr. Herbert Strauss for further information.

The experiences of the Austrian emigration in the United States, specifically on Café Éclair and Hollywood, can be found in Friedrich Torberg, *Eine tolle, tolle Zeit* (Munich, 1989). There is a full bibliography in *Handbuch der deutschsprachigen Emigration*, edited by Claus Dieter Krohn et al. (Darmstadt, 1998). A interview with Walter Roberts was also helpful.

Leo Lania, in an article in the *Aufbau*, June 11, 1943, described how he accompanied his son to the draft board in New York. There is a succinct account of the G.I. Bill of Rights in Theodore R. Mosch, *The G.I. Bill* (Hicksville, N.Y., 1975).

Individual accounts of their first (and second and third) steps in America include Frankel, *The Times of My Life*; Ruth Westheimer, *All in a Lifetime* (New York, 1985); Reinhard Bendix, *Von Berlin nach Berkeley* (Frankfurt, 1985); Hajo Funke, *Die andere Erinnerung*, on, among others, Kurt Wolff and Lewis Coser (Frankfurt, 1989); and Lewis Coser, *Refugee Scholars in America*, on, among others, Albert Hirschman (New Haven, 1984). Also on Hirschman, see Michael Schornstheimer, "Widersacher der Resignation," *Exil* 2 (1994). Peter Gay, *My German Question* (New Haven, 1998).

The study of academic emigration from Germany and Austria has been limited in the past to those who had reached the top in their country of origin. The role of the second generation is only now being investigated. Helpful introductory essays can be found in Claus Dieter Krohn, *Handbuch*. I am also grateful for information received from Gunther Stent, Arno Motulski, and others.

Among the young refugees who served in the foreign service of the United States and especially in the information service (USIA), only a few can be singled out: Richard Schifter, Walter Roberts, Robert Neuman, Edmund Schecter, Hans Tuch, Henry Kellermann, Gerard Gert, Walter Stettner, not to mention the ambassadors and assistant secretaries of the next generation born to parents from Germany, such as Dennis Ross and Richard Holbrook.

World Revolution, or the Dream That Failed

There is no comprehensive history of the groups of the far left among the young generation of German Jewry, but several interesting monographs have appeared, such as Stefanie Schueler-Springorum, "Jugendbewegung und Politik," in *Tel Aviver Jahrbuch fuer deutsche Geschichte, 1999,* and Guenter Eckstein, "Die freie deutsch-juedische Jugend 1932/3," in *Leo Baeck Year Book,* 1981. Some of the individuals involved also write about this in their recollections, including Max Fuerst, *Talisman Scheherezade* (Munich, 1976); Fritz Teppich, Der rote Pfadfinder (Berlin, 1997); Karl Kormes, in *1945, Jetzt wohin* (Berlin, 1995); Erna Nelki, in *Eine stumme Generation berichtet,* edited by G. Dischner (Berlin, 1984); and Helmut Eschwege, *Fremd unter Meinesgleichen* (Berlin, 1991).

Others who belonged to this generation include Eric Hobsbawm, who made an academic and political career in England—"Gespraech mit Eric Hobsbawm," in *Neue Rundschau* 4 (1996)—and Stefan Heym, who returned to East Germany after the war—*Nachruf* (Berlin, 1988). Kurt Goldstein survived the camps in Germany and also had a political career in East Germany; his interview can be found in Wolfgang Herzberg, *Ueberleben heisst erinnern* (Berlin, 1990). Several hundred German refugees of the left fought in Spain; see Arno Lustiger, *Schalom Libertad* (Frankfurt, 1987), and Irma Schaber, *Gerta Taro, Als Fotoreporterin im spanischen Buergerkrieg* (Marburg, 1994).

On the fate of the political emigration to the Soviet Union in general, see Carola Tischler, *Die UdSSR und die Politemigration* (Muenster, 1996). Specifically on the fate of the young generation and the role of the Liebknecht School in Moscow, see *Shkola nashikh mechtei,* catalogue of an exhibition (Moscow, 1995); Henry Karl Lewenstein, *Die Karl-Liebknechtschule in Moskau 1932–37* (Lueneburg, 1991); and an article by Christa Uhlig in *Paedagogik und Schulalltag,* 1996. Some of the younger members of the emigration among the Jews were deported to Nazi Germany after the German-Soviet nonaggression pact of 1939. See Hans Schafranek, *Zwischen NKWD und Gestapo* (Frankfurt, 1990), and Klaus Sator, "Das kommunistische Exil und der deutsch-sowjetische Nichtangriffspakt," in *Exilforschung,* 1996.

Personal recollections on the purges and the war include two widely read books: Wolfgang Leonhard, *Die Revolution entlaesst ihre Kinder* (Koeln,

1983), and Markus Wolf, *Die Troika* (Duesseldorf, 1989). An interview with Moritz Mebel appeared in *Neues Deutschland*, October 26, 1996.

The strange alleged discovery of a branch of the Hitler Youth in Moscow is related in several recent studies. See Holger Dehl and Natalia Musijenko, "Hitlerjugend," *Beitraege zur Geschichte der deutschen Arbeiterbewegung*, March 1996, and Oleg Del, *Ot illiuzii k tragedii* (Moscow, 1997). On arrests in general, see Domerius in *Exil 2* (1997).

The story of the return of German and Austrian refugees to their native countries is covered in Hans Schafranek *Kinderheim Nr. 6* (Vienna, 1998), and "Die Remigration aus der UdSSR 1945–62," in *1945, Jetzt wohin?*

The return of young Jewish Communists is mainly the story of those who came from Britain. See Alfred Fleischhacker, *Das war unser Leben: Erinnerungen und Dokumente zur Geschichte der FDJ in Grossbritannien 1933–46* (Berlin, 1996); Alice and Gerhard Zadek, *Mit dem letzten Zug aus England* (Berlin, 1992); and the autobiography of Horst Brie, *David's Odyssee* (Berlin, 1997). As for their subsequent fate, see the contributions by Schalscha, Zamory, Ursula Herzberg, and others in Fleischhacker, *Das war unser Leben*, as well as Eva Brueck, *Im Schatten des Hakenkreuzes* (Freiburg, 1993). The return of Communists from Shanghai is related in Georg Ambruester, "Exil in Shanghai," in *1945, Jetzt wohin?* (Berlin, 1995). Also *Leben im Wartesaal* (catalogue of an exhibition), as well as Guenter and Genia Nobel, "Als politische Emigranten in Schanghai," *Beitraege zur Geschichte der deutschen Arbeiterbewegung* 21 (1979). The return of several Communists from Palestine/Israel is detailed in Guenter Stillmann, *Berlin-Palaestina und zurueck* (Berlin, 1989). For a short bibliography covering the fate of those who went to the Soviet Union and perished in the camps or were executed, see Schueler-Springorum, "Jugendbewegung." On the views of the second generation of the returnees, consult the interviews in Robin Ostow, *Juden in der DDR* (Berlin, 1996), and Vincent von Wroblewsky, *Zwischen Torah und Trabant* (Berlin, 1993), as well as Robin Ostow, *Juden aus der DDR und die deutsche Wiedervereinigung; elf Gespraeche* (Berlin, 1996). Also Salomea Genin, *Scheindl und Salomea* (Berlin, 1992), and Wolfgang Benz, *Das Exil der kleinen Leute* (Munich, 1991). Very different in mood are the recollections of Ingeborg Rapoport, *Meine ersten drei Leben* (Berlin, 1997), but Rapoport belongs to the first, rather than the second, generation. It is noteworthy, but hardly surprising, that virtually all this literature appeared only after the fall of the Berlin Wall in 1989.

Britain: Forever Refugees?

On British immigration policy in the 1930s, see A. J. Sherman, *Island Refuge* (London, 1973), On the reception of the refugees from Germany in England by

Anglo-Jewry, see Amy Zahl Gottlieb, *Men of Vision* (London, 1998). The story of the Kindertransports has been described in several books and booklets, only the most important of which can be mentioned: Bertha Leverton, *I Came Alone* (Sussex, 1990); Karen Gershon, *Wir kamen als Kinder* (Frankfurt, 1966); Barry Turner, *And the Policeman Smiled* (London, 1991); Rebekka Goepfert, *Der juedische Kindertransport* (Frankfurt, 1999). Also see *Kindertransport 60th anniversary* (London, 1999), and the more analytical work by Dorit Bader Whitman, *The Uprooted* (New York, 1993).

The recollections of some of those who came not within the framework of the Kindertransport but alone or with their parents include Sylvia Rodgers, *Red Saint, Pink Daughter* (London, 1996), and the two autobiographical accounts by Charles Hannan, *Almost an Englishman* (London, 1979) and *A Boy in Your Situation* (London, 1977), as well as Vera Gissing, *Pearls of Childhood* (New York, 1981). Lore Segall's *Other People's Houses* (New York, 1964) became a bestseller when it appeared in the 1960s. Ruth Furst, *Home Is Somewhere Else* appeared even earlier (Albany, N.Y., 1945). George Wei-denfeld, *Remembering My Good Friends* (London, 1994), was a few years older, which at the time made a considerable difference.

There is only a brief study so far of the experiences of those admitted as domestic servants to Britain: Tony Kushner in *Second Chance*, edited by Werner Mosse (Tuebingen, 1991); and a few personal accounts such as that of Bronka Schneider, *Exile* (Columbus, Ohio, 1998). On the young Zionist pioneers from Germany who came to Britain, see Perez Leshem, *Strasse zur Rettung* (Tel Aviv, 1973), as well as the circular letters of Hechaluz in Britain and unpublished manuscripts by Fred Dunston and other youth leaders kept in the Wiener Library in London. In contrast, a great deal has been written about the internment of the refugees on the Isle of Man and elsewhere. Again, only the more important accounts can be listed, such as Ronald Stent, *A Bespattered Page* (London, 1980); Connery Chappell, *Island of Barbed Wire* (London, 1984); Peter and Leni Gillman, *Collar the Lot* (London, 1980); and Eric Koch, *Deemed Suspect* (Toronto, 1980), which also deals with the camps in Canada. Individual accounts include those of Josef Eissinger, who was deported to Canada, and Bern Brent, who was sent to Australia (interview with Dunera, 1989). Yakov Friedler eventually went to Palestine/Israel (*Die leisen Abchiede* [Hagen, 1994]), whereas Walter Foster remained in Britain (*All for the Best* [Bournemouth, 1993], privately published).

For the subsequent fate of the detainees, see Werner Mosse, *Second Chance*, and also the sources mentioned in the chapter on the war effort. The postwar problems of refugee existence in Britain are discussed in Marion Berghahn, *Continental Britains* (London, 1988). The monthly bulletin *AJR Information* put out by the Association of Refugees from Germany and Austria is

Bibliographical Essay 323

an indispensable source in this context. Peter Alter, *Out of the Third Reich* (London, 1998), is a collection of essays by young refugees who in later years opted for an academic career, specifically in history.

The Great Dispersal: Hotel Bolivia and Hotel Shanghai

One of the last Jewish books that could be published in Nazi Germany was the (second) *Philo Lexikon* (1938), containing information of vital interest for prospective emigrants. A general survey of Jewish emigration is given in Ruth Saris, *Brecha beterem shoah* (Ghetto Fighters House) (Israel, 1990), from which the evidence of Anneliese Borinski is quoted. For personal accounts of the dispersal of communities see Gross Breesen, *Rundbrief,* June 1946.

Latin America became one of the two main destinations. On this see Patrik von zur Muehlen, *Fluchtziel Lateinamerika* (Bonn, 1988); Achim Schrader, *Europaeische Juden in Lateinamerika* (St. Ingbert, 1989); and Leonardo Senkman, *Argentina, la segunda guerra mundial y los refugiados indeseables* (Buenos Aires, 1991). Also on Argentina, see Olga Elaine Rojer, *Exile in Argentina* (New York, 1989); and Alfredo Jose Schwarcz, *Y a peser de todo* (Buenos Aires, 1991), which deals specifically with German Jews and the younger generation, as does Elena Levin, *Historias de una emigracion* (Buenos Aires, 1991). The life of refugees in early wartime Buenos Aires is the background to Livia Neumann's German-language novel *Puerto Nuevo* (Buenos Aires, 1943).

The voyage of the *St. Louis* to the Americas is well known and has been documented in books, such as Gordon Thomas and Max Morgan Witts, *Voyage of the Damned* (London, 1994), as well as documentaries and exhibitions. There are several unpublished accounts of the odyssey of other ships, for instance Kurt and Adele Orgler, *Die Kubareise der Flandres* (Wiener Library, London). On Brazil, *Exil in Brasilien, die deutschsprachige Emigration* (no author given), Frankfurt, 1994); on Chile, Marjorie Agosin, *A Cross and a Star* (Reading, Pa., 1997); on Ecuador, Benno Weiser Varon, *Professions of a Lucky Jew* (New York, 1992); on Peru, Hans Joachim Sell, *Briefe einer Juedin aus Cuzco* (Vienna, 1978). On Bolivia, see Leo Spitzer *Hotel Bolivia* (New York, 1998), and Egon Schwarz, *Keine Zeit fuer Eichendorff* (Koenigstein, 1979). The writings of Ernesto Kroch, who went to Uruguay, have been mentioned earlier. In addition I have made use of published autobiographies, such as Guenther Holzmann, *On dit que j'ai surécu part au dela des mers* (Paris, 1997), of unpublished memoirs, and of Jewish community periodicals.

One of the largest refugee communities was in Sao Paulo, where the local Jewish scout organization consisted largely of young refugees. See Avan Handava, *60 anos de escotismo e Judaismo, 1938–98* (Sao Paulo, 1999).

The subsequent fate of the Jewish communities is the subject of Patrik von zur Muehlen, "Juedische und deutsche Identitaet von Lateinamerikanischen Emigranten," *Exilforschung* 5 (1987), and of Alice Irene Hirschberg, *Desafio e Resposta* (Sao Paulo, n.d.).

The other main destination of last-minute refugees was Shanghai. For a description of Shanghai as a shelter, see David Kranzler, *Japanese, Nazis and Jews* (New York, 1976); Ernest G. Heppner, *Shanghai Refuge* (Lincoln, Neb., 1996); Michael Blumenthal, *The Invisible Wall* (New York, 1998); Wilfried Seywald, *Journalisten im Schanghaier Exil* (Salzburg, 1987); and James R. Ross, *Escape to Shanghai* (New York, 1994). Survivors of the younger generation established a website, http://www.rickshaw.org, which includes much interesting information. I also had the benefit of the advice of Sonja Muehlberger, Ernest Heppner, Hilde Schulz, and other eyewitnesses.

A short survey of the emigration to what was then British India is given by Johannes H. Voigt, "Die Emigration von Juden aus Mitteleuropa nach Indien," in *Jahrbuch Wechselwirkung* (Stuttgart, 1991). See also Max Born, *Mein Leben* (Munich, 1975), and Anita Desai, *Baumgarten's Bombay* (London 1988).

The fullest description of the involuntary residents of the camps on Mauritius is Ronald Friedman, *Exil auf Mauritius* (Berlin, 1998). Further information is contained in Aaron Zwergbaum, "Exile in Mauritius," in *Yad Vashem Studies* (Jerusalem, 1960), and "From Internment in Bratislava . . . ," in *The Jews of Czechoslovakia: Historical Studies and Surveys.* (New York, 1971).

The then British dominions were unwilling to accept Jewish refugees, as shown in *False Havens: The British Empire and the Holocaust*, edited by Paul Bartrop (Lanham, Md., 1995), and, with specific reference to Australia in Michael Blakeney, *Australia and the Jewish Refugees* (Sydney, 1985). Other accounts of refugees to Australia are Eugen Kamenka, "On Being a German Jewish Refugee in Australia," in the special issue on refugees of the *Australian Journal of Politics and History*, 1985; *Strauss to Matilda* edited by Karl Bittman (Victoria, 1988); *Community of Fate: Memoirs of German Jews in Melbourne*, edited by John Foster (Sydney 1986); Volker E. Pilgrim, et al., *Fremde Freiheit* (Hamburg, 1992); as well as W. S. Matsdorf, *No Time to Grow: The Story of the Gross Breeseners in Australia* (Sydney, 1994).

Several hundred academics of Jewish or part-Jewish background went to Turkey. Their experience is described in Fritz Neumark, *Zuflucht am Bosporus* (Frankfurt, 1981), and in the catalogue of a Berlin exhibition, *Haymatloz*, 2000.

Lastly, concerning the strange fate of the camp in Southern Italy that was bypassed by history, see Carlo Spartaco Capogreco, *Ferramonti* (Florence, 1987). A brief version in English is in *The Italian Refuge*, edited by Ivo Herzer (Washington, D.C., 1989).

Returning to Germany

On Jews in postwar Germany, see Michael Brenner, *After the Holocaust* (Princeton, 1997); Erika Burgauer, *Zwischen Erinnerung und Verdraengung* (Hamburg, 1993); and Micha Brumlik, *Juedisches Leben in Deutschland* (Frankfurt, 1978). Most recently, Richard Schneider, *Wir sind da*, a television documentary in several installments and also a book (Berlin, 2000), consists of interviews with many of those involved in the reemergence of Jewish communities in postwar Germany. Eyewitness accounts of young refugee soldiers reurning to Germany in 1945 are found in Walter Hellendal, "Als amerikanischer Soldat in der deutschen Vaterstadt," *Aufbau*, April 6, 1945, and Arno Hamburger, "Coming Home in the Uniform of the Jewish Brigade," in Brenner, *After the Holocaust.*

Some German Jews came to resettle in Germany after 1946. Their motives and experiences are described in Karola Fings, "Rueckkehr als Politikum," in *Unter Vorbehalt* (Cologne, 1997). I have quoted from this source the impressions of Henry Green, Peter Max Blank, and Mrs. Schoenfeld, Mrs. Blank, and Mrs. Liebermann. The Ulbricht and Goodman quotations appear in *1945, Jetzt wohin?* (Berlin, 1985). Van Dam's article appeared in *Yediot chadashot*, Tel Aviv, May 29, 1959. Other refugees who returned include Alfred Moos, *Ein Ulmer Jude* (Ulm, 1995), and Malka Schmuekler *Gast im eigenen Land* (Ratingen, 1997). Another interesting collection of the accounts of young Jews who went back is Franz Juergens, *Wir waren ja eigentlich Deutsche* (Berlin, 1997). The story of the musician Helmut Stern is in *Die Erfahrung des Exils*, edited by Wolfgang Benz (Berlin, 1997), and in Stern's autobiography, *Saitenspruenge* (Berlin, n.d.).

Jewish culture in a reunited Germany is the subject of Sandor Gilman and Karen Remler, *Reemerging Jewish Culture in Berlin* (New York, 1994). Current information can be found on the website http://www.hagalil.com. The specific problems of the "second generation" in former East Germany has been the subject of a rich and interesting literature. See in particular Vincent von Wroblewsky, *Zwischen Thora und Trabant* (Berlin, 1993), for the accounts by Barbara Honigmann, Irene Runge, Jalda Rebling, Annetta Kahana, and others. See also the interviews by Thomas Kleinspehn in "Jeder muss sein Paeckchen tragen," www.Radiobremen.De/rbtext/rb2/s98/ 1209/htm.

Our study refers only to the younger refugee writers who returned, such as Hilde Domin, *Fast ein Lebenslauf* (Munich, 1996), and Marcel Reich-Ranicki; *Mein Leben* (Stuttgart, 1999); as well as Volker Hage and Mathias Schreiber, *Marcel Reich-Ranicki* (Stuttgart, 1997). Others who published in German after the war include Paul Celan (John Felstiner, *Paul Celan: Poet, Survivor, Jew* [New Haven, 1996]); Peter Weiss (Roger Ellis, *Peter Weiss in Exile* [Ann

Arbor, 1987]; and Rainer Gerlach, *Peter Weiss* [Frankfurt, 1984]); Erich Fried (Steven W. Lawrie, *Erich Fried: A Writer without a Country* (New York, 1996); Wolfgang Hildesheimer (Heinz Puknus, *Wolfgang Hildesheimer* [Munich, 1978]); and Jean Amery (Irene Heidelberger Leonard, *Ueber Jean Amery* [Heidelberg, 1990]). For Jurek Becker, see *Materialien* (Frankfurt, 1990) and Sandor Gilman, *Jurek Becker* (Washington, D.C., 1999).

Among the books of the younger generation of writers born after the war the following are more or less representative: Irene Dische, *The Jewess* (London, 1992); Esther Dischereit, *Joemi's Tisch* (Frankfurt, 1988); Maxim Biller, *Land der Vaeter und Verraeter* (Stuttgart, n.d.); Rafael Seligmann, *Rubinstein's Versteigerung* (Frankfurt, 1989), and *Eine juedische Mamme* (Frankfurt, 1990).

The Broch quotation is from *Eine schwierige Heimkehr*, edited by Johann Holzner (Innsbruck, 1991).

The organized trips to their home towns are described (with reference to the city of Bochum) in *Vom Umgang mit der Geschichte*, edited by Irmtrud Wojak and Herbert Schneider (Essen, 1996). There are several personal reports in *1945, Jetzt wohin?* by, among others, Hermann Neville, Prentki, and Martin Teich. On revisiting Vienna, see Freda Ulman Teitelbaum, *Vienna Revisited* (Santa Barbara, 1995). On her return to Prague immediately after the war, see Ruth Bondi, *Shevarim shlemim* (Tel Aviv, 1997), translated into German as *Mehr Glueck als Verstand* (Gerlingen, 1999).

Portrait of a Generation

On the reunions fifty and sixty years after the flight from Germany see, for instance, *Kindertransport 60th Anniversary* (London, 1999). On a similar meeting in the state of New York, see "Elephant in the Living Room," *Aufbau*, July 9, 1999. What is a generation? One of the classic statements is Ortega y Gasset, *El tema de nostro tiempo* (Madrid, 1923). One striking example of the revival of interest in the German Jewish origins is Orna Porat's memoir of her late husband, Josef, "The Spy Who Loved Me," *Ha'aretz*, August 6, 1999. See also Annette Leo, "Sehnsucht nach dem Exil der Eltern," *Exilforschung* 17 (1999).

In the recollections of survivors there are countless stories of the role of accident. See, for instance, Irene Kirkland in Michael Dobbs, *Madeleine Albright: A Twentieth Century Odyssey* (New York, 1999); Henry Burger's story of a young Jewish partisan in Italy, *Biancastella: A Jewish Partisan in World War Two* (Bivot, Colo., 1997); or Zvi Aharoni, *In Life and Death: The Tale of a Lucky Man* (London, 1998). The tragic story of Klaus Lebeck, a schoolmate of mine, has been related to me in detail by his sister Rosemarie Steinfeld in New York, June 1999. My account of the different fates of two neighbors from

Upper Silesia is based on Walter Gruenfeld, *Rueckblicke* (privately published in Zurich, ca. 1985), and Joanna Helander, *Breven van Polen* (Sweden, 1986), as well as personal communications from Joanna Helander and Bo Parsson. Accident often played an equally important role in the postwar careers of individuals, particularly in their access to education. See Louise Hoffman, *Without Regret* (Perth, Australia, 1994).

The issue of apostasy in historical perspective is covered in Todd Edelman, *Jewish Apostasy* (New York, 1989), and, to give but two German Jewish examples, Katie Haffner, *The House on the Bridge* (New York, 1995), as well as Victor Klemperer, *Und so sitze ich zwischen allen Stuehlen* (Berlin, 1998).

On the pressures to convert in wartime, see, on the one hand, Alfred Grosser, *Mein Deutschland* (Hamburg, 1993), and, on the other, Saul Friedlaender, *When Memory Comes* (New York, 1979).

On the problems involved in name changing: See Peter Leighton-Langer, *X steht fuer unbekannt* (Berlin, 1999). See Peter Masters, *Striking Back* (Novato, Calif., 1998), with regard to the pressures exerted in the British army. On changing names in Palestine and Israel, see Gideon and Jakob Toury, "Namensaenderungen deutschsprachiger Juden in Palaestina bis 1942," in *Menorah, Jahrbuch fuer deutsch-juedische Geschichte*, 1991.

Young German Jews had a substantial impact on religious life in the United States as outlined in Herbert A. Strauss, *Ueber dem Abgrund* (Berlin, 1998), as well as Guenter Plaut and Alfred Gottschalk, in Abraham J. Peck, *The German-Jewish Legacy in America 1938–1988* (Detroit, 1988). Others dealing with this topic were Peter Levinson, *Ein Ort ist mit wem du bist* (Berlin, 1996), and Jacob J. Petuchowski, *Mein Judesein* (Freiburg, 1991). Their impact on religious thought in Israel was minimal. See Michael Sasar, *Kehalom ya'uf* (Jerusalem, 1997).

On the central role of cultural heritage, see among many others Editha Koch in *Exil*, 1991. On the persisting interest in German literature even among very young people, see Shimon Sachs, *Hamaniot* (Tel Aviv, 1984) and *Hehalom hayarok* (Tel Aviv, 1964), as well as Hilde Domin, *Fast ein Lebenslauf* (Munich, 1996). But there were also many cases of near total rejection; see for instance Reuven Meir's memoirs, *Me Januar 1933 vead hayom*, privately published. I found helpful an interview with Nurit Meyer in Jerusalem, April 1999. See also Konrad Bloch in Herlinde Koelbl, *Juedische Portraits* (Frankfurt, 1989).

As for anxiety, guilt feelings, and other psychological issues among young survivors, see Dorit Whiteman, *The Uprooted* (New York, 1993); Aharon Appelfeld, *Sipur haim* (Tel Aviv, 1999); Klaus Scheurenberg, *Ueberleben* (Berlin, 1990) and *Ich will leben* (Berlin, 1994); as well as Ruth Elias, *Triumph of Hope* (New York, 1998), and Ruth Klueger, *Weiter Leben, eine Jugend* (Goettingen, n.d.).

On the central role of *Bildung* in the German Jewish heritage, see George L. Mosse, *German Jews beyond Judaism* (Bloomington, Ind., 1985).

Youth movement and adventure: There is a recent biography of Ulli Beyer by Wole Ogundela, *Omuluabi, Ulli Beyer, Yoruba Society and Culture* (Trenton, N.J., 1999). The exotic fates of two women of German Jewish origin are described in Eva Siao, *China mein Traum, mein Leben* (Duesseldorf, 1997), and Ronald Shepherd, *Ruth Prawer, Jhabwala in India, the Jewish Connection* (Delhi, 1994), as well as Ralph Crane, *Ruth Prawer Jhabwala* (New York, 1992). See also Guenter Holzmann's Andean adventures, and many other accounts.

Did German Jewish refugees feel cultural superiority? See the dissertation by Guy Miron, quoted earlier (Jerusalem, 1998), as well as Hermann Zondek, *Auf festem Fusse* (Stuttgart, 1973), and the Fred Lessing interview in Herlinde Koelbel, *Juedische Portraits*.

The politics of the generation of young refugees have not yet been studied in any detail, and perhaps there are few common denominators other than a distrust of political extremes. See Dorit Whiteman, *The Uprooted*.

On the changing image of the "Jecke" in Israel, see the general survey by Gershon Shaked, *Hasiporet ha'ivrit 1880–1980*, volume 5 (Tel Aviv, 1998), and specifically Nathan Shaham, *The Rosendorf Quartet* (London, 1991), and Yoram Kaniuk, *ha'yehudi ha'aharon* (Tel Aviv, n.d.).

Very little has been written about the second generation, but on certain German Jewish prejudices in the United States (for instance with regard to comic books and chewing gum), see Carol Ascher in Abraham Peck, *The German-Jewish Legacy*. For the rediscovery of their Jewish heritage by members of the second generation in contrast to the generation of their parents, see Peter Stephan Jungk, *Shabbat: A Rite of Passage in Jerusalem* (New York, 1985), and his father's interview, in Herlinde Koelbl, *Juedische Portraits*.

INDEX

Abraham, Henry, 139
Abrahamson, Zvi, 44–45
Academics. *See* Universities
Accent, 291
Achitov, Avraham, 91
Adenauer, Konrad, 81, 177
Adler, Helmuth, 139
Affidavit, 307
Agriculture: German immigrants to Palestine in, 96, 103–4, 108–9; Gross Breesen, 17, 85, 215–16, 238, 268, 308; by Latin American refugees, 219–20; training for young German Jews in, 17–18, 312
Agudat Israel, 147
Aharoni, Zvi (Hermann Aronsheim), 3–4, 271
Ahasver, 267
AJR (Association of Jewish Refugees) (Britain), 212, 213
Albright, Madeleine Korbel, 279–80
Aliens Bill (South Africa), 236
Aliya: from Central Europe up to 1940, 96; definition of, 307; emigration seen as, 13. *See also* Youth *aliya*
Aliya bet, 25, 307
Aliya Chadasha, 125, 307
Allgemeine Juedische Wochenzeitung (newspaper), 243
Aloni, Jenny, 100, 257
Alsberg, Paul, 117, 127
Altmann, Alexander, 210
Amadeus Quartet, 207
Ambassadors, 159
Amberg, Carl, 138
America. *See* United States
American Veterans Committee, 150

Amery, Jean, 258
Amichai, Yehuda, 12–13, 116, 120, 257
Anglo-Jewry: German Jewish refugees and, 212–14; German Jews compared with, 192; and the Kindertransports, 192; as not quite part of British society, 211; as poor and uneducated, 192, 200
Angress, Werner, 80, 84, 85, 138
Antisemitism: in Australia, 237; in Britain, 189; in German schools, 3; in Latin America, 220; as official policy after January 1933, 12; in rightwing parties, 161; in Russia, 242
Antonescu, Ion, 53
Appelfeld, Aharon, 290
Arandora Star (ship), 208
Aranyi (Masters), Peter, 76, 77, 78
Arendt, Hannah, 158, 290
Argentina: agriculture by refugees in, 220; antisemitism in, 220; assimilation as difficult in, 220; Buenos Aires, 143, 222, 225, 226; enters the war, 225; Jewish community in 1990s, 226; Jews' attachment to, 226–27; number of German Jewish refugees to, 218
Arieli, Joshua, 15–16
Arndt, Rudi, 69, 167
Aronsheim, Hermann (Zvi Aharoni), 3–4, 271
Aronson, Alex, 233
Ascher, Abraham, 8
Assimilationists: assimilation as difficult in Latin America, 220; European and American Jews being acculturated out of existence, 287–88; losing their patriotism, 6; name changes by, 153; as not

Temple Isaiah Library

To borrow this book when
no librarian is present, follow
the directions posted on
the librarian's desk.

DAY
BOOK